The Art of SQL Server FILESTREAM

A Quick Start Guide
for developers and administrators

By Jacob Sebastian and Sven Aelterman

First published by Simple Talk Publishing August 2012

Copyright August 2012
ISBN 978-1-906434-89-2

The right of Jacob Sebastian and Sven Aelterman to be identified as the authors of this work has been asserted by them in accordance with the Copyright, Designs and Patents Act 1988.

All rights reserved. No part of this publication may be reproduced, stored or introduced into a retrieval system, or transmitted, in any form, or by any means (electronic, mechanical, photocopying, recording or otherwise) without the prior written consent of the publisher. Any person who does any unauthorized act in relation to this publication may be liable to criminal prosecution and civil claims for damages.

This book is sold subject to the condition that it shall not, by way of trade or otherwise, be lent, re-sold, hired out, or otherwise circulated without the publisher's prior consent in any form other than that in which it is published and without a similar condition including this condition being imposed on the subsequent publisher.

Technical Review by Sven Aelterman

Cover Image by Andy Martin

Edited by Tony Davis and Heather Fielding

Typeset & Designed by Peter Woodhouse & Gower Associates

Table of Contents

Introduction — 17

Chapter 1: Storing and Managing Unstructured Data — 21
  Structured Data — 22
  Unstructured Data — 25
    CLOB data — 26
    BLOB data — 27
  Storing Unstructured Data — 28
    Storing Large Objects in SQL Server — 28
    Storing Large Objects in the file system — 30
    Database or file system? — 30
  Enter FILESTREAM — 35
    A first look at FILESTREAM — 37
    When to use FILESTREAM — 42
  Summary — 44

Chapter 2: Getting Started with FILESTREAM — 47
  The FILESTREAM Data Container — 47
  Understanding the FILESTREAM Filegroup — 49
  Creating FILESTREAM-enabled Databases — 52
    Creating a new FILESTREAM-enabled database — 52
    Enabling an existing database for FILESTREAM — 58
  Creating a Table with FILESTREAM Columns — 59
    Using SSMS table designer to create a table with FILESTREAM columns — 59
    Using T-SQL to create a table with FILESTREAM columns — 60
    Using T-SQL to add FILESTREAM columns to an existing table — 62
    Converting VARBINARY(MAX) columns to FILESTREAM and vice versa — 65
    Tables and FILESTREAM filegroups — 67
    FILESTREAM filegroup queries — 68
  FILESTREAM Data Manipulation Using T-SQL — 69
    Inserting a row with FILESTREAM data — 71

    Updating and deleting FILESTREAM data — 77
    FILESTREAM and triggers — 78
Advanced FILESTREAM DDL — 79
    The FILESTREAM data container and partitioned tables — 79
    Creating a database with multiple FILESTREAM filegroups — 82
Disabling FILESTREAM Storage on a Database — 85
Summary — 87

Chapter 3: Accessing FILESTREAM Data from Client Applications — 89

What is Streaming? — 89
Understanding Streaming Access to FILESTREAM Data — 90
    Step 1: Starting a transaction — 91
    Step 2: Retrieving the logical path name and transaction context — 92
    Step 3: Opening the FILESTREAM data file — 95
    Step 4: Reading and writing FILESTREAM data — 98
    Step 5: Closing the FILESTREAM data file — 101
    Step 6: Closing the transaction (COMMIT/ROLLBACK) — 101
Data Manipulation Using the Streaming APIs — 102
    Inserting a new record into a FILESTREAM-enabled table — 102
    Replacing the FILESTREAM data completely — 103
    Partial updates to FILESTREAM data — 104
    Reading information from the FILESTREAM store — 105
    Deleting the BLOB data stored in a FILESTREAM column — 105
    Deleting a row from a FILESTREAM-enabled table — 105
Lab 1: Reads, Writes and Partial Updates — 106
    Handling multiple FILESTREAM columns and rows — 114
Understanding the Logical Path to a FILESTREAM Data File — 115
    Formatting PathName() — 119
    PathName() and ROWGUIDCOL — 120
SqlFileStream Class Reference — 123
    Instantiating a SqlFileStream object — 123
OpenSqlFilestream API Reference — 126
Summary — 130

Chapter 4: FILESTREAM with Entity Framework and LINQ to SQL — 131

Lab 2: FILESTREAM and Entity Framework — 132
- Rebuilding the sample database — 133
- Lab 2a: A simple EF application using T-SQL access — 134
- Lab 2b: Using SqlFileStream and Entity Framework together — 144
- Adding a row to the table — 152

Lab 3: FILESTREAM and LINQ to SQL — 158
- Creating a new console application project — 158
- Adding a LINQ to SQL class — 158
- Defining object relational mappings — 159
- Adding a new row — 162
- Querying FILESTREAM data using LINQ to SQL — 162

Summary — 163

Chapter 5: FILESTREAM with ASP.NET and Silverlight — 165

Lab 4: Uploading Files to a FILESTREAM Database from an ASP.NET Web Page — 167
- Creating a new ASP.NET web application — 167
- Adding a database connection string — 168
- Designing the data entry page — 169
- Writing the "code-behind" — 171
- Running the application — 175

Lab 5: Deploying and Configuring a FILESTREAM Web Application on IIS — 176
- Running Visual Studio under an administrator account — 177
- Publishing the web application into a new virtual directory — 177
- Configuring IIS to use SQL Server Integrated Security — 181
- Running the application — 188

Lab 6: Creating a Web Handler to Serve Images from a FILESTREAM Database — 189
- Creating a stored procedure to retrieve FILESTREAM data — 189
- Creating the web page to serve images — 190
- Running and testing the application — 193

Lab 7: Displaying Thumbnail Images of Items from a FILESTREAM Database on an ASP.NET Web Page — 194
Creating the stored procedure to fetch item information — 194
Adding a new web form and data grid — 196
Adding a data source — 196

Lab 8: Using SqlFileStream in an N-Tier Scenario — 204
Creating the Visual Studio solution and projects — 205
Writing the domain object code — 207
Writing the data access code — 207
Creating an HTTP handler to serve images — 209
Adding remote calling capability — 211
Testing the application from Visual Studio — 215

Lab 9: Playing a Video Stored in a FILESTREAM Database on a Silverlight Application — 216
Setting up the data — 217
Creating a Silverlight application — 218
Creating a video handler — 219
Adding and configuring MediaElement — 222
Running and testing the application — 224

Summary — 225

Chapter 6: FILESTREAM with SSIS and SSRS — 227
FILESTREAM and SSIS — 228
Lab 10: Loading BLOB Values into a FILESTREAM Column Using SSIS — 228
Setting up the sample database — 230
Creating the SSIS package — 235

Lab 11: Exporting BLOB Values from a FILESTREAM Column Using SSIS — 256
Creating the SSIS package — 256
Setting the output folder — 256
The Execute SQL task — 257
The Foreach Loop container — 257
The Script task — 258

| Lab 12: Displaying FILESTREAM Data in SSRS Reports | 260 |
| Summary | 269 |

Chapter 7: FILESTREAM Database Administration — 271

FILESTREAM and Database Transaction Isolation Levels — 272
- READ COMMITTED, REPEATABLE READ and SERIALIZABLE isolation levels — 272
- READ UNCOMMITTED isolation level — 273
- Snapshot isolation level — 274
- Summary of FILESTREAM behavior under transaction isolation levels — 276

Detaching and Attaching FILESTREAM Databases — 277

FILESTREAM and Garbage Files — 280
- Garbage files and recovery models — 280
- FILESTREAM garbage collection and tombstone tables — 281

FILESTREAM Data Corruption and DBCC Checks — 285
- Corruption caused by missing FILESTREAM data files — 286
- Corruption caused by orphaned files — 292
- Corruption caused by deleting the garbage files manually — 293

Querying FILESTREAM Databases — 294

FILESTREAM Data and Space Management — 295
- Changing the FILESTREAM filegroup location — 296
- Adding a new partition to share the FILESTREAM storage load — 300

Migrating FILESTREAM Data — 307
- SSMS scripting — 307
- The Database Publishing Wizard — 310

Summary — 311

Chapter 8: Backup and Restore for FILESTREAM Databases — 313

Creating and Populating the Sample Database — 314

Backing up FILESTREAM Databases — 315
- Full backups — 316
- Differential backups — 316
- Transaction log backups — 317

Restoring FILESTREAM Databases 319
    Restoring from a full backup 320
    Point-in-time restore 320

File Backups and Piecemeal Restores 323

Data and Backup Compression for FILESTREAM Databases 326

Beware of Garbage Files in FILESTREAM Backups 327

Summary 329

Chapter 9: Investigating FILESTREAM Databases 331

Relevant System Catalog Views 331
    sys.all_columns, sys.columns and sys.system_columns 332
    sys.computed_columns 333
    sys.identity_columns 333
    sys.dm_repl_traninfo 333
    sys.tables 334
    sys.internal_tables 334
    sys.partitions 335
    sys.data_spaces 335
    sys.database_files 336
    sys.filegroups 336
    sys.system_internals_partition_columns 336
    sys.system_internals_partitions 337
    sys.filestream_tombstone_* 337

Useful FILESTREAM Metadata Queries 337
    SQL Server instance-level queries 338
    Database-level queries 342

FILESTREAM-related DMVs 348
    sys.dm_filestream_file_io_handles 348
    sys.dm_filestream_file_io_requests 349
    sys.dm_tran_active_transactions 350

FILESTREAM and Wait Types 350
    FS_FC_RWLOCK 350
    FS_GARBAGE_COLLECTOR_SHUTDOWN 351

FS_HEADER_RWLOCK 351
FS_LOGTRUNC_RWLOCK 351
FSA_FORCE_OWN_XACT 351
FSAGENT 352
FSTR_CONFIG_MUTEX 352
FSTR_CONFIG_RWLOCK 352
Summary 352

Chapter 10: Integrating FILESTREAM with other SQL Server Features 353

FILESTREAM and Replication 354
    Replicating FILESTREAM columns 354
    Maximum replication data size 357
    FILESTREAM replication and the UNIQUEIDENTIFIER column 359
    Managing the FILESTREAM replication flag using T-SQL 362
    Replication log reader and the FILESTREAM garbage collector 367
    FILESTREAM and synchronization methods 368
    Replicating databases with multiple FILESTREAM filegroups 369
    FILESTREAM and the different replication types 370
FILESTREAM and Log Shipping 372
FILESTREAM and Full-Text Indexing 373
FILESTREAM and Database Snapshots 377
FILESTREAM and Change Data Capture 379
FILESTREAM and Data Compression 384
FILESTREAM and Transparent Data Encryption 384
FILESTREAM and Database Mirroring 385
FILESTREAM and High Availability Disaster Recovery 386
Summary 387

Chapter 11: FileTable 389

Introduction to FileTable 389
FileTable Concepts 390
    Fixed schema 390
    Creating folder structures using the HIERARCHYID data type 394
    Root folder 397

Non-transactional access	398
FileTable namespace	400
FileTable security	402

Setting Up the Server for FileTable — 404
Creating a Database with Support for FileTable — 404
Creating a FileTable — 406

Create a FileTable using T-SQL	406
Create a FileTable using SSMS	408
Work with a FileTable using SSMS	410
Adding constraints to the FileTable	411
Restrictions on creating FileTables	412

Accessing a FileTable with Windows Explorer and Other Client Applications — 413

Creating files	413
Creating folders	415
Memory-mapped files	415
Empty database folder	416

Programming FileTable — 416

Adding rows using T-SQL	417
Using .NET file I/O APIs	422

Managing FileTables — 425

T-SQL functions	425
Catalog and Dynamic Management Views	428
Stored procedures	431

Advanced FileTable Uses — 432

Full-text search	432
Semantic search	434

Investigating FileTable — 437
Summary — 437

Chapter 12: Planning, Configuration and Best Practices — 439

Planning — 439
Optimizing your Storage Configuration for FILESTREAM — 441

Keep FILESTREAM data containers on a separate disk volume	441

Disabling short file names ... 441
Compressing FILESTREAM data ... 445
Configuring NTFS cluster size ... 446
Disabling the indexing service ... 447
Configuring antivirus ... 448
Disabling the Last Access Time attribute ... 449
Configuring the disks with the correct RAID level ... 450
Regular disk defragmentation ... 451
Setting up FILESTREAM for Remote Access ... 451
Configuring the client computer for remote access ... 452
Configuring the client application for remote access ... 452
Best Practices for FILESTREAM Development ... 453
Use FILESTREAM streaming APIs to read and write FILESTREAM data ... 453
Avoid small partial updates ... 453
Keep an additional column to store the type of file or extension ... 454
Identifying the type of file from a file header ... 454
Add a content-type column on FILESTREAM tables ... 456
Add a timestamp or date column to track last modified date for cache control ... 456
Use a computed column to retrieve the file size ... 457
Keep a default constraint on FILESTREAM columns ... 458
Summary ... 459

Appendix A: Configuring FILESTREAM on a SQL Server Instance ... 461
Understanding FILESTREAM Configuration and Access Levels ... 463
FILESTREAM access levels ... 463
Enabling and Configuring FILESTREAM During Installation ... 468
Enable FILESTREAM for Transact-SQL access ... 469
Enable FILESTREAM for file I/O streaming access ... 469
Allow remote clients to have streaming access to FILESTREAM data ... 470
Enabling and Configuring FILESTREAM After Installation ... 471
Configuring FILESTREAM at the Windows level ... 471
Configuring FILESTREAM at the SQL Server instance level ... 473

Verifying FILESTREAM Configuration 477
   Verifying Windows-level FILESTREAM configuration settings 477
   Verifying SQL Server Instance-level FILESTREAM configuration settings 479
   Using SSMS to check that FILESTREAM is enabled 479
   Using T-SQL to check that FILESTREAM is enabled 480
Disabling the FILESTREAM Feature 481
Advanced Installation and Configuration Options 483
   Unattended SQL Server installation and FILESTREAM configuration 483
   Enabling and configuring FILESTREAM from the command line 485
   Configuring FILESTREAM access level from the command line 486
   Setting up FILESTREAM on a failover cluster 487
Summary **488**

About the authors

Jacob Sebastian

Jacob Sebastian is a Microsoft MVP (SQL Server) from Ahmedabad, India, who has been working with SQL Server for almost 15 years. He works as CTO with Excellence Infonet, Ahmedabad, which focuses on building highly scalable, mission critical applications for the healthcare industry.

Jacob started his database career in the early nineties with Dbase and then moved to Clipper, FoxPro and, finally, to SQL Server, starting with version 6.5. He has presented at various SQL Server conferences, including PASS Global Summit, European PASS Conference, 24 Hour PASS, Tech-ED India, Community Techdays, Microsoft Virtual Techdays, SQL Server Saturday and more.

Jacob wrote his first book in 2009, *The Art of XSD – SQL Server XML Schema Collections* (HTTP://BRURL.COM/FS21) which delved deeply into the XSD and XML Schema collections, introduced in SQL Server 2005. He also wrote the XML chapter for the book, *SQL Server 2008 Bible* (HTTP://BRURL.COM/FS22).

When not working, Jacob spends time at BEYONDRELATIONAL.COM.

Jacob was the lead author on this book, and wrote Chapters 1 to 10.

Sven Aelterman

Sven Aelterman is a lecturer in Information Systems at Troy University in Troy, Alabama. He teaches undergraduate courses in data warehousing, network infrastructure and security. He is also the technology specialist for Troy University's Sorrell College of Business, and performs a variety of technology roles with a global scope.

He continues consulting work through Adduxis, where he assists customers with software development projects using the Microsoft .NET Framework and related technologies. Sven focuses on application design and architecture and secure coding practices. He received his MBA from Troy University and his bachelor's degree from the Hogeschool Gent (University College, Ghent) in Belgium, his native country. Sven is married to Ebony and they have a son, Edward, and a daughter, Sofia.

Sven contributed Chapter 11 to this book, and the labs in Chapters 4 and 5, as well as some additional material throughout.

Acknowledgements

Jacob Sebastian

This is my third book and, as always, the first name I would like to mention is Steve Jones at SQLServerCentral.com, who deserves the credit for igniting my passion for writing. Thereafter, I've benefited from the help of numerous mentors. Big thanks, in particular, to Jeff Moden, Madhu Nair, Kent Waldrope, Arnie Rowland, and Michael Coles, all of whom played a significant role in shaping my attitude towards the SQL Server community.

I would like to thank Tony Davis at Red Gate, who helped me to get this project started and guided me throughout this long journey. Tony not only managed the project, but also stepped in at every stage throughout the writing process, commenting, correcting, rephrasing and reorganizing to mold the content into the shape in which you see it in this book.

Sven Aelterman, technical reviewer and co-author of this book deserves major credit since this book would not have been possible without his involvement and hard work. He wrote the entire chapter on FileTable and rewrote several sections of other chapters, including many of the code samples. His expertise in SQL Server, **FILESTREAM** and various Web/.NET technologies has played a crucial role in ensuring the accuracy of information presented in the book.

Several other people contributed, directly or indirectly, to this book throughout the journey. Michael Rys and Srini Acharya at Microsoft were kind enough to answer many of my various questions, as was Paul Randal at sqlskills.com. My friend, Sudeep Raj, did a wonderful internal review of the SSIS lab and provided some valuable comments. Many times during this journey, I needed to recharge and refocus on the goal of completing the book. For helping me achieve this, I thank my friends Anil, Khyati, Pinal, Krupali, Tejas, Nakul, Vinod Kumar, and everyone else who helped motivate me along the way.

Finding time for writing such a lengthy book has been a real challenge. I ended up stealing the weekends, holidays, early mornings and late night hours from the family. I dedicate this book to my wife Jincy and daughters Julie and Jiya. Without your support, encouragement and understanding, I would not have been able to write it.

Finally, I would like to thank all the readers of my articles, blogs, and previous books, for their continuous feedback and encouragement.

Sven Aelterman

Participating in the technical review and authoring of this book has been a unique experience and one that would not have been possible without the efforts of many others. I am, first and foremost, grateful to Jacob for allowing me to share the authorship of this work with him. Jacob is, without a doubt, a leading expert in SQL Server and `FILESTREAM`. Working with him has allowed me to learn so much, including the fact that I didn't yet know everything about `FILESTREAM`. A close second is reserved for the efforts of our editor, Tony Davis. It was probably sufficient to ask him to coordinate Jacob's writing and my reviews, but his role didn't stop there. Adding an additional chapter and more content to the book doubtlessly caused him long nights. I appreciate his experience and guidance in seeing us through this venture.

As you're about to learn, SQL Server `FILESTREAM` is an exciting and intricate feature. I would like to claim that I was able to figure it all out on my own, but I would do injustice to several people who helped clarify some of the finer points (where the documentation wasn't always helpful).

First, Microsoft developer evangelist, Glen Gordon, was instrumental in connecting me to members of the SQL Server team, whom I'd like to thank for reading and responding to my wordy questions. Finally, Paul Randal at SQLskills was also called upon for some verification.

While the help of these professionals was vital to the accuracy and completeness of the book, I am equally thankful to my wife, Ebony, for her support during the late nights of researching, editing, and writing. She was very much aware of the existence of our two children. I am not so sure if she was aware of the existence of her husband anymore. (Honey, he was the one sleeping in late while you were raising the kids.)

Introduction

When I first started my database career in the early 1990s, all the applications on which I worked dealt with simple relational data, stored in a few relational tables. The most commonly used data types were strings, numbers, dates, and Boolean. Many of these were single-user applications that lived on a single computer.

Soon, however, and rapidly, applications started becoming more complex, and new and more challenging data processing requirements began to emerge. Many applications started dealing with unstructured data. Along with relational data, our applications needed to be able to generate, process and serve non-relational data such as XML, images, music, videos, and so on.

SQL Server 6.5 offered two data types for storing large chunks of text and binary data, namely `text` and `image` respectively. SQL Server 7.0 added one more data type, `ntext`, which enabled storage of Unicode text. SQL Server 2005 added the data types `VARCHAR(MAX)`, `NVARCHAR(MAX)` and `VARBINARY(MAX)`, which made reading and writing chunks of unstructured data much simpler. Despite these improvements, the basic underlying problem remained: SQL Server is primarily a relational database management system and optimized for processing relational data. Reading and writing large chunks of text/binary data within the database requires a lot of SQL Server internal memory (buffers as big as the size of the chunk being read/written), and multiple, simultaneous requests for large blocks of data can put the server under severe memory pressure.

The workaround adopted by most database architects was to store the unstructured data as disk files on the file system, and store only the path to the file in the relational table. The file system is optimized for reading and writing large files, and offers streaming capabilities. This solved the performance problems, but introduced new challenges. In this scheme, we had no way to ensure transactional consistency between relational data and data in the file system. Also, management of backups was complicated, since the normal database backups were only possible if accompanied by the corresponding backup of the file system.

When SQL Server 2008 introduced the `FILESTREAM` feature, it had my immediate attention. At last, we had a way to store the unstructured data in the file system and thus take advantage of the NTFS streaming capabilities but, at the same time, ensure transactional consistency between the relational data and the file system data. In addition, a normal database backup would now also include the file system data.

It's safe to say I was an early adopter, and my primary goal with this book is to ease the paths of others who are interested in this technology, as some aspects of its adoption proved far from plain sailing.

This book attempts to guide you, step-by-step, through every phase of `FILESTREAM` implementation, from enabling the feature, to creating `FILESTREAM` tables, to manipulating `FILESTREAM` data through the streaming APIs, to handling `FILESTREAM` data in simple ASP.NET web pages, to complex N-tier .NET applications.

It also covers, in detail, administration and troubleshooting of `FILESTREAM` databases and tables. Alongside the advantages offered by the technology, it tries to cover some of its shortcomings, and to offer practical advice on workarounds, or possible alternative solutions.

Who is this book for?

The primary audience for this book is the SQL Server developers who have to deal with more than relational data. It will help them to get started with `FILESTREAM`-enabled databases, and it provides a very detailed coverage on accessing `FILESTREAM` data through the .NET and Win32 APIs. We have provided a reasonable number of examples, sample code, and labs that demonstrate how to access `FILESTREAM` data from C#.NET, VB.NET and C++. In addition, there are several labs demonstrating `FILESTREAM` access from common application platforms/tools such as ASP.NET, Silverlight, SSIS, SSRS (SQL Server Reporting Services), Entity Framework, LINQ to SQL and so on.

The secondary audience for this book are any SQL Server administrators and technical project managers on projects requiring the storage and retrieval of BLOB (Binary Large Objects) data. The second half of the book is dedicated to `FILESTREAM` database administration-related topics covering almost everything you might need to know when dealing with `FILESTREAM`-enabled databases.

How this book is organized

Chapters 1–2 of the book provide an overview of the `FILESTREAM` feature and enough information to enable the technology and then start creating a `FILESTREAM`-enabled database, tables and columns, and manipulating `FILESTREAM` data with T-SQL.

Chapters 3–6 explain how to access `FILESTREAM` data from client applications, through the streaming APIs, targeting the interests of database developers. Topics covered include how to:

- access `FILESTREAM` data in a transactionally consistent manner using C#.NET (with equivalent code examples provided in C++ and VB.NET)
- access `FILESTREAM` data with Entity Framework and LINQ to SQL
- deploy and configure `FILESTREAM` Web Applications with IIS (Internet Information Services)
- handle `FILESTREAM` data in N-tier .NET applications.

Chapters 7–10 cover topics relating to the administration of `FILESTREAM`-enabled databases, such as backup and restore, migrating `FILESTREAM` databases and data, and investigating `FILESTREAM` databases, using Dynamic Management Views (DMVs).

Chapter 11 takes an in-depth look at an extension of `FILESTREAM`, called FileTable, which was introduced in SQL Server 2012. A FileTable can store the data on an entire NTFS folder hierarchy. Unlike a regular `FILESTREAM` column, client applications can directly access the files in a FileTable.

Chapter 12 provides a summary of some of best practices to observe when using the `FILESTREAM` feature.

Finally, there is an appendix providing advice on how to set up, review and troubleshoot `FILESTREAM` configuration-related problems.

Code examples

Throughout this book are scripts demonstrating use of the `FILESTREAM` feature. All the code you need to try out the examples in this book can be obtained from the URL below.

http://www.simple-talk.com/RedGateBooks/SebastianAelterman_ArtOfSQL-ServerFILESTREAM_Code.zip.

All examples should run on all versions and editions of SQL Server from SQL Server 2008 upwards, unless specified otherwise. You must have .NET Framework 3.5 SP 1 or later to run the .NET examples. Some of the .NET examples use the .NET 4.0 method `Stream.CopyTo()`, and you will need either .NET 4.0 for those examples, or to replace this method with equivalent code in .NET 3.5 (as explained with the relevant code listings). To run the labs, you will need the associated environment, such as Silverlight SDK (Software Development Kit) for the Silverlight Lab, SQL Server Reporting Services for the SSRS Lab, SQL Server Integration Services for the SSIS Lab, and so on. Chapter 11, on FileTable, requires SQL Server 2012.

Chapter 1: Storing and Managing Unstructured Data

One of the challenges of designing data storage of SQL Server-driven applications is that not all data fits into the relational model. The relational model expects each table to describe a discrete entity and each column in the table to define exactly one aspect of that entity. Much business data is less structured in nature; it is becoming increasingly common to need to store images, documents, and speech data (PDF, MP3, and so on) alongside the relational data.

It's been possible to store this sort of unstructured data in SQL Server for a number of years, but there have always been associated difficulties. With older, large object (LOB) data types, such as `TEXT`, `NTEXT`, and `IMAGE`, the data was generally held out of row, i.e. on a different page from the rest of the row data. Reading and modifying the data, using T-SQL functions such as `READTEXT` and `WRITETEXT` was painfully slow. The introduction of the large-value (`MAX`) data types, namely `VARCHAR(MAX)`, `NVARCHAR(MAX)` and `VARBINARY(MAX)` improved matters somewhat and made it easier to develop applications that used these LOB data types. However, it was still preferable to store these LOBs on the file system, with only a link to the data stored in the database, in order to avoid the buffer pool pollution that arose from having such data stored inline, and also to take advantage of high-performance streaming, lower rates of fragmentation during modifications, and so on, that are offered by file system storage.

Nevertheless, storing LOBs on the file system, separately from the rest of the business data, was not without problems, including the fact that the data wasn't included in database backups and, perhaps most significantly, having the data outside the transactional control of the database meant that it was possible for the LOB data, if it were subject to modification, to become out of sync with the structured, SQL Server-based data to which it related. In addition, when LOB data is stored in the file system, outside the control of the database administrator, any user or application with sufficient

Windows permissions can access the LOB data files directly. This makes it a considerable challenge to ensure that the LOB data files are accessible only to the Windows users who have access to the associated relational data.

Enter `FILESTREAM` storage, introduced with SQL Server 2008, which allows us to append a `FILESTREAM` attribute to a `VARBINARY(MAX)` data type, and so get the performance advantages of storing LOB data on the file system, combined with the many advantages of having that data under the control of SQL Server. In this chapter, we will begin our exploration of the storage of LOB data, using the new `FILESTREAM` attribute, covering:

- what we mean by structured, unstructured and semi-structured data
- advantages and disadvantages of storing LOB data in the database and file system
- what `FILESTREAM` offers, a first look at how it works, and strategic considerations for its use.

Structured Data

As database professionals, we deal with data every day; we store, manage, process, and query large volumes of data as part of our day-to-day database development and management work. Most of the data that we handle may be regarded as *structured*, meaning that it conforms fully to the formats and data models associated with the relational database. By way of its compliance with the relational data model, such data generally also conforms to more formal definitions of the term, *structured data*, which refer to:

- information that has been organized to allow identification and separation of the context of the information from its content
- data organized into semantic chunks or entities, with similar entities grouped together in relations or classes, and presented in a patterned manner

- data that can be shared electronically with customers and suppliers, because the structure and meaning of data has been standardized and usually determined by a data model.

All of these definitions point to the defining characteristic of structured data: the ability to identify and extract specific pieces of information that is included in the data. This is usually done by adding some sort of schema or data model which explains the structure of the data and makes it meaningful. It means we can query the data based on predetermined data types and well-defined and understood relationships.

Of course, there are degrees of structure; data that one application would deem unstructured, might be deemed structured enough by another. To demonstrate what I mean, consider the data presented in Listing 1-1, which is a log generated by an invoicing application.

```
Row Details
--- -------------------------------------------------------
01  Mike created invoice 101 dated 2010/01/13 with a note
    to notify James before shipping on fax number 456-098-0909
02  John created invoice 102 dated 2010/01/14 with a note to
    call Anna on 898-090-0909 after shipment is sent
```

Listing 1-1:   Unstructured log data.

If asked whether this data is structured or unstructured, most would say "unstructured," and with good justification; many pieces of vital information, stored in each row as a long text string. It is comprehensible to a human, but will be hard for software to extract those pieces of information from the text string.

So essentially, yes, this data is unstructured but even so, if this data is used just as a log of activities and the application does not need to query those vital pieces of information embedded in the text string, and extract them separately, then for that business this data is structured enough. Of course, a second application might need direct access to the invoice date, currently embedded within the string stored in the `Details` column. From this application's perspective, the data really is unstructured, and we'd need to store the information in a slightly more structured manner, as shown in Listing 1-2.

```
Inv#  SalesRep  InvDate     InvNote
----  --------  ----------  ------------------------------------------------
101   Mike      2010/01/13  Notify James before shipping on fax number 456-098-0909
102   John      2010/01/14  Call Anna on 898-090-0909 after shipment is sent
```

Listing 1-2:   Slightly more structured log data.

A third application, one that requires access to all of the individual elements in the data, would require the data to be more structured still, in fact in the sort of form we are accustomed to seeing in typical relational database tables, as shown in Listing 1-3.

```
Inv#  SalesRep  InvDate     Notify  Number        type   when
----  --------  ----------  ------  ------------  -----  ---------------
101   Mike      2010/01/13  James   456-098-0909  Fax    before shipment
102   John      2010/01/14  Anna    898-090-0909  Phone  after shipment
```

Listing 1-3:   Structured log data.

I recently encountered a perfect example of this subtlety in a real application. It was a data integration project for a health care system, where the source system stored the patient address in a single field, and so the `address` column in the source system held values such as "999-888, Kings Highway, Brooklyn, NY 11223." From the perspective of this system, the data was structured enough, since the address information was used only for mailing purpose. A mailing module picked the information from the address field and printed the mailing label. No other part of the application touched the address column.

The target system, however, was more advanced and needed to display the location of patients on a map, and so needed to extract individual elements of the address, such as street name, zip code, and so on, in order to calculate the latitude and longitude of each patient. Because the target system found the data to be unstructured, we had to build a module that parsed the source data and produced more structured output for the target application.

From here on, however, we are simply going to define "structured data" in general to mean data that meets the requirements of the relational model, such that we can extract the required information from the data easily and accurately.

> ***Semi-structured data***
>
> *Semi-structured data is a form of structured data that does not fully follow the rules and structures associated with tables and data models of relational databases. However, they do include tags and markups to separate and identify semantic elements and collections of records and fields within the data. The most common example of semi-structured data is XML. An XML document contains hierarchical data organized as elements and attributes which does not fall within the relational data model. However, a database engine such as SQL Server can read the markup information and extract values out of an XML document, and shred the data into one or more result sets. We won't cover semi-structured data any further in this book.*

Unstructured Data

From the previous section, it is clear that data can be considered to be in an unstructured form when it is hard to programmatically retrieve the information at the desired level of granularity. Such data if often not associated with a schema, or has only a very simple schema, and typical examples include images and videos. Following on from our definition of structured data, we can simply state that unstructured data is any data that **does not meet the requirements of the relational model**.

Due to the complex nature of today's business requirements, it is quite natural that applications need to handle unstructured, as well as structured, data. For example, not all the input data is generated by manual data entry nowadays. The input data may come from a variety of sources and, as discussed, data may be structured enough for the application that produces the data, but may be unstructured in terms of the requirements of the application that consumes it.

In the language of the relational database, this sort of unstructured data is a Large Object (LOB), with Character Large Objects (CLOBs) for storing plain text data, and Binary Large Objects (BLOBs) for binary data.

CLOB data

Many applications deal with some sort of CLOB data. For example:

- an email management application that stores the Base64 encoded version of the attachments
- a discussion forum that stores the questions and answers discussed in the forum threads
- a content management system (CMS) that stores the content of web pages (e.g. articles) in a relational table
- an invoicing application that stores the notes or delivery instructions.

This sort of data does have a defined structure; for example, the input controls for a forum application, which stores the questions and answers, generate data in a certain markup format (e.g. HTML or RTF). When the data is to be displayed, the application reads the data, analyzes the structure, and can recognize certain elements of the data that require specific formatting, such as URLs.

However, in the context of our definition of structured data, this CLOB data is unstructured. It is not easy for the relational database engine to understand the content stored in the CLOB column. For example, if a user wants to retrieve a list of all URLs in a set of forum posts, this is not going to be easy for a relational database query.

BLOB data

BLOBs consist of "chunks" of binary data. When you record a voice note using your personal organizer software, you are generating some BLOB data. A chunk of encrypted binary data, or the content of an executable file, is a BLOB value. More and more applications today need to handle and store BLOB data. A few examples include:

- a document management system that stores different types of documents, such as Word or Excel
- a product catalog application that stores the images of products
- a multimedia library that stores videos and music
- a software download website that stores setup files, executable or zip files.

Again, most BLOB data (Word or Excel documents, images, audio files, and so on) does have a defined structure; an application that generates or consumes these files can understand the content based on the associated, simple schema.

However, from the relational database perspective, BLOB data is most certainly unstructured. Even though the applications that read and write BLOB data from and into the database understand the structure of the data, a database engine does not really understand it.

Storing Unstructured Data

As discussed, most business applications need to store, manage and process unstructured data of various shapes and sizes. Choosing the right storage design for this data will be critical to the performance, manageability, and overall health of the application and its database. There are two basic choices: store the LOB in the database, or store it on the file system with a pointer to it from within the database. So, depending upon the nature of the data, usage pattern, workload and various other factors related to the specific application and business requirements, the designers might decide whether to keep the LOB data within the database or outside the database.

Storing Large Objects in SQL Server

Most relational database management systems provide data types that can store LOBs. One can simply create a table with columns of the appropriate data types and use the programming model provided to read, write, and update the LOB data.

Pre-SQL Server 2005, unstructured data was stored in LOB data types. CLOB data was stored in **TEXT** (and **NTEXT** for Unicode) data types. BLOB data was stored in the **IMAGE** data type. These data types could store up to 2 GB of data, which was stored separately from the relational table data.

These old LOB data types, while still available, are deprecated in SQL Server 2005 and later, in favor of the large-value data types: **VARCHAR(MAX)** for text data (and **NVARCHAR(MAX)** for Unicode character data) and **VARBINARY(MAX)** for BLOB data. Working with these new data types is much easier than working with their older counterparts. For example, reading from, or writing into, a **VARCHAR(MAX)** column is much easier than with a **TEXT** column.

```
-- Create a table and insert a row
CREATE TABLE BlobTable
    (
        TextValue TEXT ,
        VarcharMaxValue VARCHAR(MAX)
    )
INSERT  INTO BlobTable
        ( TextValue ,
          VarcharMaxValue
        )
        SELECT  'The text data type is invalid for local variables.' ,
                'However VARCHAR(MAX) is valid'

-- Reading the first 20 characters from the TEXT column
DECLARE @val VARBINARY(16)
SELECT  @val = TEXTPTR(TextValue)
FROM    BlobTable
READTEXT BlobTable.TextValue @val 0 20


-- Reading the first 20 characters from the VARCHAR(MAX) column
SELECT  LEFT(VarcharMaxValue, 20)
FROM    BlobTable
```

Listing 1-4: Working with the new LOB data types is much easier.

All of the new LOB data types introduced in SQL Server 2005 support storage of up to 2 GB of data in a single column.

```
VARBINARY(10)    -- Can store up to 10 Bytes
VARBINARY(8000)  -- Can store up to 8000 Bytes
VARBINARY(8001)  -- Error!!!
VARBINARY(MAX)   -- Can store up to 2 GB of data
```

Listing 1-5: MAX identifier raises the storage capacity from 8,000 bytes to 2 GB.

Chapter 1: Storing and Managing Unstructured Data

Storing Large Objects in the file system

Many applications that deal with LOB data store this data outside the database, in the file system. Under this approach, a `Products` table in SQL Server would simply have an additional `VARCHAR` column (called, for example, `ImagePath`), which stores the file system path to the image file associated with the current product, the image being stored as an individual disk file in a designated folder.

An application that needs to retrieve the image will first read the relational data, obtain the path to the image file, and grab the image file using file system APIs. When a new product is added, the image file is copied to the specified folder and the path to the new image file is inserted into the `ImagePath` column. When an image needs to be updated, either the existing image file is overwritten, or a new file is copied and the path is updated in the table.

Database or file system?

Architects of applications that work with LOBs need to decide whether to store this data in a column within the database or as files in the file system. To a large degree, this decision will depend on the exact nature of the data, and the business application that uses it. Fundamentally, the size of a single LOB in SQL Server 2000 and 2005 is limited to 2 GB. If your application needs to store, for example, high-definition movies or X-ray films, then you may well exceed this limit, and have little choice but to store them on the file system, where the limit, for a NTFS file system, is closer to 16 TB (unless you can split the data into multiple 2 GB columns which, in many cases, would be impossible, or very painful).

Another common consideration would be the coupling of the data to the application and to other data. For an application like Flickr, the database is actually just a repository for loosely-coupled BLOBs. It probably makes more sense to store them on the file system.

Conversely, if an application needs to store a PDF version of every quote sent to a customer, then there is tighter coupling and it may make more sense to store the LOBs in the database.

Regardless of the route that seems most appropriate for your application, there are advantages and disadvantages to each approach, based on considerations of:

- transactional consistency
- data manageability and recoverability
- security
- performance.

We'll briefly discuss these issues in the coming sections, and further details can be found in Paul Randal's white paper, *FILESTREAM Storage in SQL Server 2008* (HTTP://BRURL.COM/FSI).

Transactional consistency

One of the fundamental advantages of storing data in a relational database is that, via the implementation of various transaction isolation levels, locking mechanisms, and so on, the relational engine guarantees a transactionally-consistent view of the data, at any point in time. In other words, it guarantees that transactions within SQL Server conform to the ACID properties, and so prevents interference between transactions on the same data, and ensures that transactional operations can succeed or fail together, as a batch.

By storing LOBs within the database, we can ensure that this transactional consistency extends to the LOB data as well as other relational data within the database. For example, assume that a user uploads a document (a BLOB) into a document management application that uses SQL Server storage. The operation involves inserting a new row into a table along with the relational data (such as the document name) and the BLOB data (the content of the document). Operations on the BLOB column fall within the scope of any open transactions, and a `COMMIT` or `ROLLBACK` affects the changes to the BLOB column just like any other columns that are involved the current batch of operations (`COMMIT` will save the changes and `ROLLBACK` will discard the changes).

Conversely, when LOB data is stored outside, SQL Server cannot ensure transactional consistency between the relational data in the tables and the data in the file system. It is hard, for example, to implement an architecture that rolls back file system changes when a SQL Server transaction rolls back. This can result in situations where the relational data and LOB data get out of sync. It is common, over time, to end up with "orphaned" files that are not referenced from the relational data and, conversely, references to files that no longer exist.

Data manageability and recoverability

From a data management perspective, there are several reasons why it is a lot easier to have all the data, including LOB data, stored in the database.

Firstly, it means that when a full backup of the database is taken it will include the LOBs, which makes restoring the data to a consistent state in the event of a disaster a much easier task. Also, it eases the process of moving the data from one location to another.

Since it is quite easy to take differential backups and transaction log backups of databases, we can (at least in theory) perform point-in-time restores of all data in the database, including the LOB data. For example, in cases of accidental data loss, the DBA can return the database to a previous state, at a point in time just before the operation took place that erroneously removed the data.

When storing the LOBs in the file system, and only the path to the disk file in a relational table, the backups do not contain the LOB data, and DBAs need to take separate backups of the database and file system. When the database is to be restored on another location, the correct version of the file system backup should also be restored. This requires careful versioning to make sure the right file system data is restored with the right database backup. It is also important to make sure to keep the same file system structure in the new location so that the disk files maintain the same path as that stored in the relational tables.

When the LOB data is stored outside the database, the relational data can be restored to a given point in time, but not the file system changes, since the file system on its own does not track modifications and does not allow you to roll back the changes, once the file is saved.

Security

When LOB data is stored within the database, the security can be managed at the SQL Server level. This reduces the administrative complexity and aligns LOB security with the same security processes applied to the associated relational data.

If LOB data is stored outside the database, separate measures must be put in place to secure the file system. The relational data and LOB data are disconnected (or connected with just a weak link which stores the path to the file in a relational column), and managing user access permissions is a major challenge.

Performance

You're probably thinking that, on almost all levels, storing LOB data in the database is preferable to storing it in the file system. However, despite the numerous advantages discussed so far, of storing LOB data in the database, **performance** is the one consideration that makes it a non-feasible option for most applications.

The relational database engine is optimized to process relational data; storing and processing huge chunks of LOB data is not always done with the same ease.

One of the big advantages that the file system can offer, when handling LOB data, is **streaming**. The streaming of data refers to transferring it in a manner that allows it to be processed as the data is transferred, rather than collecting all the data before the processing begins. Streaming significantly increases the performance of read and write operations on that data.

SQL Server cannot stream LOB data. When a chunk of LOB data is written, SQL Server creates a memory buffer large enough to hold the data, accepts all the data, and only then starts writing it into the database. Similarly, when LOB data is read, SQL Server creates a memory buffer large enough to hold the LOB value, reads all the data into the buffer and then sends it to the client connection that requested the data. So, to read or write a 500 MB value from or to a column, SQL Server needs to allocate 500 MB of memory to read or write the value.

Exceptionally large objects, or multiple simultaneous requests to read or write LOB data, can cause severe memory pressure and possibly result in the dreaded "insufficient memory" error. Keep in mind that SQL Server is optimized for I/O operations involving 8 KB pages, not massive objects. In any scenario, such queries can slow down other queries and affect overall server performance.

A piece of Microsoft research which studied the performance differences between storing LOB data in the database and in the file system found that file system is the preferred option for storing LOB data **if the size is 1 MB or above**.

> **To BLOB or not to BLOB?**
>
> *You can find the Microsoft Research Paper, one of Jim Gray's last projects before he disappeared at sea, To BLOB or Not To BLOB: Large Object Storage in a Database or a File System at* HTTP://BRURL.COM/FS2.

Enter FILESTREAM

By now it should be very clear that storing LOB data in the database offers a number of benefits, but introduces performance challenges. Conversely, storing the LOB data in the file system has overriding performance advantages, but fails to offer some of the basic data integrity, security, and manageability features that are required for business data, and which SQL Server provides.

Up to now, most people have adopted file system storage by necessity, and often struggled to overcome the associated shortcomings. This is exactly where the new `FILESTREAM` feature fits in. `FILESTREAM` storage, introduced in SQL Server 2008, is implemented as an extension to the `VARBINARY(MAX)` data type. In other words, SQL Server implements `FILESTREAM` storage through `VARBINARY(MAX)` columns with an additional flag indicating that the BLOB data should be stored in the `FILESTREAM` data container. It allows BLOBs to be stored in a special folder on the NTFS file system, while bringing that data under the transactional control of SQL Server. When a `VARBINARY(MAX)` column is marked as a `FILESTREAM` column, the 2 GB storage limit SQL Server puts on large-value types is no longer applicable.

This new `FILESTREAM` attribute is only available on the `VARBINARY(MAX)` data type. It cannot be applied to the `VARCHAR(MAX)` data type. If you have large plain text values to store, you can opt to store them in a `VARBINARY(MAX) FILESTREAM` column and use the `CAST(<column> AS VARCHAR(MAX))` method, if you need access to the plain text data in a query. When accessing a CLOB stored in a `FILESTREAM` column using the `FILESTREAM` APIs (`SqlFileStream` managed class or the Win32 function, `OpenSqlFileStream`), you can use functions available in your programming language of choice to convert the byte stream to plain text. For this reason, from this point on, we'll use the generic term "BLOB" to refer to all forms of LOB data.

Note that, to access **FILESTREAM** data through the streaming API, you must connect to SQL Server using Integrated Security (Windows authentication). If you connect to SQL Server using SQL Server authentication, you will get an "Access Denied" error when you try to open the **FILESTREAM** data file.

By applying the **FILESTREAM** attribute to a **VARBINARY(MAX)** column, all data in the resulting **FILESTREAM** column is actually stored in a file system folder, known as the **FILESTREAM** data container, which SQL Server specially configures for **FILESTREAM** data storage.

The intent is to provide a "best of both worlds" solution, offering the advantages below.

- **Excellent NTFS data streaming performance** – Makes reading and writing the BLOB data much faster.

- **Faster client access methods** – Client applications can request access to the **FILESTREAM** data files directly using the Win32 API or the .NET Objects exposed by SQL Server. **FILESTREAM** data can still be modified using T-SQL methods (which is not a recommended method), but the file system API methods allow much faster read/write access to the **FILESTREAM** data.

- **Reduced overhead on SQL Server** – When accessing the **FILESTREAM** data through the Win32 API or .NET Classes, **FILESTREAM** operations no longer overload SQL Server's internal memory.

- **Transactional consistency** – BLOB data operations happen within the context of a transaction so, if the transaction rolls back, the relational data modifications *and* BLOB changes will be rolled back.

- **Significantly easier backup management** – Though the BLOB data is still stored in the file system, a database backup includes the **FILESTREAM** data as well as all the relational data. When the backup is restored, the file system data is also restored to the new location. This topic, along with a few caveats, will be covered in detail in Chapter 8, *Backup and Restore for FILESTREAM Databases*.

- **Point-in-time restores** – With `FILESTREAM` enabled, changes to the BLOB data in the file system are captured in the transaction log, and the log can be backed up, enabling DBAs to restore all the data to a state as of a specific date and time.

- **Improved security management** – Permissions can be granted or denied on a `FILESTREAM` column just as for any other SQL Server columns.

There are also a few limitations arising from the use of `FILESTREAM`. For example, database mirroring does not support `FILESTREAM` data; Transparent Data Encryption (TDE) does not work with `FILESTREAM` data; and database snapshots cannot be created for `FILESTREAM` filegroups. These limitations are discussed further in Chapter 10, and on Books Online (http://brurl.com/fs3).

A first look at FILESTREAM

Chapter 2 goes into much greater depth on how `FILESTREAM` works, how to create new databases and tables that can store `FILESTREAM` data, how to insert, update, and delete `FILESTREAM` data, and so on.

However, to whet your appetite, we'll walk through a very simple example here of how to start using `FILESTREAM` on an existing SQL Server instance, covering:

- enabling the `FILESTREAM` feature for a given SQL Server instance
- setting the access level for the `FILESTREAM` data
- adding `FILESTREAM` storage to an existing database
- adding a `FILESTREAM` column to an existing table
- inserting `BLOB` data into the `FILESTREAM` column.

Chapter 1: Storing and Managing Unstructured Data

FILESTREAM is a hybrid feature that requires both the Windows Administrator and the SQL Server Administrator to perform actions before the feature is enabled. Because of this, the configuration is often a two-step process.

The Windows Administrator manages the Windows-related configuration changes needed for the FILESTREAM feature. For example, Windows Administrator privileges are required to create a Windows file share for the FILESTREAM feature. The Windows Administrator uses the SQL Server Configuration Manager to enable, disable, and configure FILESTREAM.

The SQL Server Administrator manages the configuration changes within the boundaries of the given SQL Server instance. The SQL Administrator enables, disables, and configures the FILESTREAM Access Level, either by using SQL Server Management Studio or by running sp_configure.

Appendix A describes in great detail how to enable and configure the FILESTREAM feature, both during a SQL Server installation and for existing instances and databases. If you encounter any difficulties, or need further information, please refer there.

Enabling FILESTREAM

Our first step is to enable the FILESTREAM feature at the instance level. Briefly, on the machine on which the SQL Server 2008 instance is installed, navigate as follows (this path may change in future versions): **Start | All Programs | Microsoft SQL Server 2008 | Configuration Tools | SQL Server Configuration Manager**, then select **SQL Server Services**. Right-click on the appropriate instance, select **Properties** then move to the **FILESTREAM** tab. In here, you can enable the instance for T-SQL and file I/O streaming access.

Setting the access level

All the rest of the work can be done from within SQL Server Management Studio (SSMS), so open it up and connect to the instance you just FILESTREAM enabled. Since we are enabling FILESTREAM access on an instance that did not have FILESTREAM enabled as part of the SQL Server installation process, we will also need to set the FILESTREAM Access Level, as demonstrated in Listing 1-6.

```
EXEC sp_configure filestream_access_level, 2;
GO
RECONFIGURE
GO
```

Listing 1-6: Setting the FILESTREAM access level for the instance.

Here, we've enabled both T-SQL and file I/O streaming access for the instance. Alternatively, by setting the `filestream_access_level` to 1, we could have enabled T-SQL access only (a value of 0 means disabled).

This same process can be performed through the SSMS GUI (see Appendix A).

Adding FILESTREAM storage

Next, we need to add a FILESTREAM filegroup and FILESTREAM file (data container) to the `NorthPole` database, as shown in Listing 1-7.

```
ALTER DATABASE NorthPole
   ADD FILEGROUP NorthPole_fs
   CONTAINS FILESTREAM;
GO

ALTER DATABASE NorthPole
   ADD FILE (
     NAME = NorthPole_fs,
```

```
        FILENAME = 'C:\ArtOfFS\Demos\Chapter1\NorthPole_fs')
TO FILEGROUP NorthPoleFS;
GO
```

Listing 1-7: Adding a `FILESTREAM` filegroup and data container.

Note that the `C:\ArtOfFS\Demos\Chapter1` directory must exist on the appropriate SQL Server instance machine (see Appendix A for more discussion of NTFS file system configuration).

Adding a FILESTREAM column

Having done this, we can now create a table in this database that has a `FILESTREAM` column, as shown in Listing 1-8.

```
CREATE TABLE [dbo].[Authors]
    (
        [AuthorID] UNIQUEIDENTIFIER ROWGUIDCOL
                                    NOT NULL
                                    UNIQUE ,
        [AuthorName] VARCHAR(50) ,
        [AuthorImage] VARBINARY(MAX) FILESTREAM
                                    NULL
    )
```

Listing 1-8: Creating an `Authors` table with a `FILESTREAM` column.

For reasons that will be discussed in much more detail in Chapter 3, a `FILESTREAM` column can be created only on a table that has a `UNIQUEIDENTIFIER` column with the `ROWGUIDCOL` attribute. Notice, also, that the table contains an `AuthorImage` column of type `VARBINARY(MAX)` to which we've applied the `FILESTREAM` attribute.

Inserting BLOB data

In Listing 1-9, we insert an image of the famous Simple-Talk author, Phil Factor, into this column, and the image will be automatically stored in the `NorthPole_fs` data container, on the file system, specified in Listing 1-7.

```sql
-- Insert the data to the table
INSERT  INTO [dbo].[Authors]
        ( AuthorID ,
          AuthorName ,
          AuthorImage
        )
        SELECT  NEWID() ,
                'PhilFactor' ,
                bulkcolumn
        FROM OPENROWSET(BULK 'C:\temp\philFactor.gif', SINGLE_BLOB) AS x

SELECT  *
FROM    dbo.authors


AuthorID                              AuthorName            AuthorImage
------------------------------------  --------------------  -------------
C0B1E727-40B3-48FE-B83A-2FD6C1261695  PhilFactor            0x474946383761C8001B01F7000004...

(1 row(s) affected)
```

Listing 1-9:   Inserting an image into the `Authors` table.

Notice that we use the `NEWID()` function to assign a new unique value to our `AuthorID` column. We use the `OPENROWSET` function, with the `BULK` rowset provider, to read in our image file. The `SINGLE_BLOB` argument specifies that the file is returned as a single-row, single-column rowset, called `bulkcolumn`, of type `VARBINARY(MAX)`. We then simply insert this image into the `AuthorImage` column.

We now have an image, stored in the file system, but under the transactional control of SQL Server, and which would be included in database backups, and so on. We are also now ready to take advantage of the performance benefits of streaming and fast file system API access methods when reading and modifying this data, as we will see in Chapter 2.

When to use FILESTREAM

Despite the obvious advantages of `FILESTREAM` to SQL Server applications that use BLOB data, the decision of where and how to use it should be taken only after carefully analyzing the storage requirements, data usage patterns, possible administrative overheads, and so on.

Size of the files

The previously-referenced Microsoft Research paper, *To BLOB or Not To BLOB: Large Object Storage in a Database or a File System*, suggests that, for BLOBs that are smaller than 256 KB, the best performance will probably be obtained by simply storing the data directly in the relational tables. Files larger than 1 MB are better stored in the file system, and managed through SQL Server using `FILESTREAM`. In that in-between region of 256 KB to 1 MB, the decision of which way to go can only be taken after analyzing the specific data usage scenarios.

Generally speaking, though, if the average size of the BLOB values that you expect your application to process is below 1 MB, then direct storage in the database, using a normal `VARBINARY(MAX)` column, is likely to perform better in most cases. However, this may vary based on how write-intensive the workload is. Even 256 KB files that are read/updated many times per second in a `VARBINARY(MAX)` column will cause memory exhaustion. The best way to take this decision is by running some tests that involve real workload and usage patterns, and see what fits best in your specific environment.

Data usage patterns

`FILESTREAM` does not support in-place (also referred to as "partial") updates of BLOB data files. Instead, every time a BLOB value is modified, SQL Server creates an entirely new copy of the file with the modified content, and discards the old file. The old file will be deleted by an asynchronous garbage collector process.

If your business requirement includes making frequent changes to the BLOB data values, then `FILESTREAM` may not be the right option. However, this decision should be taken only after running some tests with the expected usage pattern and deciding whether to go with `FILESTREAM` or `VARBINARY(MAX)` storage.

Administrative overhead

Though `FILESTREAM` offers a number of benefits to the database administrators, there may be cases when it adds unacceptable administrative and storage overhead.

As discussed earlier, when you take a full database backup of the `FILESTREAM`-enabled database, all the `FILESTREAM` data will, by default, come along with your backup. When you restore the backup to a different location, the `FILESTREAM` data will be restored as well.

This is great from a management perspective but, if you have terabytes of `FILESTREAM` data, this will add a huge storage overhead to your backup files, and greatly increase the time and server resources required to perform the backups. For example, let's say you have a 10 GB database and 20 Terabytes of `FILESTREAM` data. Your SLA requires a daily full backup of the database to be taken, but the `FILESTREAM` data is seldom modified. You will be adding massively to the size and overhead of your daily full backups, with most of the space taken up by `FILESTREAM` data that hasn't changed since last time.

In such cases, it probably makes sense to exploit the fact that `FILESTREAM` data is stored in a separate, dedicated filegroup, and that SQL Server supports partial backups, whereby only selected filegroups are backed up. We could take backups excluding the `FILESTREAM` filegroups, and then less-frequent backups that include only the `FILESTREAM` data.

In short, it is recommended that you analyze the workload and the type of data to be processed, and undertake some performance tests before deciding whether or not to use `FILESTREAM`.

Summary

As business applications become ever more versatile, the smooth handling of unstructured, LOB data, alongside the normal (and normalized) relational data is becoming an increasingly common requirement.

Storing such data in the database (in a `VARBINARY(MAX)` column) offers a number of advantages, including transactional consistency, point-in-time recovery, manageability and better security administration. However, these benefits come with a large memory overhead and, often, a severe performance penalty. Microsoft research shows that the file system is the preferred storage medium for files over 1 MB in size.

Storing BLOB data in the file system offers performance benefits, taking advantage of the streaming capabilities of NTFS, but it does not provide transactional consistency, point-in-time recovery, security, and so on, and this is a big drawback for many business applications.

`FILESTREAM` is a new storage feature introduced in SQL Server 2008. It stores the BLOB data in the file system and allows you to take advantage of the NTFS stream capabilities. At the same time, `FILESTREAM` ensures transactional consistency between the relational data and BLOB data stored in the file system.

Furthermore, administering and safeguarding the data is much simpler, since the BLOB data is included in normal database backups, and any modifications to that data are included in the transaction log file, so point-in-time recovery is supported.

Any BLOB data that is under 1 MB is probably still best stored in a `VARBINARY(MAX)` column, directly in the database. However, for all other BLOB data, `FILESTREAM` storage is the way to go.

Chapter 2: Getting Started with FILESTREAM

As we discussed in the previous chapter, `FILESTREAM` enables you to store BLOB data in the file system so that you can take advantage of the streaming and caching capabilities of NTFS. By accessing the BLOB data using the Win32 streaming APIs exposed by SQL Server 2008, you can offload the processing overhead from SQL Server.

In this chapter, we look in detail at how `FILESTREAM` data is stored, and how you set up a `FILESTREAM` database, table, and column. We then provide an example of inserting data into the column.

The FILESTREAM Data Container

SQL Server stores the `FILESTREAM` data in a file system folder which is known as the `FILESTREAM` data container. Each `FILESTREAM`-enabled database must have its own unique data container. The location of the `FILESTREAM` data container is specified when you create a `FILESTREAM`-enabled database or when you enable `FILESTREAM` on an existing database.

SQL Server creates a number of subfolders in the data container to manage the `FILESTREAM` data; a folder is created for each table, with one or more `FILESTREAM` columns. If a table is partitioned, a folder is created for each partition. Within the folder for each table or partition, a subfolder is created for each of the `FILESTREAM`-enabled columns, to store the BLOB data.

Chapter 2: Getting Started with FILESTREAM

When SQL Server configures a file system folder as the `FILESTREAM` data container, it creates a file named **filestream.hdr**, and a folder named **$FSLOG**. Both of these file system objects are used by SQL Server internally and it is strongly recommended that you do not access or modify them outside SQL Server.

The **filestream.hdr** file stores the internal information that SQL Server uses to manage the BLOB data stored in the `FILESTREAM` data container, and to associate it with the relational data stored in the database tables. The **$FSLOG** folder is used to keep track of the changes applied on the BLOB data stored in the `FILESTREAM` data container, similar to a transaction log in a SQL Server database.

It is important to remember that two databases cannot share the same file system location to store their `FILESTREAM` data. It is not permitted even to use a subfolder within the `FILESTREAM` data container of one database to store the `FILESTREAM` data container of another database.

For example, assume that you have a `FILESTREAM`-enabled database named `NorthPole` with a `FILESTREAM` data container located in `C:\FS\NorthPole`. Table 2-1 shows some examples of valid and invalid `FILESTREAM` data container locations for another `FILESTREAM`-enabled database called `Southpole`, assuming the `NorthPole` database already exists.

FILESTREAM Data Container	Comments
`C:\FS\SouthPole`	Valid
`C:\FS\NorthPole`	**Invalid:** `C:\FS\NorthPole` is already used by the `SouthPole` database.
`C:\FS\NorthPole\SouthPole`	**Invalid:** `C:\FS\NorthPole` is already used by the `NorthPole` database; therefore the data container cannot be created as a subfolder.

Table 2-1:   Valid and invalid `FILESTREAM` data container locations.

Note that SQL Server does not prevent you from storing your own data in the `FILESTREAM` data container; for example, you can create additional files and folders in a `FILESTREAM` data container. However, you should not touch the folders and files created by SQL Server directly; only access the `FILESTREAM` data container using the APIs provided by SQL Server.

Understanding the FILESTREAM Filegroup

A SQL Server database requires a minimum of two filegroups to store its data: the **data filegroup** and the **log filegroup**. Most real-world databases have more than one data filegroup, usually placed on different disk drives to improve the I/O performance.

To store `FILESTREAM` data, a database must have a new type of filegroup known as a **`FILESTREAM` filegroup**. A separate filegroup is needed because the `FILESTREAM` BLOB data is not stored within the database; it is stored in the `FILESTREAM` data container. So a `FILESTREAM`-enabled database needs to have at least three filegroups:

- a data filegroup to store relational data
- a log filegroup to store transactional logs
- a `FILESTREAM` filegroup to store `FILESTREAM` data.

As with the data filegroups, you might decide to have more than one `FILESTREAM` filegroup in a database, to distribute the `FILESTREAM` I/O load into multiple disk volumes. In such cases, one of those filegroups must be marked as the default filegroup. When you create a table, you can choose the filegroup in which you want SQL Server to store the `FILESTREAM` data (described later in the section *Creating a database with multiple FILESTREAM filegroups*).

Chapter 2: Getting Started with FILESTREAM

To further understand the `FILESTREAM` filegroup, let's take a look at the minimal T-SQL script that creates a `FILESTREAM`-enabled database (Listing 2-1).

```
/*01*/ CREATE DATABASE NorthPole ON
/*02*/ PRIMARY (
/*03*/     NAME = NorthPole,
/*04*/     FILENAME = 'C:\ArtOfFS\Demos\Chapter2\NorthPole.mdf'
/*05*/ ), FILEGROUP NorthPole_fs CONTAINS FILESTREAM(
/*06*/     NAME = NorthPole_fs,
/*07*/     FILENAME = 'C:\ArtOfFS\Demos\Chapter2\NorthPole_fs')
/*08*/ LOG ON (
/*09*/     NAME = NorthPole_log,
/*10*/     FILENAME = 'C:\ArtOfFS\Demos\Chapter2\NorthPole_log.ldf')
```

Listing 2-1: Sample T-SQL script to create a `FILESTREAM`-enabled database.

Lines 05, 06, and 07 specify the configuration parameters for the `FILESTREAM` filegroup. A closer look will highlight a few differences between a `FILESTREAM` filegroup definition and the definition of a data or log filegroup.

First of all, the `FILESTREAM` filegroup uses the additional clause `CONTAINS FILESTREAM` which tells SQL Server to treat the filegroup as a `FILESTREAM` filegroup. This is important, because SQL Server needs to do some additional work to configure the `FILESTREAM` filegroup.

Next, notice the value of the `FILENAME` parameter in line 07; while the `FILENAME` parameters of data files and log files point to a disk file, for a `FILESTREAM` filegroup it points to a **folder**. The `FILESTREAM` data will be stored in multiple files, with one file for each data value. Therefore, it makes sense that the `FILESTREAM` filegroup points to a folder, rather than a single file.

When you create a `FILESTREAM`-enabled database, SQL Server will create and configure the folder specified as the `FILESTREAM` data container. It is very important to ensure that the leaf-level folder within the path that you provide does not already exist, so that SQL Server can go ahead and create it. Please also note that SQL Server will create only the leaf-level folder and assume that the rest of the folder structure already exists. The operation will fail if the leaf-level folder exists, or if top level folders do not exist, or if the folder structure specified is within the `FILESTREAM` data container of another database.

In the above example, `C:\ArtOfFS\Demos\Chapter2\NorthPole_fs` is specified as the `FILESTREAM` data container. Therefore, the folder structure `C:\ArtOfFS\Demos\Chapter2` should already exist at the time of running the above script. If this folder structure does not exist, the operation will fail with the error:

```
The path specified by 'C:\ArtOfFS\Demos\Chapter2\NorthPole_fs' is not in a valid directory.
```

It is not possible to create a `FILESTREAM` data container as a child folder of another `FILESTREAM` data container. If you attempt, for example, to create a `FILESTREAM` data container called `FS2` within an existing `FILESTREAM` data container, SQL Server will fail the operation with the error:

```
The path specified by 'C:\ArtOfFS\Demos\Chapter2\Northpole_fs\FS2' cannot be used for a
FILESTREAM container since it is contained in another FILESTREAM container.
```

The folder **NorthPole_fs** should not exist within `C:\ArtOfFS\Demos\Chapter2` because SQL Server needs to create it. If the folder already exists, the operation will fail with the error:

```
Cannot create file 'C:\ArtOfFS\Demos\Chapter2\NorthPole_fs' because it already exists. Change
the file path or the file name, and retry the operation.
```

It may be interesting to examine how SQL Server identifies whether or not the `FILESTREAM` data container specified is within the `FILESTREAM` container of another database. It appears that SQL Server looks for the existence of the `FILESTREAM` header file in any of the upper level folders. The name of the `FILESTREAM` header file is **filestream.hdr**. SQL Server creates this file within the `FILESTREAM` data container of every `FILESTREAM`-enabled database when the database is created, and keeps an exclusive lock on it as long as the database is running.

Chapter 2: Getting Started with FILESTREAM

What is very interesting to know is that SQL Server only checks for the filename and not the data or a signature inside the file. So, if you create a file named **filestream.hdr** and place it in one of the folders, SQL Server thinks that it is a `FILESTREAM` data container and will not allow you to configure any of its subfolders as a `FILESTREAM` data container. Filegroups are discussed in more detail later in this chapter, in the *Tables and FILESTREAM filegroups* section.

Creating FILESTREAM-enabled Databases

A `FILESTREAM`-enabled database is one that has one or more `FILESTREAM` filegroups. Such a database can be used to create relational tables that contain `FILESTREAM` columns. BLOB data that you insert into a `FILESTREAM` column is stored in the `FILESTREAM` data container within the specified `FILESTREAM` filegroup.

You can enable `FILESTREAM` when you create a database, or you can enable it on an existing database. However, before you do either, you must ensure that the `FILESTREAM` feature is enabled and correctly configured at the SQL Server instance level. Detailed information about how to do this is provided in Appendix A: *Configuring FILESTREAM on a SQL Server Instance*.

Note that the configuration demonstrated in this chapter, when creating a new `FILESTREAM`-enabled database, will get you started, but is rather basic and probably not suitable for a production deployment. In Chapter 7, we discuss how to adapt filegroup architectures for very large `FILESTREAM` databases. In this chapter, we also don't consider any aspects of the configuration of the underlying file system; see Chapter 12 for a discussion of this topic.

Creating a new FILESTREAM-enabled database

Once you have ensured that the SQL Server instance is `FILESTREAM` enabled, you can create a new `FILESTREAM`-enabled database. It is possible to do this using either SSMS or T-SQL.

Using SSMS to create a new FILESTREAM-enabled database

When creating a FILESTREAM-enabled database using SSMS, you create the database in the usual way, but then there are two additional steps: creating a FILESTREAM filegroup for the new database, and adding a FILESTREAM data file that points to the FILESTREAM filegroup.

You create the filegroup using the **Filegroups** page of the **New Database** dialog box. You will see a **Filestream** section in the lower half of the page, where you can create one or more FILESTREAM filegroups for the new database being created, as shown in Figure 2-1.

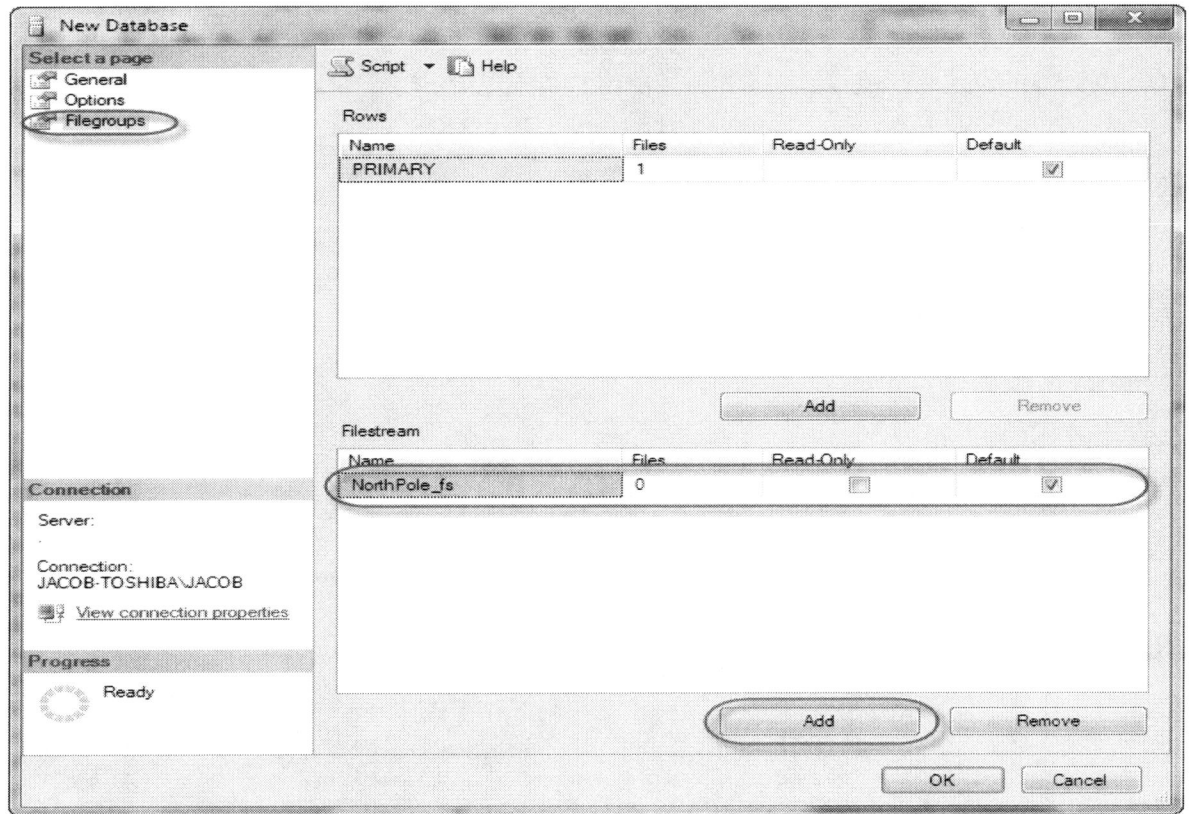

Figure 2-1:   Adding FILESTREAM filegroups to a database.

Chapter 2: Getting Started with FILESTREAM

Next, you add a new file to the database to point to the FILESTREAM filegroup. You do this on the **General** tab. The **File Type** of this file should be set to the **Filestream Data** file type and should point to a valid FILESTREAM filegroup, as shown in Figure 2-2.

Note that under SQL Server 2008 and 2008 R2, only one FILESTREAM data file can be added to a FILESTREAM filegroup. This limitation has been removed in SQL Server 2012 which allows creating more than one FILESTREAM data file per FILESTREAM filegroup.

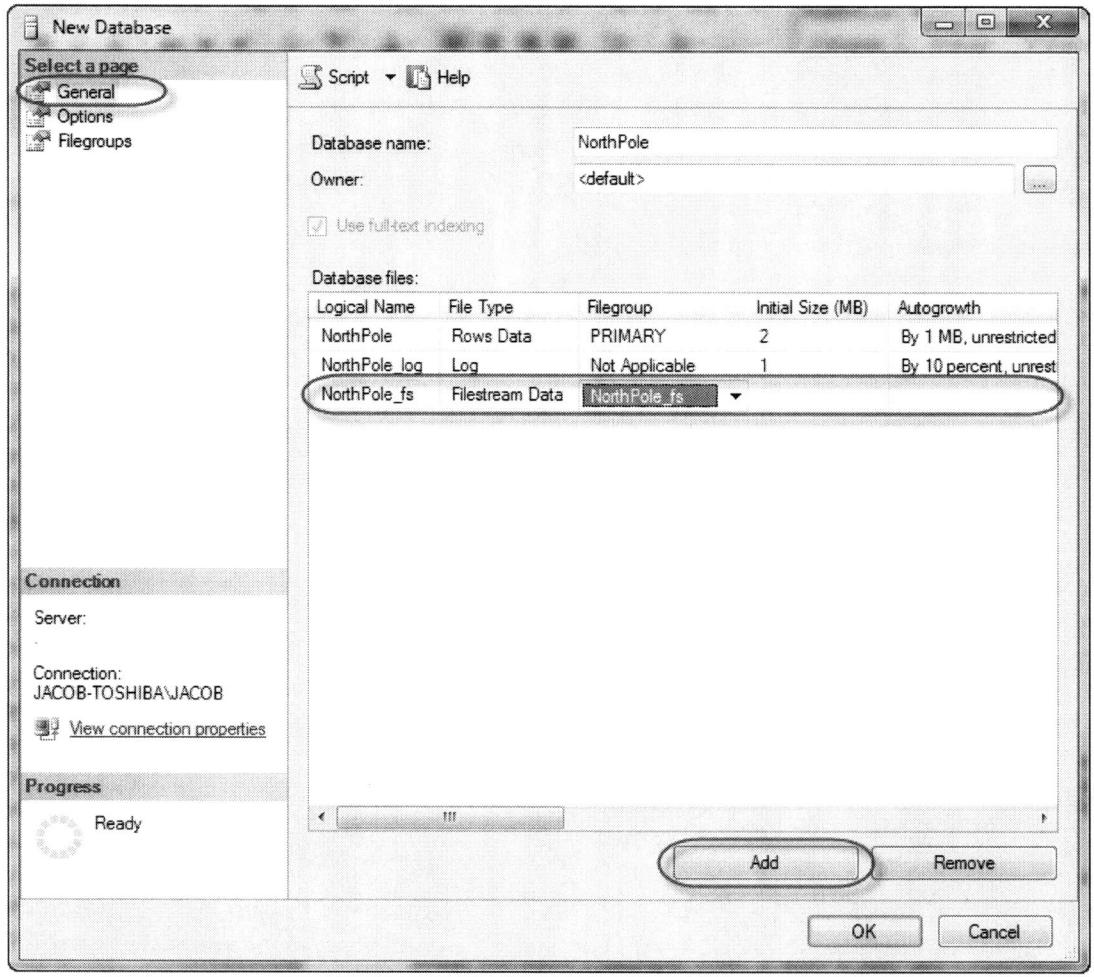

Figure 2-2: Adding a Filestream Data-type file to a database.

When you select **Filestream Data**, the **Filegroup** column is automatically filled with the name of the default FILESTREAM filegroup specified in the **Filegroups** page. If your database has more than one FILESTREAM filegroup and you want to change the filegroup associated with a newly-added FILESTREAM data file, you can do it by selecting a different filegroup from the drop-down control. However, this can be done only at the time of adding a new FILESTREAM data file into the database. Once the changes are saved, it cannot be modified further.

There is something more to note here. When adding a FILESTREAM data file to the database, the **Path** column should point to the folder in which the FILESTREAM data container for the database will be created, as shown in Figure 2-3. Note that you specify the *parent* folder of the data container in **Path**. SSMS creates a subfolder in the parent folder for the FILESTREAM data container, with the same name as the FILESTREAM logical name of the data file.

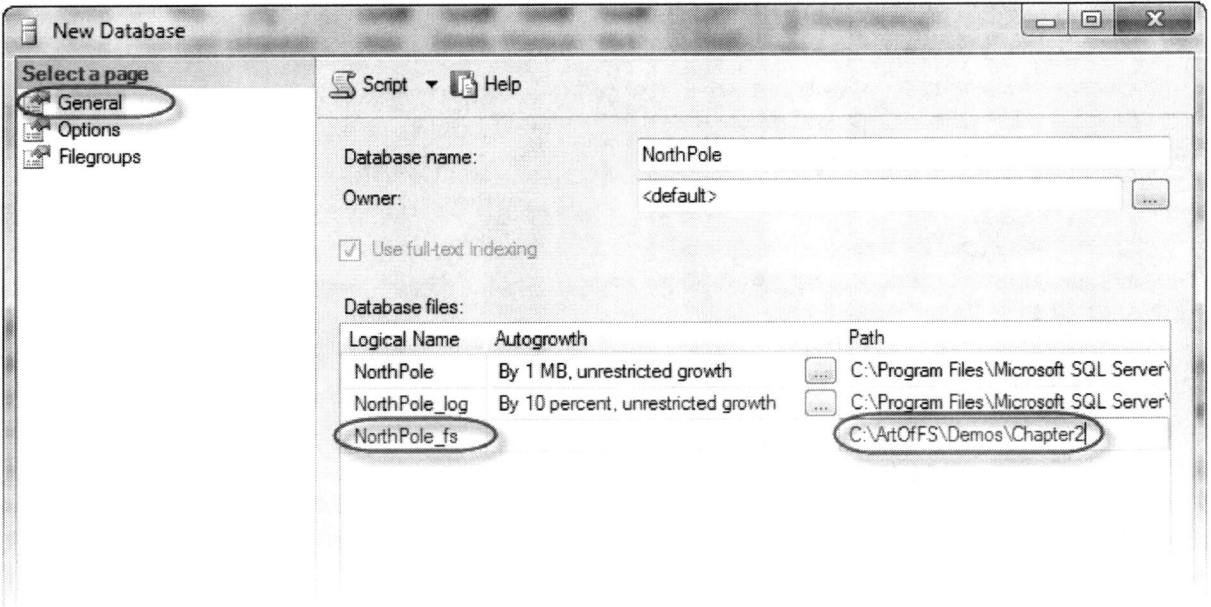

Figure 2-3: Specifying the FILESTREAM data file path.

In this example, a new folder named `NorthPole_fs` will be created in `C:\ArtOfFS\Demos\Chapter2`. SQL Server will configure `C:\ArtOfFS\Demos\Chapter2\NorthPole_fs` as the `FILESTREAM` data container (see *The FILESTREAM Data Container*, earlier in this chapter).

When using SSMS to create a `FILESTREAM`-enabled database, the name of the `FILESTREAM` data container folder will always be the logical name of the filegroup. When creating a `FILESTREAM`-enabled database using T-SQL, you can explicitly specify a folder name which can be different from the logical filegroup name.

Using T-SQL to create a FILESTREAM-enabled database

In the previous section we saw how to create a `FILESTREAM`-enabled database using SSMS. We will now do the same using T-SQL, so let's look in more detail at the minimum script for creating a `FILESTREAM`-enabled database.

```sql
-- If the 'NorthPole' exists, drop it
IF DB_ID('NorthPole') IS NOT NULL BEGIN
    DROP DATABASE NorthPole;
END

-- Create NorthPole database
CREATE DATABASE NorthPole ON
PRIMARY (
    NAME = NorthPole,
    FILENAME = 'C:\ArtOfFS\Demos\Chapter2\NorthPole.mdf'
), FILEGROUP NorthPole_fs CONTAINS FILESTREAM(
    NAME = NorthPole_fs,
    FILENAME = 'C:\ArtOfFS\Demos\Chapter2\NorthPole_fs' )
LOG ON (
    NAME = NorthPole_log,
    FILENAME = 'C:\ArtOfFS\Demos\Chapter2\NorthPole_log.ldf')
```

Listing 2-2: T-SQL code to create a `FILESTREAM`-enabled database.

Chapter 2: Getting Started with FILESTREAM

The script is the same one we would use to create a regular database, except for the following part that creates an additional filegroup to store the FILESTREAM data.

```
FILEGROUP NorthPole_fs CONTAINS FILESTREAM(
    NAME = NorthPole_fs,
    FILENAME = 'C:\ArtOfFS\Demos\Chapter2\NorthPole_fs' )
```

Listing 2-3: Code snippet to show the definition of a FILESTREAM filegroup.

The first line in the above listing creates a FILEGROUP named NorthPole_fs. The syntax is the same as creating or adding a regular data or log filegroup to a database. The clause CONTAINS FILESTREAM is new in SQL Server 2008; it specifies that the filegroup is to be added as a FILESTREAM filegroup. The next line, NAME = NorthPole_fs, specifies the logical name of the filegroup.

The FILENAME parameter in the third line specifies the file system location to be configured as the FILESTREAM data container. When creating a new FILESTREAM-enabled database using T-SQL, you must provide the complete path to the FILESTREAM data container (C:\ArtOfFS\Demos\Chapter2\NorthPole_fs in the above example). The parent folder (C:\ArtOfFS\Demos\Chapter2) must exist at the time of executing the T-SQL script; however, the last subfolder in the path (NorthPole_fs) must *not* exist – if the folder already exists, the T-SQL script will fail, as described previously. Remember, you must not tamper with the FILESTREAM data container folder. Any change you make directly to this folder could corrupt your database.

Note also the following, with regard to a FILESTREAM filegroup:

- it cannot be named PRIMARY
- SIZE, MAXSIZE, and FILEGROWTH attributes are inapplicable
- it cannot point to a UNC path; it must refer to a path on the local server, a storage area network or an iSCSI target
- it can be placed on a compressed disk volume.

Enabling an existing database for FILESTREAM

We have seen how to add `FILESTREAM` storage capabilities when creating a new database. Next, we will examine the process of adding `FILESTREAM` capabilities to an existing database.

When the `FILESTREAM` feature is enabled at the SQL Server instance level, the next step is to check whether the database already has a `FILESTREAM` filegroup, by running the query in Listing 2-4.

```sql
IF EXISTS ( SELECT  *
            FROM    sys.filegroups
            WHERE   type = 'FD' )
    BEGIN
        PRINT 'FILESTREAM Filegroup Exists!'
    END
ELSE
    BEGIN
        PRINT 'FILESTREAM Filegroup does not exist!'
    END
```

Listing 2-4: Checking for a default `FILESTREAM` filegroup on the database.

You can then use T-SQL in Listing 2-5 to add a new `FILESTREAM` filegroup to the database.

```sql
ALTER DATABASE NorthPole
ADD FILEGROUP NorthPole_fs
CONTAINS FILESTREAM ;
GO
```

Listing 2-5: Adding a new `FILESTREAM` filegroup to a database.

Once the `FILESTREAM` filegroup has been added to the database, you can add a `FILESTREAM` file (which points to the `FILESTREAM` data container) using the T-SQL command in Listing 2-6.

```
ALTER DATABASE NorthPole
ADD FILE (
NAME = NorthPole_fs,
FILENAME = 'C:\ArtOfFS\Demos\Chapter2\NorthPole_fs')
TO FILEGROUP NorthPole_fs ;
GO
```

Listing 2-6:   Adding a `FILESTREAM` data container to a database.

The database is now `FILESTREAM` enabled. We can go ahead and start creating tables that contain `FILESTREAM` data.

Creating a Table with FILESTREAM Columns

Once we have a `FILESTREAM`-enabled database, we are ready to go ahead and create tables containing `FILESTREAM` columns. A `FILESTREAM` column is a `VARBINARY (MAX)` column that has the `FILESTREAM` attribute enabled.

Using SSMS table designer to create a table with FILESTREAM columns

You will be surprised if you try to create a table with `FILESTREAM` columns using SSMS table designer in SQL Server 2008 and SQL Server 2008 R2 – it appears that the SSMS team missed this feature, as there is no way to do this in the latest version at the time of writing (SQL Server 2012). You can create a table with a `VARBINARY (MAX)` column, but there is no way to set the `FILESTREAM` flag on the column.

Therefore, the recommended method for creating tables with `FILESTREAM` columns is to write the `CREATE TABLE` statements using T-SQL (as described in the following section). Alternatively, you can do this in a two-step process: create all columns except the `FILESTREAM` columns using the table designer, and then use T-SQL `ALTER TABLE` statements to create the `FILESTREAM` column (see *Using T-SQL to add FILESTREAM columns to an existing table*, later in this chapter).

Using T-SQL to create a table with FILESTREAM columns

The script in Listing 2-7 creates a table with a `FILESTREAM` column. The `FILESTREAM` column is created by adding the `FILESTREAM` attribute to the `VARBINARY(MAX)` column called `ItemImage`. Only `VARBINARY(MAX)` columns can be used for `FILESTREAM` storage.

```sql
CREATE TABLE [dbo].[Items]
    (
        [ItemID] UNIQUEIDENTIFIER ROWGUIDCOL
                                    NOT NULL
                                    UNIQUE ,
        [ItemNumber] VARCHAR(20) ,
        [ItemDescription] VARCHAR(50) ,
        [ItemImage] VARBINARY(MAX) FILESTREAM
                                    NULL
    )
```

Listing 2-7: Creating a table with a `FILESTREAM` column.

Notice that `FILESTREAM` is not a data type; it is an attribute that you can set on a `VARBINARY(MAX)` column. Setting this attribute adds `FILESTREAM` storage capabilities to the column.

The `ItemID` column in the above listing is very significant. A `FILESTREAM` column can be created only on a table that has a `UNIQUEIDENTIFIER` column marked as `ROWGUIDCOL`. The limitations for the `ROWGUIDCOL` are as follows:

- cannot allow `NULL`
- should have either the `UNIQUE` attribute or be the entire primary key
- needs to be `UNIQUEIDENTIFIER` data type
- cannot be modified or dropped as long as `FILESTREAM` columns exist in the table.

SQL Server will create a subfolder in the `FILESTREAM` data container for each table that contains a `FILESTREAM` column. Within each table subfolder, another subfolder will be created for each `FILESTREAM`-enabled column in the table. If the table has multiple partitions, a folder will be created for each partition.

Listing 2-8 shows the structure of the `FILESTREAM` data container after creating a database and table using the example scripts in this chapter (the folder names have been shortened to simplify the listing). The folder for the table and the `FILESTREAM` column are always GUID values, so these folder names will be different on your computer if you have followed the example.

```
c:\
 |-ArtOfFS\
   |-Demos\
     |-Chapter2\
       |-NorthPole_fs\          -- FILESTREAM Data Container
         |-$FSLOG\              -- Log Folder
         |-filestream.hdr       -- Metadata File
         |-6488cba4...6eaad3\   -- Root folder for "Items" table
           |-7761f220...b204f1\ -- Folder for "ItemImage" column
```

Listing 2-8: Example `FILESTREAM` data container structure.

Note that the file locations in which SQL Server stores the BLOB data are irrelevant to us, because no direct access to these files is recommended. Any read/write operation to the BLOB data should be done either through T-SQL (in which you access the BLOB data as if it is a `VARBINARY(MAX)` column in the table) or through the Win32 API (in which you access the BLOB data using a logical identifier). This chapter provides examples using T-SQL, and the Win32 API is discussed further in Chapter 3: *Accessing FILESTREAM Data from Client Applications*.

Using T-SQL to add FILESTREAM columns to an existing table

Adding a `FILESTREAM` column to an existing table can be simple or complex, depending upon the current schema of the table. In the simplest case, the `ALTER TABLE` command could be as shown in Listing 2-9.

```
ALTER TABLE [dbo].[Items]
ADD ItemImage VARBINARY(MAX) FILESTREAM NULL
GO
```

Listing 2-9: `ALTER TABLE` T-SQL script to add a `FILESTREAM` column to an existing table.

This script adds a new `FILESTREAM` column named `ItemImage` to the `Items` table. For the script to execute successfully, the table must already have a `UNIQUEIDENTIFIER` column that meets all requirements outlined above.

In most cases, you can look into the table schema to verify whether or not the table already has a `UNIQUEIDENTIFIER` column with the required characteristics. The easiest way may be to right-click on the table in SSMS and generate the `CREATE` script for the table. You can see the current attributes of all the columns in the script output.

There may be times when you are required to check the table schema programmatically. You can query the system metadata tables to see if a table has all the required characteristics to have a **FILESTREAM** column. Querying `is_rowguidcol` in **sys.columns** will tell you whether the column is marked as **ROWGUIDCOL**. Similarly, the `is_nullable` column can be queried to see if the column allows **NULL** values. Additional information, such as whether the column has a unique constraint or single column primary key, can be retrieved from **sys.key_constraints**, **sys.indexes** and **sys.index_columns**. Listing 2-10 shows the T-SQL code to find out whether the **Items** table has a **ROWGUIDCOL** with the required attributes to have **FILESTREAM** columns.

```sql
IF EXISTS ( SELECT  *
            FROM    sys.key_constraints sc
                    INNER JOIN sys.indexes si
                        ON sc.unique_index_id = si.index_id
                           AND si.object_id = OBJECT_ID('items')
                    INNER JOIN ( SELECT * ,
                                        COUNT(*) OVER ( PARTITION BY index_id,
                                                        object_id ) AS ColCount
                                        /* number of columns in the index */
                                 FROM   sys.index_columns
                               ) ic ON ic.index_id = si.index_id
                                       AND ic.object_id = si.object_id
                    INNER JOIN sys.columns c
                        ON c.column_id = ic.column_id
                           AND c.object_id = ic.object_id
                           AND c.is_rowguidcol = 1   -- ROWGUIDCOL
                           AND c.is_nullable = 0     -- NOT NULL
            WHERE   is_unique_constraint = 1  -- UNIQUE constraint
                    OR ( is_primary_key = 1
                         AND ColCount = 1
                       ) -- SINGLE COLUMN Primary Key
          )
    BEGIN
        PRINT 'Table can have FILESTREAM columns'
    END
ELSE
    BEGIN
        PRINT 'Table is not ready to have FILESTREAM columns'
    END
```

Listing 2-10: Checking whether a table is **FILESTREAM** ready.

Chapter 2: Getting Started with FILESTREAM

If the table already has a UNIQUEIDENTIFIER column with all the required characteristics, you can simply go ahead and add the FILESTREAM column using the ALTER TABLE script in Listing 2-9. However, if the table does not have a UNIQUEIDENTIFIER column then you need to add one, with all the required attributes. Listing 2-11 shows how to do this.

```
ALTER TABLE [dbo].[Items]
ADD ItemID UNIQUEIDENTIFIER ROWGUIDCOL NOT NULL UNIQUE
GO
```

Listing 2-11: Adding a UNIQUEIDENTIFIER column with all the required attributes.

A third possible outcome is that the table already has a UNIQUEIDENTIFIER column, but it does not have all the required attributes. For example, the column may allow NULLS, or it may not be marked as a ROWGUIDCOL, and so on. Depending upon your design requirements, you could either add a new column with the required attributes, as shown in Listing 2-11, or you could change the existing column, as shown in Listing 2-12; note, though, that a table can have only one ROWGUIDCOL.

```
-- Create a table with a UNIQUEIDENTIFIER Column
CREATE TABLE [dbo].[Items]
    (
       [ItemID] UNIQUEIDENTIFIER ,
       [ItemNumber] VARCHAR(20) ,
       [ItemDescription] VARCHAR(50)
    )

-- Alter the UNIQUEIDENTIFIER column to NOT NULL
ALTER TABLE Items
ALTER COLUMN ItemID UNIQUEIDENTIFIER NOT NULL

-- Add a UNIQUE Constraint
ALTER TABLE Items
ADD CONSTRAINT IX_ItemID UNIQUE(ItemID)

-- Create a ROWGUIDCOL
ALTER TABLE Items
ALTER COLUMN ItemID ADD ROWGUIDCOL
```

```
--NOT NULL UNIQUE

-- Add FILESTREAM column
ALTER TABLE [dbo].[Items]
ADD ItemImage VARBINARY(MAX) FILESTREAM NULL
```

Listing 2-12: Configures a UNIQUEIDENTIFIER column to make the table FILESTREAM ready.

Converting VARBINARY(MAX) columns to FILESTREAM and vice versa

One of the common requirements found on environments where an older version of SQL Server is migrated to SQL Server 2008 or later is to convert the existing VARBINARY(MAX) columns to FILESTREAM. It is also quite possible that you would want to convert a FILESTREAM column to VARBINARY(MAX), for some reason. For example, if it turns out that most of the values being stored in the FILESTREAM column are small (less than 1 MB) then it may be beneficial to convert the column to VARBINARY(MAX), since FILESTREAM columns only perform better for larger data. However, this is a decision that can be taken only after performing adequate performance tests.

Unfortunately, changing the FILESTREAM attribute is not just a simple metadata operation; SQL Server does not permit you to change the FILESTREAM attribute of an existing column (the ALTER COLUMN command cannot SET or CLEAR the FILESTREAM flag on a column).

When you change a VARBINARY(MAX) column to FILESTREAM, the data in the column needs to be moved to the FILESTREAM data container in the NTFS. Similarly, when the FILESTREAM attribute is removed, the FILESTREAM data should be moved from the file system into the data files of the database. That explains why SQL Server does not allow you to modify the FILESTREAM flag of a VARBINARY(MAX) column.

As such, the following steps are required, in case you want to convert an existing **VARBINARY(MAX)** column to **FILESTREAM**.

1. Create a new **VARBINARY(MAX)** column with the **FILESTREAM** attribute.
2. Copy the data from the **VARBINARY(MAX)** column to the **FILESTREAM** column using an **UPDATE** statement. This will create a **FILESTREAM** file for each non-**NULL** value being copied to the new column.
3. Drop the original **VARBINARY(MAX)** column.
4. Rename the new **FILESTREAM** column to the original name.

The T-SQL script in Listing 2-13 demonstrates how to do this.

```sql
-- Add FILESTREAM column
ALTER TABLE [dbo].[Items]
ADD ItemImage_New VARBINARY(MAX) FILESTREAM NULL

-- Copy data to the new column
UPDATE [dbo].[Items] SET
    ItemImage_New = ItemImage

-- Drop the original column
ALTER TABLE [dbo].[Items]
DROP COLUMN ItemImage

-- Rename the new column to original name
EXECUTE sp_rename
    @objname = '[dbo].[Items].[ItemImage_New]',
    @newname = 'ItemImage',
    @objtype = 'COLUMN'
```

Listing 2-13: Altering a **VARBINARY(MAX)** column to a **FILESTREAM** column.

A similar approach can be used to change a **FILESTREAM** column to a regular **VARBINARY(MAX)** column.

Note that, after deleting the `FILESTREAM` column, the table will still be associated with the `FILESTREAM` filegroup. Even if you delete all the `FILESTREAM` columns and try to drop the `FILESTREAM` file or filegroup, you will get an error stating that the file or filegroup is not empty. After dropping all the `FILESTREAM` columns, you have to set `FILESTREAM_ON` to `NULL`, using `ALTER TABLE ... SET (FILESTREAM_ON = "NULL")`.

If you have created `FILESTREAM` columns on a table and later on decide to move back to `VARBINARY(MAX)`, you might also want to drop the `GUID` column you created on the table. This is relevant in cases where the `GUID` column was added only to fulfill the `FILESTREAM` requirement.

Tables and FILESTREAM filegroups

Each table that contains `FILESTREAM` columns must be associated with at least one `FILESTREAM` filegroup. A table can be associated with more than one `FILESTREAM` filegroup if it is partitioned.

As discussed earlier, depending upon your design requirements, all tables can be associated with a single `FILESTREAM` filegroup, or they can each be associated with a separate filegroup (or some combination). This decision may be made based on the `FILESTREAM` load that you expect to have in each table; using separate filegroups can distribute the `FILESTREAM` I/O load if they are located on different devices.

You can specify the `FILESTREAM` filegroup in which you would like to store the `FILESTREAM` data when you create a table. If you do not specify the `FILESTREAM` filegroup, SQL Server will associate the default `FILESTREAM` filegroup with that table and all the `FILESTREAM` data for that table will be stored there. When a table is associated with a `FILESTREAM` filegroup, all the `FILESTREAM` data from all `FILESTREAM` columns that exist in that table will go to the same filegroup. It is not possible to configure two `FILESTREAM` columns in the same table to store their data in two separate `FILESTREAM` filegroups.

Listing 2-7 demonstrated how to create a `FILESTREAM`-enabled table called `Items` that uses the default `FILESTREAM` filegroup. If you do not want to use the default `FILESTREAM` filegroup, you use the `FILESTREAM_ON` clause of the `CREATE TABLE` statement to specify the filegroup, as shown in Listing 2-14.

```
CREATE TABLE [dbo].[Items]
    (
        [ItemID] UNIQUEIDENTIFIER ROWGUIDCOL
                                    NOT NULL
                                    UNIQUE ,
        [ItemNumber] VARCHAR(20) ,
        [ItemDescription] VARCHAR(50) ,
        [ItemImage] VARBINARY(MAX) FILESTREAM
                                    NULL
    ) FILESTREAM_ON [NorthPole_fs]
```

Listing 2-14: Creating a table with `FILESTREAM` columns using a specified filegroup.

For an example that shows how to change the `FILESTREAM` filegroup associated with an existing table, see the section *Creating a database with multiple FILESTREAM filegroups*, later in this chapter.

FILESTREAM filegroup queries

There are some system views that you can use to query `FILESTREAM`-related information on your SQL Server 2008 database. We will see many of them in the coming chapters, but a couple of examples are included here.

You might need to find out the `FILESTREAM` filegroup that is associated with a specific table. You can do this by querying the catalog view `sys.data_spaces` as shown in Listing 2-15.

```
SELECT   d.name AS [FILESTREAM Filegroup]
FROM     sys.tables t
         INNER JOIN sys.data_spaces d ON t.filestream_data_space_id = d.data_space_id
WHERE    t.name = 'Items'

/*
FILESTREAM Filegroup
-------------------------------------------------
NorthPole_fs
*/
```

Listing 2-15: Retrieving the FILESTREAM filegroup associated with a table.

Listing 2-16 queries the catalog view `sys.filegroups` and retrieves the default FILESTREAM filegroup of the current database.

```
SELECT   name
FROM     sys.filegroups
WHERE    type_desc = 'FILESTREAM_DATA_FILEGROUP'
         AND is_default = 1
/*
name
-------------------------------------------------
NorthPole_fs
*/
```

Listing 2-16: Retrieving the FILESTREAM filegroup of the current database.

FILESTREAM Data Manipulation Using T-SQL

We have so far spent quite some time discussing FILESTREAM-enabled databases, FILESTREAM filegroups, and tables with FILESTREAM columns. Enough DDL for now! It is time to see some DML operations.

Chapter 2: Getting Started with FILESTREAM

A T-SQL batch or stored procedure can access `FILESTREAM` columns as if they are regular `VARBINARY(MAX)` columns. However, accessing large BLOB data stored in a `FILESTREAM` column from T-SQL does not perform well, for the reasons below.

- One of the features that `FILESTREAM` offers is the I/O streaming capability for faster `FILESTREAM` operations. When accessing `FILESTREAM` data through T-SQL, the benefits of streaming I/O are not available.

- When accessing `FILESTREAM` data using T-SQL, SQL Server memory is used for buffering the `FILESTREAM` data. This will add memory overhead to the SQL Server instance.

- To T-SQL, a `FILESTREAM` column appears as a `VARBINARY(MAX)` column with a 2 GB size limitation. Therefore, if the data stored in the `FILESTREAM` column is larger than 2 GB, T-SQL can only access the first 2 GB of it.

Therefore, for best performance and optimum usage of the SQL Server resources, `FILESTREAM` data should *not* generally be accessed using T-SQL. Instead, we should use the streaming APIs exposed by SQL Server, as described in Chapter 3: *Accessing FILESTREAM Data from Client Applications*.

However, as always, there are exceptions to the rule. Most significantly, unless the `FILESTREAM` column is assigned a default value, then a client application *has* to execute a T-SQL `INSERT` statement in order to add a new row into a `FILESTREAM`-enabled table, rather than use the streaming APIs. The reason for this is that streaming access can be made only to rows that contain non-`NULL` BLOB data in the `FILESTREAM` column. So, T-SQL `INSERT` statements on `FILESTREAM`-enabled tables usually store dummy `VARBINARY` data in the `FILESTREAM` column, or a default value can be set on the `FILESTREAM` column. For example, we could insert a dummy value, or use a default value, of `0x`. This will create a zero-length file, which can then be replaced by actual `FILESTREAM` BLOB data using streaming I/O (or T-SQL).

Beyond this, there are a few cases where it is acceptable to access and manipulate data using T-SQL. In most cases, it is fine to store small BLOB data values in a `FILESTREAM` column and retrieve it using T-SQL. The question you might ask now is, "What size is considered to be small?" There is no absolute definition but, generally speaking, anything below 1 MB may be considered to be small; please refer to the Microsoft Research Paper available at HTTP://BRURL.COM/FS2 for a more in-depth discussion that demonstrates how the BLOB size affects performance when stored inside the database as well as in the file system. If the BLOB data being stored, updated, or retrieved from the `FILESTREAM` storage is large (generally speaking, bigger than 1 MB) it is not advisable to manipulate the data using T-SQL.

The following operations require T-SQL because there are no equivalent operations in the streaming APIs:

- deleting rows from a table with `FILESTREAM` columns
- truncating a `FILESTREAM`-enabled table
- updating one or more `FILESTREAM` columns to `NULL`.

Inserting a row with FILESTREAM data

We're going to walk through an example of creating a new `FILESTREAM` column and then inserting an image into that column using T-SQL. We'll then explore the contents of the `FILESTREAM` data container, in order to gain some insight into how this data is stored.

Please note, right from the start, that this example is for illustrative and learning purposes *only*. Firstly, the most benefit is gained from the `FILESTREAM` feature when accessing it using the streaming APIs instead of T-SQL, as we'll discuss in Chapter 3. Secondly, you would never, in a production system, delve directly into the contents of the `FILESTREAM` data container, as we will do here.

Chapter 2: Getting Started with FILESTREAM

With this in mind, let's get started! If you have followed all the sample scripts so far and executed them in SSMS, you will have a `FILESTREAM`-enabled table containing a `FILESTREAM` column. So, before we move ahead with storing BLOB data in the `FILESTREAM` column of our table, let us rebuild it to make sure that everything is set up correctly (Listing 2-17).

```sql
-- Drop the table if exists
IF OBJECT_ID('Items', 'U') IS NOT NULL
    BEGIN
        DROP TABLE Items
    END
GO

-- Create the table
CREATE TABLE [dbo].[Items]
    (
        [ItemID] UNIQUEIDENTIFIER ROWGUIDCOL
                                    NOT NULL
                                    UNIQUE ,
        [ItemNumber] VARCHAR(20) ,
        [ItemDescription] VARCHAR(50) ,
        [ItemImage] VARBINARY(MAX) FILESTREAM
                                    NULL
    )
GO
```

Listing 2-17:   Creating a table with a `FILESTREAM` column.

SQL Server 2005 enhanced the `OPENROWSET()` function with a very powerful attribute: `BULK`. The `BULK` attribute can be used to load the content of an image file on disk into a `VARBINARY(MAX)` column, and then insert it into a `FILESTREAM` column.

We'll use the `BULK` attribute to load the image of a Microsoft mouse (Figure 2-4) into the `FILESTREAM` column of the `Items` table. (You can find this image in the sample image download file available at HTTP://BRURL.COM/FS4 and extract it into `C:\TEMP` folder if you do not want to change the code given in the sample snippet.)

Chapter 2: Getting Started with FILESTREAM

Figure 2-4: Image of Microsoft mouse to be loaded into a FILESTREAM column.

Note again that, in most real-world scenarios, we would not insert this image directly using T-SQL. Instead, we'd insert a record with a dummy (generally 0x) value into the FILESTREAM column, and then update the column with the required image using the streaming APIs.

Listing 2-18 shows the T-SQL script to load the image.

```
-- Declare a variable to store the image data
DECLARE @img AS VARBINARY(MAX)

-- Load the image data
SELECT  @img = CAST(bulkcolumn AS VARBINARY(MAX))
FROM    OPENROWSET(BULK 'C:\temp\MicrosoftMouse.jpg', SINGLE_BLOB) AS x

-- Insert the data to the table
INSERT  INTO Items
        ( ItemID ,
          ItemNumber ,
          ItemDescription ,
          ItemImage
        )
        SELECT  NEWID() ,
                'MS1001' ,
                'Microsoft Mouse' ,
                @img
```

Listing 2-18: Loading the content of a disk file into a VARBINARY(MAX) column and inserting into a FILESTREAM column.

Chapter 2: Getting Started with FILESTREAM

Loading the content to the **VARBINARY(MAX)** variable is unnecessary in the above example. This additional step was added to make the code easier to follow. Listing 2-19 shows another version of the code that does not use a staging variable, but instead inserts the data directly into the table.

```
-- Insert the data to the table
INSERT  INTO Items
        ( ItemID ,
          ItemNumber ,
          ItemDescription ,
          ItemImage
        )
        SELECT  NEWID() ,
                'MS1001' ,
                'Microsoft Mouse' ,
                CAST(bulkcolumn AS VARBINARY(MAX))
        FROM    OPENROWSET(BULK 'C:\temp\MicrosoftMouse.jpg', SINGLE_BLOB) AS x
```

Listing 2-19: Loading a disk file directly into a **FILESTREAM** column.

So, where did the data go? Well, the data we just loaded into the **FILESTREAM** column goes to the **FILESTREAM** data container. The *exact* content of the source file is copied to the *correct location* within the **FILESTREAM** data container; when SQL Server stores BLOB data in the **FILESTREAM** data container, an exact copy of the original binary chunk is stored in the file system. SQL Server does not change the content; nothing is added, modified, or removed. Also, there is a specific location for every **FILESTREAM** column in the database. Listing 2-20 shows the file system map.

```
C:\
 |-ArtOfFS\
   |-Demos\
     |-Chapter2\
       |-NorthPole_fs\            -- Filestream Data Container
         |-$FSLOG\                -- Log Folder
         |-filestream.hdr         -- Metadata File
         |-5a032731…dfeff9\       -- Root folder for "Items" table
            |-e943c1e6…5fc1f5\    -- Folder for "ItemImage" column
```

Listing 2-20: Sample **FILESTREAM** data container structure.

Chapter 2: Getting Started with FILESTREAM

So, in this example, the image that was loaded into the `FILESTREAM` column of the `Items` table is stored in the file system folder `e943c1e6...5c1f5`. Note that the name of the folder may be different if you are following this example on your computer, but the hierarchy will be the same.

Let's get adventurous and explore this folder. But before that, a statutory warning!

***

In a production system, never touch the `FILESTREAM` files directly!

Never update the `FILESTREAM` data directly. I am showing this here only for demonstration purposes, and it should never be done on a production system. If you do, you may corrupt your database. The `FILESTREAM` data files should be accessed only using the Win32 interface exposed by SQL Server, as explained in Chapter 3: Accessing FILESTREAM Data from Client Applications.

***

Bearing in mind the risks of playing with the `FILESTREAM` data container, let's go ahead and do it anyway, as it will shed some light on how the files are stored in the file system. If we navigate to the file system location for the `ItemImage` column, we will see something very similar to Figure 2-5.

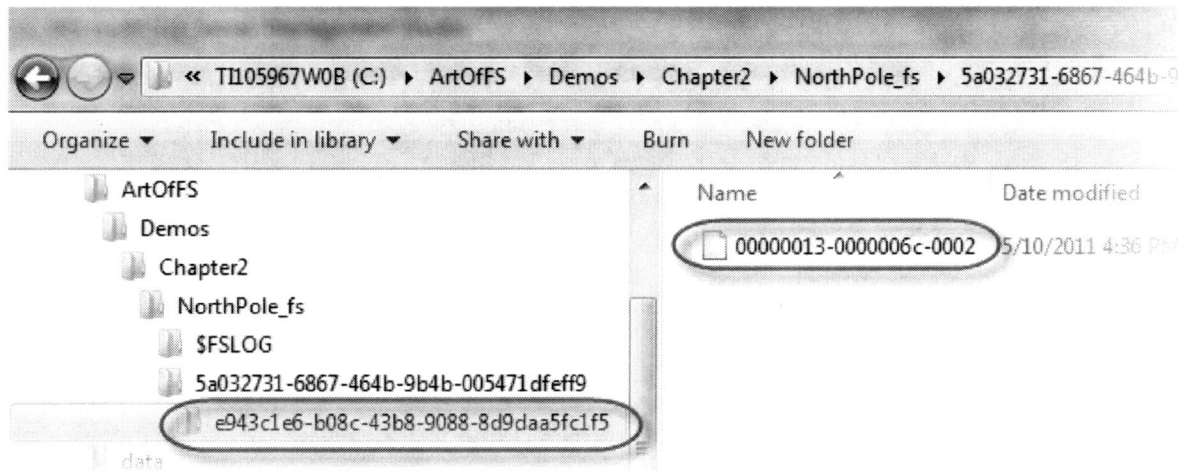

Figure 2-5: The contents of a `FILESTREAM` data container.

Chapter 2: Getting Started with FILESTREAM

A new file has been created inside the subfolder that SQL Server created for the `ItemImage` column. The content of the file will be the same as the content of the original file. To make sure that we don't corrupt the database, we'll copy this file to another folder and open it in MS Paint to view its contents. The file opens correctly (Figure 2-6). This indicates that SQL Server stores the content of the file "as is" in the `FILESTREAM` data file.

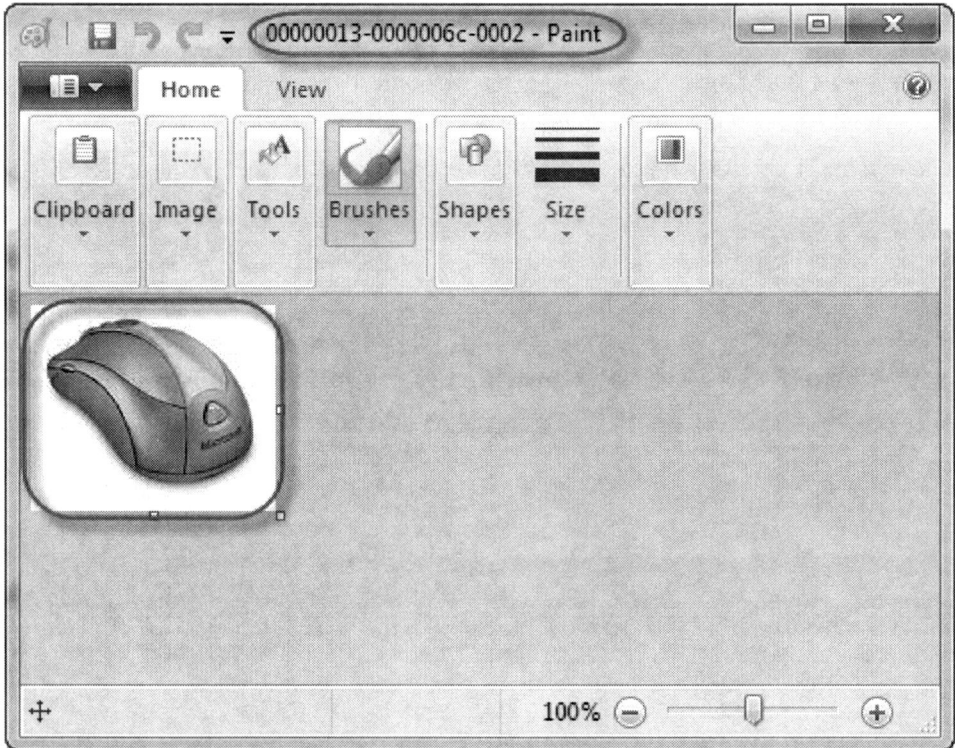

Figure 2-6: Opening the `FILESTREAM` data in MS Paint.

Updating and deleting FILESTREAM data

Only rarely will you modify `FILESTREAM` data using T-SQL, since it is much more efficient to do it using the streaming APIs, as demonstrated in Chapter 3. Note that SQL Server does not support a partial update to the `FILESTREAM` data. If you want to make changes to your BLOB data, the entire content must be replaced.

However, it is more common to delete `FILESTREAM` data from a column by setting it to `NULL`, using T-SQL.

```
UPDATE Items SET
    ItemImage = NULL
```

Listing 2-21: Updating a `FILESTREAM` column to `NULL` to delete the data.

The BLOB file is not removed from the `FILESTREAM` data container immediately. This is done by a garbage collector background thread, so there is a delay before the physical file is deleted from the file system. You can force a garbage collection using the `CHECKPOINT` command but that does not guarantee that the garbage collector will remove the unwanted file. The garbage collector will remove the unwanted `FILESTREAM` data files only after the transaction log is truncated past the log entry that created the garbage files.

If you intend to delete the entire row containing the `FILESTREAM` data from the table, a regular `DELETE` command will delete the row from the table and remove all the `FILESTREAM` data associated with that record from the `FILESTREAM` data container. Again, there may be a delay before the physical data is deleted from the data container by the garbage collector.

FILESTREAM and triggers

Just like other columns, `FILESTREAM` columns are accessible from within DML triggers. The `FILESTREAM` columns can be accessed from a trigger in the same way as a regular `VARBINARY(MAX)` column. DML triggers get fired even when modifying the `FILESTREAM` data using Win32 I/O streaming.

It is not good practice to print debug information from a trigger. However, for the purpose of showing that the `FILESTREAM` columns are accessible from a trigger, we'll create an `INSERT` trigger that prints the size of the `FILESTREAM` data value being inserted (Listing 2-22).

```
CREATE TRIGGER TGR_Items ON dbo.Items
    AFTER INSERT
AS
    BEGIN
        DECLARE @size INT
        SELECT  @size = DATALENGTH(ItemImage)
        FROM    INSERTED
        PRINT   'FILESTREAM Size :' + STR(@size)
    END
```

Listing 2-22: An `INSERT` trigger that prints the size of the `FILESTREAM` data value being inserted.

Now we'll insert a new record into the `FILESTREAM` column of the `Items` table using the script in Listing 2-23.

```
-- Insert the data to the table

INSERT  INTO Items
        ( ItemID ,
          ItemNumber ,
          ItemDescription ,
          ItemImage
        )
```

```
        SELECT  NEWID() ,
                'MS1001' ,
                'Microsoft Mouse' ,
                CAST(bulkcolumn AS VARBINARY(MAX))
        FROM    OPENROWSET(BULK 'C:\temp\MicrosoftMouse.jpg', SINGLE_BLOB) AS x
/*
OUTPUT From Trigger:

FILESTREAM Size :       2288
*/
```

Listing 2-23: Inserting a row into the `Items` table with `FILESTREAM` data.

The code within the trigger prints the size of the `FILESTREAM` data value when the new value is inserted.

Advanced FILESTREAM DDL

In this section, we'll briefly review some slightly more advanced requirements for `FILESTREAM`-enabled databases and tables, namely using `FILESTREAM` with partitioned tables, and creating databases with multiple `FILESTREAM` filegroups, for scalability.

The FILESTREAM data container and partitioned tables

We saw earlier that SQL Server creates a folder at the root of the `FILESTREAM` data container for every `FILESTREAM`-enabled table in the `FILESTREAM` database. If a table is partitioned, a folder will be created for every partition in the table. Within each of these folders, a subfolder will be created for every `FILESTREAM` column in the table.

Chapter 2: Getting Started with FILESTREAM

Let's create a partitioned table and see this in action. First, we'll drop the table we created earlier by running the script shown in Listing 2-24.

```
IF OBJECT_ID('Items', 'U') IS NOT NULL
    BEGIN
        DROP TABLE Items
    END
GO
```

Listing 2-24: Dropping the Items table.

When you drop a table with FILESTREAM columns, the FILESTREAM data container for that table is removed from the FILESTREAM data container. Note, however, that this is done by a garbage collector and you might experience some delay in getting the file removed.

If we now go to the FILESTREAM data container and take a look at the content of the folder, the FILESTREAM folders have been removed and the folder is empty except for the metadata objects (Figure 2-7).

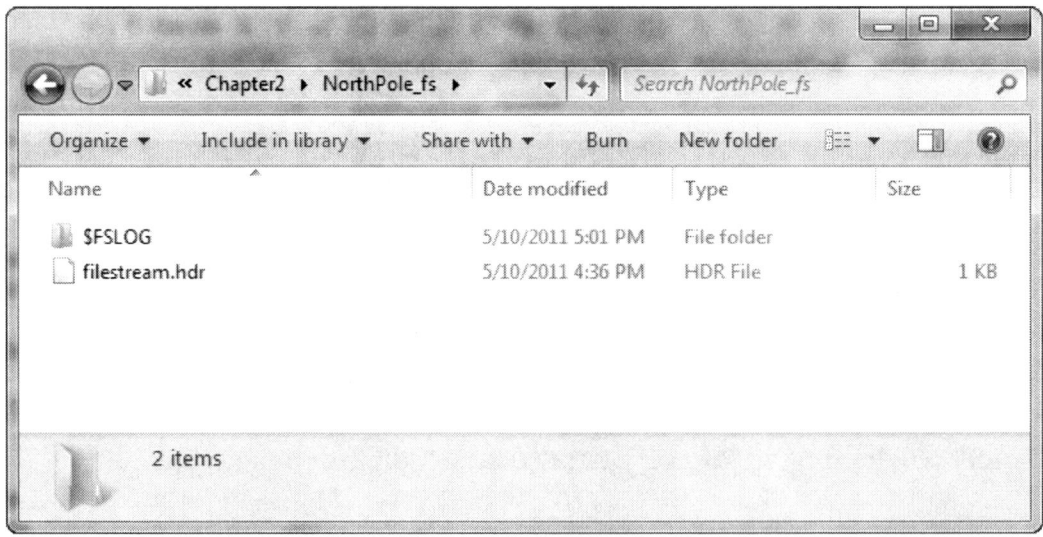

Figure 2-7: Verifying that the FILESTREAM data container contains only metadata.

Now we'll create a partitioned table. The script in Listing 2-25 creates a new version of the `Items` table with three partitions. (Remember that the aim of this script is to create a **FILESTREAM** table with three partitions for demonstration purposes; the way this table is partitioned does not make much business sense.)

```sql
-- Create partition function
CREATE PARTITION FUNCTION
ItemPartitionFn (INT)
AS RANGE RIGHT FOR VALUES (1, 2) ;

-- Create partition scheme for ItemID
CREATE PARTITION SCHEME
ItemPartitionSch
AS PARTITION ItemPartitionFn ALL TO ([PRIMARY]) ;

-- Create partition scheme for FILESTREAM
CREATE PARTITION SCHEME
ItemFSPartitionSch
AS PARTITION ItemPartitionFn ALL TO (Northpole_fs) ;

-- Create Item table with FILESTREAM column
CREATE TABLE Items
    (
        ItemGUID UNIQUEIDENTIFIER ROWGUIDCOL
                            NOT NULL
                            UNIQUE ON [PRIMARY] ,
        ItemID INT ,
        ItemName VARCHAR(50) ,
        ItemImage VARBINARY(MAX) FILESTREAM
    )
ON   ItemPartitionSch(ItemID) FILESTREAM_ON ItemFSPartitionSch ;
GO
```

Listing 2-25: Creating a `FILESTREAM` table with `PARTITION`.

After running the script, if we return to the **FILESTREAM** data container, there are three new folders; one for each partition in the `Items` table (Figure 2-8).

Chapter 2: Getting Started with FILESTREAM

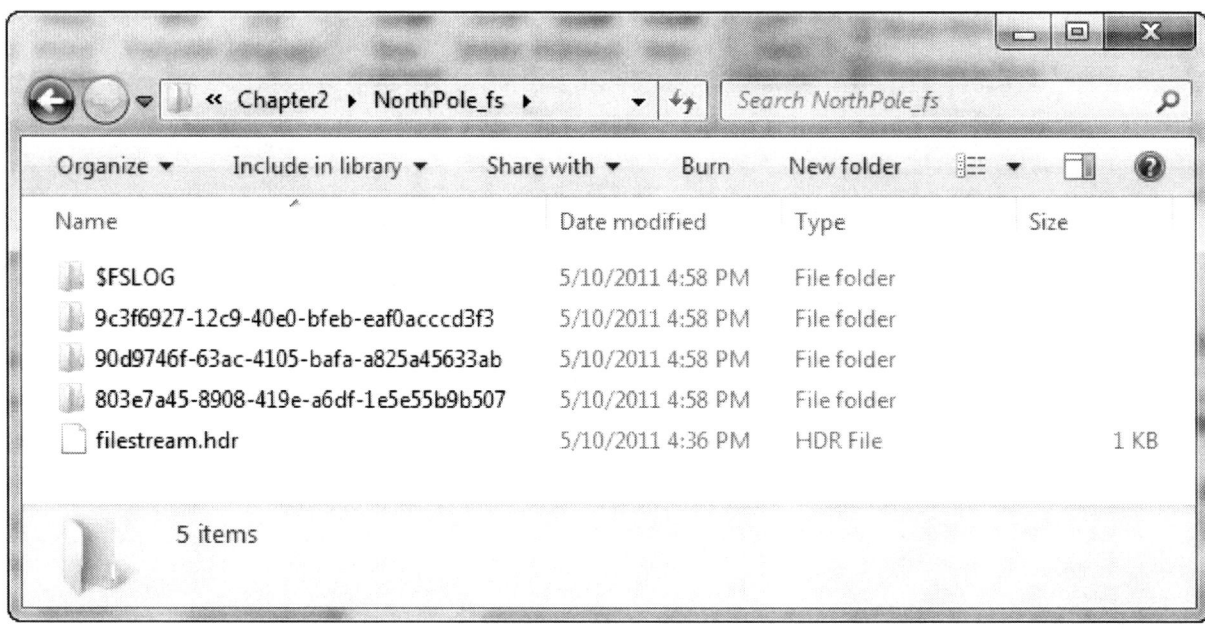

Figure 2-8: Data container showing a folder for each partition in the Items table.

Creating a database with multiple FILESTREAM filegroups

Depending upon your database design requirements, you might decide to have more than one FILESTREAM filegroup. If you have a few tables for which you expect a very high volume of FILESTREAM reads and writes, you might decide to have FILESTREAM filegroups on different disk volumes, and set up each table to use a different disk for its FILESTREAM storage. This will give you more throughput as each disk can be used in parallel.

The script in Listing 2-26 creates a database with two FILESTREAM filegroups.

Chapter 2: Getting Started with FILESTREAM

```sql
CREATE DATABASE NorthPole ON PRIMARY (
   NAME = NorthPole,
    FILENAME = 'C:\ArtOfFS\Demos\Chapter2\NorthPole.mdf'
), FILEGROUP NorthPole_fs1 CONTAINS FILESTREAM DEFAULT(
   NAME = NorthPole_fs1,
    FILENAME = 'C:\ArtOfFS\Demos\Chapter2\NorthPole_fs1'
), FILEGROUP NorthPole_fs2 CONTAINS FILESTREAM(
   NAME = NorthPole_fs2,
    FILENAME = 'C:\ArtOfFS\Demos\Chapter2\NorthPole_fs2'
) LOG ON (
   NAME = NorthPole_log,
    FILENAME = 'C:\ArtOfFS\Demos\Chapter2\NorthPole_log.ldf')
GO
```

Listing 2-26: Creating a database with two FILESTREAM filegroups.

Note that, if you have more than one FILESTREAM filegroup, you need to specify one of them as the default filegroup; SQL Server will use the default filegroup for the FILESTREAM storage if you create a table without specifying the FILESTREAM filegroup. In Listing 2-29, NorthPole_fs1 is specified as the default.

To specify the FILESTREAM filegroup for the table you are creating, use the FILESTREAM_ON clause, as shown in Listing 2-27, in which two tables are created, each using a different filegroup.

```sql
-- Store FILESTREAM data on "NorthPole_fs1"
CREATE TABLE [dbo].[Items1]
    (
      [ItemID] UNIQUEIDENTIFIER ROWGUIDCOL
                                NOT NULL
                                UNIQUE ,
      [ItemNumber] VARCHAR(20) ,
      [ItemDescription] VARCHAR(50) ,
      [ItemImage] VARBINARY(MAX) FILESTREAM
                                NULL
    ) FILESTREAM_ON NorthPole_fs1
GO
```

Chapter 2: Getting Started with FILESTREAM

```sql
-- Store FILESTREAM data on "NorthPole_fs2"
CREATE TABLE [dbo].[Items2]
    (
        [ItemID] UNIQUEIDENTIFIER ROWGUIDCOL
                                    NOT NULL
                                    UNIQUE ,
        [ItemNumber] VARCHAR(20) ,
        [ItemDescription] VARCHAR(50) ,
        [ItemImage] VARBINARY(MAX) FILESTREAM
                                    NULL
    ) FILESTREAM_ON NorthPole_fs2
GO
```

Listing 2-27: Creating two tables that store the FILESTREAM data in different filegroups.

You can change the FILESTREAM filegroup of a table even after the table is created. However, this is possible only if the table does not contain any FILESTREAM columns. Therefore, you must remove any FILESTREAM columns before you reset the FILESTREAM_ON flag, as shown in Listing 2-28.

```sql
-- Store FILESTREAM data on "NorthPole_fs1"
CREATE TABLE [dbo].[Items]
    (
        [ItemID] UNIQUEIDENTIFIER ROWGUIDCOL
                                    NOT NULL
                                    UNIQUE ,
        [ItemNumber] VARCHAR(20) ,
        [ItemDescription] VARCHAR(50) ,
        [ItemImage] VARBINARY(MAX) FILESTREAM
                                    NULL
    ) FILESTREAM_ON NorthPole_fs1
GO

-- Drop the FILESTREAM column
ALTER TABLE Items DROP COLUMN ItemImage

-- Reset the FILESTREAM_ON flag
ALTER TABLE Items SET
(FILESTREAM_ON = "NULL"
)
```

```
-- Change the FILESTREAM filegroup
ALTER TABLE Items SET
(FILESTREAM_ON = NorthPole_fs2
)

-- Add the FILESTREAM column back
ALTER TABLE Items
ADD [ItemImage] VARBINARY(MAX) FILESTREAM NULL
```

Listing 2-28: Changing the FILESTREAM filegroup of a table.

Disabling FILESTREAM Storage on a Database

Disabling FILESTREAM storage on a database involves removing the FILESTREAM files and filegroups from the database. This can be done by using an ALTER DATABASE statement.

If the database contains any tables that use FILESTREAM storage, all references to the FILESTREAM filegroups must be removed before the FILESTREAM filegroups are removed. The procedure is summarized below.

1. Drop all FILESTREAM columns from all tables using ALTER TABLE.

2. Set the FILESTREAM_ON attribute on all the tables to NULL using ALTER TABLE.

3. Remove the FILESTREAM file using ALTER DATABASE.

4. Remove the FILESTREAM filegroup using ALTER DATABASE.

Assume that the NorthPole database has a table with a FILESTREAM column, created using Listing 2-7. SQL Server will not allow the FILESTREAM filegroup to be removed until all the other steps have been made.

Chapter 2: Getting Started with FILESTREAM

First, you have to drop the `FILESTREAM` column from the table (Listing 2-29).

```
-- Drop the FILESTREAM column
ALTER TABLE Items DROP COLUMN ItemImage
```

Listing 2-29: Dropping the `FILESTREAM` column from the `Items` table.

Note that the association between the `FILESTREAM` filegroup and the table remains, even after dropping the `FILESTREAM` column; SQL Server still thinks that the `FILESTREAM` filegroup is not empty. The table is still linked to its `FILESTREAM` filegroup even though there are no `FILESTREAM` columns in the table.

Next, you must disassociate the table from its `FILESTREAM` filegroup by setting the `FILESTREAM_ON` attribute to `NULL`. Listing 2-30 shows how to do this.

```
-- Disassociate table "items" from its FILESTREAM filegroup
ALTER TABLE Items SET (FILESTREAM_ON = "NULL")
```

Listing 2-30: Disassociating a table from its `FILESTREAM` filegroup.

Now you can remove the `FILESTREAM` file and filegroup using `ALTER DATABASE`. Listing 2-31 shows how to remove the `FILESTREAM` capabilities from the example database.

```
-- Remove the File
ALTER DATABASE NorthPole REMOVE FILE NorthPoleFS ;

-- Remove the Filegroup
ALTER DATABASE NorthPole REMOVE FILEGROUP NorthPoleFS ;
```

Listing 2-31: Removing `FILESTREAM` features from a database.

If a database does not contain any tables that use FILESTREAM storage, removing the FILESTREAM feature from a database is much simpler, and comprises only two steps:

1. Remove the FILESTREAM data container.
2. Remove the FILESTREAM filegroup.

Summary

In this chapter, we started with an exploration of the world of FILESTREAM data containers and filegroups, and a look at how to create FILESTREAM-enabled databases. The FILESTREAM data container is the file system location in which SQL Server stores the BLOB data in a FILESTREAM-enabled database. SQL Server stores FILESTREAM data in special filegroups known as FILESTREAM filegroups.

We saw that a database can have more than one FILESTREAM filegroup, but that one of the filegroups should be marked as the default filegroup. When you create a table with FILESTREAM columns you can specify the FILEGROUP in which to store the FILESTREAM data for that table. If the table has multiple FILESTREAM columns, all of them will be stored in the same filegroup, which will be the default filegroup, unless you specify otherwise.

We also looked at how to insert data into our FILESTREAM columns. Unless a DEFAULT value is assigned to a FILESTREAM column, when creating the table, the data must be initially inserted using T-SQL. However, inserting or updating FILESTREAM data using T-SQL may not be beneficial in terms of performance, since SQL Server's memory buffers are used for processing the BLOB data, which might create memory pressure on production systems. As such, it is better to set an initial default value on the FILESTREAM column, and then modify the data to the required values using the Win32 streaming APIs exposed by SQL Server, which we'll discuss in the next chapter.

Finally, we looked at how to disable FILESTREAM storage, noting in particular that setting the FILESTREAM column to NULL will delete the associated FILESTREAM data from the FILESTREAM data container.

Chapter 3: Accessing FILESTREAM Data from Client Applications

As discussed in the previous chapters, `FILESTREAM` storage is ideal for BLOB data values that are relatively large (larger than 1 MB). This data can be accessed either through T-SQL code or through the `FILESTREAM` APIs exposed by SQL Server, though the latter is more efficient than the former.

The `FILESTREAM` APIs come in two flavors, Win32 and .NET, and in this chapter we'll walk through several examples using each of these I/O streaming APIs.

What is Streaming?

Streaming, in simple terms, means "continuous flow." Within the context of reading and writing BLOB data, it refers to a continuous flow of bytes to and from the physical disk, without local buffering (i.e. without collecting bytes in an intermediate location before transmitting the data to the target). Performing `FILESTREAM` operations with streaming offers two immediate benefits. Firstly, it means that only a small memory buffer is needed. Without streaming, potentially large files will be stored in the memory buffer. This could overload the server by incurring excessive paging and loss of cached execution plans. It could also affect other processes running on the server. It is also possible that the file will be bigger than the available memory on the server.

Secondly, streaming gives better performance in several cases. Your process can start sending bytes to the target location even before the entire contents of the file are read from the source location. This performance benefit may be particularly evident if you are serving the BLOB data to a client over the Internet (such as streaming an audio file or downloading a file from a client browser).

Understanding Streaming Access to FILESTREAM Data

In order to gain streaming access to the `FILESTREAM` data, SQL Server exposes a managed object for the .NET developers and a Win32 API for the Windows programmers. Having instantiated an `SqlFileStream` object, representing the `FILESTREAM` data file (in case of .NET), or opened a `FILESTREAM` data file (using the SQL Server Win32 API), you can read or write to the `FILESTREAM` data file using the `FILE` manipulation functions provided by the client library or the .NET programming language.

So how does this differ from the traditional model of storing the BLOB data in the file system and storing the path to the data file in a relational table? How does SQL Server maintain transactional consistency between the relational and the `FILESTREAM` data?

Well, when using the `FILESTREAM` streaming APIs, you are not accessing the `FILESTREAM` data directly; SQL Server opens the file handle and passes it to you through its own wrapper APIs. This allows SQL Server to keep total control over the operations and maintain transactional consistency between the relational data in the tables and the BLOB data in the `FILESTREAM` store.

Accessing `FILESTREAM` data through the streaming APIs involves the steps below, irrespective of the client library or programming language you use.

1. **Start a transaction** – You need a transaction to gain streaming access to the `FILESTREAM` data.

2. **Retrieve the path name and transaction context** – You need to obtain a logical path name to the `FILESTREAM` data file and a pointer to the current transaction context to access the `FILESTREAM` data.

3. **Open the FILESTREAM data file** – Gain access to the `FILESTREAM` data file either using the .NET wrapper class or the Win32 `FILESTREAM` API.

4. **Read/Write FILESTREAM data** – Read or write FILESTREAM data using the file I/O functions.

5. **Close the FILESTREAM data file** – Gracefully close the FILESTREAM data file.

6. **Commit/rollback the transaction** – Commit or roll back the transaction when you have finished.

Let's examine each of these steps in detail.

Step 1: Starting a transaction

All streaming access to FILESTREAM data, even just read access, must be done within the context of a database transaction so, before accessing the FILESTREAM data, your application should start a SQL Server transaction.

The exact manner in which you start a transaction on the current database connection will vary depending on the client library in use (ADO.NET, Open Database Connectivity, etc.). There is nothing FILESTREAM-specific in this step, you can just begin a transaction in the same way as for a T-SQL DML operation.

We will see more detailed examples and fully functional sample code later in this chapter but, for now, Listing 3-1 shows a simple example of how to start a transaction on an ADO.NET connection object using C#.

```
// Create a SqlConnection object
SqlConnection con = new SqlConnection("database=NorthPole;server=(local);
integrated security=sspi;");

//Open a connection to the database
con.Open();

//Start a transaction
SqlTransaction transaction = con.BeginTransaction("ItemTran");
```

Listing 3-1: Using C# to start a transaction on an ADO.NET connection object.

Chapter 3: Accessing FILESTREAM Data from Client Applications

Non-.NET programming languages like C++ can use the Win32 Open Database Connectivity (ODBC) APIs to create a connection to the desired database and begin a database transaction. Listing 3-2 shows an example.

```
//Connect to SQL Server through ODBC using DSN "NorthPole"
SQLConnect(hdbc, TEXT("NorthPole"), SQL_NTS, NULL, 0, NULL, 0);

//Start a transaction by setting AUTO_COMMIT attribute to OFF
SQLSetConnectAttr(hdbc, SQL_ATTR_AUTOCOMMIT, (SQLPOINTER)SQL_AUTOCOMMIT_OFF,
                  SQL_IS_UINTEGER);
```

Listing 3-2: Using C++ to start a transaction on an ODBC connection.

When the `AUTO_COMMIT` attribute is turned `OFF` on an ODBC connection, the next T-SQL statement starts an explicit transaction. The transaction stays active until `SQL_COMMIT` or `SQL_ROLLBACK` is called explicitly using `SQLEndTran()`.

Step 2: Retrieving the logical path name and transaction context

Before accessing a `FILESTREAM` data value, we must retrieve, from SQL Server, the logical path to the disk file associated with the `FILESTREAM` data, and the transaction context that represents the current database transaction, and then include these values in the data access request.

> **FILESTREAM *data values and cells***
>
> *In this chapter, the terms* `FILESTREAM` *cell and* `FILESTREAM` *data value refer, respectively, to a specific cell in a* `FILESTREAM` *table (i.e. the intersection of a given row and column) and the BLOB data stored in a* `FILESTREAM` *cell.*

Chapter 3: Accessing FILESTREAM Data from Client Applications

`PathName()` is a new intrinsic function available on the `FILESTREAM`-enabled column of a SQL Server 2008 database. Note that, unlike other T-SQL functions, `PathName()` is case sensitive. It returns the logical path to the physical file associated with a `FILESTREAM` data value. The example in Listing 3-3 retrieves the `PathName()` of the `ItemImage` column from the `Items` table. The `PathName()` value returned by each `FILESTREAM` cell will be unique, pointing to the specific disk file associated with the data in the given `FILESTREAM` cell.

```
SELECT
    ItemNumber,
    ItemImage.PathName() AS LogicalPath
FROM Items
/*
Item#   LogicalPath
------  -----------------------------------------------------
MS1001  \\JACOB-LAPTOP\SQL2008R2NOV\v1\          <= wrapped
        NorthPole\dbo\Items\ItemImage\           <= for
        E76D878F-0B2D-48EE-906E-58349797D6EC     <= readability
*/
```

Listing 3-3:   Using T-SQL to retrieve the logical path name of the `FILESTREAM` data value.

The logical path returned by the `PathName()` function should be passed back to SQL Server to access the `FILESTREAM` data value. SQL Server uses this value to identify the correct `FILESTREAM` data file when you request streaming access to the `FILESTREAM` data value of a column.

The `PathName()` function returns `NULL` if the value stored in the `FILESTREAM` cell is `NULL`. Streaming access is possible only to a `FILESTREAM` cell that has non-`NULL` value. A very detailed discussion of the `PathName()` function is provided later in this chapter.

The `FILESTREAM` transaction context associated with the current transaction can be retrieved by calling another new T-SQL function in SQL Server 2008: `GET_FILESTREAM_TRANSACTION_CONTEXT()`. This is the second piece of

Chapter 3: Accessing FILESTREAM Data from Client Applications

information that needs to be sent to SQL Server, along with the request, in order to gain streaming access to a `FILESTREAM` data value. Listing 3-4 shows an example.

```sql
-- Start an explicit transaction
BEGIN TRAN

-- returns the FILESTREAM TRANSACTION CONTEXT associated with the current session
SELECT GET_FILESTREAM_TRANSACTION_CONTEXT()

/*
output
------------------------------------
0xEC138B4813D41841A7360E5236D7CEDB
*/
```

Listing 3-4:   Using T-SQL to retrieve the `FILESTREAM` transaction context.

If an active transaction context exists in the current session, then the return value is a byte array of type `VARBINARY(MAX)`. If there is no active transaction in the current session, `NULL` is returned.

Note that, although the example in Listing 3-4 demonstrates how to call the `GET_FILESTREAM_TRANSACTION_CONTEXT()` function using T-SQL, the return value is meaningless in T-SQL; it has meaning only to a client application that wants to access the `FILESTREAM` data using the streaming APIs.

Listing 3-5 shows how to retrieve the current transaction context and the logical path to the `FILESTREAM` data value prior to requesting streaming access, from C#.

```csharp
// Retrieve the PathName() and transaction context
SqlCommand cmd = new SqlCommand();
cmd.Connection = con;
cmd.CommandText = ("SELECT TOP 1 "
                + ("    ItemImage.PathName() AS filePath, "
                + ("    GET_FILESTREAM_TRANSACTION_CONTEXT() AS txContext "
                + ("FROM Items"))));
```

```
// Begin a transaction
SqlTransaction trn = con.BeginTransaction("ItemTran");
cmd.Transaction = trn;

// Execute the query
SqlDataReader reader;
reader = cmd.ExecuteReader();
```

Listing 3-5: Using C# to retrieve the transaction context and logical path name of a FILESTREAM data value.

Step 3: Opening the FILESTREAM data file

The next step is to open the FILESTREAM data file, using the wrapper function/class provided by SQL Server. Direct access to the physical files stored in the FILESTREAM data container can corrupt the database, so it's always advisable to access the data through these streaming APIs.

.NET developers can use the SqlFileStream object to access the FILESTREAM data. SqlFileStream exposes SQL Server data that is stored with the FILESTREAM column as a sequence of bytes. It resides within the namespace System.Data.SqlTypes and within the assembly System.Data.dll. You must have .NET Framework 3.5 SP 1 or later to use SqlFileStream class.

SqlFileStream is derived from System.IO.Stream. Once you have a valid SqlFileStream object representing the desired FILESTREAM data file, you can use the Read(), Write() or the other "stream" functions available within the class to manipulate your FILESTREAM data.

Listing 3-6 shows how to open a FILESTREAM data file for reading.

Chapter 3: Accessing FILESTREAM Data from Client Applications

```
// Open and read file using SqlFileStream Class
string filePath = reader.GetString(0);
object objContext = reader.GetValue(1);
byte[] txContext = (byte[])objContext;

SqlFileStream fs = new SqlFileStream(filePath, txContext, FileAccess.Read);
```

Listing 3-6: Using C# to open a FILESTREAM data file for read access.

The parameter `filePath` is the logical path name of the FILESTREAM data file we obtained using the `PathName()` method call, and `txContext` is the FILESTREAM transaction context associated with the current transaction.

The third parameter specifies the file access mode. It can be one of `Read`, `Write`, or `ReadWrite`. `Read` opens the FILESTREAM data file for reading all the content. When `Write` is specified, the `SqlFileStream` object will point to a zero-byte file and existing data will be overwritten when the object is closed and transaction is committed. When `ReadWrite` is used, the file is opened for both reading and writing, and the file pointer is placed at the beginning of the file. By using the `Seek()` method, you can move the file pointer to any location in the file to overwrite the existing content, or you can move it to the end of the file to append more data. See *SqlFileStream Class Reference*, later in this chapter, for a detailed discussion of the different constructors and member functions of the `SqlFileStream` class.

Non .NET programming languages can use the FILESTREAM Win32 API to obtain a Windows file handle to the requested FILESTREAM data file, and use the file handle to read or write FILESTREAM data. SQL Server 2008, or later, Native Client exposes a new Win32 API, `OpenSqlFilestream()`, which returns a Windows file handle to the requested FILESTREAM data file. Just like the .NET example we saw earlier, you need to pass the FILESTREAM transaction context and logical path to the desired FILESTREAM data value when calling this function, as shown in Listing 3-7.

Chapter 3: Accessing FILESTREAM Data from Client Applications

```cpp
//Get a handle to the FILESTREAM data using OpenSqlFileStream API
SQLCHAR transactionToken[32];
SQLINTEGER cbTransactionToken = sizeof(transactionToken);
HANDLE srcHandle = INVALID_HANDLE_VALUE;
srcHandle = OpenSqlFilestream (
     dstFilePath, SQL_FILESTREAM_READ,
     SQL_FILESTREAM_OPEN_NONE , transactionToken,
     cbTransactionToken, 0);
```

Listing 3-7: Using C++ to open a FILESTREAM data file for read access.

The first parameter is the logical path to the FILESTREAM data file obtained from a call to the PathName() function. The second argument specifies file access mode. It can be one of SQL_FILESTREAM_READ, SQL_FILESTREAM_WRITE, or SQL_FILESTREAM_READWRITE (for read, write, and read/write operations respectively).

The third parameter allows you to specify the file attributes and flags. These are additional hints that tell the system about the usage pattern, and the system will use this information to optimize caching and performance. In Listing 3-7 we have set it to SQL_FILESTREAM_OPEN_NONE which indicates that the file needs to be opened with no specific flags.

The fourth argument is the transaction context we retrieved, and the fifth specifies the size (in bytes) of the transaction context buffer.

The last argument allows you to specify the initial allocation size of the data file in bytes; this is ignored when the file is opened for read operation.

See *OpenSqlFilestream API Reference*, later in this chapter, for a detailed discussion of this API function.

Step 4: Reading and writing FILESTREAM data

Once you have a valid `FILESTREAM` file handle (if you are using Win32 API) or a valid `SqlFileStream()` object (if you are using Managed API) you can go ahead and read or write `FILESTREAM` data. The read/write operations you perform on the Win32 handle or the `SqlFileStream` object will affect the disk file associated with the given `FILESTREAM` data value.

Listing 3-8 reads data from a `FILESTREAM` data file and copies it to a disk file. This example targets .NET Framework Version 4 or later, which adds the `CopyTo()` method to the `Stream` class. For earlier versions of the .NET Framework, one can write a helper method that will perform a similar buffered copy between two streams.

```
//Open the FILESTREAM data file
SqlFileStream fs = new SqlFileStream(filePath, txContext, FileAccess.Read);

//Create the target data file
FileStream fStream = new FileStream("C:\\temp\\MicrosoftMouse2.jpg",
                                    FileMode.CreateNew);

//Transfer data from FILESTREAM data file to disk file using a 4KB buffer size
fs.CopyTo(fStream, 4096);

//Close the source file
fStream.Close();
```

Listing 3-8:   Using C# to read a `FILESTREAM` data file and write to a disk file.

Listing 3-9 demonstrates a write operation where the data is read from a disk file and copied into a `FILESTREAM` column.

```
//Open the FILESTREAM data file for writing
SqlFileStream fs = new SqlFileStream(filePath, txContext, FileAccess.Write);
// Open the source file for reading
FileStream fStream = new FileStream("C:\\temp\\MicrosoftMouse2.jpg",
                                    FileMode.Open, FileAccess.Read);
```

```
//Transfer data from disk file into the FILESTREAM column
fStream.CopyTo(fs, 4096);

//Close the source file
fStream.Close();
```

Listing 3-9: Using C# to read a disk file and write into a FILESTREAM column.

It is apparent that the `SqlFileStream` object makes FILESTREAM data manipulation much simpler. It is a little bit more complicated when reading FILESTREAM data using the Win32 API function, as shown in Listing 3-10.

```
//Get a handle to the FILESTREAM data using OpenSqlFileStream API
fsHandle = OpenSqlFilestream(
                fsFilePath, SQL_FILESTREAM_READ, 0, tkn, tknSize,     0);

//Create the disk file to copy data
fileHandle = CreateFile(TEXT("C:\\temp\\microsoftmouse2.jpg"), GENERIC_WRITE,
            FILE_SHARE_WRITE, NULL, CREATE_NEW, FILE_FLAG_SEQUENTIAL_SCAN,
NULL);

const int COPYBUFFERSIZE = 4096;
DWORD bytesRead = 0;
DWORD bytesWritten = 0;
do
{
    //Read from FILESTREAM
    ReadFile(fsHandle, buffer, COPYBUFFERSIZE, &bytesRead, NULL);

    //Write to disk file
    if (bytesRead > 0)

    {
        WriteFile(fileHandle, buffer, bytesRead, &bytesWritten, NULL);
    }
} while (bytesRead == COPYBUFFERSIZE);

//close the disk file handle
if ( fileHandle != INVALID_HANDLE_VALUE )      CloseHandle(fileHandle);
```

Listing 3-10: Using C++ to read a FILESTREAM data file and write to a disk file.

Chapter 3: Accessing FILESTREAM Data from Client Applications

Listing 3-11 opens a disk file and copies the contents of the file into a FILESTREAM column.

```cpp
//Get a handle to the FILESTREAM data using OpenSqlFileStream API
fsHandle = OpenSqlFilestream(
                dstFilePath, SQL_FILESTREAM_WRITE, 0, tkn, tknSize,  0);

//Open the disk file to read
fileHandle = CreateFile(TEXT("C:\\temp\\microsoftmouse2.jpg"), GENERIC_READ,
            FILE_SHARE_READ, NULL, OPEN_EXISTING,
            FILE_FLAG_SEQUENTIAL_SCAN, NULL);

const int COPYBUFFERSIZE = 4096;
DWORD bytesRead = 0;
DWORD bytesWritten = 0;
do
{
   //Read from the disk file
   ReadFile(fileHandle, buffer, COPYBUFFERSIZE, &bytesRead, NULL);

   //Write to the FILESTREAM column
   if (bytesRead > 0)

   {
      WriteFile(fsHandle, buffer, bytesRead, &bytesWritten, NULL);
   }
} while (bytesRead == COPYBUFFERSIZE);

//close the disk file handle before closing the transaction
if ( fileHandle != INVALID_HANDLE_VALUE )     CloseHandle(fileHandle);
```

Listing 3-11:   Using C++ to read from a disk file and write into a FILESTREAM column.

Step 5: Closing the FILESTREAM data file

After the desired operation is completed, it is important to close the `FILESTREAM` data file. The `FILESTREAM` handle should be closed before the transaction is committed or rolled back. Listing 3-12 shows how to close the `FILESTREAM` file handle.

```
//close the file handle
fs.Close();
```

Listing 3-12:   Using C# to close the `FILESTREAM` file handle.

Any `UPDATE` triggers on the table will be fired when the `FILESTREAM` data file that was opened for the `Write` operation is closed.

Step 6: Closing the transaction (COMMIT/ROLLBACK)

After closing the `FILESTREAM` data file, the current transaction should be committed or rolled back depending upon the status of the operation. When the transaction is committed, the changes made to the `FILESTREAM` data file will be permanently written to the `FILESTREAM` data file. A rollback will undo the changes done in the current transaction. Listing 3-13 commits the current transaction.

```
//Commit the transaction
cmd.Transaction.Commit();
```

Listing 3-13:   Using C# to commit the transaction associated with an ADO.NET command object.

Data Manipulation Using the Streaming APIs

On a FILESTREAM-enabled table, a client application might perform one or more of the database operations below.

- Insert a new record into a FILESTREAM-enabled table.
- Replace the FILESTREAM data completely.
- Replace the FILESTREAM data partially.
- Append more data to an existing FILESTREAM data value.
- Read the information stored in a FILESTREAM column.
- Delete the FILESTREAM data value from a column.
- Delete a row from a FILESTREAM-enabled table.

Some of these operations must be done using T-SQL, whereas some of them are best done using the streaming APIs. We'll examine each one in detail, and recommend the best approach. We'll then present a worked lab that demonstrates how to insert, read, and partially update FILESTREAM data via the streaming APIs.

Inserting a new record into a FILESTREAM-enabled table

As discussed in Chapter 2, unless the FILESTREAM column is assigned a default value, a client application will need to execute a T-SQL INSERT statement in order to add a new row into a FILESTREAM-enabled table, rather than use the streaming APIs. The reason for this is that streaming access can be made only to rows that contain non-NULL BLOB data in the FILESTREAM column.

To avoid additional round trips to the database, the stored procedure or T-SQL batch that is used to perform the `INSERT` operation can also return the `FILESTREAM` transaction context of the current transaction and the logical path to the `FILESTREAM` data file associated with the newly inserted record. The client application can then use these values to access the `FILESTREAM` data.

Since it is not possible to use the streaming API to create a new `FILESTREAM` data file and associate it with a `FILESTREAM` column, to create a new record and save the BLOB data into the `FILESTREAM` column the client application must use two steps.

1. Execute a T-SQL statement to create a new record along with a dummy `FILESTREAM` value. Inserting a fake value such as `0x` into the `FILESTREAM` column will force SQL Server to create a `FILESTREAM` data file and associate it with the column.
2. Once the `FILESTREAM` data file has been created, the client application can use the `PathName()` value of the `FILESTREAM` column in the newly inserted record to access the `FILESTREAM` data file and write the BLOB data into it.

An alternative solution involves not allowing `NULL` values in the `FILESTREAM` column and providing a default value of `0x`. This ensures that the `FILESTREAM` cell will always be associated with a valid file, and can remove some repetitive code from the application that is writing `FILESTREAM` data.

Replacing the FILESTREAM data completely

When the `FILESTREAM` data is to be replaced completely, this is usually done using the streaming APIs. A client application can perform a write operation using either the `SqlFileStream` class (.NET) or the `OpenSqlFilestream()` Win32 API function. When the `FILESTREAM` data file is opened for write access, the file pointer is at the beginning of the file. The write operation will write into a new disk file, and the reference on the `FILESTREAM` column will be updated to point to the new file when the file handle is closed and transaction is committed. The old `FILESTREAM` data file will be removed by an asynchronous garbage collector thread.

Note that any `UPDATE` triggers that exist on the target table will be fired when the `FILESTREAM` file handle is closed.

Partial updates to FILESTREAM data

A partial update involves replacing a part of an existing `FILESTREAM` data file with new content, or appending to the end of an existing BLOB file. Unlike partial updates on `VARBINARY(MAX)` columns, attempting partial updates on `FILESTREAM` cells is a very slow operation because a new disk file will be created with the new file content every time the contents change. This adds a lot of additional I/O requirements. In effect, there is no such thing as a partial update to a `FILESTREAM` data file so, if your business or application requires frequent small partial updates to the BLOB data, you might want to use `VARBINARY(MAX)` columns rather than `FILESTREAM` storage.

If necessary to support a legacy application, partial updates can be simulated by opening the `FILESTREAM` data file for read-write access and then moving the file pointer to the appropriate position before writing the new data to the desired location, either overwriting existing data, or appending the data to the end of the file.

Any `UPDATE` triggers that exist on the target table will be fired when the `FILESTREAM` file handle is closed.

Reading information from the FILESTREAM store

.NET applications can access the `FILESTREAM` data file for read access using the `SqlFileStream()` class and specifying the `READ` flag.

Win32 applications can use the `OpenSqlFilestream()` Win32 API function to obtain a handle to the `FILESTREAM` data file associated with the `FILESTREAM` cell.

Just like the write operation, read will also require a two-step approach; the client application must retrieve the `FILESTREAM` transaction context and the logical path name for the `FILESTREAM` cell before accessing the `FILESTREAM` data file associated with the column.

Deleting the BLOB data stored in a FILESTREAM column

The recommended way to delete the BLOB data stored in a `FILESTREAM` column is by using a T-SQL `UPDATE` statement, as was described in Chapter 2. The BLOB data associated with a `FILESTREAM` column is deleted when the value of the column is set to `NULL`.

Deleting a row from a FILESTREAM-enabled table

Just like the `INSERT` operation, deleting a row from a `FILESTREAM`-enabled table must be done using T-SQL. This can be achieved directly, by using a `DELETE` query, or indirectly, in which a client library such as ADO.NET runs a `DELETE` query.

Lab 1: Reads, Writes and Partial Updates

It is time for us to write some fully functional sample code that reads and writes FILESTREAM data to perform the FILESTREAM operations below.

1. Inserting a new record (with T-SQL) and storing FILESTREAM data in the column.
2. Reading information from a FILESTREAM column.
3. Performing partial updates on the BLOB data stored in a FILESTREAM column.

In the following sections, we'll provide the sample code and step-by-step explanations for each of these operations in C# using the Managed API. The sample code for VB.NET (using the Managed API) and C++ (using the Win32 API) is supplied separately in the download. Though the syntax and code used in each of these programming languages differ a little, the overall flow of the operations remains the same across all these programming languages.

Inserting a new record with FILESTREAM data

Let us see an example that reads the content of a disk file and stores it in the FILESTREAM data container. We will load the content of the Microsoft Mouse image file that we used in Chapter 2.

The first step is to create a connection to the desired target SQL Server 2008 instance that hosts the database with the FILESTREAM-enabled table in which we want to store the BLOB data, as shown in Listing 3-14.

```
//References at the top of the file
using System;
using System.Data;
using System.Windows.Forms;
using System.Data.SqlClient;
```

Chapter 3: Accessing FILESTREAM Data from Client Applications

```csharp
using System.Data.SqlTypes;
using System.IO;

public void SaveItemImage()
{
    byte[] txContext = null;
    string filePath = string.Empty;

    // Create a connection to the database
    string ConStr = ("Data Source=(local);" +
                    "Initial Catalog=NorthPole;Integrated Security=True");
    SqlConnection con = new SqlConnection(ConStr);
    con.Open();
```

Listing 3-14: Creating a connection to the SQL Server instance.

Note that to access `FILESTREAM` data through the streaming API, you must connect to SQL Server using Integrated Security (Windows authentication). If you connect to SQL Server using SQL Server authentication, you will get an "Access Denied" error when you try to open the `FILESTREAM` data file.

Next, we insert a row with a dummy value into the `FILESTREAM` column in the `Items` table, using the T-SQL `INSERT` statement shown in Listing 3-15. Notice the `OUTPUT` clause, which returns the path name associated with the `FILESTREAM` column of the newly inserted row, along with the current `FILESTREAM` transaction context.

```csharp
// Insert a record to the table and retrieve the PathName()
// A dummy value is inserted to the ItemImage column to obtain a valid PathName()

SqlCommand cmd = new SqlCommand();
cmd.Connection = con;
cmd.CommandText = "INSERT INTO Items " +
                  "(ItemID, ItemNumber, ItemDescription, ItemImage)" +
                  "OUTPUT GET_FILESTREAM_TRANSACTION_CONTEXT() AS txContext," +
                  "       inserted.ItemImage.PathName() AS filePath " +
                  "SELECT NEWID(), 'A0001', 'Microsoft Mouse', 0x";
```

Chapter 3: Accessing FILESTREAM Data from Client Applications

```
SqlTransaction transaction = con.BeginTransaction("ItemTran");
cmd.Transaction = transaction;
SqlDataReader reader = cmd.ExecuteReader();

if (reader.Read())
{
    txContext = (reader["txContext"] as byte[]);
    filePath = reader["filePath"].ToString();
}
reader.Close();
```

Listing 3-15:   Inserting a record and retrieving the FILESTREAM file path and transaction context.

Once we have the logical path to the FILESTREAM data file and the FILESTREAM transaction context, we can write the binary data (the content of the disk file that stores the image) into the FILESTREAM store, as shown in Listing 3-16.

```
//Open the FILESTREAM data file for writing
SqlFileStream fs = new SqlFileStream(filePath, txContext,
                                FileAccess.Write);

// Open the disk file for reading
FileStream localFile = new FileStream("C:\\temp\\microsoftmouse.jpg",
                                FileMode.Open, FileAccess.Read);

//Copy data from disk file to FILESTREAM column
localFile.CopyTo(fs, 4096);
```

Listing 3-16:   Writing the content of a byte array into a FILESTREAM data file.

And finally, we close the FILESTREAM file, commit the transaction, and close the database connection to complete the exercise (Listing 3-17).

```
//Close the files
localFile.Close();
fs.Close();
```

```
//Commit the transaction and close the connection
cmd.Transaction.Commit();
con.Close();
```

Listing 3-17:   Cleanup code.

As previously mentioned, the full listings for this exercise using C#, VB.NET, and C++ can be found in the download files.

Reading FILESTREAM data

Now we'll look an example that reads the BLOB data from the `FILESTREAM` store in the `Items` table and creates a disk file with the BLOB data.

First, we need to create a connection to the SQL Server 2008 instance. The next step is to write a `SELECT` query that retrieves the path name and `FILESTREAM` transaction context of the desired record in the `Items` table (Listing 3-18). To make the code listing simpler, we will just select the `TOP 1` row from the table. In real life, you might be querying for a specific record based on a search criteria.

```
public void ReadItemImage()
{
    string filePath = string.Empty;
    byte[] txContext = null;
    string ConStr;

    ConStr = ("Data Source=(local);Initial Catalog=NorthPole"
            + ";Integrated Security=True");
    SqlConnection con = new SqlConnection(ConStr);
    con.Open();

    SqlCommand cmd = new SqlCommand();
    cmd.Connection = con;
    cmd.CommandText = "SELECT TOP 1 " +
                      "     ItemImage.PathName() AS filePath, " +
                      "     GET_FILESTREAM_TRANSACTION_CONTEXT() AS txContext " +
                      "FROM Items";
```

```
SqlTransaction trn = con.BeginTransaction("ItemTran");
cmd.Transaction = trn;
SqlDataReader reader;
reader = cmd.ExecuteReader();

// Retrieve the FilePath() of the image file
if (reader.Read())
{
    txContext = (reader["txContext"] as byte[]);
    filePath = reader["filePath"].ToString();
}
reader.Close();
```

Listing 3-18: Retrieving the FILESTREAM logical path name and transaction context.

We can now go ahead and open the FILESTREAM data file. The sample code in Listing 3-19 opens a FILESTREAM data file for read operation.

```
//Open the FILESTREAM data file
SqlFileStream fs = new SqlFileStream(filePath, txContext, FileAccess.Read);
```

Listing 3-19: Opening a FILESTREAM data file for read operation.

Next, we open the target file into which we will write the data being read from the FILESTREAM data file (Listing 3-20).

```
//Create the target data file
FileStream localFile = new FileStream("C:\\temp\\MicrosoftMouse2.jpg",
                                      FileMode.CreateNew);
```

Listing 3-20: Creating a disk file to store the BLOB data.

In Listing 3-21, we read from the FILESTREAM data file and write into the disk file we just created.

```
// Transferring data from FILESTREAM data file to disk file
fs.CopyTo(localFile, 4096);
```

Listing 3-21:   Reading from the `FILESTREAM` data file and writing to the disk file.

This should be followed by the cleanup operation to close the `FILESTREAM` file, commit the transaction, and close the database connection (Listing 3-17).

Performing partial updates

A partial update is performed by opening the `FILESTREAM` data file for read-write operation, and then moving the file pointer to the desired location using the `Seek()` function, or to the end of the file to append new content.

In order to verify the result of the operation manually, we will use some text data instead of the binary image file from the previous examples. We will perform the actions below.

1. Create a text file on a local folder.
2. Open the `FILESTREAM` data file for write access and store the content of the text file in it.
3. Open the `FILESTREAM` data file for read-write access, and then move to the end of the file and write the content of the text file (created at Step 1) into the file again. There will be two copies of the text in the `FILESTREAM` data file.
4. Open the `FILESTREAM` data file for read access, and then read the contents of the data file and write it into a disk file.
5. Open the disk file created at Step 4 and verify that it contains two copies of the original text.

Chapter 3: Accessing FILESTREAM Data from Client Applications

To start with, let's create a text file with some simple text data in C:\temp folder, and name the file original.txt (Figure 3-1).

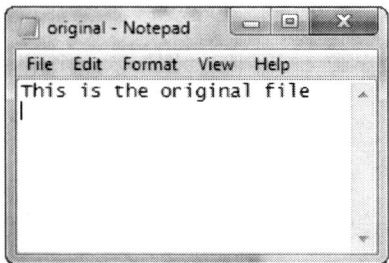

Figure 3-1:   Creating a text file.

Next, we need to write the content of this file into the FILESTREAM data store. As previously, we need to connect to SQL Server, start a transaction, and retrieve the FILESTREAM column logical path name and the FILESTREAM transaction context.

Next, we will read the content of original.txt and write it into the FILESTREAM file. We will open the FILESTREAM data file for write access and write the content of the source file into it (Listing 3-22).

```
//Open the FILESTREAM data file and store the content of source file
SqlFileStream fs = new SqlFileStream(filePath, txContext,
                                    FileAccess.Write);
FileStream localFile = new FileStream("C:\\temp\\original.txt",
                                    FileMode.Open, FileAccess.Read);
localFile.CopyTo(fs, 4096);

localFile.Close();
fs.Close();
```

Listing 3-22:   Reading the content of original.txt and writing it to the FILESTREAM data store.

Next, we'll perform the partial update. In Listing 3-23, we open the file for read-write access, move to the end of the file, and write the content of original.txt again.

Chapter 3: Accessing FILESTREAM Data from Client Applications

```
//Re-open the FILESTREAM data file and move to the end of file
fs = new SqlFileStream(filePath, txContext, FileAccess.ReadWrite);
fs.Seek(0, SeekOrigin.End);

localFile = new FileStream("C:\\temp\\original.txt",
                                     FileMode.Open, FileAccess.Read);

//Append the content of original.txt again
localFile.CopyTo(fs, 4096);
localFile.Close();
fs.Close();
```

Listing 3-23: Performing a partial update.

We just performed a partial update on the `FILESTREAM` column. We will now verify that the information is stored as expected, by reading the contents of the `FILESTREAM` data file and creating a new text file with the data. We can then open the text file and verify that the partial update took place correctly (Listing 3-24).

```
//Open the FILESTREAM data file for 'READ' and copy contents
//into a disk file
fs = new SqlFileStream(filePath, txContext, FileAccess.Read);
localFile = new FileStream("C:\\temp\\copy.txt", FileMode.Create);
fs.CopyTo(localFile, 4096);

localFile.Close();
fs.Close();
```

Listing 3-24: Reading from the `FILESTREAM` data file and writing to a disk file.

Let's now open the text file (`copy.txt`) and verify that it contains two copies of the text data that was present in `original.txt` (Figure 3-2).

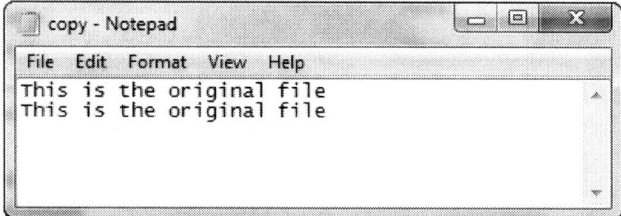

Figure 3-2:   Verifying that the copy contains two copies of the original text.

We can see that the partial update has taken place as expected.

Handling multiple FILESTREAM columns and rows

One of the interesting features T-SQL programming offers is the ability to perform set-based operations. A set operation allows you to process more than one row and column in a single T-SQL query.

However, when it comes to accessing `FILESTREAM` data through the streaming APIs, set-based operations are not applicable. In the examples discussed above, we saw how to read or write a single `FILESTREAM` cell using I/O streaming. If you want to read or write more than one `FILESTREAM` column or row, you must process each, one by one. The pseudocode in Listing 3-25 shows an approximate representation of how to read `FILESTREAM` data from more than one row and column.

```
/*
Connect to database
Begin a transaction
Retrieve 10 rows from a table that has 3 FILESTREAM columns
    SELECT TOP 10
        GET_FILESTREAM_TRANSACTION_CONTEXT(),
        FileStreamColumn1.PathName(),
        FileStreamColumn2.PathName(),
        FileStreamColumn3.PathName()
```

```
        FROM Items
For each row in the result set
    For column 1 to 3
        Open the FILESTREAM data file
        Read from FILESTREAM data File
        Do something with the data
        Close the FILESTREAM data file
    Next column
Next row
Commit transaction
Close database connection
*/
```

Listing 3-25:   Pseudocode that shows how to read BLOB data from more than one row and column.

Understanding the Logical Path to a FILESTREAM Data File

You may have noticed by now that FILESTREAM deals with a lot of logical identifiers! For example, the FILESTREAM file share, configured while enabling the FILESTREAM feature (see Appendix A) is not mapped to a physical directory on the system; it is simply a logical identifier that SQL Server uses internally to point to the FILESTREAM data container. If you try to explore the FILESTREAM share name by double-clicking on it from Windows Explorer, you will realize that it does not open any folder, as would be expected for a "normal" file share.

Just like the FILESTREAM file share, the logical path to a FILESTREAM data file (returned by the PathName() function) is an internal identifier that SQL Server uses to point to the disk file associated with a FILESTREAM data value. When a client application wants to read or write FILESTREAM data through the streaming APIs, it needs to have a way to exactly pinpoint the FILESTREAM value on a specific table, row, or column. The PathName() function make this simpler. A client application can run a T-SQL query that locates the specific FILESTREAM value and calls the PathName() function to retrieve a logical identifier pointing to it.

Chapter 3: Accessing FILESTREAM Data from Client Applications

The client application can then pass this value to the **FILESTREAM** API method call to open the NTFS data file represented by the logical identifier returned by the `PathName()` function.

To illustrate this point, let's return to the example we first saw in Chapter 2, and create a new **FILESTREAM**-enabled database (Listing 3-26).

```
CREATE DATABASE NorthPole ON
PRIMARY (
    NAME = NorthPoleDB,
    FILENAME = 'C:\ArtOfFS\Demos\Chapter3\NorthPoleDB.mdf'
), FILEGROUP NorthPoleFS CONTAINS FILESTREAM(
    NAME = NorthPole_fs,
    FILENAME = 'C:\ArtOfFS\Demos\Chapter3\'NorthPole_fs')
LOG ON (
    NAME = NorthPole_log,
    FILENAME = 'C:\ArtOfFS\Demos\Chapter3\NorthPole_log.ldf')
```

Listing 3-26: Creating a FILESTREAM-enabled database.

In Listing 3-27, we create a table with a **FILESTREAM** column and insert some data.

```
-- Create "Items" table
CREATE TABLE [dbo].[Items](
    [ItemID] UNIQUEIDENTIFIER ROWGUIDCOL NOT NULL UNIQUE,
    [ItemNumber] VARCHAR(20),
    [ItemDescription] VARCHAR(50),
    [ItemImage] VARBINARY(MAX) FILESTREAM NULL
)
GO
-- Insert the data to the table
INSERT INTO Items (ItemID, ItemNumber, ItemDescription, ItemImage)
SELECT
    NEWID(), 'MS1001', 'Microsoft Mouse',
    CAST(bulkcolumn AS VARBINARY(MAX))
FROM OPENROWSET(
    BULK 'C:\temp\MicrosoftMouse.jpg', SINGLE_BLOB
) AS x
```

Listing 3-27: Creating a table with a FILESTREAM column and populating it with sample data.

Let us now try to query the table and see the data we just inserted (Listing 3-28).

```
SELECT * FROM Items
/*
ItemID          Item#   ItemDescription  ItemImage
-----------     ------  ---------------  ------------------
E76D878F-0..    MS1001  Microsoft Mouse  0xFFD8FFE000104A4..
*/
```

Listing 3-28: Querying the `Items` table.

The column `ItemImage` stores the `FILESTREAM` data we just inserted. To a T-SQL query, the `FILESTREAM` column appears as a `VARBINARY(MAX)` column. However, the data is stored in the `FILESTREAM` data container as a disk file. Every BLOB value in every `FILESTREAM` column (in every non-`NULL` `FILESTREAM` field) has a disk file associated with it in the `FILESTREAM` data container.

The logical path name refers to the disk file associated with each BLOB data value, and can be retrieved by using the new intrinsic function `PathName()`, as shown in Listing 3-29. Note that `PathName()` is case sensitive. You will get an error if the correct case is not used when invoking this method.

```
SELECT
    ItemNumber,
    ItemImage.PathName() AS LogicalPath
FROM Items

/*
Item#   LogicalPath
------  --------------------------------------------------
MS1001  \\localhost\MSSQLSERVER\v1\              <= wrapped
        NorthPole\dbo\Items\ItemImage\           <= for
        E76D878F-0B2D-48EE-906E-58349797D6EC     <= readability
*/
```

Listing 3-29: Retrieving the logical path associated with a `FILESTREAM` data value.

The example above shows the logical path to the `FILESTREAM` data inserted into the `Items` table using the script in Listing 3-27 on the author's computer. If you run the code on your computer, you might see a slightly different result.

Table 3-1 dissects the various different component parts of the logical path name of a `FILESTREAM` data file.

`\\localhost`	Computer name.
`\MSSQLSERVER`	`FILESTREAM` share name.
`\v1`	`FILESTREAM` version number (used internally). On SQL Server 2008 and 2008 R2 the version number shows up as "v1." On SQL Server 2012, the version number shows up as "v02" which is part of a more complex value such as "v02-A60EC2F8-2B24-11DF-9CC3-AF2E56D89593."
`\NorthPole\dbo\Items\`	Fully qualified object name (Database\Schema\Table).
`\ItemImage`	Column name.
`\E76D878F-0B2D-48EE-906E-58349797D6EC`	File identifier. This is the value of the ROWGUIDCOL of the current row.
`VolumeHint-HarddiskVolume2`	This additional value is seen only in SQL Server 2012.

Table 3-1: The components of the logical path name.

Note that the logical path name is useful only to SQL Server; you cannot reliably identify the disk file using this information. SQL Server installs a filter driver which translates the logical path name to the correct disk file when you try to access it using the streaming API functions.

The `PathName()` function returns `NULL` if the `FILESTREAM` column is `NULL`. This means that a `FILESTREAM` column with `NULL` value cannot be accessed using the Win32 streaming APIs.

Formatting PathName()

When invoking the `PathName()` function, you can specify additional flags to format the output that is returned. `PathName()` takes an integer parameter 0, 1, or 2; the default is 0.

The only difference is in the server name. Table 3-2 shows the way in which `PathName()` formats the server name with the different flags that it supports.

`PathName()` `PathName(0)`	\\JACOB-LAPTOP	Converts the server name to NetBIOS format.
`PathName(1)`	\\jacob-laptop	Does not perform any conversion.
`PathName(2)`	\\jacob-laptop.beyondrelational.com	If the server is part of a domain, returns the fully qualified domain name. If the server is not part of a domain, does not perform any conversion, as for `PathName(1)`.

Table 3-2:   Pathname parameters.

In most cases this formatting may not be helpful for us as database administrators or developers. According to Srini Acharya, a Senior Program Manager in the Relational Engine development group at Microsoft SQL Server, this formatting is intended for the use of testing and support engineers at Microsoft.

PathName() and ROWGUIDCOL

In Chapter 1, we stated that a `FILESTREAM` column could be created only on a table that has one (and only one) `UNIQUEIDENTIFIER` column, with the `ROWGUIDCOL` attribute, which indicates that the value in that column can be used to uniquely identify each row in the table. However, since the database engine does not do anything to enforce this uniqueness, the `NOT NULL` and `UNIQUE` attributes are also required on this column.

The value stored in the column marked as `ROWGUIDCOL` can even be accessed without knowing the name of the column. For example, if a table named `Customers` exists, and the `UNIQUEIDENTIFIER` column, with the `ROWGUIDCOL` attribute, is called `CustomerID`, then values from the `CustomerID` column can be retrieved using `SELECT $ROWGUID FROM Customers`.

Not only must this `ROWGUIDCOL` column of the table exist, it must also be visible to the query that uses the `PathName()` function. If we create a view or common table expression (CTE) that does not include the `ROWGUIDCOL` column, executing the `PathName()` function on the view or CTE will generate an error (Books Online clearly explains the reason for this restriction).

Listing 3-30 creates a `VIEW` of the `Items` table, but does not include the `ROWGUIDCOL` in the view.

```
-- Create a VIEW
CREATE VIEW ItemInfo AS
SELECT ItemNumber, ItemImage FROM Items
GO

-- SELECT from the VIEW
SELECT
    ItemNumber,
    ItemImage.PathName()
FROM ItemInfo

/*-- Output
Msg 5539, Level 16, State 1, Line 3
The ROWGUIDCOL column associated with the FILESTREAM being used is not visible
where method PathName is called.
*/
```

Listing 3-30: Using a view to show that the ROWGUIDCOL must be visible to the PathName() query.

The ItemInfo view does not include the ROWGUIDCOL column, so a call to the PathName() on any of the columns will generate an error. To fix this problem, we must include the ItemID column (which is marked as ROWGUIDCOL) in the view, as shown in Listing 3-31.

```
ALTER VIEW ItemInfo AS
SELECT
    ItemNumber,
    ItemImage,
    ItemID     --This is needed for PathName()
FROM Items
```

Listing 3-31: Adding the ROWGUIDCOL column to the view.

Similarly, the query on the CTE in Listing 3-32 will fail because the ROWGUIDCOL is not visible to the PathName() function.

Chapter 3: Accessing FILESTREAM Data from Client Applications

```
;WITH cte AS (
    SELECT
        ItemNumber,
        ItemImage
    FROM Items
)
SELECT
    ItemNumber,
    ItemImage.PathName()
FROM cte

/*-- Output
Msg 5539, Level 16, State 1, Line 1
The ROWGUIDCOL column associated with the FILESTREAM being used is not visible
*/
```

Listing 3-32: Using a CTE to show that the ROWGUIDCOL must be visible to the PathName() query.

Again, because the CTE does not include the ROWGUIDCOL column, a call to the PathName() on any of the columns will generate an error. For the same reason, the query in Listing 3-33 will also fail.

```
SELECT
    ItemNumber,
    ItemImage.PathName()
FROM (
    SELECT
        ItemNumber,
        ItemImage
    FROM Items
) a

/*-- Output
Msg 5539, Level 16, State 1, Line 1
The ROWGUIDCOL column associated with the FILESTREAM being used is not visible
where method PathName is called.
*/
```

Listing 3-33: The ROWGUIDCOL must be visible to the PathName() query.

The SELECT statement does not include the ROWGUIDCOL column, so the PathName() query generates an error.

SqlFileStream Class Reference

The `SqlFileStream` class represents the `FILESTREAM` data file associated with the BLOB data stored in a `FILESTREAM` cell. This class exposes the BLOB as a sequence of bytes.

`SqlFileStream` is derived from `System.IO.Stream` and resides in the `System.Data.Sqltypes` namespace. To use the `SqlFileStream` class, you need a reference to assembly `System.Data` in `System.Data.dll`. (`SqlFileStream` was added to the Framework with .NET Framework 3.5 SP 1 or later, which also includes 2.0 SP 2 and 3.0 SP 2.)

Instantiating a SqlFileStream object

`SqlFileStream` provides two constructors that you can use to instantiate an object with different levels of control over the file being accessed. We have seen an example of the basic constructor earlier in this chapter. Listing 3-34 shows the simple constructor that we saw earlier.

```
// Open and read file using SqlFileStream Class
SqlFileStream fs = new SqlFileStream(filePath, txContext, FileAccess.Read);
```

Listing 3-34: C# code that opens a `FILESTREAM` data file for read access.

- **filePath** – This is the logical path to the physical file associated with the `FILESTREAM` data value. The logical path is retrieved by a call to the `PathName()` function on the `FILESTREAM` column on the specific row in the table.

- **txContext** – This is the `FILESTREAM` transaction context associated with the current transaction. Note that you need an active transaction even to read `FILESTREAM` data when accessing through I/O streaming.

Chapter 3: Accessing FILESTREAM Data from Client Applications

- **FileAccess** – This parameter specifies the required file access mode. The possible values are:

  - **FileAccess.Read** – Opens the FILESTREAM data file for reading. The file pointer is placed at the beginning of the file.

  - **FileAccess.Write** – Opens the FILESTREAM data file for writing.

  - **FileAccess.ReadWrite** – Opens the FILESTREAM data file for reading and writing. The file pointer is placed at the beginning of the file. You can use the Seek() method to move the file pointer to specific locations in the file and make partial updates, or to move to the end of the file to append content.

SqlFileStream provides another version of the constructor that gives more control over the FILESTREAM data file being opened. Listing 3-35 shows an example that demonstrates the advanced SqlFileStream constructor.

```
// Open and read file using SqlFileStream Class
SqlFileStream fs = new SqlFileStream(filePath, txContext, FileAccess.Read,
                                     FileOptions.SequentialScan, 0);
```

Listing 3-35: Using the advanced FILESTREAM constructor.

This version of the SqlFileStream constructor allows you to specify more options when opening the FILESTREAM data file. The additional parameters enable you to optimize the FILESTREAM operations.

The first three parameters are the same as for the basic FILESTREAM constructor which we discussed earlier. The FileOptions parameter enables you to specify additional flags that inform the system about your intended file access pattern and optimize the operations accordingly. For example, Listing 3-35, above, tells the system that you intend to use the file sequentially; the system uses this information to optimize FILESTREAM access because it knows in advance that you will not move the file pointer backwards or jump into a random location in the file.

The other options that you can specify are:

- **FileOptions.None** – Indicates that you do not want to specify any additional flags.
- **FileOptions.WriteThrough** – Instructs the system to send writes directly to disk, bypassing any intermediate caches.
- **FileOptions.Asynchronous** – Informs the system that you intend to use the file for asynchronous reading and writing.
- **FileOptions.RandomAccess** – Informs the system that you might access the file randomly. The system will use this information to optimize file caching for random access.
- **FileOptions.SequentialScan** – Informs the system that you will use the file sequentially. When this flag is specified, the system optimizes the file operations on the basis that you will not access the file backwards or jump into a random location in the file.

Note that using any option other than those listed above will result in an `ArgumentOutOfRangeException` error.

The last parameter in Listing 3-35 specifies the default file allocation size while creating the file. You can specify 0 to instruct the system to use the default size specified by the NTFS volume.

Note, also, that if an error occurs when calling the constructor, the current transaction should be rolled back.

`SqlFileStream` exposes a number of methods that enable you to manipulate the `FILESTREAM` data described below.

- **BeginRead()** – Begins an asynchronous read operation.
- **BeginWrite()** – Begins an asynchronous write operation.

- **Close()** – Closes the `FILESTREAM` data file. This should be done before the transaction is committed or rolled back.
- **CopyTo()** – Copies all the bytes from the current stream to a destination stream.
- **EndRead()** – Waits for a pending asynchronous read to complete.
- **EndWrite()** – Ends an asynchronous write operation.
- **Flush()** – Clears buffers and forces the data to be written to the `FILESTREAM` data file.
- **Read()** – Reads a sequence of bytes from the `FILESTREAM` data file.
- **ReadByte()** – Reads a byte from the `FILESTREAM` data file.
- **SetLength()** – Sets the length of the current stream.
- **Write()** – Writes a sequence of bytes into the `FILESTREAM` data file.
- **WriteByte()** – Writes a byte into the `FILESTREAM` data file.

For additional reference, see the MSDN documentation at: HTTP://BRURL.COM/FS5.

OpenSqlFilestream API Reference

`OpenSqlFilestream()` is a Win32 API function exposed by the SQL Server Native Client that gives you access to the `FILESTREAM` data file. This function returns a Win32 file handle pointing to the `FILESTREAM` data file associated with a given `FILESTREAM` data value.

The `OpenSqlFilestream` API is exposed from the dynamic link library `sqlncli.dll`. The declaration of the various symbols for accessing the `OpenSqlFilestream` API function is found in header file `sqlncli.h`, and the static library that you need to link is `sqlncli.lib`. These files can be found in the `Include` and `Lib` folders of your SDK directory respectively.

Chapter 3: Accessing FILESTREAM Data from Client Applications

The default location is `C:\Program Files\Microsoft SQL Server\100\SDK\Include`, but you might find it in a different location, depending upon where you installed SQL Server 2008.

The code snippet in Listing 3-36 shows an example that opens a FILESTREAM data file using the `OpenSqlFilestream` API function.

```
//Get a handle to the FILESTREAM data using OpenSqlFileStream API
HANDLE srcHandle = INVALID_HANDLE_VALUE;
srcHandle = OpenSqlFilestream ( dstFilePath, SQL_FILESTREAM_READ, 0,
                                transactionToken,cbTransactionToken, 0);
```

Listing 3-36: Opening a FILESTREAM data file for READ access with C++ using Win32 API OpenSqlFileStream().

The first argument (`dstFilePath`) is the logical path to the FILESTREAM data file, retrieved by a call to the `PathName()` function on the FILESTREAM column. The second argument specifies the file access level required. This argument can take one of the values listed below.

- **SQL_FILESTREAM_READ** – Opens the FILESTREAM data file for reading. The file pointer is placed at the beginning of the file.

- **SQL_FILESTREAM_WRITE** – Opens the FILESTREAM data file for writing. The file pointer is placed at the beginning of the file. A write operation will overwrite the existing content in the file.

- **SQL_FILESTREAM_READWRITE** – Opens the FILESTREAM data file for reading and writing. The file pointer is placed at the beginning of the file. You can use the `Seek()` method to move the file pointer to specific locations in the file and make partial updates, or to move to the end of the file to append content.

Chapter 3: Accessing FILESTREAM Data from Client Applications

The next argument in Listing 3-36 specifies additional flags that help the system to optimize the requested file operation. The different values this parameter can take are described below.

- **SQL_FILESTREAM_OPEN_NONE** – Indicates that you do not want to specify any additional flags.

- **SQL_FILESTREAM_OPEN_FLAG_NO_WRITE_THROUGH** – Instructs the system to send writes directly to disk, bypassing any intermediate caches.

- **SQL_FILESTREAM_OPEN_FLAG_ASYNC** – Informs the system that you intend to use the file for asynchronous reading and writing.

- **SQL_FILESTREAM_OPEN_FLAG_RANDOM_ACCESS** – Informs the system that you might access the file randomly. The system will use this information to optimize file caching for random access.

- **SQL_FILESTREAM_OPEN_FLAG_SEQUENTIAL_SCAN** – Informs the system that you will use the file sequentially. When this flag is specified, the system optimizes the file operations on the basis that you will not access the file backwards or jump into a random location in the file.

- **SQL_FILESTREAM_OPEN_FLAG_NO_BUFFERING** – Requests the system to open the file with no buffering support.

The next argument in Listing 3-36 (`transactionToken`) is the FILESTREAM transaction context retrieved by calling T-SQL function GET_FILESTREAM_TRANSACTION_CONTEXT(). This is followed by another parameter, `cbTransactionToken`, which specifies the size of the buffer that stores the FILESTREAM transaction context.

The final parameter in Listing 3-36 specifies the initial allocation size of the data file in bytes. This parameter is ignored when the file is opened for READ operation. If this parameter is NULL, the system will use the default allocation size.

Chapter 3: Accessing FILESTREAM Data from Client Applications

Note that `FILESTREAM` data can be accessed using the `OpenSqlFilestream()` function only if the application connects to SQL Server using Windows authentication.

If `OpenSqlFilestream()` succeeds, it returns a valid handle to the `FILESTREAM` data file associated with the logical path name passed into the function as the first parameter. If the function fails, it returns `INVALID_HANDLE_VALUE`. The handle value returned by this function can be used to manipulate the `FILESTREAM` data associated with the handle. The Win32 API functions below can be used on the handle returned by `OpenSqlFilestream()` function.

- **ReadFile()** – Reads information from the `FILESTREAM` data file.
- **WriteFile()** – Writes information into the `FILESTREAM` data file.
- **TransmitFile()** – Used to transmit `FILESTREAM` data over a socket.
- **SetFilePointer()** – Moves the file pointer to a desired location in the disk file associated with the handle. The next read/write operation will start from the new location.
- **SetEndOfFile()** – Truncates the file at the current file pointer position.
- **FlushFileBuffers()** – Writes the data in all the buffers associated with a file into the disk.
- **CloseHandle()** – Closes the `FILESTREAM` file handle. If the table has `UPDATE` triggers, they will be fired when the `FILESTREAM` file handle is closed.

Note that the `FILESTREAM` data handle cannot be used with any Win32 APIs other than those listed above. If you pass the handle to any other Win32 API function, you will get an `ERROR_ACCESS_DENIED` error.

The `FILESTREAM` file handle should be closed by calling `CloseHandle()` before the current transaction is committed or rolled back.

Summary

When accessing `FILESTREAM` data through the Win32 or .NET interfaces exposed by SQL Server, you can get better performance in most cases because SQL Server memory is not used for processing the BLOB data. In addition, your code can benefit from the caching and streaming capabilities of the NTFS. Any .NET applications can use the `SqlFileStream()` class and Win32 applications can use the `OpenSqlFilestream()` API to gain streaming access to the `FILESTREAM` data.

A `FILESTREAM` transaction context, and the logical path name to the `FILESTREAM` data file to be processed, are two basic ingredients that you will need prior to accessing a BLOB value stored in the `FILESTREAM` cell. Once an explicit SQL Server transaction has been started, the `FILESTREAM` transaction context can be retrieved by calling the T-SQL function `GET_FILESTREAM_TRANSACTION_CONTEXT()`. The logical path name to the `FILESTREAM` data file can be retrieved by calling the new case-sensitive intrinsic function `PathName()` on the `FILESTREAM` column.

`OpenSqlFilestream()` returns a file handle to the `FILESTREAM` data file, which can be used to read and write information stored in the `FILESTREAM` data file. The .NET class `SqlFileStream` encapsulates the `FILESTREAM` data file and provides a number of methods that allow you to read and write information into the `FILESTREAM` data file. The `FILESTREAM` file handle, or the `SqlFileStream` object, should be closed before the transaction is committed or rolled back.

Chapter 4: FILESTREAM with Entity Framework and LINQ to SQL

In this chapter, we run through some labs that demonstrate how applications that employ ADO.NET Entity Framework (EF) or LINQ to SQL in their data access layer can interact with the `FILESTREAM` feature.

The focus will be on the `FILESTREAM` end of the equation, rather than on the specifics of the given data access framework or technology, and the chapter adopts a highly practical approach, consisting of the worked labs below.

- **Lab 2:** Using `FILESTREAM` data with EF. This lab actually comprises two separate examples:
    - **Lab 2a**: a simple application that adopts the "default" EF approach of using T-SQL to access the `FILESTREAM` data
    - **Lab 2b**: a custom approach that allows continued used of streaming I/O access with `SqlFileStream`.
- **Lab 3:** Using `FILESTREAM` data with LINQ to SQL.

As you can see, there is greater emphasis in this chapter on EF than on LINQ to SQL. The latter has been characterized by Microsoft as being for *"strongly-typed LINQ access to SQL Server, for rapidly developed applications"* or, less formally by members of the Microsoft developer community, as "the quick and dirty way to do it." In contrast, ADO.NET Entity Framework *"provides strongly-typed LINQ access for applications requiring a more flexible Object Relational mapping, across Microsoft SQL Server and third-party databases."*

Chapter 4: FILESTREAM with Entity Framework and LINQ to SQL

If it sounds like LINQ to SQL plays second fiddle to EF's lead violin, then I'd say that this is a fair reflection of community opinion and of the development of the two technologies by Microsoft; the former is being "supported" on an ongoing basis, the latter is being actively developed and improved. Nevertheless, LINQ to SQL has an endearing simplicity that continues to make it popular among its users, hence its inclusion here.

Before we get started, a note of sensible caution: the labs in this chapter demonstrate a particular way to accomplish tasks with these technologies; they don't attempt to cover all possible approaches, nor do we guarantee that the approach shown will be the best one for your specific environment. Use the labs as a starting point, then adapt them as necessary for your needs, and bear in mind that you'll also need to rework the code to take into account the specific nature of your security architecture, and so on.

Lab 2: FILESTREAM and Entity Framework

ADO.NET EF has become one of the most widely discussed and used object relational mapping (ORM) frameworks for .NET, and many questions have been raised on various forums regarding the use of EF with **FILESTREAM** columns.

As we have seen, one of the key benefits of **FILESTREAM** storage is that the data can be accessed using Win32 or Managed APIs, which provide streaming performance. Though EF allows you to access **FILESTREAM** columns, the access is provided through the T-SQL interface. At the time of writing this, EF does not provide a built-in way to access **FILESTREAM** data through Win32 or Managed APIs, so you might want to reconsider your decision to use EF to access **FILESTREAM** data and instead write some custom code that performs the **FILESTREAM** operations within an EF project.

Our labs demonstrate both approaches. Lab 2a creates a basic application that uses EF to access **FILESTREAM** data directly, and hence access the **FILESTREAM** data using T-SQL. Lab 2b shows a technique that allows us to continue to use the `SqlFileStream` class to access the **FILESTREAM** data through EF.

Each lab will follow the same basic structure.

1. Create a stored procedure through which EF will access the `FILESTREAM` data.
2. Create a console application project.
3. Add an Entity Data Model Object to the project.
4. Create the ORM.
5. Insert a row with `FILESTREAM` data into the table.
6. Retrieve rows along with `FILESTREAM` data.

In both cases, the goal is to help you to get started with writing EF applications that read and write `FILESTREAM` data. We will examine only a few basic features offered by ADO.NET EF, a more detailed discussion of which is beyond the scope of this book.

Rebuilding the sample database

Before we get started with the labs, we need to create a new sample database. Run the T-SQL script in Listing 4-1 to rebuild the NorthPole sample database.

```
USE master
GO


-- ---------------------------------------------------
-- If the sample database exists, drop it and re-create
-- ---------------------------------------------------
IF DB_ID('NorthPole') IS NOT NULL
    DROP DATABASE NorthPole
GO
CREATE DATABASE NorthPole ON
```

```
PRIMARY (
    NAME = NorthPoleDB,
    FILENAME = 'C:\ArtOfFS\Demos\Chapter4\NorthPoleDB.mdf'
), FILEGROUP NorthPole_fs CONTAINS FILESTREAM(
    NAME = NorthPole_fs,
    FILENAME = 'C:\ArtOfFS\Demos\Chapter4\NorthPole_fs')
LOG ON (
    NAME = NorthPole_log,
    FILENAME = 'C:\ArtOfFS\Demos\Chapter4\NorthPole_log.ldf')
GO
```

Listing 4-1:   Rebuilding the sample `NorthPole` database.

Next, create a table to store the `FILESTREAM` data using the code in Listing 4-2.

```
USE NorthPole
GO

CREATE TABLE [dbo].[Items](
    [ItemID] INT IDENTITY PRIMARY KEY,
    [ItemGuid] UNIQUEIDENTIFIER ROWGUIDCOL NOT NULL UNIQUE,
    [ItemNumber] VARCHAR(20),
    [ItemDescription] VARCHAR(50),
    [ItemImage] VARBINARY(MAX) FILESTREAM NULL
)
GO
```

Listing 4-2:   Creating a table for the `FILESTREAM` data.

Lab 2a: A simple EF application using T-SQL access

In this lab we'll create a simple application that will treat the `FILESTREAM` column as a plain `VARBINARY(MAX)` column. This is the default way Entity Framework handles `FILESTREAM` data. For applications that seek to leverage the streaming benefits of `FILESTREAM`, this isn't a suitable approach, so you may want to review the alternative approach in Lab 2b.

Create the stored procedure interface

Our first step is to create a stored procedure for adding new items into the table (Listing 4-3). This stored procedure will be invoked from the EF project.

```sql
CREATE PROCEDURE [dbo].[SaveItem] (
    @ItemNumber VARCHAR(20),
    @ItemDescription VARCHAR(50),
    @ItemImage VARBINARY(MAX)
) AS
INSERT INTO dbo.Items(
    ItemGuid,
    ItemNumber,
    ItemDescription,
    ItemImage
)
SELECT
    NEWID(),
    @ItemNumber,
    @ItemDescription,
    @ItemImage

RETURN SCOPE_IDENTITY()
```

Listing 4-3: Creating a stored procedure to add items to the table.

Note that this procedure accepts item information including the image, which will go to the **FILESTREAM** column of the table. Because we are using the T-SQL interface for writing into the **FILESTREAM** column, a **VARBINARY(MAX)** variable is used. Remember that the **FILESTREAM** columns appear as **VARBINARY(MAX)** data type values when accessing them from T-SQL.

Creating a console application project

The next step is to create a simple application. For simplicity, we will create a console application. Open Visual Studio, select **File | New | Project**, and then select **Console Application**. You might want to select your favorite .NET programming language (VB or C#) at this stage. The programming language will not make much difference because there is not much code in this lab. We present C# code in this chapter; the sample code for VB is supplied separately in the download.

Adding an Entity Data Model

The next step is to add an ADO.NET Entity Data Model to the project. Right-click on your project in Solution Explorer, and select **Add | New Item**. Then select **ADO.NET Entity Data Model** (Figure 4-1).

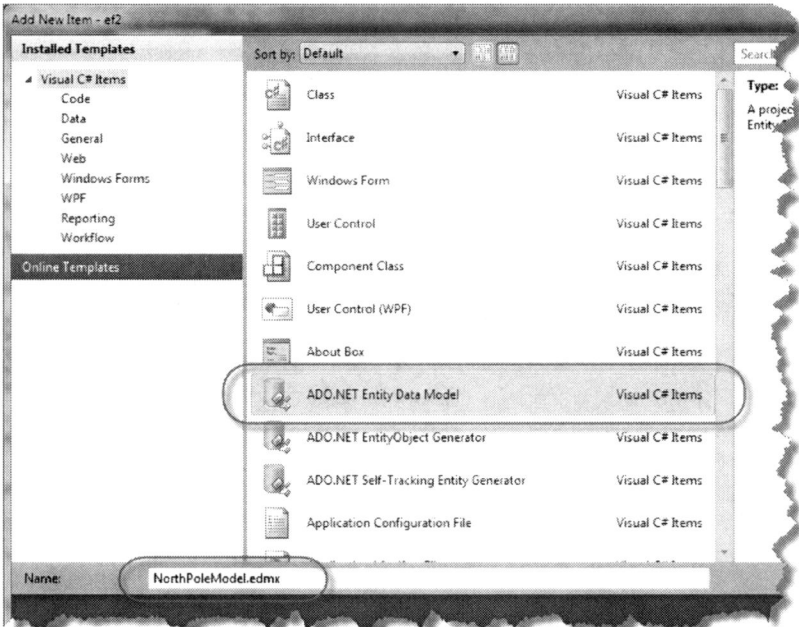

Figure 4-1: Add New Item dialog box.

Chapter 4: FILESTREAM with Entity Framework and LINQ to SQL

We will name the Entity Data Model **NorthPoleModel.edmx**. Click **OK** to proceed to the Entity Data Model Wizard (Figure 4-2).

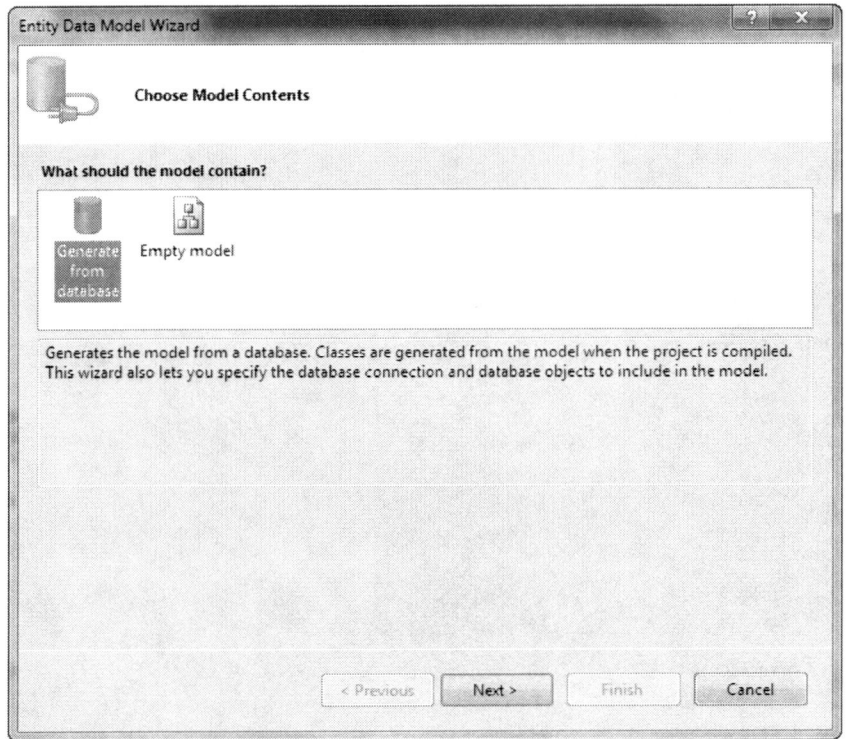

Figure 4-2: Generating the model.

Select **Generate from database**, because we have already created the database needed for this lab. The wizard will generate EF wrapper classes for the selected database objects when completed. Next, we choose the data connection (Figure 4-3).

Chapter 4: FILESTREAM with Entity Framework and LINQ to SQL

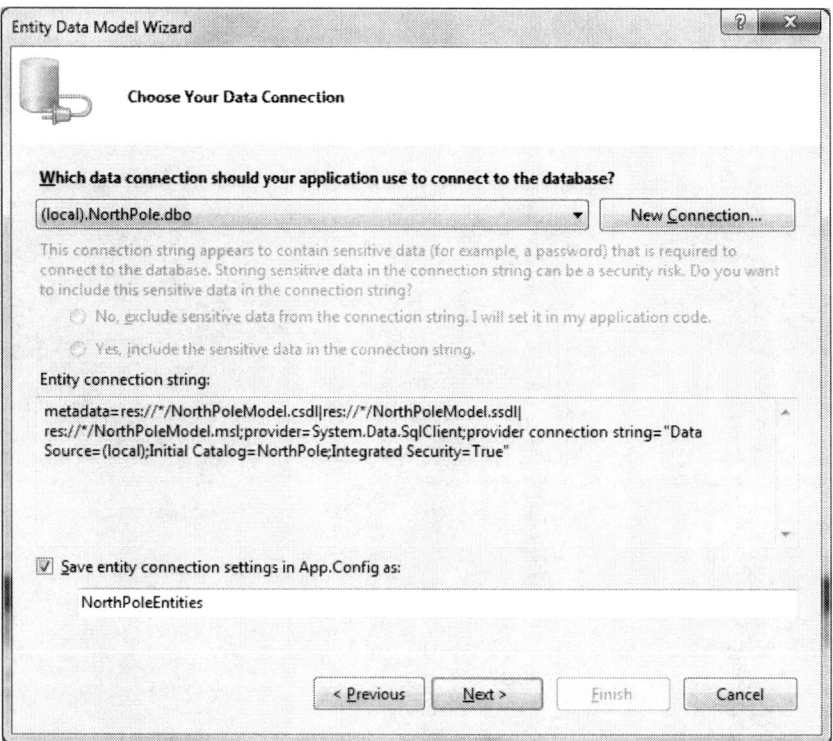

Figure 4-3: Choosing the data connection.

You may remember that, for accessing `FILESTREAM` through Win32 or Managed APIs, Windows authentication was necessary. However, as mentioned earlier, EF accesses `FILESTREAM` data through T-SQL only. Therefore, when you enter your database credentials, you can use either Windows authentication or SQL Server authentication.

The next step allows you to select the database objects you wish to include in your data model (Figure 4-4). We'll select the `Items` table and the stored procedure `SaveItem`, and name the data model `NorthPoleModel`.

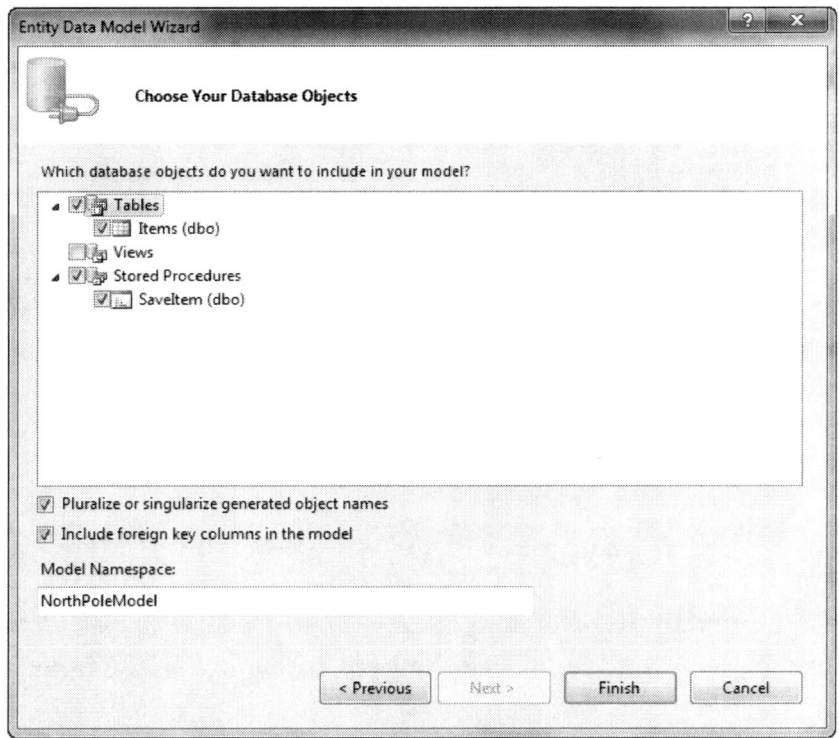

Figure 4-4: Choosing the database objects.

Clicking **Finish** saves the information and opens the Model Designer window.

Configuring object relational mapping

The next step is to review and configure the mapping of properties and functions. The Entity Data Model designer creates data model objects based on the selections we made using the wizard. In our case, we selected the `Items` table, so you will see a model object named **Item** that represents each row in the `Items` table (Figure 4-5).

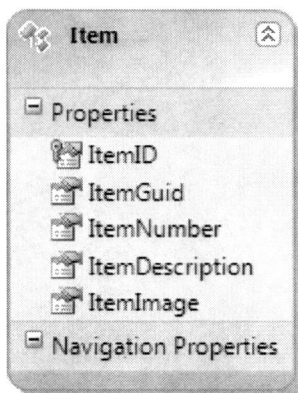

Figure 4-5: The Item data model object.

Click on the **Item** object to open the **Mapping Details** window (Figure 4-6). If the window does not open automatically on your system, right-click the **Item** entity and select **Table Mapping** from the shortcut menu.

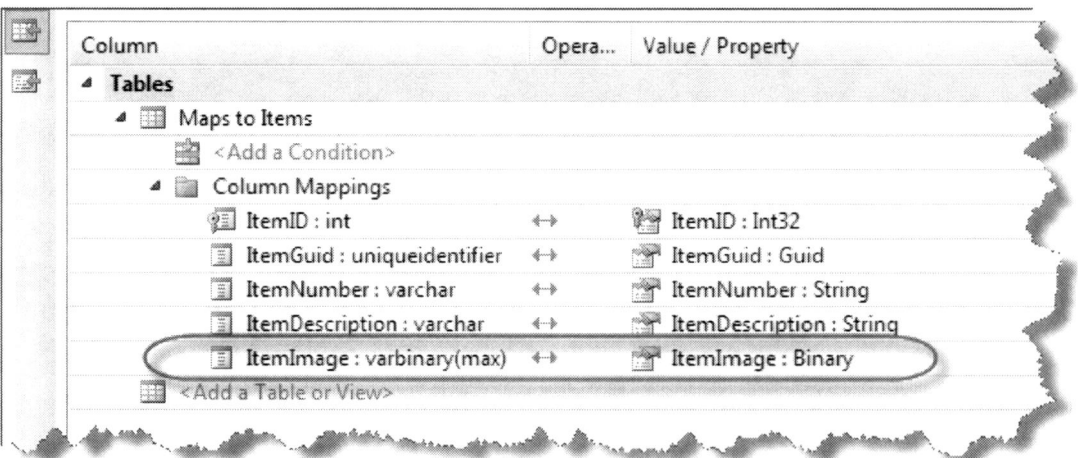

Figure 4-6: The Mapping Details window.

Take a look at the mapping of the `ItemImage` column; it is a `FILESTREAM` column but it is mapped to the Binary data type. EF does not understand `FILESTREAM` values. It sees `FILESTREAM` columns as `VARBINARY(MAX)` data type values.

The next step is to create a mapping for the stored procedure we created for saving items. Click on the **Map Entity to Functions** button on the left side of the **Mapping Details** window, and select the stored procedure from the drop-down list provided for the insert operation (Figure 4-7).

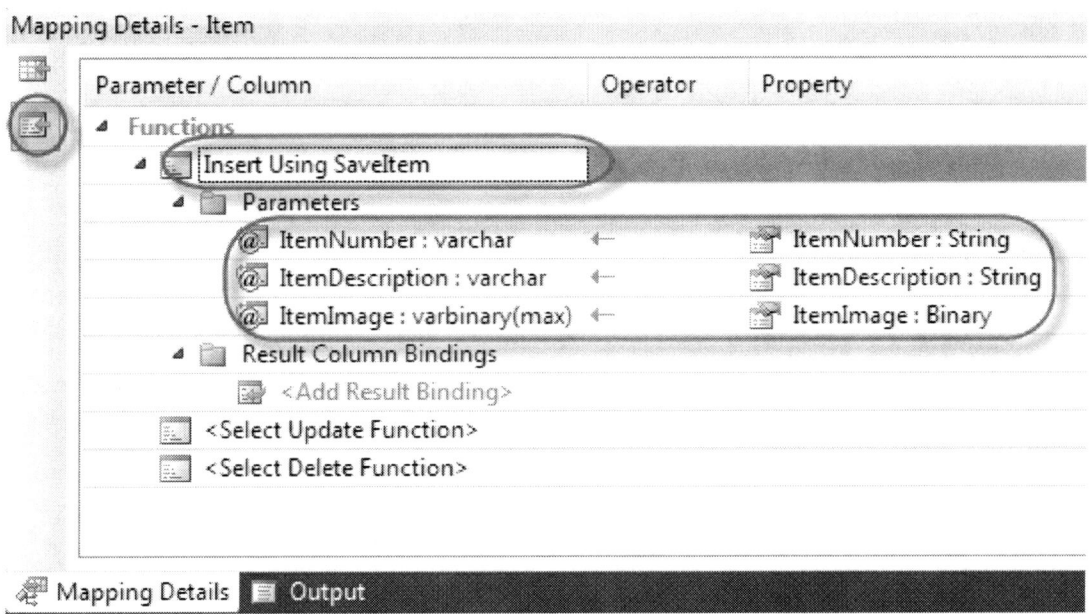

Figure 4-7: Creating a mapping for the stored procedure.

With this, we are done with the mapping and it is time to go ahead and write the code that adds a new item into the table using EF.

Adding a row to the table

Having completed the object relational mapping, it is quite easy to perform operations that manipulate the data stored in the associated tables. The C# code in Listing 4-4 adds a new record into the `Items` table. One of the columns being populated is a `FILESTREAM` column. The content of a disk file is read and copied into the `ItemImage` property of the EF class `Item`, which represents the `FILESTREAM` column in the table.

```csharp
static void Main(string[] args)
{
    Item itm = new Item();
    itm.ItemNumber = "IT001";
    itm.ItemDescription = "Microsoft Mouse";
    itm.ItemImage =
            System.IO.File.ReadAllBytes("c:\\temp\\microsoftmouse.jpg");

    NorthPoleEntities npe = new NorthPoleEntities();
    npe.AddObject("Items", itm);
    try
    {
        npe.SaveChanges();
    }
    catch (Exception ex)
    {
        Console.Write(ex.Message);
    }

    npe.Dispose();
}
```

Listing 4-4: Adding a new record to the `Items` table using EF.

Note that there is nothing `FILESTREAM`-specific in this code. Though the column being populated is a `FILESTREAM` column, the code treats it as a `VARBINARY(MAX)` column.

Retrieving information from the database

Now, let us see how to retrieve data from `FILESTREAM` columns using EF. Just as we saw in the previous example, there is no `FILESTREAM`-specific code involved in this step either. EF treats `FILESTREAM` columns as `VARBINARY(MAX)` columns, and therefore the code that we will write will be the same for `FILESTREAM` and `VARBINARY(MAX)` columns.

The code in Listing 4-5 searches for a record with `ItemNumber IT001`, and returns an Item object that contains the information about the given record. The last part of the code reads the `FILESTREAM` value stored in the `ItemImage` column and writes to a disk file. Add the code to the `Main()` method in the `Program` class. You must also import the `System.Data.Objects` namespace at the top of your code file.

```
NorthPoleEntities npe = new NorthPoleEntities();
foreach (Item itm in npe.Items.Where(
                "it.ItemNumber == IT001"))
{
    System.IO.File.WriteAllBytes("c:\\temp\\mm.jpg", itm.ItemImage);
}
npe.Dispose();
```

Listing 4-5:   Retrieving BLOB values stored in a `FILESTREAM` column.

That completes Lab 2, in which we created a very simple console application that demonstrated how to read and write `FILESTREAM` values using EF. Run the application, or debug and step through the code, to see our code in action.

Lab 2b: Using SqlFileStream and Entity Framework together

In this lab, we'll create an application similar to the one from Lab 2a but one that can still use the `SqlFileStream` class to access the `FILESTREAM` data, while at the same time maintaining the object oriented features of Entity Framework for accessing the relational data. This is done by retrieving the structured data using EF's mapping capabilities and the `FILESTREAM` data using custom code developed in an application's data access layer.

Modifying the stored procedure interface

To help support the needs of the application, we will create two additional stored procedures in the sample database.

The first, `Items_Insert`, effectively replaces the `SaveItem` stored procedure from the previous lab. It is used to create a new row in the `Items` table and ensures that the `FILESTREAM` data file for the row is created by setting a dummy value (Listing 4-6).

```sql
CREATE PROCEDURE [dbo].[Items_Insert]
    @ItemGuid uniqueidentifier,
    @ItemNumber nvarchar(20),
    @ItemDescription nvarchar(50)
AS
BEGIN
    -- SET NOCOUNT ON added to prevent extra result sets from
    -- interfering with SELECT statements.
    SET NOCOUNT ON;

    INSERT INTO [Items] (ItemGuid, ItemNumber, ItemDescription, ItemImage)
    VALUES (@ItemGuid, @ItemNumber, @ItemDescription, 0x);

    SELECT SCOPE_IDENTITY() AS NewItemID;
END
```

Listing 4-6: Creating a stored procedure to create a row with a dummy `FILESTREAM` value.

Chapter 4: FILESTREAM with Entity Framework and LINQ to SQL

The stored procedure takes three arguments that are mapped directly to fields in the `Items` table. There is no input parameter for the `ItemImage` field because we provide a default dummy value of `0x` (zero-length binary value). This ensures that a `FILESTREAM` data file will be created for the new record, but the file is a zero-length (empty) file. We also select the value of the `SCOPE_IDENTITY()` function as a new field with name `NewItemID`. Because `ItemID` is an `IDENTITY` column, we will use the value of that field to update the `ItemID` scalar property value of the stored **Item** object instance with the value assigned by the database engine.

The second new stored procedure, `GetSqlFileStreamInfo` (Listing 4-7), will return the values necessary to create a `SqlFileStream` object instance for the `FILESTREAM` data of a given item (identified by the `ItemID` parameter). The stored procedure will return a single row containing the path name of the `FILESTREAM` data file, the transaction context of a previously started transaction and the length of the `FILESTREAM` data file.

```
CREATE PROCEDURE [dbo].[GetSqlFileStreamInfo]
    @ItemID int
AS
BEGIN
    -- SET NOCOUNT ON added to prevent extra result sets from
    -- interfering with SELECT statements.
    SET NOCOUNT ON;

    -- Insert statements for procedure here
    SELECT I.ItemImage.PathName() AS FilePath,
        GET_FILESTREAM_TRANSACTION_CONTEXT() AS "Context",
        DATALENGTH(I.ItemImage) AS "Size"
    FROM Items I
    WHERE I.ItemID = @ItemID
END
```

Listing 4-7: Creating a stored procedure to retrieve the `SqlFileStream` constructor values.

Creating a console application project

The next step is to create a simple application. We will create another console application. Open Visual Studio, select **File | New | Project**, and then select **Console Application**. You might want to select your favorite .NET programming language (VB or C#) at this stage. The programming language will not make much difference because there is not much code in this lab. We present C# code in this chapter; the sample code for VB is supplied separately in the download.

Provide a suitable name for your project and solution, such as *FILESTREAM Chapter 4 Lab 2b*.

Adding an Entity Data Model

The next step is to add an ADO.NET Entity Data Model to the project. Right-click on your project in Solution Explorer, and select **Add | New Item**. Then select **ADO.NET Entity Data Model** (Figure 4-8).

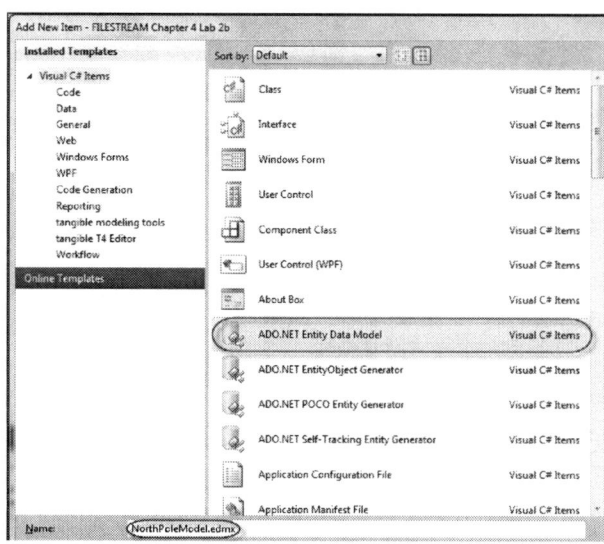

Figure 4-8:   The Add New Item dialog box.

We will name the Entity Data Model **NorthPoleModel.edmx**. Click **OK** to proceed to the Entity Data Model Wizard (Figure 4-9).

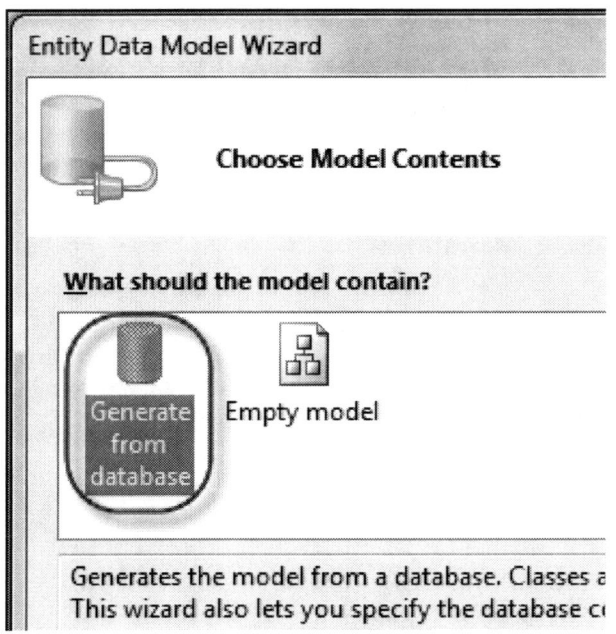

Figure 4-9: Generating the model.

Select **Generate from database**, because we have already created the database needed for this lab. The wizard will generate EF wrapper classes for the selected database objects when completed. Next, we choose the data connection (Figure 4-10).

In Lab 2a, it was noted that using SQL Server authentication to connect to the database was acceptable because we would only access the `FILESTREAM` data using T-SQL. In this lab, we must use Windows authentication because the application will access the `FILESTREAM` data using the Managed APIs.

Chapter 4: FILESTREAM with Entity Framework and LINQ to SQL

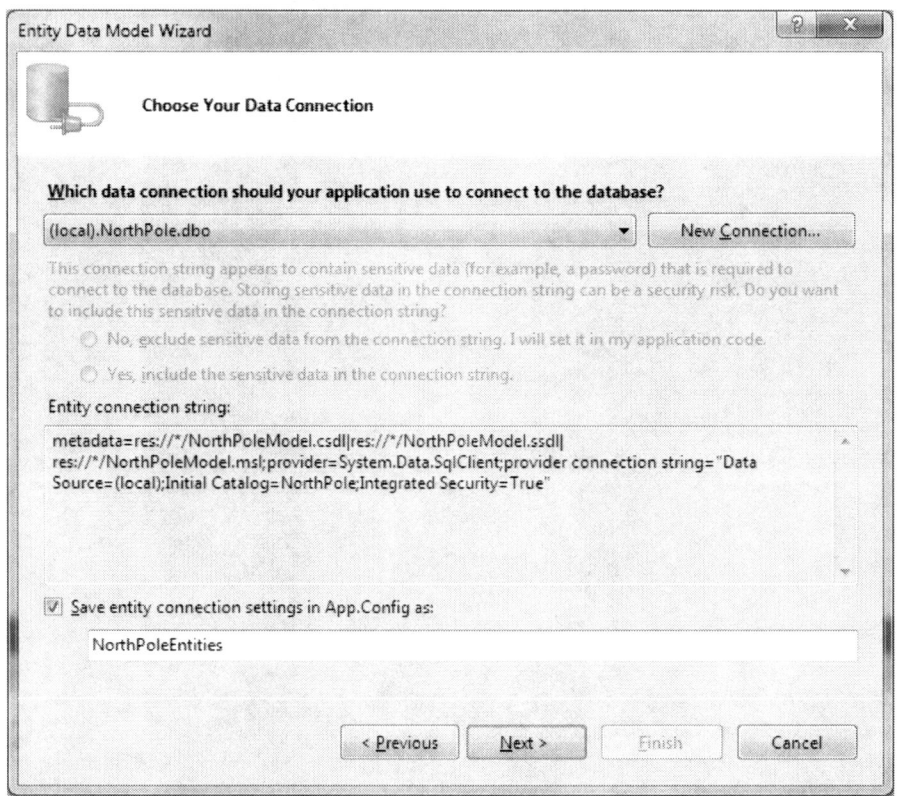

Figure 4-10: Choosing the data connection.

The next step allows us to select the database objects we wish to include in our data model (Figure 4-11). We'll select the **Items** table and the stored procedures **Insert_Items** and **GetSqlFileStreamInfo**, and name the data model **NorthPoleModel**.

Chapter 4: FILESTREAM with Entity Framework and LINQ to SQL

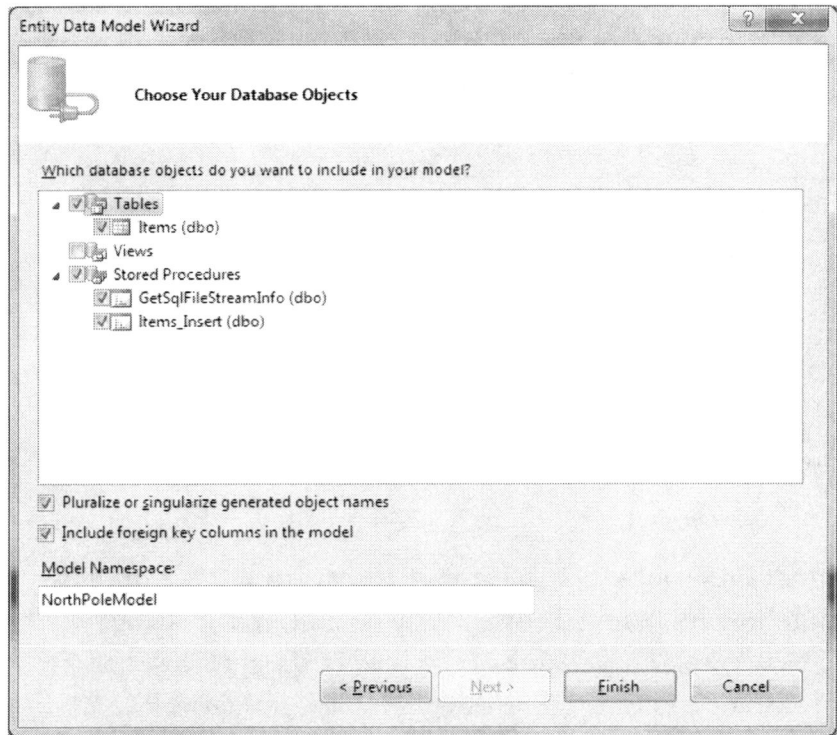

Figure 4-11: Choosing the database objects.

Clicking **Finish**, saves the information and opens the **Model Designer** window.

Configuring object relational mapping

We will now make some modifications to the default object relational mapping that was created. Most importantly, we will remove the mapping of the `ItemImage` field so that it will not be included in the standard `SELECT` statements generated by Entity Framework.

Right-click on the **ItemImage** scalar property in the **Item** entity on the entity diagram and click **Delete**. This effectively removes the **ItemImage** field from the mapping.

Next, we will map the `Items_Insert` stored procedure so that it becomes the Insert Function for the `Items` table. In the **Mapping Details** window click on the **Map Entity to Functions** button, found on the right-hand side of the window (Figure 4-12).

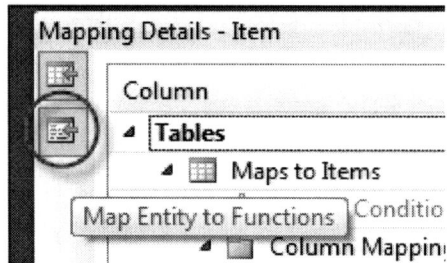

Figure 4-12: The **Map Entity to Functions** button.

Click on the **<Select Insert Function>** row and select **Items_Insert** from the drop-down list. The parameters for the function are mapped correctly by default. In the **Result Column Bindings** node, type **NewItemID** (the name of the field in the return set of our **Items_Insert** stored procedure) and press **Enter**. The designer will automatically and correctly map this value to the **ItemID** scalar property.

Finally, we will map the `GetSqlFileStreamInfo` stored procedure to a function in the data access layer. To add a function, right-click empty space in the Entity Model designer and click **Add > Function Import**. The **Add Function Import** dialog box (Figure 4-13) opens. Select the `GetSqlFileStreamInfo` stored procedure from the **Stored Procedure Name** drop-down list. Create a suitable name for the function, which in our example we will keep the same as the stored procedure name.

Our stored procedure returns a single row containing three columns. The structure of that row does not map to our Item entity though, so we will let the Entity Framework designer create a new class whose scalar properties map to the fields returned by the stored procedure.

First, click the **Get Column Information** button, then click the **Create New Complex Type** button. This will automatically change the **Returns a Collection Of** option group value to **Complex**. The designer will assign a default name of `GetSqlFileStreamInfo_Result` to the new complex type.

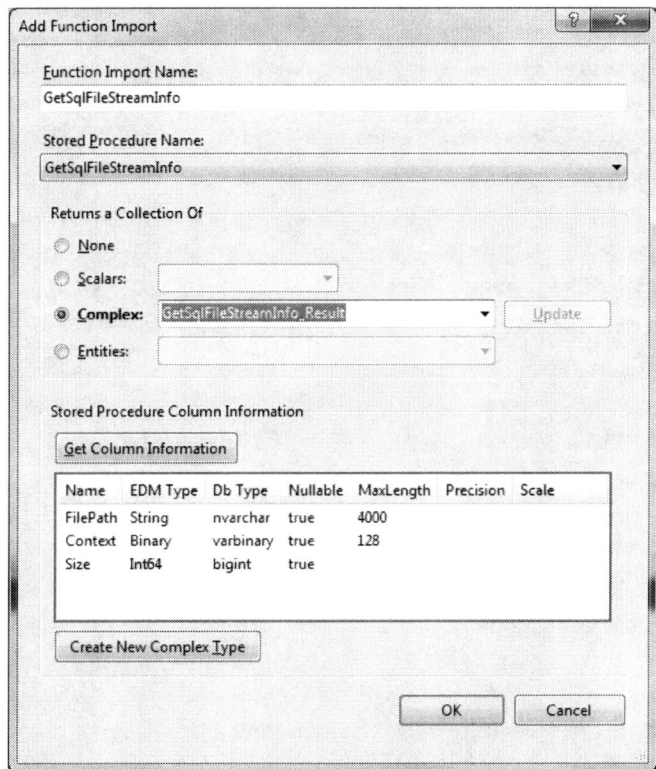

Figure 4-13: The **Add Function Import** dialog box.

You can see the effects of these steps in the **Model Browser** window.

Adding a row to the table

We will create a new method in the **Program.cs** file to insert a new item in the database. The code for this method is shown in Listing 4-8. This code will go in the `Program` class.

```
static int InsertItem()
{
  Item NewItem = new Item();

  NewItem.ItemNumber = "IT002";
  NewItem.ItemGuid = System.Guid.NewGuid();
  Console.WriteLine("New  Item GUID: {0}",
    NewItem.ItemGuid.ToString());
  NewItem.ItemDescription = "Microsoft Mouse";

  using (NorthPoleEntities e = new NorthPoleEntities())
  {
    bool OpenedConn = false;

    if (e.Connection.State != System.Data.ConnectionState.Open)
    {
      e.Connection.Open();
      OpenedConn = true;
    }

    try
    {
      // Start a transaction explicitly to ensure adding the row and
      // creating the BLOB are part of the same transaction
      // System.Transactions.TransactionScope can be used if required
      using (System.Data.Common.DbTransaction tran =
             e.Connection.BeginTransaction())
      {
        e.Items.AddObject(NewItem);
        // Because this uses a stored procedure (instead of
        // generated T-SQL)
        // this will create a FILESTREAM data file
        // If adding records using a stored proc is not desired,
        // then this can be set as a DEFAULT
        e.SaveChanges();
```

```csharp
      // Now read the item using SqlFileStream, leveraging
      // the stored procedure that's mapped as a function
      GetSqlFileStreamInfo_Result info =
        e.GetSqlFileStreamInfo(NewItem.ItemID).ToList()[0];

      // If the path is NULL, a BLOB file does not exist
      // and a BLOB must be created first
      using (SqlFileStream fs = new SqlFileStream(
              info.FilePath, info.Context, FileAccess.Write,
              FileOptions.WriteThrough, 0L))
      using (FileStream local = new FileStream(
              "C:\\temp\\MicrosoftMouse.jpg",
              FileMode.Open, FileAccess.Read))
      {
        local.CopyTo(fs);
      }

      tran.Commit();
    }
  }
  finally
  {
    // If the connection was opened by this procedure, close it
    if (OpenedConn) e.Connection.Close();
  }
}

return NewItem.ItemID;
}
```

Listing 4-8: `InsertItem` method.

This code first creates a new instance of the `Item` class and, for demonstration purposes, assigns values to the `ItemNumber`, `ItemGuid` and `ItemDescription` properties. Then, an instance of the Entity Framework Object Context (`NorthPoleEntities` class) is created. If the object context does not have an open connection to the database, we open the connection and keep track of the fact that we did so (this means that we can properly close it when the method ends).

As we have already discussed, access to `FILESTREAM` data must occur in the context of a SQL Server transaction, so we start a transaction using the `BeginTransaction()` method on the `Connection` object associated with the object context. As part of that transaction, we add the newly created **Item** object to the object context and save the changes to the database.

Saving the changes to the database causes the `ItemID` property of the `NewItem` object to be set to the value assigned by the database engine (recall the mapping we modified earlier). We use this value as the parameter for the `GetSqlFileStreamInfo` method. Even though we know that the `GetSqlFileStreamInfo` method can only return a single object instance, because the `SELECT` statement in the stored procedure filters by the table's primary key (`ItemID`), the framework doesn't have that knowledge and will return a set of `GetSqlFileStreamInfo_Result` objects. We will simply take the first and only item in that list.

Using the values in the `GetSqlFileStreamInfo_Result` object, we can create a new `SqlFileStream` instance for write access. From the local file system, we open a sample image file using standard .NET file I/O APIs. We then copy the bytes from the local file to the `SqlFileStream`.

Finally, we commit the transaction and, if we opened it, close the database connection.

Retrieving information from the database

To end this lab, we are going to add some code that can retrieve a specific item (row) from the database. We will use the Entity Framework object relational mapping to retrieve the relational data, but use streaming I/O access to work with the `FILESTREAM` data.

Listing 4-9 shows the `ReadItem` method to be added to the `Program` class. This code requires that you import two namespaces in your code file: `System.Data.SqlTypes` and `System.IO`.

Chapter 4: FILESTREAM with Entity Framework and LINQ to SQL

```csharp
static void ReadItem(int itemId)
{
  // Obtain info about the object
  using (NorthPoleEntities e = new NorthPoleEntities())
  {
    // This does not cause the BLOB to be read with T-SQL as long as
    // the BLOB column is in a different object,
    // or excluded from the model altogether (preferred)
    Item i = e.Items.SingleOrDefault(itm => itm.ItemID == itemId);

    if (i != null)
    {
      Console.WriteLine("Read Item GUID: {0}", i.ItemGuid.ToString());
      bool OpenedConn = false;

      try
      {
        // Ensure the connection is open before
        // attempting to start a transaction
        // NOTE: connection is probably closed
        if (e.Connection.State != System.Data.ConnectionState.Open)
        {
          e.Connection.Open();
          OpenedConn = true;
        }

        // There are also ways to use
        // Systems.Transactions.TransactionScope
        // to enlist in an existing transaction
        // at the business logic level if desired
        using (System.Data.Common.DbTransaction tran =
          e.Connection.BeginTransaction())
        {
          // Now read the item using SqlFileStream,
          // leveraging the stored
          // procedure that's mapped as a function
          GetSqlFileStreamInfo_Result info =
            e.GetSqlFileStreamInfo(i.ItemID).ToList()[0];

          // If there is a BLOB, there is a file path
          if (!string.IsNullOrEmpty(info.FilePath) &&
              info.Size > 0)
          {
            using (MemoryStream ms = new MemoryStream())
```

Chapter 4: FILESTREAM with Entity Framework and LINQ to SQL

```
            {
                using (SqlFileStream fs = new SqlFileStream(
                    info.FilePath, info.Context, FileAccess.Read,
                    FileOptions.WriteThrough, (long)info.Size))
                {
                    fs.CopyTo(ms);
                }

                // TODO: Do some things with the memory stream,
                // or convert to byte array if serialization is required
            }
        }

        tran.Commit();
    }

  }
  finally
  {
     if (OpenedConn) e.Connection.Close();
  }
 }
 }
}
```

Listing 4-9:   `ReadItem` method.

This method first creates an Entity Framework object context (`NorthPoleEntities` class) and retrieves the desired item. In this case, we used a lambda expression to indicate which item we are looking for. Lambda expressions may look a little intimidating, but the basics can be learned easily. Here, we are indicating that, in the collection of all Items, we are looking for a single item that matches the predicate (think `WHERE`-clause) `ItemID == ItemID`, where the first `ItemID` is the scalar property and the second `ItemID` is the parameter value of the `ReadItem` function. We use the `.SingleOrDefault()` method to ensure that if there is no item with the specified `ItemID`, the object context will return a null reference instead of throwing an exception.

Chapter 4: FILESTREAM with Entity Framework and LINQ to SQL

If we successfully retrieved the item's relational data from the database, we will create a new SQL Server transaction after ensuring that we have an open database connection (much like we did for the `InsertItem` method). We again leverage the `GetSqlFileStreamInfo` method that maps to the `GetSqlFileStreamInfo` stored procedure to retrieve the information we need to create a `SqlFileStream` instance. Before we create the instance, we check if there is a valid `filePath` value (a null value would indicate there is no **FILESTREAM** data file for this data row) and that the size of the file is greater than zero (there is no sense in reading a zero-length file). We are copying the `SqlFileStream` contents to a `MemoryStream` which can then be used for other purposes.

To test the functionality in this lab, add the code in Listing 4-10 to the `Main()` method in the `Program` class.

```
int NewItemId = 0;

NewItemId = InsertItem();
ReadItem(NewItemId);

Console.Write("Done...");
Console.ReadKey();
```

Listing 4-10: Sample code for `void Main()`.

Now compile and run the code. You should find that the program outputs the same `Item GUID` twice, indicating that the item that was saved to the database using the `InsertItem()` method was successfully read back using the `ReadItem()` method.

Lab 3: FILESTREAM and LINQ to SQL

This lab presents a very basic example that will help you to get started writing applications that use LINQ to SQL classes to access the `FILESTREAM` data. Just as we saw with the default EF approach in Lab 2a, LINQ to SQL also accesses `FILESTREAM` data through T-SQL interfaces only; it is not capable of accessing the `FILESTREAM` data using Win32 or Managed APIs.

To complete this lab, we will follow the procedure below.

1. Create a console application project.
2. Add a LINQ to SQL class object to the project.
3. Create a LINQ to SQL wrapper class for the `Items` table.
4. Use LINQ to SQL to add a new row with a `FILESTREAM` value to the table.
5. Query the table using LINQ to SQL and retrieve `FILESTREAM` data.

Creating a new console application project

Let's get started. Open Visual Studio, and create a new console application project by selecting **File | New | Project** as demonstrated in the previous labs.

Adding a LINQ to SQL class

The next step is to add a LINQ to SQL class to the project. Right-click on the project in the Solution Explorer and select **Add | New Item**. Then, in the **Add New Item** dialog box, select **LINQ to SQL Classes**, and rename the class to `NorthPoleDB` (Figure 4-14).

Chapter 4: FILESTREAM with Entity Framework and LINQ to SQL

Figure 4-14: Adding a LINQ to SQL class.

Click **Add** to add the class to the current project. This will open the Object Relational Designer. The designer window will be empty because we have not yet done any mapping.

Defining object relational mappings

The next step is to define object relational mappings for the Items table. Open the Server Explorer window by clicking the **Server Explorer** hyperlink in the Object Relational Designer window (Figure 4-15).

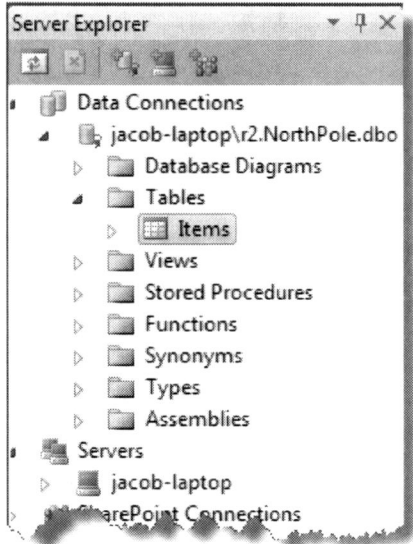

Figure 4-15: The Server Explorer.

Locate the **Items** table under the **Tables** node, then drag and drop the **Items** table into the Object Relational Designer window (Figure 4-16).

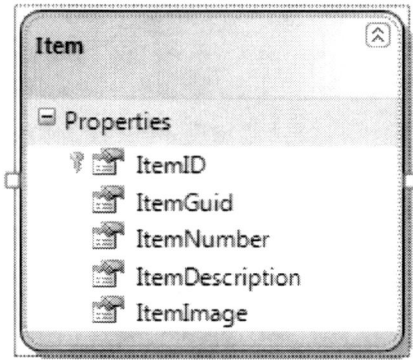

Figure 4-16: The **Items** table in the Object Relational Designer.

Chapter 4: FILESTREAM with Entity Framework and LINQ to SQL

Notice that LINQ to SQL automatically maps `FILESTREAM` columns to `System.Data.Linq.Binary` data type. You can see this by looking at the properties of the `ItemImage` property of the mapping object, as shown in Figure 4-17.

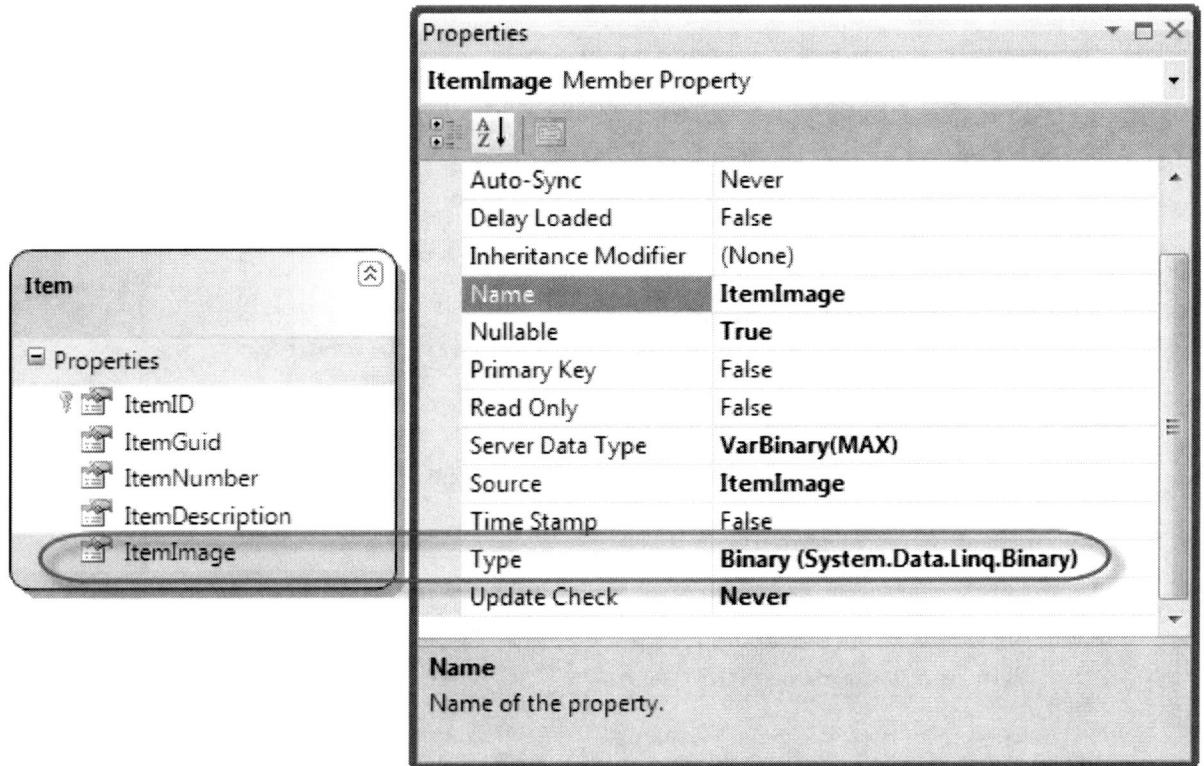

Figure 4-17: `FILESTREAM` mapping to the `System.Data.Linq.Binary` data type.

That is all you need to do. We are ready to write the code that performs `FILESTREAM` data manipulation using LINQ to SQL classes.

Adding a new row

Let us see how to add a new row into the `Items` table using LINQ to SQL classes, and populate the `FILESTREAM` column. Listing 4-11 shows the C# code to do this.

```
static void SaveItem()
{
    Item itm = new Item();

    itm.ItemDescription = "Microsoft Mouse";
    itm.ItemGuid = System.Guid.NewGuid();

    System.Data.Linq.Binary img;
    img = new System.Data.Linq.Binary(
            System.IO.File.ReadAllBytes("c:\\temp\\MicrosoftMouse.jpg"));
    itm.ItemImage = img;
    itm.ItemNumber = "IT001";

    NorthPoleDBDataContext db = new NorthPoleDBDataContext();
    db.Items.InsertOnSubmit(itm);
    db.SubmitChanges();
    db.Dispose();
}
```

Listing 4-11:   Adding a new row using LINQ to SQL.

Querying FILESTREAM data using LINQ to SQL

The final step in this lab is to see how to query and retrieve `FILESTREAM` data using LINQ to SQL classes. Listing 4-12 searches for an item with a specific item number and retrieves the `FILESTREAM` value associated with the row.

```
static void Main(string[] args)
{
    NorthPoleDBDataContext db = new NorthPoleDBDataContext();
    var itms = from p in db.Items
               where p.ItemNumber == "IT001"
               select p;

    foreach (var itm in itms)
    {
        Console.WriteLine("Item Description = {0}",
                          itm.ItemDescription);
        System.IO.File.WriteAllBytes(
            "c:\\temp\\MicrosoftMouse.jpg",
            itm.ItemImage.ToArray()
            );
    }
    db.Dispose();
}
```

Listing 4-12: Querying a FILESTREAM table using LINQ to SQL.

Now run your application or debug and step through the code to see how it works.

Remember, LINQ to SQL accesses FILESTREAM data through the T-SQL interface. Streaming access to the FILESTREAM data is not available when accessing it through LINQ to SQL. This might result in performance problems on systems that perform a large number of FILESTREAM operations using LINQ to SQL.

Summary

We have seen how to write applications that access FILESTREAM data using ADO.NET EF and LINQ to SQL. The former is one of the most popular object relational mapping frameworks available for .NET. The latter offers simplicity and remains a viable data access option, but has become less prevalent following the introduction of Entity Framework.

Chapter 4: FILESTREAM with Entity Framework and LINQ to SQL

Neither of these frameworks is ideal for working with **FILESTREAM** data. Both EF and LINQ to SQL use the T-SQL interface to access the **FILESTREAM** data by default. This means that the performance benefits offered by the streaming APIs are not available to applications that use these frameworks "out of the box" to access the **FILESTREAM** data. Performance may be really bad if the application performs a huge volume of **FILESTREAM** operations using the native **FILESTREAM** mappings of either of these frameworks.

We demonstrated an approach using EF (but that is equally valid for LINQ to SQL) that uses specialized code in order to use the technology in conjunction with streaming access to **FILESTREAM**.

Chapter 5: FILESTREAM with ASP.NET and Silverlight

This chapter will explain how to access `FILESTREAM` data from applications built using ASP.NET and Silverlight. It will adopt a very hands-on approach, consisting of the six labs below.

- **Lab 4**: Uploading files to a `FILESTREAM` database from an ASP.NET web page.
- **Lab 5**: Deploying and configuring a `FILESTREAM` web application on IIS.
- **Lab 6**: Creating a web handler to serve images from a `FILESTREAM` database.
- **Lab 7**: Displaying thumbnail images of items from a `FILESTREAM` database on an ASP.NET web page.
- **Lab 8**: Using `SqlFileStream` in an N-tier scenario.
- **Lab 9**: Playing a video stored in a `FILESTREAM` database on a Silverlight application.

The functionalities that we try to implement in these labs are probably familiar to most of you. The first five labs in this chapter deal with uploading and downloading image files. Most developers will have done this numerous times in their applications, by uploading those files to a location on the server and serving the files upon client request later. What is different in these labs is that we will store the data in the `FILESTREAM` column of a database table, then serve client requests from there.

We'll use the same sample database for Labs 4–8 in this chapter, as shown in Listing 5-1.

Chapter 5: FILESTREAM with ASP.NET and Silverlight

```sql
USE master
GO

IF DB_ID('NorthPole') IS NOT NULL
    DROP DATABASE NorthPole
GO

CREATE DATABASE NorthPole ON PRIMARY (
    NAME = NorthPole,
    FILENAME = 'C:\ArtOfFS\Demos\Chapter5\NorthPole.mdf'
), FILEGROUP NorthPole_fs CONTAINS FILESTREAM(
    NAME = NorthPole_fs,
    FILENAME = 'C:\ArtOfFS\Demos\Chapter5\NorthPole_fs') LOG ON (
    NAME = NorthPole_log,
    FILENAME = 'C:\ArtOfFS\Demos\Chapter5\NorthPole_log.ldf')
GO
```

Listing 5-1: Rebuilding the sample `NorthPole` database.

Listing 5-2 creates the usual `Items` table, with a `FILESTREAM` column.

```sql
USE NorthPole
GO

CREATE TABLE [dbo].[Items]
    (
        [ItemID] INT IDENTITY
                    PRIMARY KEY ,
        [ItemGuid] UNIQUEIDENTIFIER ROWGUIDCOL
                                    NOT NULL
                                    UNIQUE ,
        [ItemNumber] VARCHAR(20) ,
        [ItemDescription] VARCHAR(50) ,
        [ItemImage] VARBINARY(MAX) FILESTREAM
                                    NULL
    )
GO
```

Listing 5-2: Creating the `Items` table.

Lab 4: Uploading Files to a FILESTREAM Database from an ASP.NET Web Page

Most websites provide some sort of functionality to upload files to the web server, usually storing them in a disk folder and serving the files later upon client requests. In this lab, we will see how to upload a file from an ASP.NET web page to the FILESTREAM column of a table.

To do this, we will follow the procedure below.

1. Create an ASP.NET web application.
2. Add a database connection string to the configuration file web.config.
3. Design a data entry page with a file upload control.
4. Write the code to upload the file into a FILESTREAM database.
5. Run the web application and verify that the code works.

Creating a new ASP.NET web application

Open Visual Studio, and select **File | New | Project**. Select **ASP.NET Web Application** from the project templates, and then click **OK** to create the project (Figure 5-1).

If you are using Visual Studio 2010, you will see options to create projects targeting a number of different .NET frameworks such as 2.0, 3.0, 3.5, and 4.0. The features we will explore in this lab are available in all of these .NET Framework versions but, to keep the complexity to the minimum, we will create this project in .NET 2.0. When using FILESTREAM in projects targeting .NET Framework versions 2.0 or 3.0, Service Pack 2 is required.

Chapter 5: FILESTREAM with ASP.NET and Silverlight

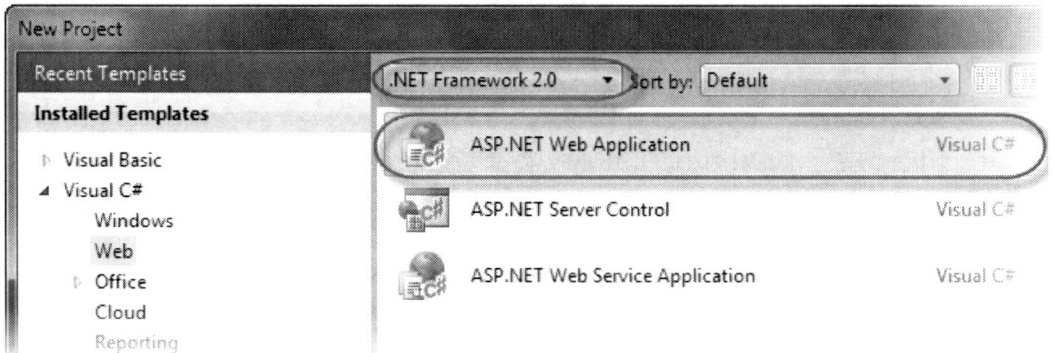

Figure 5-1: Creating a new project.

Visual Studio automatically creates a web page named `default.aspx`, and we will use that page for this lab.

Adding a database connection string

The next step is to add a database connection string to the configuration file of the web application, `web.config`. Locate `web.config` in the Solution Explorer, and double-click on it to open the configuration file in the Visual Studio editor.

Locate the section, `connectionStrings`, and add a connection string that points to the `FILESTREAM` database you would like to use for the labs. Listing 5-3 shows how the code should look after the connection string has been added to the configuration file (but you should use the data source appropriate to your own connection).

Ensure the connection string uses Windows authentication (`Integrated Security=SSPI`); we have already learnt that Windows authentication is required to access the `FILESTREAM` data using Win32 or Managed APIs.

```
<connectionStrings>
    <add name="NorthPoleDB"
        connectionString="Data Source=(local);Initial
                          Catalog=NorthPole;
                          Integrated Security=SSPI"
        providerName="System.Data.SqlClient" />
</connectionStrings>
```

Listing 5-3: Adding a connection string to point to the `FILESTREAM` database.

Designing the data entry page

Next, we'll build a very simple data entry page that allows a user to enter product information and save it into the database along with an image of the product. We will add an HTML table to the web page and put two text boxes (for **Item Number** and **Item Description**), a file upload control for the item image file, and a button to submit the data.

Depending upon your preference, you might want to write your code in the XML source editor or using the UI designer. The source code of the ASPX page is shown in Listing 5-4.

```
<%@ Page Language="c#" AutoEventWireup="false" CodeBehind="Default.aspx.cs"
    Inherits="fsweb._Default" %>

<html xmlns="http://www.w3.org/1999/xhtml">
<head id="Head2" runat="server">
    <title>ASP.NET FILESTREAM Application</title>
</head>
<body>
    <form id="form2" runat="server">
        <table>
        <tr>
            <td>Item Number:</td>
            <td><asp:TextBox runat="server" ID="txtItemNumber"/></td>
        </tr>
```

```
            <tr>
                <td>Item Description:</td>
                <td><asp:TextBox runat="server" ID="txtItemDescription"/></td>
            </tr>
            <tr>
                <td>Item Image:</td>
                <td>
                    <asp:FileUpload ID="fpItemImage" runat="server" Width="300px" />
                </td>
            </tr>
            <tr>
                <td><asp:Button runat="server" ID="btnSave"  Text="Save"/></td>
            </tr>
            </table>
        </form>
    </body>
</html>
```

Listing 5-4: The source code for the data entry page.

Figure 5-2 shows how your page should look after the controls have been added to the page.

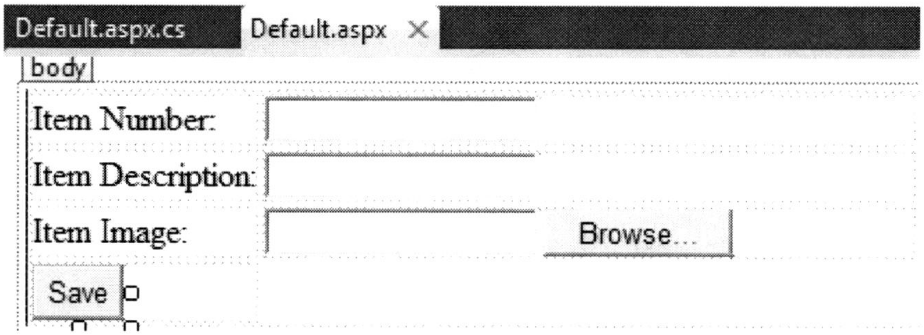

Figure 5-2: The data entry page.

Writing the "code-behind"

The next task is to write the code that runs behind the web page. When the user clicks the **Save** button, we need to save the item information, including the image file, into the database. In this section, we will see the code required to implement this functionality.

We will start with the import statements. Add the import statements in Listing 5-5 to the code file associated with your web page.

```
using System.IO;
using System.Data.SqlClient;
using System.data;
```

Listing 5-5: Import statements.

To make our code run when the user clicks the **Save** button, we'll add a handler for the `Click` event on the button. In a real-world scenario, you might want to do a number of validations before saving the information into the database, such as checking whether the user has entered all the mandatory fields. To keep the code simple in this lab, we will skip these validations and validate only the file upload control; we will proceed with the database call only if the user has selected a file using the file upload control provided on the web page. This can be verified by checking the `HasFile` property of the file upload control, as shown in Listing 5-6.

```
protected void btnSave_Click(object sender, EventArgs e)
{
    if (fpItemImage.HasFile)
    {
        SaveItem();
    }
}
```

Listing 5-6: Handler for `Click` event of the button.

The code in Listing 5-6 calls the `SaveItem()` function to perform the database operations, which we have not yet created. Saving the data into the database involves two steps.

1. Save the relational data (`ItemNumber`, `ItemDescription`).
2. Save the `FILESTREAM` data (`ItemImage`).

Relational data is always saved using T-SQL interface, whereas we can use either T-SQL or Win32/Managed APIs to save the `FILESTREAM` data. We have learned earlier that the `FILESTREAM` read-write operations should always be done using Win32 or Managed APIs for performance reasons, so that is exactly what we will do in this lab.

Saving the relational data

The first step is to save the relational data, in this case using the `SaveItemImage` stored procedure in Listing 5-7, which we can call from our web application.

```sql
CREATE PROCEDURE [dbo].[SaveItemImage]
    (
        @ItemNumber VARCHAR(20) ,
        @ItemDescription VARCHAR(50)
    )
AS
    BEGIN
        INSERT  INTO dbo.Items
                ( ItemGuid ,
                  ItemNumber ,
                  ItemDescription ,
                  ItemImage
                )
        OUTPUT  GET_FILESTREAM_TRANSACTION_CONTEXT() AS txContext ,
                inserted.ItemImage.PathName() AS filePath
                SELECT  NEWID() ,
                        @ItemNumber ,
                        @ItemDescription ,
                        0x
    END
```

Listing 5-7: Stored procedure to save item information.

Note that this stored procedure inserts a dummy value into the `FILESTREAM` column because, as we have already seen in Chapter 3, Win32/Managed API access to a `FILESTREAM` column is possible only if the column is non-`NULL`.

The stored procedure returns a result set that contains the `PathName()`, the logical identifier pointing to the disk file associated with the `FILESTREAM` column in the newly inserted row, and a `FILESTREAM` transaction context of the currently active transaction. This is done to avoid an additional database call when writing the code to save the `FILESTREAM` data. For more information, refer back to Chapter 3.

Saving the FILESTREAM data

After the relational data is saved, we will execute the code to save the `FILESTREAM` data using the `FILESTREAM` Managed API. We saw in Chapter 3 an example of how to load the content of a disk file into the `FILESTREAM` column. In this case, we will obtain a stream pointing to the file selected by the user through the `FileContent` property of the file upload control (Listing 5-8).

```
private void SaveItem()
{
    //Create and open a database connection
    SqlConnection cn = new SqlConnection();
    cn.ConnectionString =
            System.Configuration.ConfigurationManager.ConnectionStrings[
                                            "NorthPoleDB"].ToString();
    Cn.Open();

    //Create a Command object
    SqlCommand cmd = new SqlCommand();
    cmd.CommandText = "SaveItemImage";
    cmd.Connection = cn;
    cmd.CommandType = CommandType.StoredProcedure;
    cmd.Parameters.AddWithValue("@ItemNumber", txtItemNumber.Text);
    cmd.Parameters.AddWithValue("@ItemDescription",
                                            txtItemDescription.Text);
```

```csharp
//Begin a transaction
SqlTransaction transaction = cn.BeginTransaction("ItemTran");
cmd.Transaction = transaction;

byte[] txContext = null;
string filePath = string.Empty;
try
{

    //Execute the command
    SqlDataReader reader = cmd.ExecuteReader();
    if (reader.Read())
    {
        txContext = (reader["txContext"] as byte[]);
        filePath = reader["filePath"].ToString();
    }
    Reader.Close();

    //Open the FILESTREAM data file for writing
    SqlFileStream fs = new SqlFileStream(filePath, txContext,
                                        FileAccess.Write);

    //Get a stream object pointing to the content to be uploaded
    Stream localFile = fpItemImage.FileContent;

    //Start transferring data into FILESTREAM data file
    // If you are using .NET 4.0 the next 11 lines of code can be
    // replaced with a single call to "localFile.CopyTo(fs, 4096);"
    BinaryWriter bw = new BinaryWriter(fs);
    const int bufferSize = 4096;
    byte[] buffer = new byte[bufferSize];
    int byteCount = localFile.Read(buffer, 0, bufferSize);
    while (byteCount == bufferSize)
    {
        bw.Write(buffer, 0, bytes);
        bw.Flush();
        byteCount = localFile.Read(buffer, 0, bufferSize);
    }
    Bw.Close();

    //Close the files
    localFile.Close();
    fs.Close();
}
```

```
        catch (Exception ex)
        {
            //Do something with the exception
        }
        finally
        {
            //Commit the transaction and close the connection
            Cmd.Transaction.Commit();
            cn.Close();
        }
    }
}
```

Listing 5-8: Saving item information to a `FILESTREAM` database.

Running the application

We have successfully completed the coding for this lab, so it is time for us to run the application and see it in action: press **F5** or click the **Start Debugging** button on the toolbar. This will open the web page in a new web browser instance, as shown in Figure 5-3.

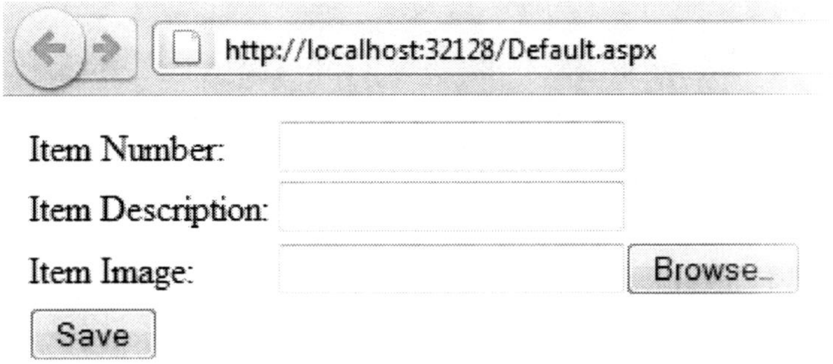

Figure 5-3: The web page.

Enter an item number and description, select an image file using the **Browse** button, and then click **Save** to insert the information into the database.

The code we wrote in the **Click** event of the **Save** button will insert a row into the **Items** table along with the **FILESTREAM** data. Verify that the information is correctly saved in the database by running **SELECT * FROM Items** in SSMS. If everything is set up correctly, you will see that the data you entered in the web page shows up in the SSMS result window.

Lab 5: Deploying and Configuring a FILESTREAM Web Application on IIS

In Lab 4, we created, ran, and tested a web application, all within Visual Studio. By default, when you run a web application from Visual Studio it runs on a built-in web server, which is designed for debugging and testing web applications in a development environment.

In a production environment, we usually configure our web application on more robust web servers, such as Microsoft IIS. Configuring and running a web application that deals with **FILESTREAM** data on IIS needs some careful attention.

In this lab, we will see how to deploy the web application we created in Lab 4 on IIS 7.0. There are different ways of deploying a web application on a web server; we will use the inbuilt functionality provided by Visual Studio to keep the process simple.

To do this, we will:

- run Visual Studio under an administrator account
- publish the web application to a new virtual directory on local IIS
- configure security for **FILESTREAM** access
- run and test the application.

Running Visual Studio under an administrator account

To deploy a web application from Visual Studio, you need to run Visual Studio under an administrator account. With administrative privileges on the computer, we can do this by right-clicking on the Visual Studio option in the Start menu and selecting **Run as administrator**.

Publishing the web application into a new virtual directory

In this step, we will publish the web application to a new virtual directory on local IIS. Right-click on the project name in Solution Explorer, and select **Publish**. This will open the **Publish Web** dialog box (Figure 5-4).

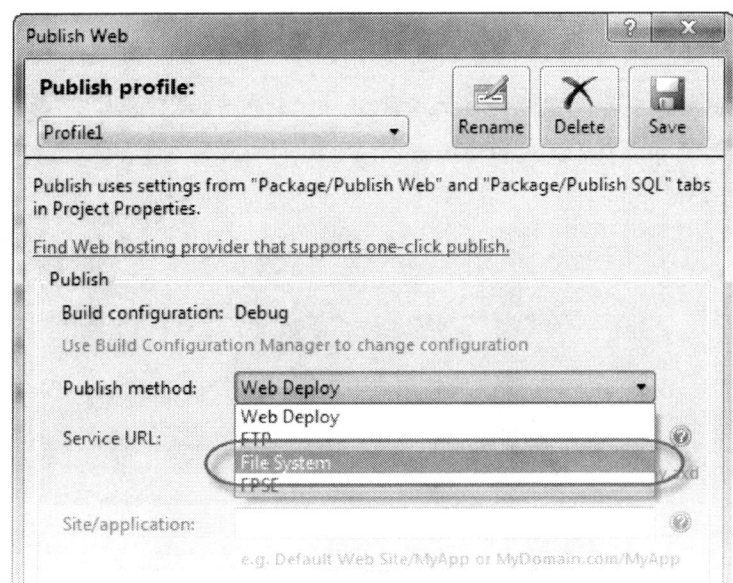

Figure 5-4:   The **Publish Web** dialog box.

Chapter 5: FILESTREAM with ASP.NET and Silverlight

The **Publish Web** dialog box provides a number of different publication options. We are going to deploy it into a local IIS virtual directory, so we will select **File System** from the drop-down list. Click on the [...] button and it will open a dialog box that enables us to select a virtual directory under the local IIS server.

Next, we create a new virtual directory for our application. Click the **Local IIS** button and then click the **New Virtual Directory** button on the top right of the page to create a new virtual directory (Figure 5-5).

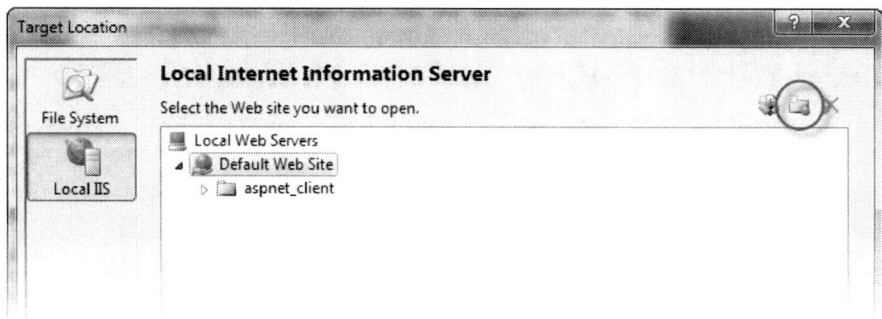

Figure 5-5: Selecting a virtual directory under the local IIS server.

We'll call the new virtual directory `fsweb`. Choose the file system location for the published files and click **OK** to return to the parent window (Figure 5-6).

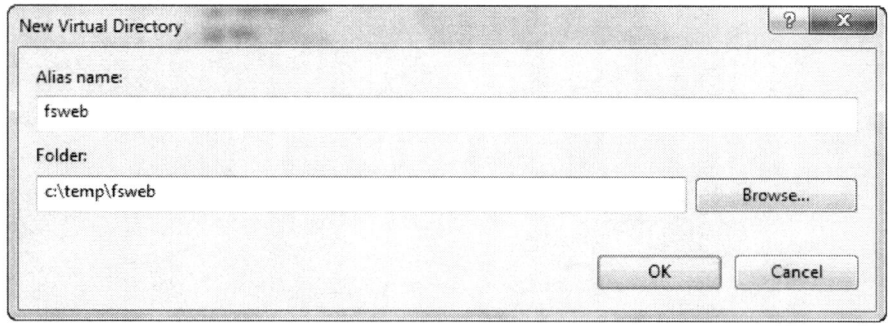

Figure 5-6: Creating the new virtual directory.

Chapter 5: FILESTREAM with ASP.NET and Silverlight

Select the new virtual directory that we just created (**fsweb**) (Figure 5-7).

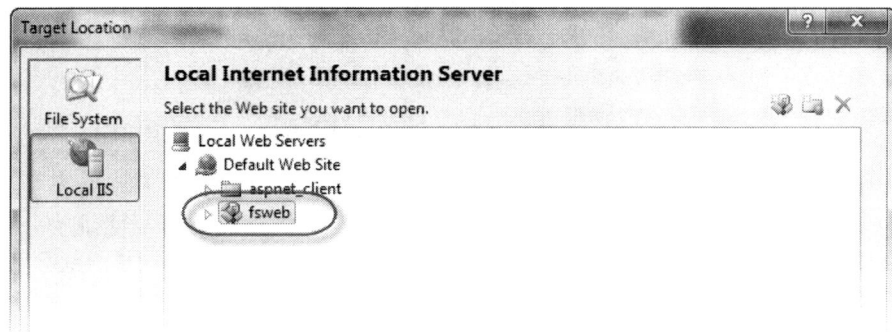

Figure 5-7: Selecting the target location.

Click **OK** to proceed to the next step. The **Publish Web** dialog box is displayed again, showing our selections (Figure 5-8).

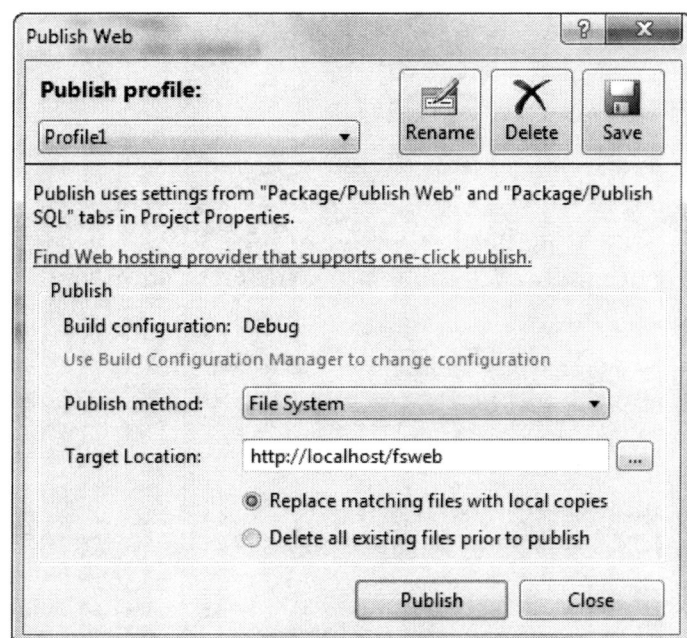

Figure 5-8: Starting the publication.

179

Chapter 5: FILESTREAM with ASP.NET and Silverlight

We have selected the **Publish Method** and **Target Location**, so now click the **Publish** button to start the publication process. The project is published into the `fsweb` virtual directory under the local IIS web server. The Visual Studio status bar will show the progress of the operation.

When the operation completes, we can go ahead and run the application from the browser. Open a web browser and enter: HTTP://LOCALHOST/FSWEB/DEFAULT.ASPX (or the appropriate URL if your local configuration is different). This will open the web page we created in the previous lab (Figure 5-9).

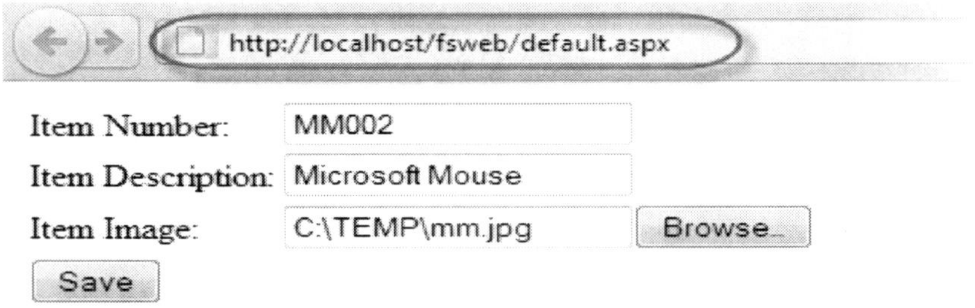

Figure 5-9: The resulting web page.

Now fill the data entry page with information for a new item, and click **Save** to send the information to the database. Surprisingly, in most cases you will see the error shown in Figure 5-10 (or similar) when you click **Save**.

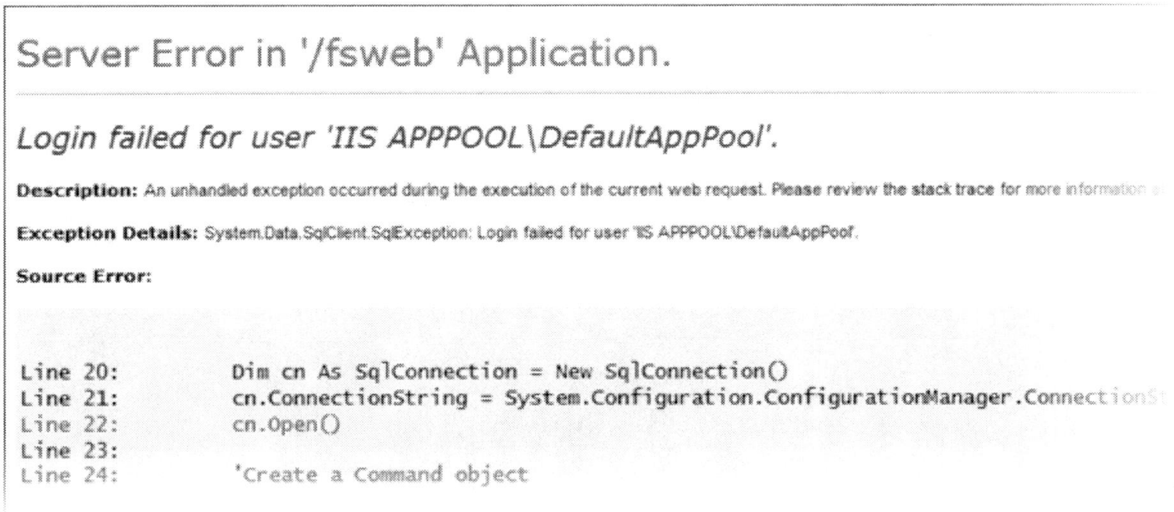

```
Server Error in '/fsweb' Application.

Login failed for user 'IIS APPPOOL\DefaultAppPool'.

Description: An unhandled exception occurred during the execution of the current web request. Please review the stack trace for more information

Exception Details: System.Data.SqlClient.SqlException: Login failed for user 'IIS APPPOOL\DefaultAppPool'.

Source Error:

Line 20:        Dim cn As SqlConnection = New SqlConnection()
Line 21:        cn.ConnectionString = System.Configuration.ConfigurationManager.ConnectionS
Line 22:        cn.Open()
Line 23:
Line 24:        'Create a Command object
```

Figure 5-10: Error displayed when you click **Save**.

The `Open()` method of the connection object raises an error. This is because we have configured the connection to use Integrated Security (Windows authentication), but the user account under which the web application runs does not have permissions to access the database. However, Windows authentication is necessary for accessing the `FILESTREAM` data through the Managed or Win32 APIs, which means we need to persevere with Integrated Security. So, we now need to fix this error by reconfiguring the security settings.

Configuring IIS to use SQL Server Integrated Security

There are a number of ways to fix the login error we saw in the previous section, and the most suitable method depends upon the security level required, the type of application, the way users access the application, and so on. We'll use one of the simpler options here.

Chapter 5: FILESTREAM with ASP.NET and Silverlight

To begin, open IIS Manager by typing **inetmgr** in the **Run** window, or by selecting it from the **Administrative Tools** section of the control panel. Then, in the **IIS Manager** window, right-click on the **Application Pools** node and select **Add Application Pool** to open the **Add Application Pool** dialog box.

Now, we can create a new application pool for our **FILESTREAM** web application. We'll call the application pool **fsweb** and select .NET version 2.0, since we created a .NET 2.0 application (Figure 5-11).

Figure 5-11:   The **Add Application Pool** dialog box.

Click **OK**, and IIS Manager creates a new application pool, which will show up in the list of application pools (Figure 5-12).

Chapter 5: FILESTREAM with ASP.NET and Silverlight

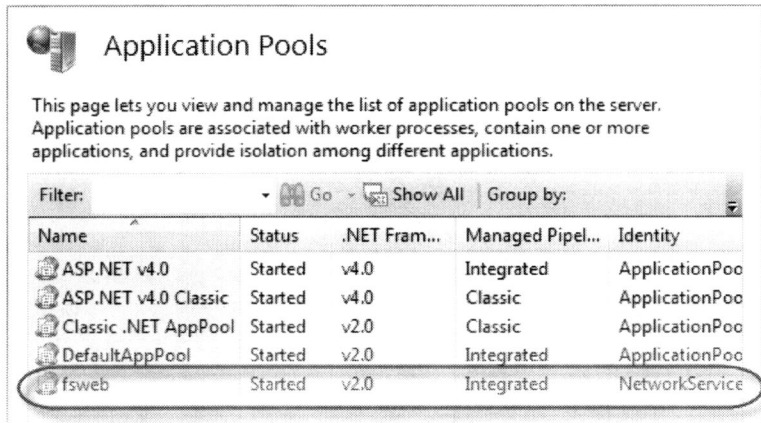

Figure 5-12: The new application pool.

In the list of application pools, right-click **fsweb** and select **Advanced Properties**, or select **fsweb** and click the **Advanced Properties** link on the right-hand side of the IIS Manager window. In the **Advanced Settings** dialog box, select the **Identity** property and click on the button on the right to change the value of the property (Figure 5-13).

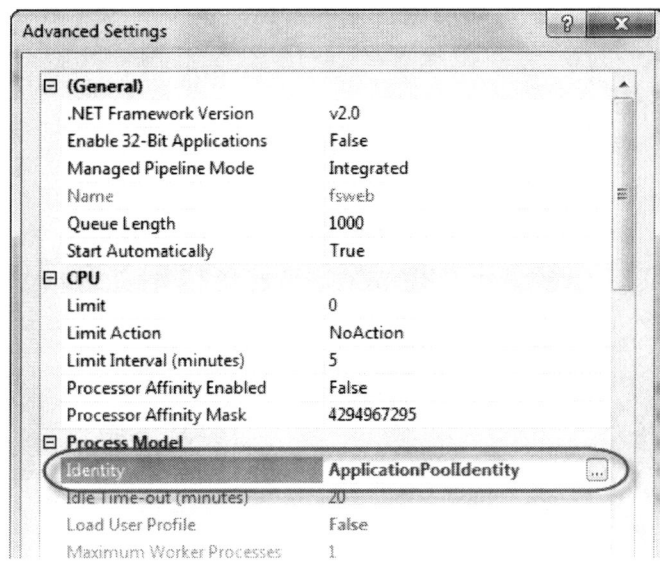

Figure 5-13: **Advanced Settings** dialog box.

In the **Application Pool Identity** window, select **Built-in account**, and then select **NetworkService** from the drop-down list (Figure 5-14).

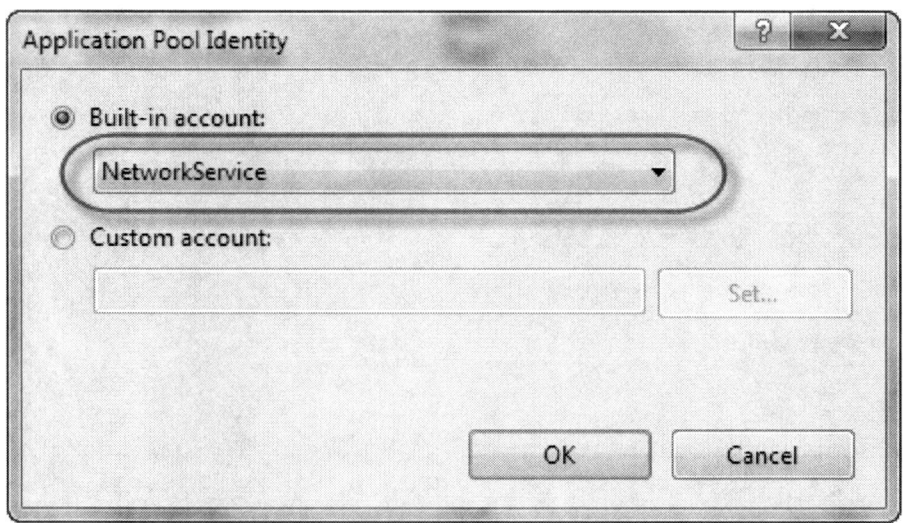

Figure 5-14: Changing the **Identity** setting.

Click **OK** to save the settings, and close the **Advanced Settings** dialog box.

We have created a new application pool with the identity of `NetworkService`. Now we'll associate this newly created application pool with our web application. In the IIS Manager, select the virtual directory we created earlier (`fsweb`), and select the **Basic Settings** option from the **Actions** section on the right-hand side. Then, on the **Edit Application** dialog box, click **Select** to change the application pool associated with our web application (Figure 5-15).

Chapter 5: FILESTREAM with ASP.NET and Silverlight

Figure 5-15: Changing the application pool.

In the **Select Application Pool** dialog box, select the new fsweb application pool (Figure 5-16).

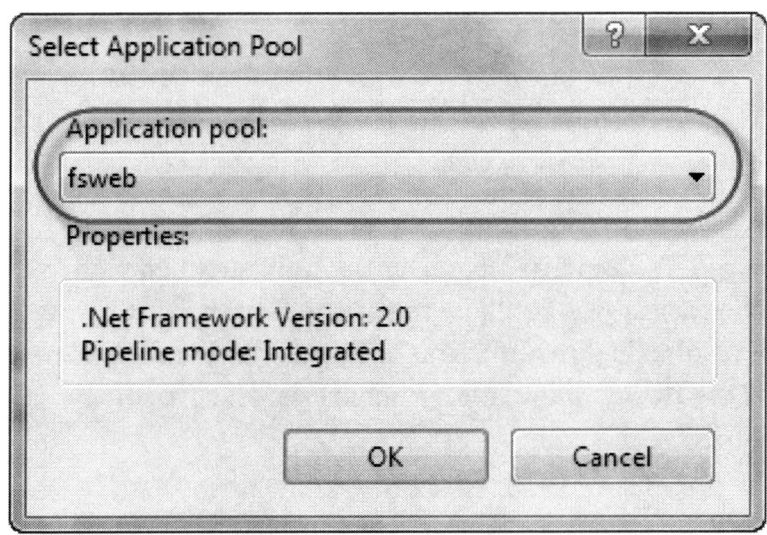

Figure 5-16: Selecting the fsweb application pool.

Click **OK** to return to the parent window, and click **OK** again to save the changes and return to the IIS Manager. After completing this step, our application is now configured to run under the identity of `NetworkService`.

The next step is to make sure that the Network Service account has permissions to access our database. If it does not have access to the SQL Server instance, we need to create a new login with the required permissions. We can do this using SSMS, by right-clicking on **Logins** in the SQL Server instance tree and selecting **New Login** (Figure 5-19).

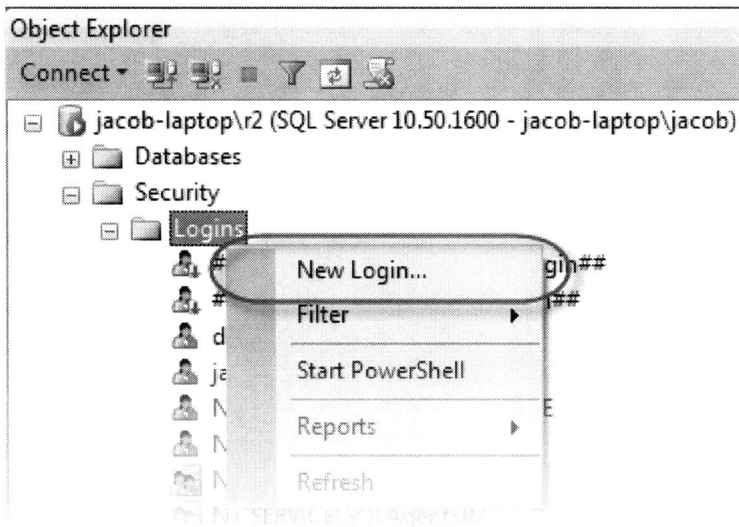

Figure 5-17:   Creating a new login for the Network Service account.

The **New Login** dialog box is displayed. In **Login name**, select the fully qualified name of the Network Service account. The easiest way could be to use the **Search** button and select the account from the search results (Figure 5-18). This assumes that the SQL Server is running on the same machine as the IIS app pool. If not, the web server's machine account needs to be given permissions.

Chapter 5: FILESTREAM with ASP.NET and Silverlight

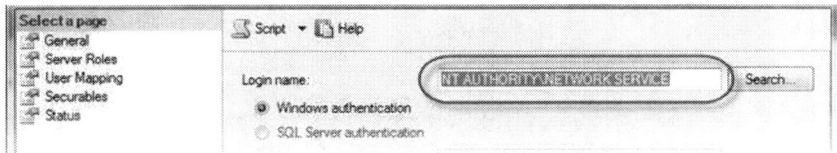

Figure 5-18: Specifying the name of the Network Service account.

Now go to the **User Mapping** page. We will give the new account permissions to access the `NorthPole` database. For the purpose of this lab, I am assigning the `db_owner` role to the newly created login (Figure 5-19). However, in most real-world scenarios you would probably assign a lesser set of permissions; it is very important to make sure you give only those permissions that are absolutely necessary. In a typical production environment, the database administrator will do this based on the security policy of the organization.

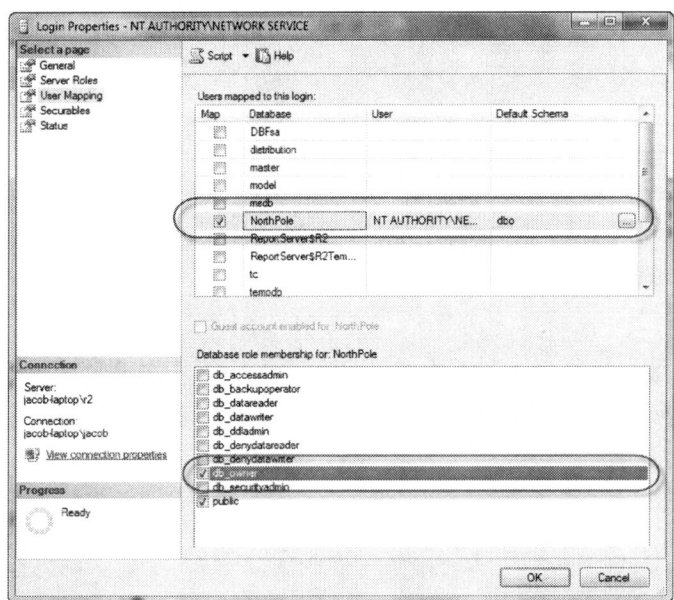

Figure 5-19: Assigning permissions to the Network Service login.

With this, we are done with security configuration and it is time to test the website and verify that it works.

Chapter 5: FILESTREAM with ASP.NET and Silverlight

Running the application

Run the application again on your favorite web browser. Enter the item information, including the location of an image file to load into the `FILESTREAM` column, and click **Save** to push the information to the database (Figure 5-20).

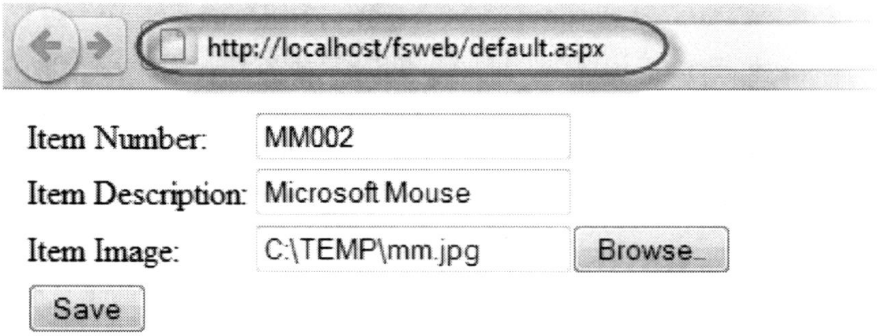

Figure 5-20: Running the application.

This time, the information should be successfully added into the database. You can verify this by looking in the `Items` table; in SSMS, run a `SELECT * from Items` query on the `Items` table to see whether the newly entered data shows up in the table.

Congratulations! You have successfully completed the second ASP.NET lab. It is time to move on to the next lab and explore some more interesting stuff.

Lab 6: Creating a Web Handler to Serve Images from a FILESTREAM Database

In Lab 4, we saw how to upload files into the `FILESTREAM` column of a SQL Server database from a web page. In this lab, we will see how to serve those files back to the client applications, upon request.

We will create a web page to retrieve images from the database and send them to the client browser. A web page is not the best way to implement such a handler, but at this stage we want to minimize complexity, so that we can focus on `FILESTREAM` and not on ASP.NET features. In a later lab, we will develop a similar solution using a generic handler, which is a much better approach.

To do this, we will:

- create a stored procedure to retrieve the `FILESTREAM` information
- create the web page that serves item images
- run and test the application.

Creating a stored procedure to retrieve FILESTREAM data

Start by creating a stored procedure that will retrieve the logical path name of the `FILESTREAM` value, and the `FILESTREAM` transaction context. This stored procedure, shown in Listing 5-9, will take an item number as input parameter and will return the `FILESTREAM` information.

```sql
CREATE PROCEDURE GetItemImageInfo
    (
      @ItemNumber VARCHAR(20)
    )
AS
    BEGIN
        SELECT  ItemImage.PathName() AS filePath ,
                GET_FILESTREAM_TRANSACTION_CONTEXT() AS txContext
        FROM    Items
        WHERE   ItemNumber = @ItemNumber
    END
```

Listing 5-9: Creating the stored procedure.

Creating the web page to serve images

The next step is to create a web page that can serve images to the client browsers. Add a new ASP.NET web form to the project and name it `GetItemImage.aspx`.

The design part of this page does not need any changes because this page is not used as a UI element; its purpose is only to serve the image of the specified item to the client browser. In most cases, we'd use a generic handler (`.ashx` file) for this type of scenario, which will be slightly faster than using an `ASPX` page. However, we will use an `ASPX` page for simplicity.

Let's start writing the code for this page. We'll begin by adding the necessary import statements to the code file `GetItemImage.aspx.cs`.

```csharp
using System.IO;
using System.Data.SqlClient;
using System.Data;
using System.Data.SqlTypes;
```

Listing 5-10: The import statements.

Chapter 5: FILESTREAM with ASP.NET and Silverlight

The web page expects a parameter in the query string named `ItemNumber` (Listing 5-11).

```csharp
protected void Page_Load(object sender, EventArgs e)
{
    string ItemNumber;
    ItemNumber = Request.QueryString["ItemNumber"].ToString();

    //Create and open a database connection
    SqlConnection cn = new SqlConnection();
    cn.ConnectionString =
            System.Configuration.ConfigurationManager.ConnectionStrings[
                                            "NorthPoleDB"].ToString();
    cn.Open();

    //Create a Command object
    SqlCommand cmd = new SqlCommand();
    cmd.CommandText = "GetItemImageInfo";
    cmd.Connection = cn;
    cmd.CommandType = System.Data.CommandType.StoredProcedure;
    cmd.Parameters.AddWithValue("@ItemNumber", ItemNumber);

    //Begin a transaction
    SqlTransaction trn = cn.BeginTransaction("ItemTran");
    cmd.Transaction = trn;

    string filePath = null;
    byte[] txContext = null;

    try
    {
        //Execute the command
        SqlDataReader reader = cmd.ExecuteReader();
        if (reader.Read())
        {
            txContext = (reader["txContext"] as byte[]);
            filePath = reader["filePath"].ToString();
        }
        reader.Close();

        // Open the FILESTREAM data file for reading
        SqlFileStream fs = new SqlFileStream(filePath, txContext,
                                            FileAccess.Read);
```

```csharp
        // Start transferring data from the FILESTREAM data file
        Response.BufferOutput = false;
        Response.ContentType = "image/jpeg";
        BinaryWriter bw = new BinaryWriter(Response.OutputStream);

        const int bufferSize = 4096;
        byte[] buffer = new byte[bufferSize];
        int byteCount = fs.Read(buffer, 0, bufferSize);

        while (byteCount == bufferSize)
        {
            bw.Write(buffer, 0, byteCount);
            byteCount = fs.Read(buffer, 0, bufferSize);
        }

        //Close the files
        Response.End();
        bw.Close();
        fs.Close();
    }
    catch (Exception ex)
    {
        //do some error handling
    }
    finally
    {
        // Commit the transaction and close the connection
        cmd.Transaction.Commit();
        cn.Close();
    }
}
```

Listing 5-11: Code to serve images stored in a FILESTREAM column.

What is interesting and worth noticing here is how we are sending the data back to the web server. We do this through the ASP.NET Response object. We first set the content type to image/jpeg to tell the browser that we are sending back an image. Then we access the OutputStream property of the Response object and write the content of the FILESTREAM file into it (Listing 5-12).

```
Response.BufferOutput = false;
Response.ContentType = "image/jpeg";
BinaryWriter bw = new BinaryWriter(Response.OutputStream);
```

Listing 5-12: Accessing the `OutputStream` property of the `Response` object.

Refer to Chapter 12, in the section entitled *Best Practices for FILESTREAM Development*, to learn about the potentially useful addition of a timestamp column to allow for caching `FILESTREAM` data that is sent over the web.

Running and testing the application

We have finished the code, so we can now verify that the application is working as expected. In Visual Studio, set the web page that we created in this lab as the default page, and run the application.

When the web page is open in the browser, add a parameter to the query string. Enter the item number of a record that exists in the table. This will retrieve the image associated with the specified item, and the image will be displayed on your browser (Figure 5-21).

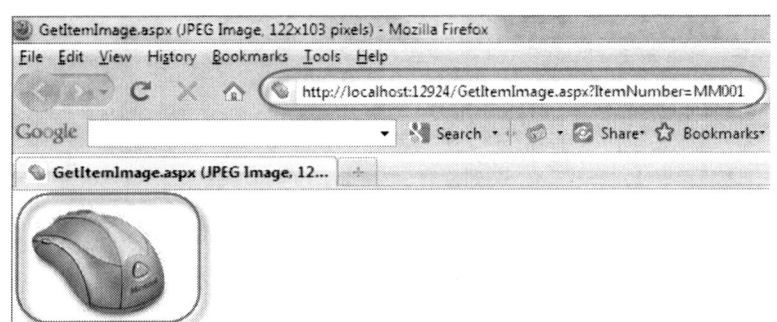

Figure 5-21: Running the application.

In the next lab we will see how to use this page as the URL source for item thumbnail images we display on a web page.

Chapter 5: FILESTREAM with ASP.NET and Silverlight

Lab 7: Displaying Thumbnail Images of Items from a FILESTREAM Database on an ASP.NET Web Page

In this lab, we will create a web page that will display a list of items along with their thumbnail images. We will use the web handler we created in the previous lab to fetch images stored in the `FILESTREAM` column of a SQL Server database.

To do this, we will:

- create a stored procedure to fetch item details
- add a new web form and a Grid View
- create a data source that retrieves item information, and bind it to the Grid View
- configure the Grid View
- run and test the web page.

Creating the stored procedure to fetch item information

The first step is to create a stored procedure that returns the list of all the items in the `Items` table. However, before you begin, add a few records to the `Items` table (I'll leave this as an exercise for the reader – I have populated my sample table with four rows, with four different products and their thumbnail images).

Now, in the SSMS window run the code in Listing 5-13 to create the stored procedure.

```
CREATE PROCEDURE GetItemList
AS
    BEGIN
        SELECT  ItemNumber ,
                ItemDescription ,
                '/GetItemImage.aspx?ItemNumber=' + ItemNumber AS ImageURL
        FROM    Items
    END
```

Listing 5-13: Creating a stored procedure to retrieve item information.

Notice the third column returned by the stored procedure; the value returned by this column points to the page we created in the previous lab to return images from the database. The value returned by this column will be used to bind the image control on the grid that will display the thumbnails. Run the application we created in the previous lab and load a few more images into the **FILESTREAM** table.

Listing 5-14 shows an example results set from the stored procedure, based on the data I entered for this demonstration.

```
ItemNumber  ItemDescription  ImageURL
----------  ---------------  --------------------------------
1001        Microsoft Mouse  /GetItemImage.aspx?ItemNumber=1001
3001        Dell Laptop      /GetItemImage.aspx?ItemNumber=3001
4005        Apple iPad       /GetItemImage.aspx?ItemNumber=4005
6009        Amazon Kindle    /GetItemImage.aspx?ItemNumber=6009
```

Listing 5-14: Example results from the stored procedure.

Adding a new web form and data grid

Next, add a new web form named **ItemList.aspx** to the project, then drag a `GridView` control from the toolbox and drop it on the web form (Figure 5-22).

Column0	Column1	Column2
abc	abc	abc
abc	abc	abc
abc	abc	abc
abc	abc	abc
abc	abc	abc

Figure 5-22: A `GridView` control.

Adding a data source

In this step, we will create a data source that fetches the item details, and binds it to the `GridView` control. Go to the properties of the `GridView` control, and locate the `DataSourceID` property. From the drop-down list, select **New data source** (Figure 5-23).

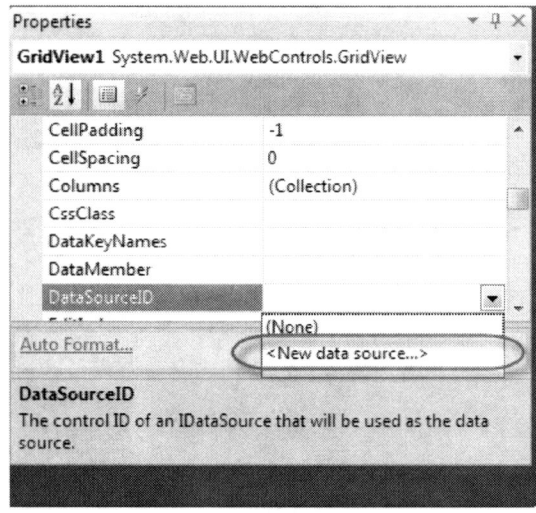

Figure 5-23: Creating a new data source.

This will open the **Data Source Configuration Wizard**, which will take you through the configuration process. From the list of data source types available, select **Database**. We'll name the data source `itemds` (Figure 5-24).

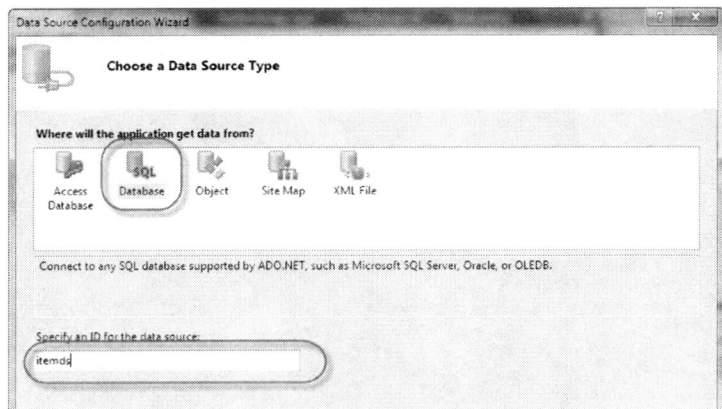

Figure 5-24: Specifying an ID for the data source.

In the next dialog box, click **New Connection** to create and configure a new connection to the database. The **Add Connection** dialog box is displayed (Figure 5-25).

Note that I have used Windows authentication for consistency only; Windows authentication is not necessary for this connection because it is used to execute the stored procedure that fetches item details, but not the images. We will use the handler page we created in the previous lab to fetch the actual images, and that page is already using Windows authentication.

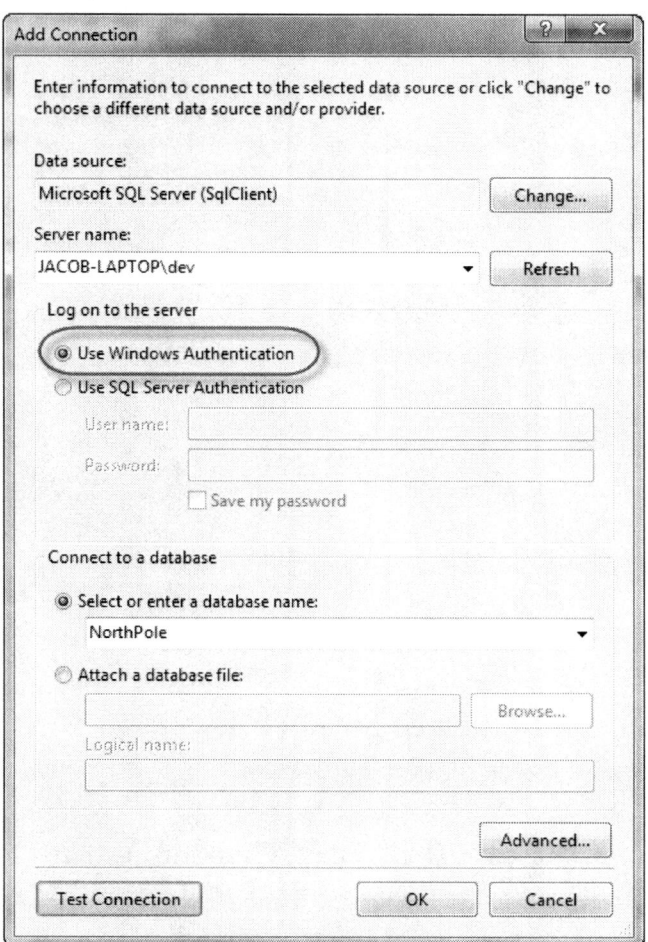

Figure 5-25: The **Add Connection** dialog box.

Click **OK** on the **Add Connection** dialog box, and then click **Next** to move to the next step in the wizard. Click **Next** again, to save the connection string to the application configuration file.

Chapter 5: FILESTREAM with ASP.NET and Silverlight

When you see the **Configure the Select Statement** step, select **Specify a custom SQL statement or stored procedure**, because we already created the stored procedure to retrieve item information (Figure 5-26).

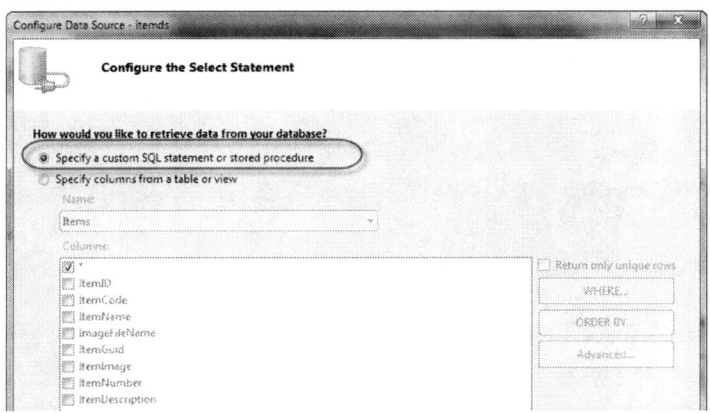

Figure 5-26: Configuring the Select Statement.

In **Define Custom Statements or Stored Procedures**, select **Stored procedure**, and from the list of stored procedures select **GetItemList** (Figure 5-27). Then click **Next**.

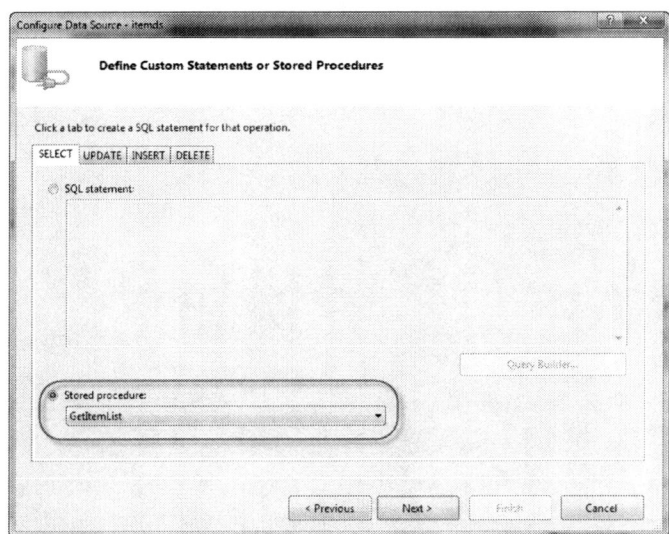

Figure 5-27: Selecting the stored procedure.

199

Chapter 5: FILESTREAM with ASP.NET and Silverlight

In the next step, click the **Test Query** button to verify that the stored procedure returns the expected results (Figure 5-28).

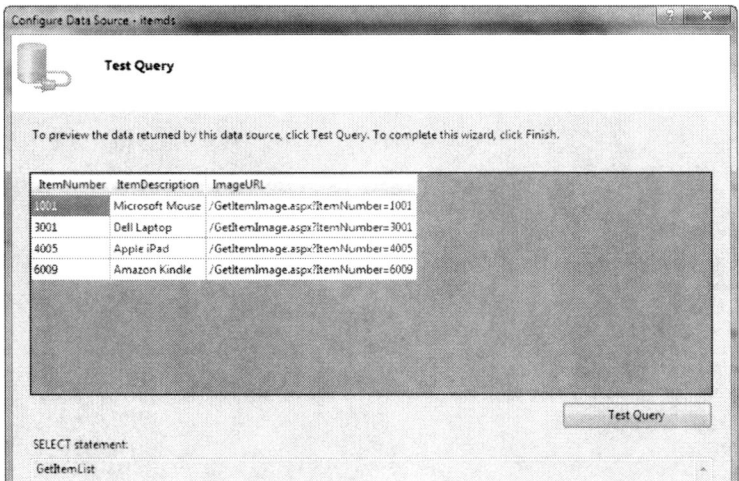

Figure 5-28: Previewing the data.

This is the last step of the wizard. Click **Finish** to return to the web page designer window. When the wizard exits, it automatically binds the columns returned by the stored procedure with the columns in the grid control. By default, all columns are bound to text boxes (Figure 5-29).

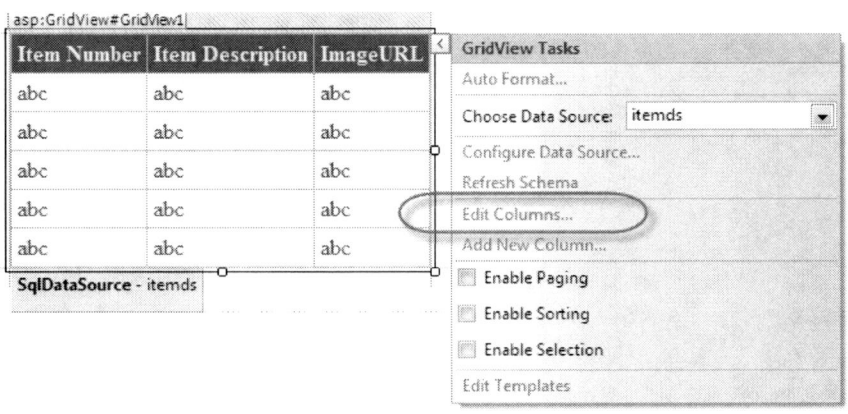

Figure 5-29: Selecting the **Edit Columns** option.

This default is alright for the first two columns, but on the last column we need an image control. We need to edit the grid control and change the third column from text box to image control. Click the **Edit Columns** link to open the column editor window. In the **Fields** dialog box, remove the **ImageURL** column that the wizard automatically added (Figure 5-30).

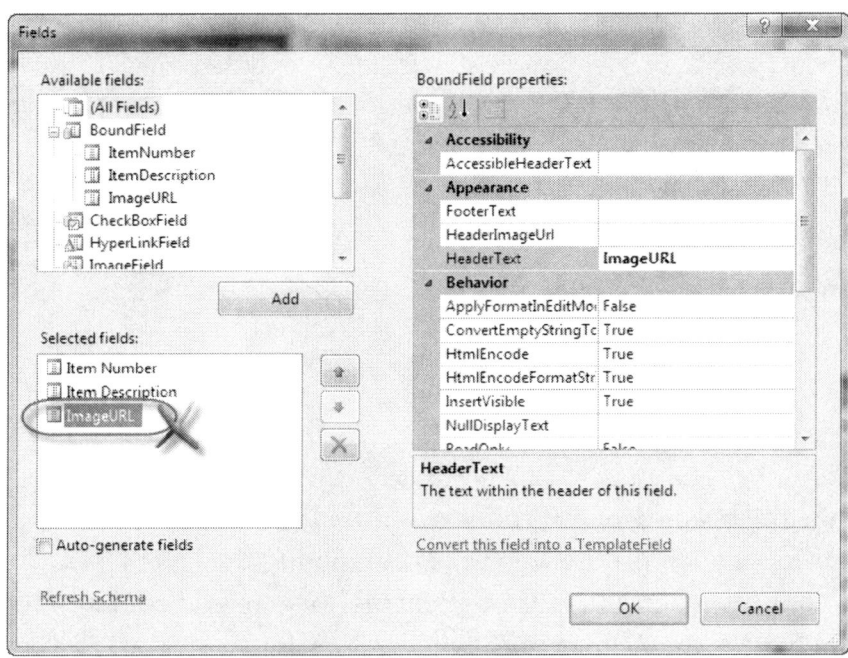

Figure 5-30: Removing the `ImageURL` text column.

Now, add an **ImageField** from the **Available fields** list, and then set the `DataImageUrlField` property of the image field to the **ImageURL** column of the data source (Figure 5-31).

Chapter 5: FILESTREAM with ASP.NET and Silverlight

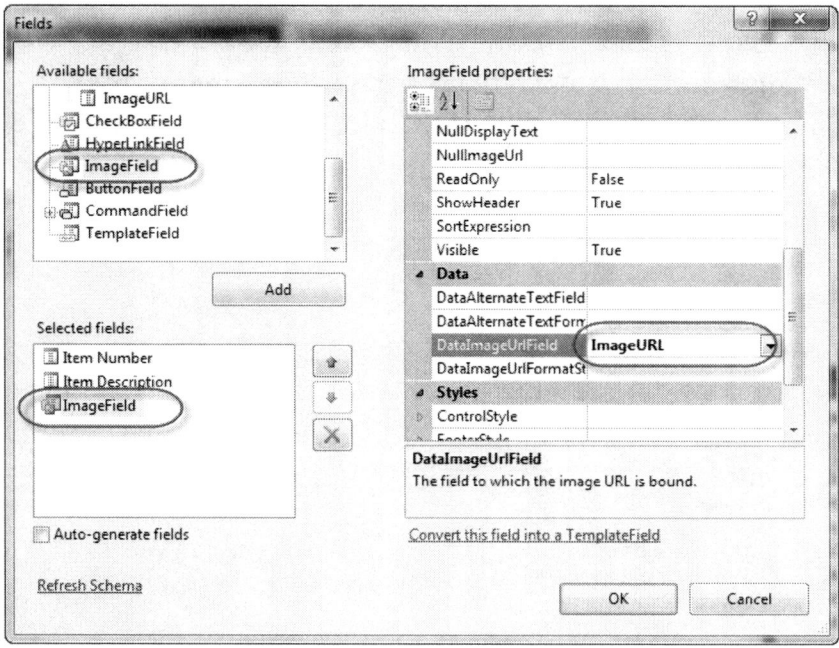

Figure 5-31: Adding an `ImageField`.

You might also want to change the heading of the columns, and set the height and width of the image control so that it looks good on the web page, and modify the layout and format of the text to make it look even better. Figure 5-32 shows how my grid control looks in the designer after applying some formatting changes.

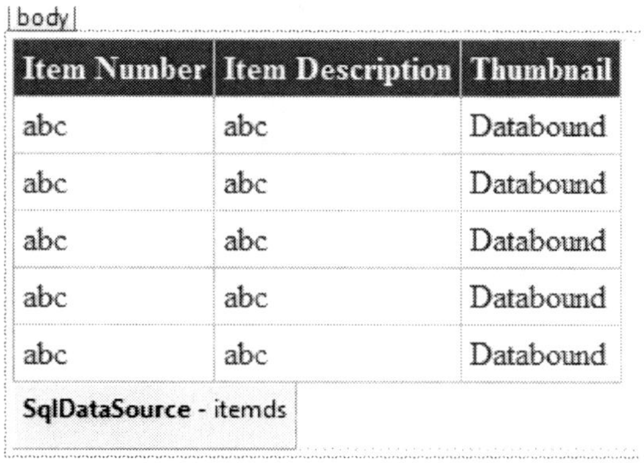

Figure 5-32: The grid control.

Chapter 5: FILESTREAM with ASP.NET and Silverlight

That is all we need to do in this lab. Our web page is ready. Let's build the project, set the default page to the newly created web form, and run the application (Figure 5-33).

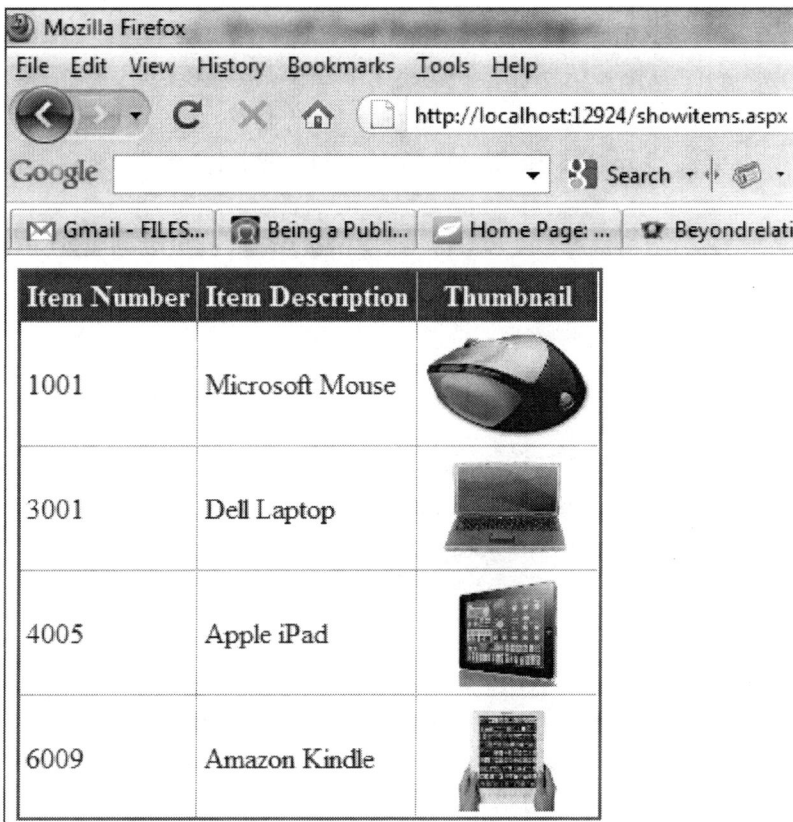

Figure 5-33: Running the application.

You will see the web page load the details of the items in the database and display the thumbnail images associated with those items.

Chapter 5: FILESTREAM with ASP.NET and Silverlight

Lab 8: Using SqlFileStream in an N-Tier Scenario

For many reasons, today's web applications are often architected to run across multiple physical computers, referred to as tiers. Using `FILESTREAM` in a multi-tier design requires attention to an important detail: in order to achieve the most benefit from `FILESTREAM`, it should be accessed using the Win32 streaming APIs. However, using `SqlFileStream` also requires an active transaction in the SQL Server database. The consumer of the `FILESTREAM` data is most often the tier closest to the client – and furthest away from the database. If the `SqlFileStream` API is used, this requires that this tier has at least some knowledge of the data store. In general, this violates good architectural practices.

In this lab, we will create a solution that makes the presentation tier as independent on this database transaction as possible, while maintaining the performance benefits offered by streaming access to `FILESTREAM` data. To fully understand the problem involved, let's consider the following example scenario. A web application must handle requests from clients for which the response includes data stored in a SQL Server `FILESTREAM` column. The web application will be hosted on a front-end IIS web server, while the SQL Server database is hosted on a back-end server. The web application's developers aim to make the application as efficient as possible, and want to use the `SqlFileStream` class and copy the stream's contents to the Response object's `OutputStream` (as shown in Listing 5-11 as part of Lab 6). They have four options, as shown below.

- **Start the `SqlTransaction` required for the `SqlFileStream` to use in the presentation tier.**
  This solution requires that the web application has intimate knowledge of the database's configuration and details. Generally, one of the architectural goals of a multi-layered web application is to avoid this.

- **Start a `SqlTransaction` and create the `SqlFileStream` in the data access layer and pass the `SqlFileStream` back to the client application.**
  This solution does not address the concern that the `SqlTransaction` must be active while the presentation layer uses the `SqlFileStream` object. The client, however, has

no control over the `SqlTransaction`, and cannot guarantee, either that the transaction will still be active, or that the transaction will be properly disposed when the work is done.

- **Create a custom class that will act as a domain object that encapsulates the required database objects and the `SqlFileStream`.**
  An object of this custom class will be instantiated in the data access layer and passed on to the presentation layer. This object will implement `IDisposable` to ensure that the `SqlTransaction` and the `SqlConnection` objects encapsulated will be properly disposed when the client is finished with the work. This may ensure somewhat better performance than the fourth solution which, as we will see in a moment, requires an additional stream copy. However, it does not fully abstract the data access method.

- **Perform all data access, including the streaming access to FILESTREAM data, in the data access layer and copy the stream data to a `MemoryStream`. Then return the `MemoryStream` to the caller.**
  This is the most appropriate solution and will be demonstrated in this lab. We create the `SqlFileStream` object in the data access layer and copy the contents to a `MemoryStream`. We then pass the `MemoryStream` reference through the tiers. This involves an extra step (the stream copy from `SqlFileStream` to `MemoryStream`), which, in my view, provides more than sufficient benefits because the client is completely unaware of the source of the streamed data.

Creating the Visual Studio solution and projects

For this lab, we will use the same sample database created previously. We will create a new Visual Studio solution and create three projects: one for domain classes, one for a data access layer, each implemented as a class library, and a third for a presentation layer, implemented as a web application.

Open Visual Studio and create a blank solution by selecting **File | New | Project...** from the menu. In the **New Project** dialog box, under **Other Project Types**, select **Visual Studio Solutions** and then **Blank Solution**. Click **OK** to create the new, blank solution.

In Solution Explorer, right-click the solution and select **Add | New Project....** Select the **ASP.NET Empty Web Application** project template. In this lab, we will give this project the name **Presentation**. Click **OK** to create this new project as part of the solution.

Follow the same process for adding a second new project to the solution, this time using the **Class Library** template. Name this project **DataAccess**. Delete the default `Class1.cs` file from the project. Repeat this process one more time to create another class library with the name **Domain**.

We will now add references to the appropriate projects. The web application will call into the data access layer to retrieve information from the SQL Server database. Both the web application and the data access layer will use the domain objects. We must therefore add the following references in the **Presentation** project:

- **Domain**
- **DataAccess**.

And in the **DataAccess** project:

- **Domain**
- **System.Configuration**.

In order to start the web application showing an image using the handler we will develop, we must change the start page. Right-click on the web application and select **Properties**. In the **Web** tab, change the **Start Action** to **Specific Page** and enter `GetItemImage.ashx?itemID=1` as the value. We are now ready to start coding the solution.

Writing the domain object code

In a real-world project, you would create a domain object class for every entity your application will use. Because our database stores little in the way of entities and our sample web application will not actually use it, we will skip this step altogether. We did create the **Domain** project, but only to illustrate the typical architectural setup of such a solution.

Writing the data access code

In the **DataAccess** project, create a single class with the name `ItemData`. Change the access modifier of the class to `public`. At the top of the code file, import the namespaces `System.Configuration`, `System.Data.SqlClient`, `System.Data.SqlTypes` and `System.IO`. The class will have one method, which retrieves the `FILESTREAM` data for a specified `ItemID` (Listing 5-15).

```
public class ItemData
{
  public MemoryStream GetItemImage(string itemID)
  {
    MemoryStream ms = null;

    string ConnectionString = ConfigurationManager.ConnectionStrings[
      "NorthPoleDB"].ToString();

    string CmdText = @"SELECT ItemImage.PathName(),
            GET_FILESTREAM_TRANSACTION_CONTEXT()
            FROM Items WHERE ItemID = @itemID";

    using (SqlConnection conn = new SqlConnection(ConnectionString))
    using (SqlCommand cmd = new SqlCommand(CmdText, conn))
    {
      conn.Open();

      using (SqlTransaction tran = conn.BeginTransaction())
```

```csharp
      {
        cmd.Transaction = tran;
        cmd.Parameters.Add(new SqlParameter("itemID",
          System.Data.SqlDbType.VarChar, 20));
        cmd.Parameters["itemID"].Value = itemID;

        using (SqlDataReader dr = cmd.ExecuteReader())
        {
          if (dr.HasRows && dr.Read())
          {
            using (SqlFileStream sfs = new SqlFileStream(dr.GetString(0),
                            (byte[])dr.GetValue(1), FileAccess.Read))
            {
              // This construct is used to avoid problems with a
              // FILESTREAM data file that exceeds 4 GB in size
              ms = new MemoryStream(
                 (int)System.Math.Min(sfs.Length, int.MaxValue));

              // Copy the SqlFileStream contents to the
              // MemoryStream (requires .NET 4.0 and later)
              sfs.CopyTo(ms);
            }
          }
        }
      }

      return ms;
  }
}
```

Listing 5-15: Code for the `ItemData` class.

In this method, new `SqlConnection` and `SqlTransaction` objects are created. Those are then used to retrieve the information necessary to create an instance of the `SqlFileStream` class. Recall that in Chapter 4, as part of the second Entity Framework lab, we created a stored procedure that encapsulates this. That stored procedure could be reused here instead of the embedded SQL statement. Then the contents of the `SqlFileStream` are copied to a new instance of `System.IO.MemoryStream`, which is then used as the return value of the method.

Alternative to the `Stream.CopyTo()` *method*

The copy of the stream content in this lab is done using the `Stream.CopyTo()` *method, which was introduced with the .NET Framework Version 4. If your application targets an older Framework version, refer to the other code samples in this chapter for a way of copying the contents of one stream to another using a 4 KB buffer (which is what* `Stream.CopyTo()` *also does).*

Creating an HTTP handler to serve images

The concept of showing the web page in a web browser will be very similar to the one used in Lab 6, but the code will look different. There will be no reference to any SQL types at all; any data access is completely abstracted in the data access layer (the **DataAccess** project).

To drive this point home, in the **Presentation** web application, remove the reference to the `System.Data` assembly. Then we will also modify the `web.config` file to include the database connection string. Refer to Listing 5-3 for this code. In the final version of the application, this connection string can be removed. Because we are taking a step-by-step approach to this implementation, we will initially test the code whereby the web application calls into the data access component directly, and the web application's configuration file will provide the required connection string information.

To illustrate a slightly more advanced ASP.NET concept, for this lab we will implement a generic handler, rather than repurposing a web form as a handler. Right-click on the **Presentation** project, and select **Add | New Item** and in the **Add New Item** dialog box, select the **Generic Handler** template and give the new item the name `GetItemImage.ashx`. At the top of the file, add namespace import statements for the `DataAcess` and `System.IO` namespaces.

We will write our code in `ProcessRequest()`, which is the method called by the ASP.NET runtime if the handler is invoked. The code is shown in Listing 5-16.

```
public void ProcessRequest(HttpContext context)
{
  context.Response.ContentType = System.Net.Mime.MediaTypeNames.Image.Jpeg;
  context.Response.BufferOutput = false;

  ItemData data = new ItemData();

  MemoryStream ms = data.GetItemImage(context.Request.QueryString["itemID"]);

  if (ms != null && ms.Length > 0)
  {
    context.Response.AddHeader("content-length", ms.Length.ToString());
    // Reset the current position in the MemoryStream
    ms.Position = 0;
    // .NET 4.0 and later method only
    ms.CopyTo(context.Response.OutputStream);
  }
}
```

Listing 5-16: `ProcessRequest()` method code.

This code contains no references to SQL, connection strings, or other database access.

This code will run as is, but we have not yet enabled remote access to the **DataAccess** component. However, at this time, you may want to run and test the web application to ensure that it returns the image as expected, even though we do not yet have a way to split the data access layer from the web application.

Adding remote calling capability

If we want to truly separate the web application from the data access layer, we must have a way to call the methods in the data access class `ItemData` remotely. Windows Communication Foundation (WCF) is one .NET technology that allows inter-process and inter-machine communication. WCF was introduced with .NET Framework Version 3 and has seen upgrades in more recent releases. An older technology for calling remote code is called .NET Remoting. Even though the .NET Framework still fully supports remoting, WCF is generally recommended. WCF services are easier to implement because less "plumbing" code is required. A thorough discussion of the concepts of WCF is beyond the scope of this book. However, the lab should be easy to follow with a basic understanding of the "ABCs" of WCF: Address + Binding + Contract = Service, as provided by this MSDN article: HTTP://BRURL.COM/FS6.

To add remote calling capability to our application, we will first create a component that will contain the definition of our WCF service contract. Then, we create a console application to host the data access component as a WCF service. Finally, we will modify the web application to call the data access component running in the console host.

Creating and implementing the service interface

In Solution Explorer, right-click the solution node and select **Add, New Project...**. In the **Add New Project** dialog box, select **Class Library** and name it **ServiceInterfaces**. Add a reference to the **System.ServiceModel** assembly and **DataAccess** project to the new project. Remove the default `Class1.cs` file and add a new interface (right-click the project, select **Add | New Item... | Interface**) with the name `IItemData`. At the top of the code file, import the `System.IO` and `System.ServiceModel` namespaces. The definition of the `IItemData` interface is shown in Listing 5-17.

```
[ServiceContract()]
Public interface IItemData
{
   [OperationContract()]
   MemoryStream GetItemImage(string itemID);
}
```

Listing 5-17: `IItemData` interface definition.

We now need to modify the `DataAccess.ItemData` class to implement this new interface. First, add a reference to the new **ServiceInterfaces** project in the **DataAccess** project. Then, modify the definition of the `ItemData` class as shown in Listing 5-18. No change is required, other than to write the interface name, because the `ItemData` class already implicitly has a `GetItemImage()` method with the correct signature.

```
Public class ItemData : ServiceInterfaces.IItemData
{
   /* Other code ommitted for brevity */
}
```

Listing 5-18: `ItemData` class implements `IItemData` interface.

Creating the WCF service host

For this basic lab, we will self-host a WCF service in a console application. In a real-world scenario, you might consider creating a Windows Service or hosting the WCF service under IIS.

Chapter 5: FILESTREAM with ASP.NET and Silverlight

Create another new project using the **Console Application** template. Name this project **ConsoleHost**. Add a reference to the **ServiceInterfaces** and **DataAccess** project and also to the **System.ServiceModel** assembly.

At the top of the `Program.cs` code file, import the namespaces `System.ServiceModel`, `System.ServiceModel.Description`, `DataAccess` and `ServiceInterfaces`. Create the following code in the `Main()` method (Listing 5-19).

```
Uri a = new Uri("net.tcp://localhost:4133/itemData");

using (ServiceHost svchost = new ServiceHost(typeof(ItemData), a))
{
  ServiceEndpoint sep = svchost.AddServiceEndpoint(typeof(IItemData),
    new NetTcpBinding(), "");

  svchost.Open();

  Console.WriteLine("The following EndpointListeners are active:\n");

  foreach (ServiceEndpoint l in svchost.Description.Endpoints)
    Console.WriteLine(l.Address);

  Console.Write("\nListening for requests. Press any key to stop...");
  Console.ReadKey();

  svchost.Close();
}
```

Listing 5-19: Creating a WCF service hosted in a console application.

Depending on your system configuration, you may need to select a TCP port different than 4133 if that port is already in use on your system (Port 4133 was arbitrarily selected for this example). We are using the TCP transport here, because we need to transport a `MemoryStream` object, which is not serializable. We are implementing the ABCs of WCF in these lines of code: after creating a `ServiceHost` instance (S) at our base URI (A), we are creating the TCP-based endpoint (B) that uses the `IItemData` interface as the contract (C). We can then open the communication channel and wait for clients to call.

Because our data access component is now effectively hosted in this console application, we need to provide the database connection string in the application's `App.config` file. Add a new application configuration file named `App.config` and add the connection string information like in Listing 5-3.

Modifying the web application to call the WCF service

We are now ready to modify the web application. If we did not have control over the service, we might choose to create a Service Reference with a proxy class. This requires a few extra configuration steps on the service side. Because we do have control over the service, we will share the `IItemData` interface between the service and the client by adding a reference to the **ServiceInterfaces** project in the web application. We must also add a reference to the **System.ServiceModel** assembly, but we can remove the reference to the **DataAccess** project.

In the `GetItemImage.ashx` handler, we need to modify the code so that we no longer create an instance of the `ItemData` class directly, but rather call a remote instance using WCF. Listing 5-20 shows the new code for the `ProcessRequest()` method. The changed lines of code are in bold format and underlined. Also add a namespace import for `System.ServiceModel` at the top of the code file.

```
public void ProcessRequest(HttpContext context)
{
   context.Response.ContentType = System.Net.Mime.MediaTypeNames.Image.Jpeg;
   context.Response.BufferOutput = false;

   EndpointAddress a = new EndpointAddress("net.tcp://localhost:4133/itemData");

   ServiceInterfaces.IItemData data =
      ChannelFactory<ServiceInterfaces.IItemData>.CreateChannel(
      new NetTcpBinding(), a);

   MemoryStream ms = data.GetItemImage(context.Request.QueryString["itemID"]);
```

```
    if (ms != null && ms.Length > 0)
    {
      context.Response.AddHeader("content-length",
          ms.Length.ToString());
      // Reset the current position in the MemoryStream
      ms.Position = 0;
      // .NET 4.0 and later method only
      ms.CopyTo(context.Response.OutputStream);
    }
  }
}
```

Listing 5-20: Updated `ProcessRequest()` method using a WCF call to obtain the `FILESTREAM` data.

Because the interface definition of `IItemData` matches that of the `ItemData` class we used to call, there is no difference in the code beyond the creation of the channel. In essence, we have replaced the call to the constructor of the `ItemData` class with a WCF call over TCP.

Be sure to make the URI of the `EndpointAddress` in this code match up with the URI created in the console application. If you will be running this code actually across different machines, replace `localhost` with the name or IP address of the computer running the WCF service. To avoid hard-coding the name or IP address of the server, the WCF client configuration can also be created in the `web.config` file, but that is not demonstrated here.

Testing the application from Visual Studio

To test this code from Visual Studio, first right-click the **ConsoleHost** project and select **Debug**, **Start new instance**. This will start the console application and, with it, the WCF service. Next, right-click the web application and start a new instance of it, also in debug mode.

If everything is set up correctly, the web application will make a remote call to the WCF service to obtain the `MemoryStream` containing the image. Other than a possible slight delay, the application is functionally the same as Lab 6. Architecturally, however, the application looks very different because the web application displaying the image no longer relies on knowledge of the data store.

If you have access to two computers (perhaps using virtualization), deploy the WCF console host application to the computer running your `NorthPole` database instance and deploy the web application to the other computer. Be sure to open up the port number specified in the host's configuration file in the computer's firewall software.

Lab 9: Playing a Video Stored in a FILESTREAM Database on a Silverlight Application

In this lab we will create a Silverlight application that will play a video stored in a `FILESTREAM` database.

To do this, we will:

- create a new table in the `NorthPole` database and load a video
- create a Silverlight application
- create the video handler
- add a `MediaElement` and configure it
- run and test the application.

Setting up the data

First, we'll set up the table and data required for this lab. Create a table in the `NorthPole` database to store the video files using the T-SQL code shown in Listing 5-21.

```
CREATE TABLE Videos(
    VideoID UNIQUEIDENTIFIER ROWGUIDCOL NOT NULL UNIQUE,
    VideoName VARCHAR(100),
    VideoData VARBINARY(MAX) FILESTREAM
)
```

Listing 5-21: Creating a table to hold the video data.

Now, we'll add some videos to the table. For this demo, I will use the sample video file that comes with the Windows 7 operating system. Listing 5-22 loads a video file into the table we just created. Make sure that you change the location of the file to point to a `.wmv` file that exists on the local computer.

```
-- Insert the data into the table
INSERT INTO Videos (VideoID, VideoName, VideoData)
SELECT NEWID(), 'Windows7 Sample Video', CAST(bulkcolumn
                                             AS VARBINARY(MAX))
FROM OPENROWSET(
    BULK
    'C:\Users\Public\Videos\Sample Videos\Wildlife.wmv',
    SINGLE_BLOB ) AS x
```

Listing 5-22: Loading a video into the table.

Next, create a stored procedure that returns the logical path name of the `FILESTREAM` column, along with the `FILESTREAM` transaction context (Listing 5-23).

Chapter 5: FILESTREAM with ASP.NET and Silverlight

```
CREATE PROCEDURE GetVideoInfo(
    @videoid UNIQUEIDENTIFIER
)
AS
BEGIN
    SELECT
        VideoData.PathName() AS filePath,
        GET_FILESTREAM_TRANSACTION_CONTEXT() AS txContext
    FROM Videos
    WHERE VideoID = @videoid
END
```

Listing 5-23: Creating a stored procedure to return the logical path and FILESTREAM transaction context.

This procedure accepts a `VideoID` and returns the `FILESTREAM` information from the associated record.

Creating a Silverlight application

The next step is to create a Silverlight application. In Visual Studio, open the new project page by selecting **File | New | Project** (Figure 5-34).

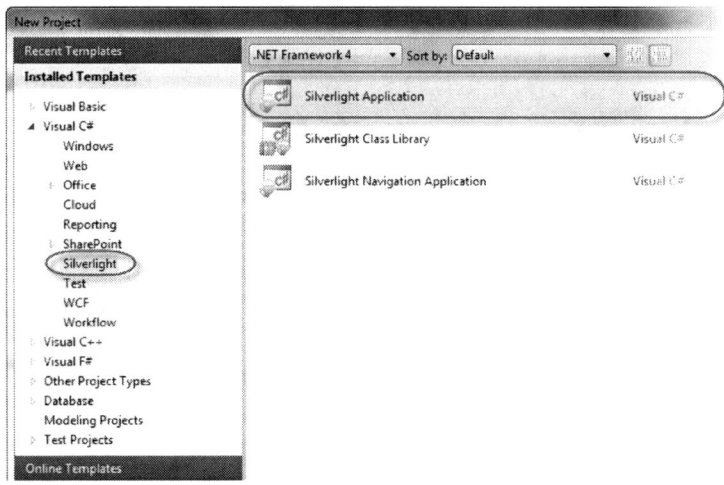

Figure 5-34: Creating a Silverlight application.

Select **Silverlight Application** from the project templates and click **OK** to create a new Silverlight application project. Visual Studio prompts us to select the project type and Silverlight version (Figure 5-35).

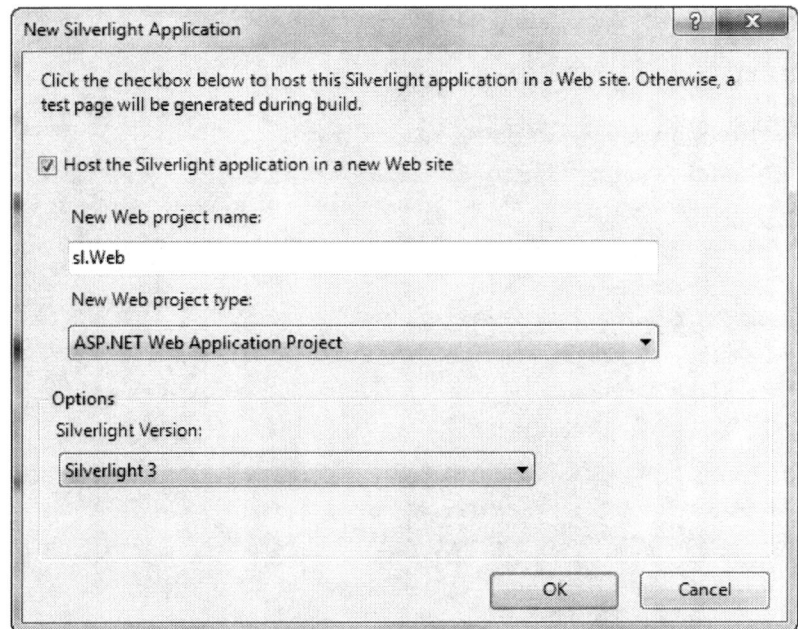

Figure 5-35: Selecting the Web project type and Silverlight Version.

Creating a video handler

The next step is to create a handler that can read the FILESTREAM data from the database and server the client requests. As before, we'll use an ASPX page for simplicity, even though in the real world you would probably create an ASP.NET handler as a code item and register it in `web.config`.

To create the video handler, right-click on the project in the Solution Explorer and select **Add New Item**. Select **ASP.NET Web Form** and name it `getvideo.aspx`. The code that

Chapter 5: FILESTREAM with ASP.NET and Silverlight

you need to add into the web form is very much the same as we have seen in the previous lab, when we created a handler for the images:

- change the name of the query string parameters and local variable
- change the name of the stored procedure
- change the content type returned by the handler.

Listing 5-24 shows the code with the changes in bold and underlined.

```
protected void Page_Load(object sender, EventArgs e)
{
    string VideoID;
    VideoID = Request.QueryString["VideoID"].ToString();

    //Create and open a database connection
    SqlConnection cn = new SqlConnection();
    cn.ConnectionString =
            System.Configuration.ConfigurationManager.ConnectionStrings[
                                            "NorthPoleDB"].ToString();
    cn.Open();

    //Create a Command object
    SqlCommand cmd = new SqlCommand();
    cmd.CommandText = "GetVideoInfo";
    cmd.Connection = cn;
    cmd.CommandType = CommandType.StoredProcedure;
    cmd.Parameters.AddWithValue("@videoid", VideoID);

    //Begin a transaction
    SqlTransaction trn = cn.BeginTransaction("VideoTran");
    cmd.Transaction = trn;

    string filePath = string.Empty;
    byte[] txContext = null;

    try
    {
        //Execute the command
        SqlDataReader reader = cmd.ExecuteReader();
        if (reader.Read())
```

Chapter 5: FILESTREAM with ASP.NET and Silverlight

```csharp
        {
            txContext = (reader["txContext"] as byte[]);
            filePath = reader["filePath"].ToString();
        }
        reader.Close();

        //Open the FILESTREAM data file for reading
        SqlFileStream fs = new SqlFileStream(filePath, txContext,
                                             FileAccess.Read);

        //Start transferring data into filestream data file
        Response.BufferOutput = false;
        Response.ContentType = "video/x-ms-wmv";
        BinaryWriter bw = new BinaryWriter(Response.OutputStream);

        const int bufferSize = 4096;
        byte[] buffer = new byte[bufferSize];
        int byteCount = fs.Read(buffer, 0, bufferSize);

        while ( byteCount == bufferSize )
        {
            bw.Write(buffer, 0, bytes);
            byteCount = fs.Read(buffer, 0, bufferSize);
        }

        //Close the files
        Response.End();
        bw.Close();
        fs.Close();
    }
    catch(Exception ex)
    {
        //Do some error handling
    }
    finally
    {
        // Commit the transaction and close connection
        cmd.Transaction.Commit();
        cn.Close();
    }
}
```

Listing 5-24: Code that serves video files stored in a FILESTREAM database.

Chapter 5: FILESTREAM with ASP.NET and Silverlight

Make sure that you add a connection string named `NorthPoleDB` to the `web.config` (Listing 5-25).

```
<add
    name="NorthPoleDB"
    connectionString="Data Source=(local);
                Initial Catalog=NorthPole; Integrated Security=SSPI"
    providerName="System.Data.SqlClient" />
```

Listing 5-25:   Adding a connection string.

Adding and configuring MediaElement

Next, we will add a `MediaElement` to the Silverlight application. The `MediaElement` component will be responsible for playing the video data that our handler will serve to the Silverlight application. Open `MainPage.xaml` in the designer window and drag a `MediaElement` object into it. Resize it so that it will look like in Figure 5-36.

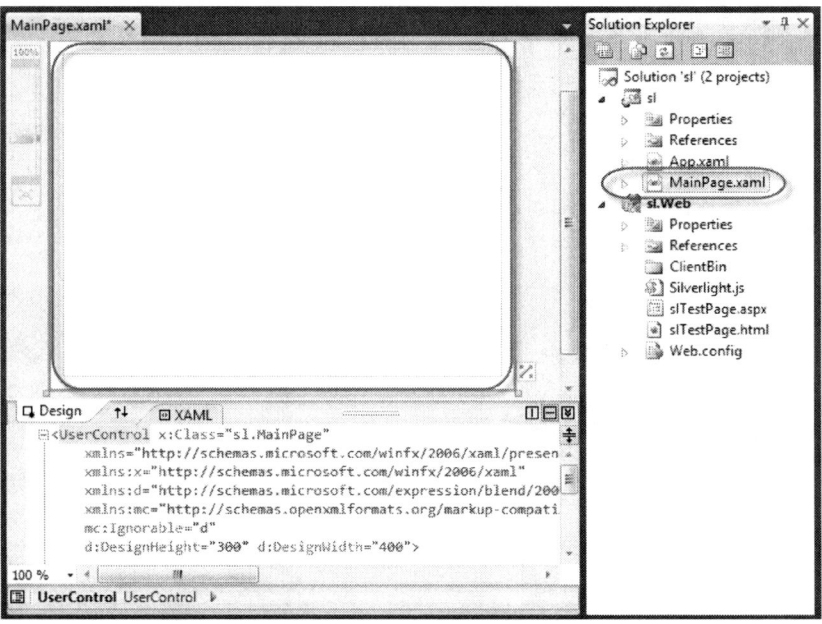

Figure 5-36:   Adding a `MediaElement` object.

The next step is to set the source of the MediaElement to the video handler we created in the previous step. Open the property page of the MediaElement, set the **AutoPlay** property to **True** and configure the **Source** property as demonstrated in Figure 5.37.

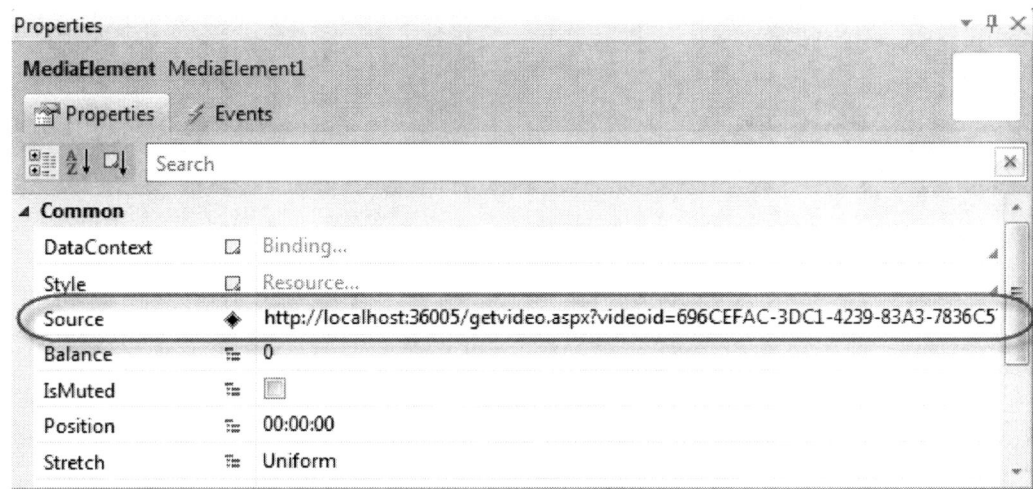

Figure 5-37: Setting the Source property of the MediaElement.

In this lab we are using a static URL as the source of the video, which can play only one video configured at design time. We can easily change it to dynamic value by programmatically setting the Source property at run time. Note also that the URL will need changes after deploying the application on a web server.

Let's take a look at the structure of the URL specified in the **Source** property. To build this URL, we need to know the port on which Visual Studio runs the built-in web server (HTTP://LOCALHOST:36005) and the GUID value stored in the **VideoID** column of the row that contains the video to be played (videoid=696CEFAC-3DC1-4239-83A3-7836C5).

By default, Visual Studio runs a web application using a built-in web server when you run a project from the IDE. The default configuration identifies a dynamic port and binds the web server to it. We can configure the web application project to use a specific port from the **Web** tab of the project properties page (Figure 5-38).

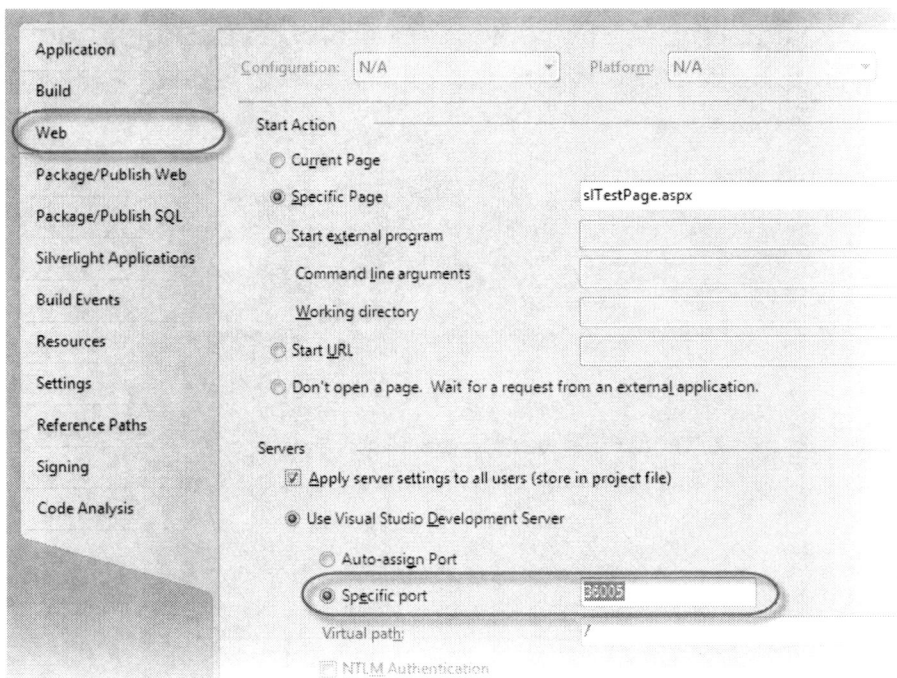

Figure 5-38: Configuring a web project to run on a specific port when executing from Visual Studio IDE.

Running and testing the application

The final step is to run and test the Silverlight application. Build the project and run the application. This will open the Silverlight application test page (which is part of the project) in the default browser and load the application. The media element we added will invoke the video handler, which will stream video data to the `MediaElement`. This, in turn, will play it on the browser (Figure 5-39).

Chapter 5: FILESTREAM with ASP.NET and Silverlight

Figure 5-39: Running the application.

Summary

ASP.NET and Silverlight are two of the most popular web application development platforms available for .NET programmers today. The labs presented in this chapter were created with the intention of helping the ASP.NET and Silverlight developer community to get started with developing web applications that deal with FILESTREAM data.

In Lab 4, we created an ASP.NET web page which demonstrated how to create web applications that allow the user to upload files into a FILESTREAM database. In Lab 5, we saw that web applications that deal with FILESTREAM storage might break when deployed on the web server (IIS). Applications that deal with FILESTREAM should use Windows authentication when connecting to SQL Server. In most cases, the user account under which the application is configured on IIS may not have access to the SQL Server database, and causes an application failure. We saw how to fix this in Lab 5.

Chapter 5: FILESTREAM with ASP.NET and Silverlight

Lab 6 demonstrated how to serve images stored in a `FILESTREAM` database to the web clients. For simplicity, we created an ASP.NET web form to do this. However, a more appropriate way would be by using an ASP.NET handler, and the `FILESTREAM`-related code that we wrote in the handler web form can be added to a generic handler with no additional changes. Lab 7 used the web handler to display image files. Lab 8 then took the next step and separated the implementation of the data store from the client. We also used an actual ASP.NET handler in that lab.

In Lab 9, we saw how to create a Silverlight application that plays video files stored in a `FILESTREAM`-enabled SQL Server database. We created another handler web page for serving the video files stored in the database. A `MediaElement` component added to the Silverlight application invoked the video handler which streamed the video data to the client web page.

Chapter 6: FILESTREAM with SSIS and SSRS

This chapter will demonstrate how to access `FILESTREAM` data from SQL Server Business Intelligence (BI) projects, namely with SQL Server Integration Services (SSIS) and SQL Server Reporting Services (SSRS). We will complete the labs below.

- **Lab 10**: Loading BLOB values into a `FILESTREAM` column using SSIS.
- **Lab 11**: Exporting BLOB values from a `FILESTREAM` column using SSIS.
- **Lab 12**: Building a product catalog in SSRS that displays images stored in a `FILESTREAM` column.

The focus of the labs is to demonstrate how to access `FILESTREAM` data from SSIS and SSRS. In SSIS, we will use a Script task rather than a Data Flow task to transfer `FILESTREAM` data. That way we can use the streaming APIs and increase performance. In SSRS, there are no special accommodations that can be made to use streaming access to the `FILESTREAM` data.

These labs do not even attempt to cover the core SSIS and SSRS features. For example, in the case of SSIS, features like configurations and parameters are not used. In the case of SSRS, no time is spent on designing a proper layout for the report. The goal of these labs is simply to provide you with basic examples that you can enhance further to fit into your specific application needs.

FILESTREAM and SSIS

SSIS is a popular choice for moving data in and out of SQL Server. While it is quite easy to create SSIS packages that import and export SQL Server data, it is a little tricky to handle scenarios in which `FILESTREAM` values are involved. This is because, if we choose the current "standard" connection type for SSIS applications (the OLEDB connection), then we are forced to access the `FILESTREAM` data using T-SQL which, as discussed, is not ideal for performance reasons. Instead, in our labs, we'll use the ADO.NET connection in our SSIS packages, allowing us to import and export `FILESTREAM` data using the streaming APIs.

Lab 10: Loading BLOB Values into a FILESTREAM Column Using SSIS

In this example, "North Pole Corporation" has a product catalog application that is used to print occasional product catalogs. The catalog application has a very simple database with only one table (`Items`), which stores product information. This table is synchronized with the `Products` table in their main inventory management application using a nightly batch process.

The nightly batch process updates the `Items` table with the most recent information about the products that are currently available in the warehouse. It also copies the images of items into a file system folder and stores the path to the image files in the `Items` table. The catalog application uses the information in the `Items` table and the images stored in the file system to build the catalogs.

Listing 6-1 shows what the data in the `Items` table looks like. (To keep the example simple, I have omitted other columns such as SKU, Case Code, Price, and so on.)

Chapter 6: FILESTREAM with SSIS and SSRS

```
ItemID  ItemCode    ItemName         ImageFileName
------  ----------  ---------------  ---------------------
1       1001        Microsoft Mouse  C:\Images\IMG_5383.jpg
2       3001        Dell Laptop      C:\Images\IMG_5384.jpg
3       4005        Apple iPad       C:\Images\IMG_5385.jpg
4       6009        Amazon Kindle    C:\Images\IMG_5386.jpg
```

Listing 6-1:   The data in the `Items` table.

North Pole Corporation has recently decided to upgrade their catalog application to SQL Server 2008 R2. One of the reasons for the migration is to take advantage of the `FILESTREAM` storage feature introduced in SQL Server 2008. They want to store the images of products in a `FILESTREAM` column for better manageability.

The development team does not want to disturb the existing nightly job that synchronizes product information. They decide to add one more job that runs after the nightly synchronization job. The new job is responsible for loading the images of products into a `FILESTREAM` column in the `Items` table.

To achieve this, they identified the steps below.

- Make appropriate database modifications to support storing `FILESTREAM` data:
  - enable the `FILESTREAM` feature on the SQL Server instance
  - add a `FILESTREAM` filegroup to the product catalog database
  - add a `FILESTREAM` column to the `Items` table
  - create the necessary stored procedures.
- Create an SSIS package that loads the files into the `FILESTREAM` column.

Setting up the sample database

Listing 6-2 rebuilds the sample database for use with this lab.

```
USE master
GO
-- ------------------------------------------------------
-- If the sample database exists, drop it and re-create it
-- ------------------------------------------------------
IF DB_ID('NorthPole') IS NOT NULL
    DROP DATABASE NorthPole
GO

CREATE DATABASE NorthPole ON PRIMARY (
    NAME = NorthPole,
    FILENAME = 'C:\ArtOfFS\Demos\Chapter6\NorthPole.mdf'
) LOG ON (
    NAME = NorthPole_log,
    FILENAME = 'C:\ArtOfFS\Demos\Chapter6\NorthPole_log.ldf')
GO
```

Listing 6-2:   Rebuilding the sample database.

Listing 6-3 creates the **Items** table and populates it with the sample data shown in Listing 6-1. Note that you need to change the file names used in the script to point to image files that exist on your computer. You can download the images used in the example from HTTP://BRURL.COM/FS4. Download the file and extract into the **C:\images** folder.

```
USE NorthPole
GO

CREATE TABLE Items
    (
        ItemID INT IDENTITY ,
        ItemCode VARCHAR(10) ,
        ItemName VARCHAR(50) ,
        ImageFileName VARCHAR(100)
    )
```

Chapter 6: FILESTREAM with SSIS and SSRS

```sql
GO

INSERT  INTO Items
        ( ItemCode ,
          ItemName ,
          ImageFileName
        )
        SELECT  '1001' ,
                'Microsoft Mouse' ,
                'C:\Images\IMG_5383.jpg'
        UNION ALL
        SELECT  '3001' ,
                'Dell Laptop' ,
                'C:\Images\IMG_5384.jpg'
        UNION ALL
        SELECT  '4005' ,
                'Apple iPad' ,
                'C:\Images\IMG_5385.jpg'
        UNION ALL
        SELECT  '6009' ,
                'Amazon Kindle' ,
                'C:\Images\IMG_5386.jpg'

SELECT * FROM Items
/*
ItemID  ItemCode    ItemName          ImageFileName
------  ----------  ----------------  ----------------------
1       1001        Microsoft Mouse   C:\Images\IMG_5383.jpg
2       3001        Dell Laptop       C:\Images\IMG_5384.jpg
3       4005        Apple iPad        C:\Images\IMG_5385.jpg
4       6009        Amazon Kindle     C:\Images\IMG_5386.jpg
*/
```

Listing 6-3: Populating the sample table.

We'll assume at this stage that the team has enabled the FILESTREAM feature on the SQL Server instance where the catalog application database is hosted. For a detailed explanation of how to do this, see Appendix A: *Configuring FILESTREAM on a SQL Server Instance*. Once FILESTREAM has been enabled in the current database, we can add a new FILESTREAM filegroup to the current database (Listing 6-4).

231

Chapter 6: FILESTREAM with SSIS and SSRS

```
ALTER DATABASE NorthPole
ADD FILEGROUP NORTHPOLE_FS
CONTAINS FILESTREAM ;
GO

ALTER DATABASE NorthPole
ADD FILE (
NAME = NorthPoleFS,
FILENAME = 'C:\ArtOfFS\Demos\Chapter6\NorthPole_fs')
TO FILEGROUP NorthPole_fs ;
GO
```

Listing 6-4:   Adding a FILESTREAM filegroup to the database.

As we discussed previously, there are a number of prerequisites for adding a FILESTREAM column to an existing table; for full details on what is involved, refer back to Chapter 2. Otherwise, go ahead and use the script in Listing 6-5 to add the column.

```
USE Northpole
GO

-- Add a UNIQUEIDENTIFIER column
ALTER TABLE Items
ADD ItemGuid UNIQUEIDENTIFIER NOT NULL
DEFAULT (NEWID())

-- Add a UNIQUE constraint
ALTER TABLE Items
ADD CONSTRAINT IX_ItemGuid UNIQUE(ItemGuid)

-- Create ROWGUIDCOL
ALTER TABLE Items
ALTER COLUMN ItemGUID ADD ROWGUIDCOL

-- Add the FILESTREAM column
ALTER TABLE [dbo].[Items]
ADD ItemImage VARBINARY(MAX) FILESTREAM NULL
```

Listing 6-5:   Adding a FILESTREAM column to a table.

When you have added the FILESTREAM column, run a SELECT query on the Items table; you will see results similar to Listing 6-6. (Of course, the ItemGuid and ImageFileName columns might show a different value.)

```
It.. ItemName ImageFileName        ItemGuid             ItemImage
---- -------- -------------------- -------------------- ---------
1001 Micros.. C:\..\IMG_5383.jpg   53C15E09-79CC-4..    NULL
3001 Dell L.. C:\..\IMG_5384.jpg   AFA5D604-68EA-4..    NULL
4005 Apple .. C:\..\IMG_5385.jpg   B6A6EE8D-7ED6-4..    NULL
6009 Amazon.. C:\..\IMG_5386.jpg   6EFF334C-B2C1-4..    NULL
```

Listing 6-6: The Items table with the FILESTREAM column.

What we are planning to do in this lab is to run a loop over all the rows in the Items table to read the content of each image file specified in the ImageFileName column, and then store it in the FILESTREAM column, ItemImage. Listing 6-7 creates the stored procedure that the SSIS package will use to retrieve item information.

```
USE NorthPole
GO

CREATE PROCEDURE [dbo].[GetItems]
AS
    SELECT  ItemID
    FROM    Items ;
```

Listing 6-7: Creating a stored procedure to retrieve the ItemID column of all the rows.

The above stored procedure returns the ItemID of all the rows to be processed. The SSIS package will loop through each row returned by this procedure and execute the FILESTREAM-related code to load the images into the FILESTREAM column of the table.

All FILESTREAM operations should take place within the context of a SQL Server transaction. You might want to do it in one of the two ways illustrated below.

1. Start a SQL Server transaction at the beginning, process all the rows and commit.
2. Start a SQL Server transaction before processing each row and commit when the given row is processed.

We will take Option 2 for this lab because, with this approach, locks are placed on each row only for a minimal period of time. A row will be locked only when the processing starts and the lock will be released as soon as the given row is processed.

To load each image file into the `FILESTREAM` column, we will need the pieces of information below:

- the `FILESTREAM` transaction context
- the `FILESTREAM` logical path (the `PathName()` value)
- the name and location of the image file on the disk (to be loaded into the `FILESTREAM` column).

We'll create another stored procedure that accepts the `ItemID` and returns the above information. Listing 6-8 shows how to create the stored procedure.

```
USE [NorthPole]
GO

CREATE PROCEDURE [dbo].[GetItemInfo] ( @ItemID INT )
AS
-- ---------------------------------------------------------------
-- If the FILESTREAM column is NULL, we cannot retrieve PathName().
-- In such a case, we need to use a dummy value
-- ---------------------------------------------------------------
    UPDATE  dbo.items
    SET     ItemImage = 0x
    WHERE   ItemID = @ItemID
            AND ItemImage IS NULL
```

```
-- ---------------------------------------------------------------
-- SELECT the required information
-- ---------------------------------------------------------------
    SELECT TOP 1
            GET_FILESTREAM_TRANSACTION_CONTEXT() AS FSContext ,
            ItemImage.PathName() AS FSPath ,
            ImageFileName
    FROM    Items
    WHERE   ItemID = @ItemID
```

Listing 6-8: Creating a stored procedure to retrieve information about the item.

Creating the SSIS package

We're now ready to create the SSIS package that loads the files into the `FILESTREAM` column. We'll proceed as shown below.

1. Create an SSIS project.
2. Add an **Execute SQL** task to retrieve all the rows from the `Items` table.
3. Add a **Foreach Loop** container, which will help us to run a loop over all the rows returned by the previous task.
4. Add a **Script** task into the **Foreach Loop** container, in which we will write the .NET code to load the content of the disk file into the `FILESTREAM` column of the table using `FILESTREAM` Managed APIs.

Creating a new SSIS project

Run **SQL Server Business Intelligence Development Studio**, and create a new SSIS project. The **New Project** dialog box is shown in Figure 6-1. Enter a **Name**, **Location**, and **Solution Name**, and click **OK**.

Chapter 6: FILESTREAM with SSIS and SSRS

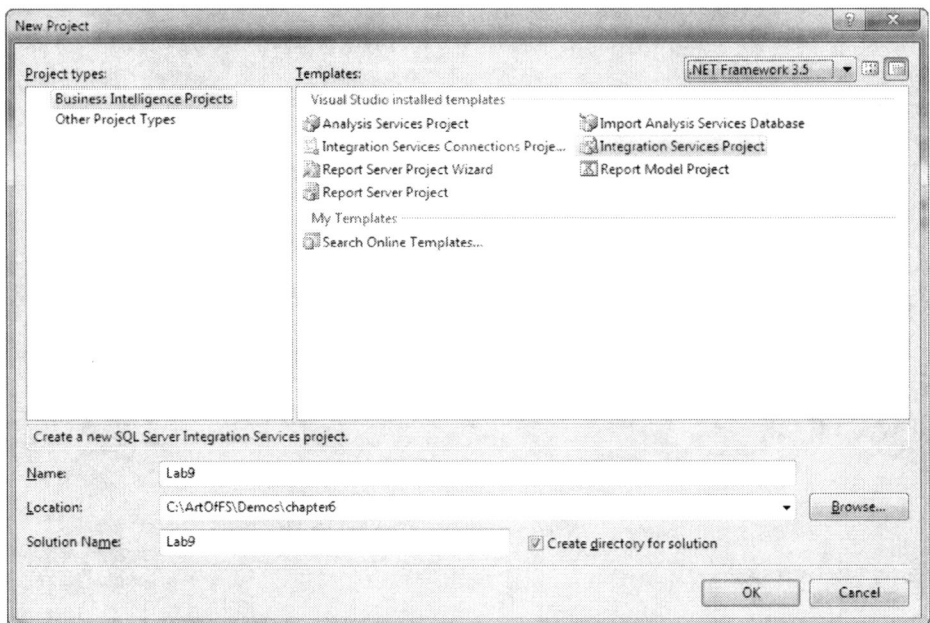

Figure 6-1: Creating a new SSIS project.

When you create a new SSIS project, an empty SSIS package is automatically added to the project. We'll rename the package **FILESTREAM Stream In.dtsx**; right-click on the package name in the **Solution Explorer** and select **Rename** (Figure 6-2).

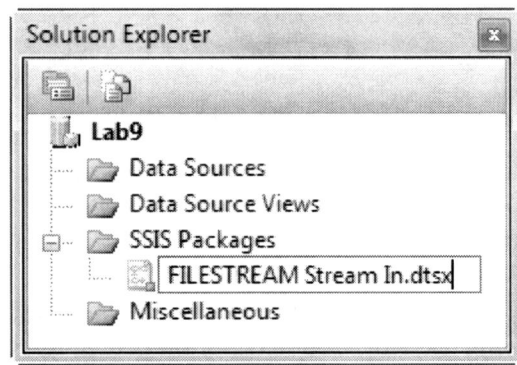

Figure 6-2: Renaming the SSIS package.

When renaming a package file, a message box will verify whether you would like to rename the package object as well. Select **Yes**, and continue.

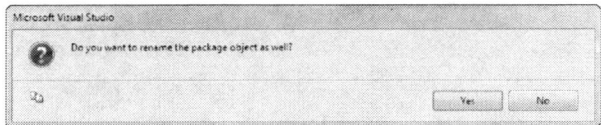

Figure 6-3:   Package object rename prompt.

Creating an ADO.NET connection to the NorthPole database

Next, let's create a connection to the catalog application database. SSIS Connection Manager allows you to create different types of connections. Streaming access to the `FILESTREAM` data should be done within the context of a SQL Server transaction. Therefore, we will choose an ADO.NET connection instead of the usually preferred OLE DB connection type.

Right-click on the **Connection Managers** window at the bottom of the SSIS Designer and select **New ADO.NET Connection**. This opens the **Configure ADO.NET Connection Manager** dialog box, where we can create and configure ADO.NET connections (Figure 6-4).

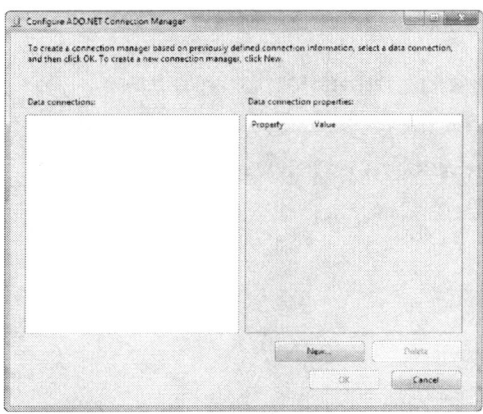

Figure 6-4:   The **Configure ADO.NET Connection Manager**.

Chapter 6: FILESTREAM with SSIS and SSRS

Click the **New** button to create a new connection. This opens the **Connection Manager** dialog box (Figure 6-5). Make sure that the **Provider** selected is **.Net Providers\SqlClient Data Provider**. Then specify the server and database names. Ensure you connect using Windows authentication, because Win32 and Managed API access to the FILESTREAM data is possible only with Windows authentication.

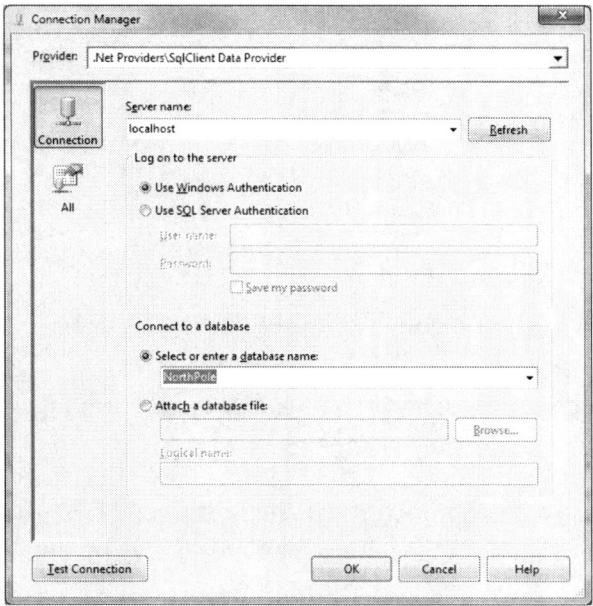

Figure 6-5: The **Connection Manager** dialog box.

You can click **Test Connection** to check that the connection information you have entered is correct. Click **OK** to save the information, and then click **OK** again on the parent dialog box to save the configuration changes and return to Package Designer. You will see a new connection object in the **Connection Managers** window (Figure 6-6).

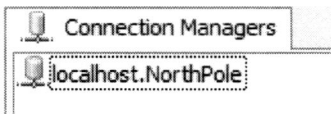

Figure 6-6: The new connection in the **Connection Managers** window.

For the sake of simplicity, we'll rename the connection `NorthPole`, so right-click on the Connection object and select **Rename**, or simply select the object and press F2 (Figure 6-7).

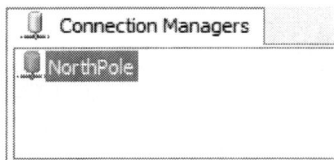

Figure 6-7:   Renaming the connection object.

Adding an Execute SQL task

The next step is to add an **Execute SQL** task. You can find it in the toolbox under **Control Flow Items**; drag and drop it onto the Package Designer window (Figure 6-8).

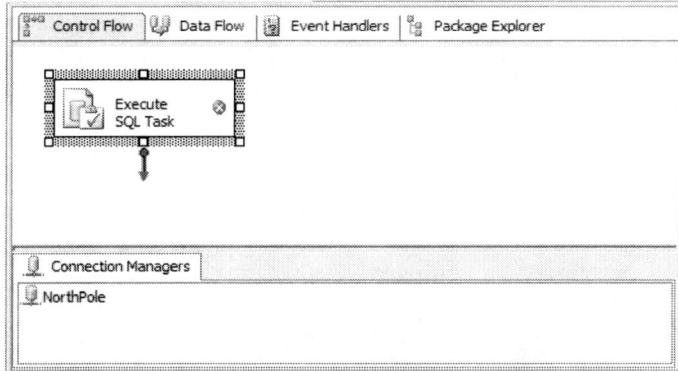

Figure 6-8:   Adding the **Execute SQL** task.

Now we'll configure the **Execute SQL** task to retrieve the item information. First, we'll use the stored procedure to retrieve the `ItemID` from the `Items` table. We only need the `ItemID` column because the information retrieved at this stage is used only for iterating

Chapter 6: FILESTREAM with SSIS and SSRS

over the rows; the **Script** task that we will create later will fetch additional information based on the `ItemID` being processed at each iteration through the loop.

Now, in the Package Designer, double-click on the **Execute SQL** task and configure the following properties on the **General** tab of the Execute SQL Task Editor (Figure 6-9):

- **Name:** Get Item List
- **Description:** Get list of items to be processed
- **Result Set:** Full result set
- **Connection Type:** ADO.NET
- **Connection:** NorthPole
- **SQLSourceType:** Direct input
- **SQL Statement:** GetItems
- **IsQueryStoredProcedure:** True.

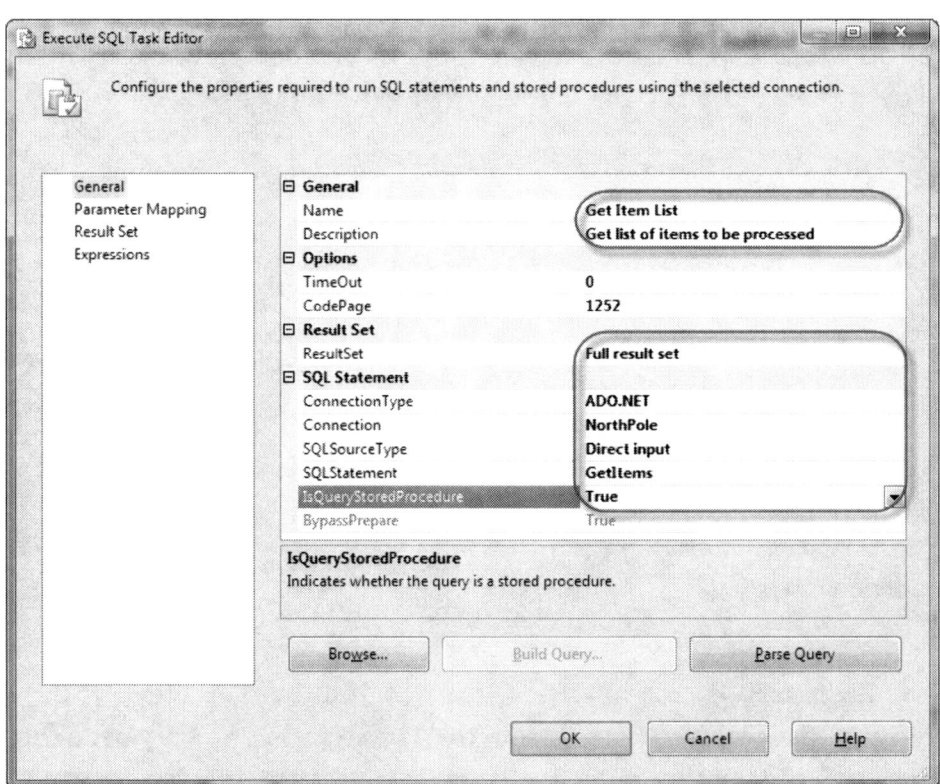

Figure 6-9: Configuring the properties of the **Execute SQL** task.

Chapter 6: FILESTREAM with SSIS and SSRS

We need to store the result set returned by the stored procedure in a local variable, and iterate over it. On the **Result Set** page, click the **Add** button to add a new result set, and then change the **Result Name** to **0** to map it to the first result set returned by the stored procedure (Figure 6-10).

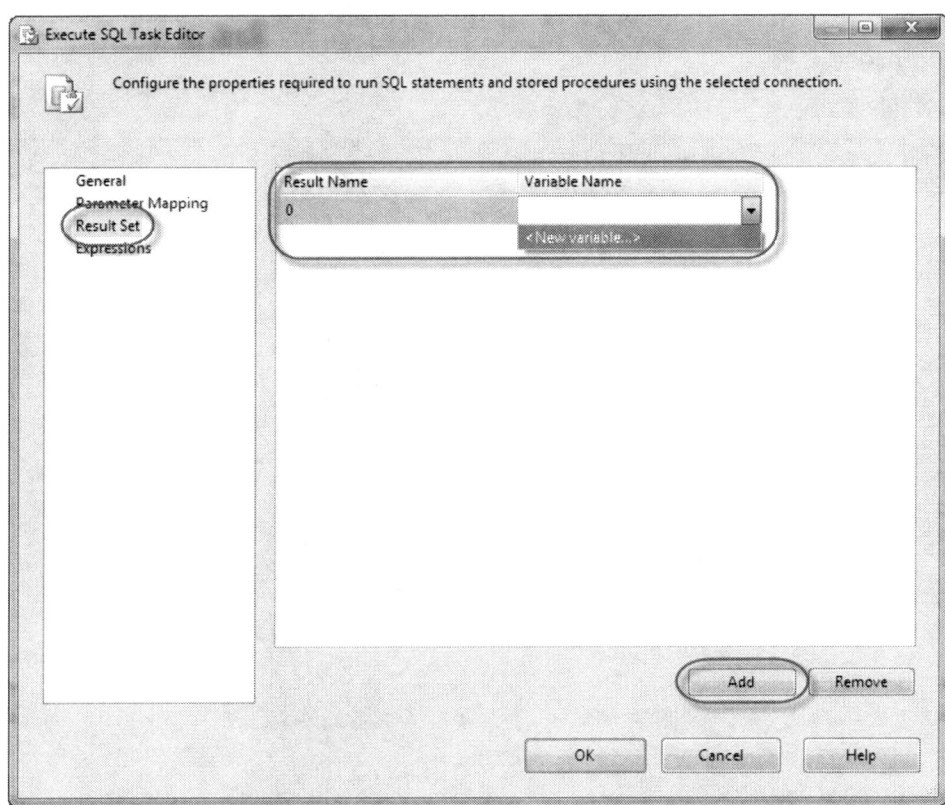

Figure 6-10: Configuring the Result Set.

Chapter 6: FILESTREAM with SSIS and SSRS

From the **Variable Name** drop-down list, select **<New Variable>** to create a new variable to hold the result set returned by the stored procedure. This opens the **Add Variable** dialog box (Figure 6-11).

Change the **Name** to items and **Value type** to Object. The **Foreach Loop** that we will add to the package in the next step will iterate over this variable to process all the rows returned by the stored procedure.

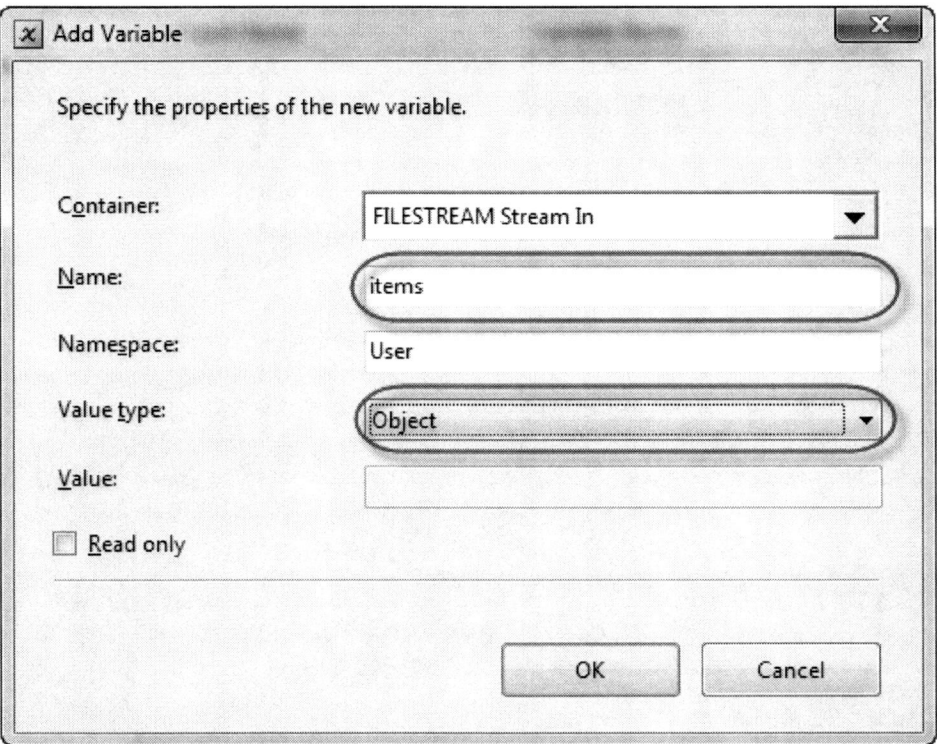

Figure 6-11:   Adding the items variable to the Execute SQL task.

Click **OK** to create the new variable. Make sure **items** is selected under **Variable Name** in the Result Set page (Figure 6-12), and click **OK** to save the configuration.

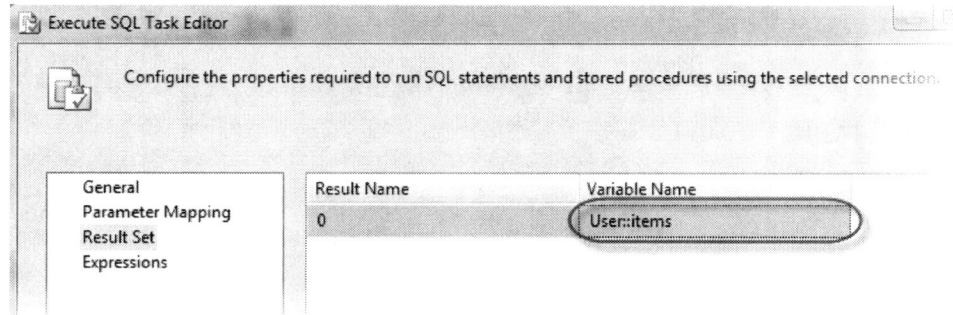

Figure 6-12: Mapping the new variable to the Result Set.

Adding a Foreach Loop container

The next step is to add a **Foreach Loop** container to the package. You can find it in the toolbox under **Control Flow Items**; drag and drop it onto the Package Designer window, then connect it with the Execute SQL task (Figure 6-13).

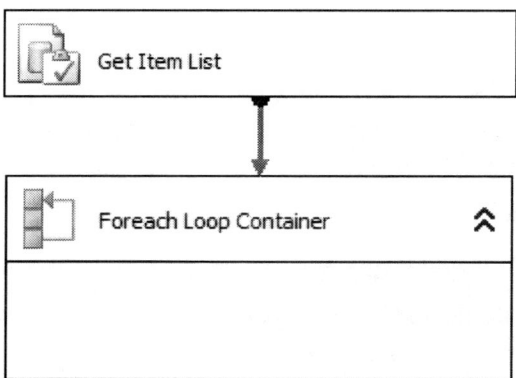

Figure 6-13: Connecting the **Get Item List** and **Foreach Loop Container** objects.

Chapter 6: FILESTREAM with SSIS and SSRS

Double-click the header of the **Foreach Loop** container to open its configuration dialog box (Figure 6-14). Then, in the **Collection** tab, set the following properties:

- **Enumerator**: Foreach ADO Enumerator
- **ADO object source variable**: User::items
- **Enumeration Mode**: Rows in the first table.

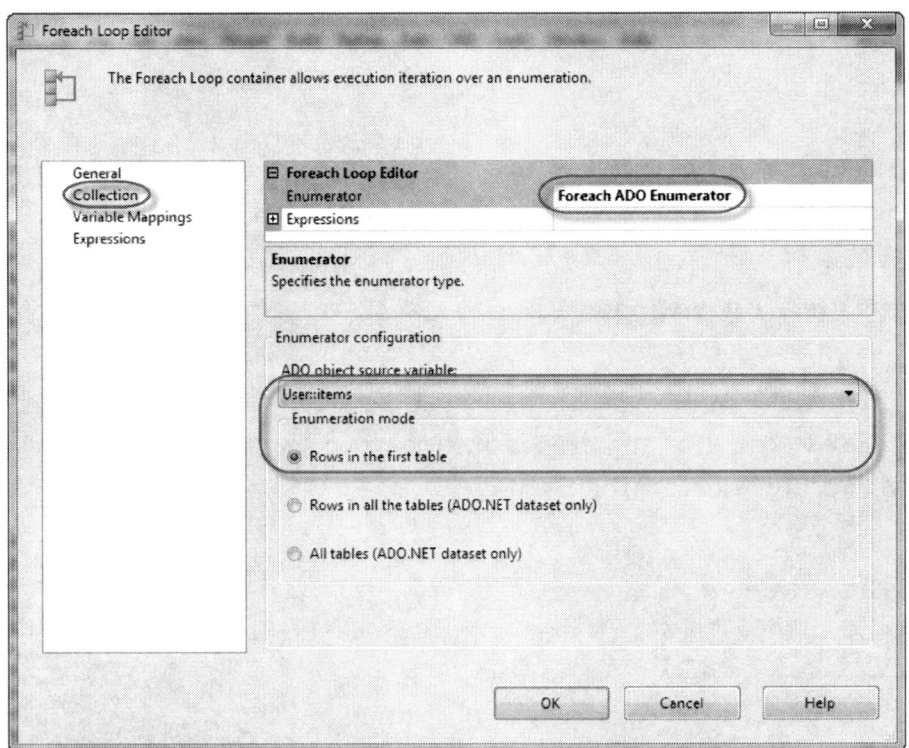

Figure 6-14: Configuring the properties of the **Foreach Loop**.

This configuration asks the enumerator to loop through all the rows in the first table contained in the object variable `User::items`. We have just configured the **Execute SQL** task to assign the result set returned by the stored procedure into this variable, therefore the **Foreach Loop** will iterate over the rows returned by the stored procedure.

Chapter 6: FILESTREAM with SSIS and SSRS

For each iteration of the loop, we will execute the .NET code that loads the image file into the `FILESTREAM` column of the Items table. The code that we execute within the loop needs to know the `ItemID` of the row currently being processed. This can be achieved by creating one more user variable, into which the **Foreach Loop** component can store the `ItemID` value of the current row. You can do this from the **Variable Mappings** tab of the **Foreach Loop Editor** (Figure 6-15).

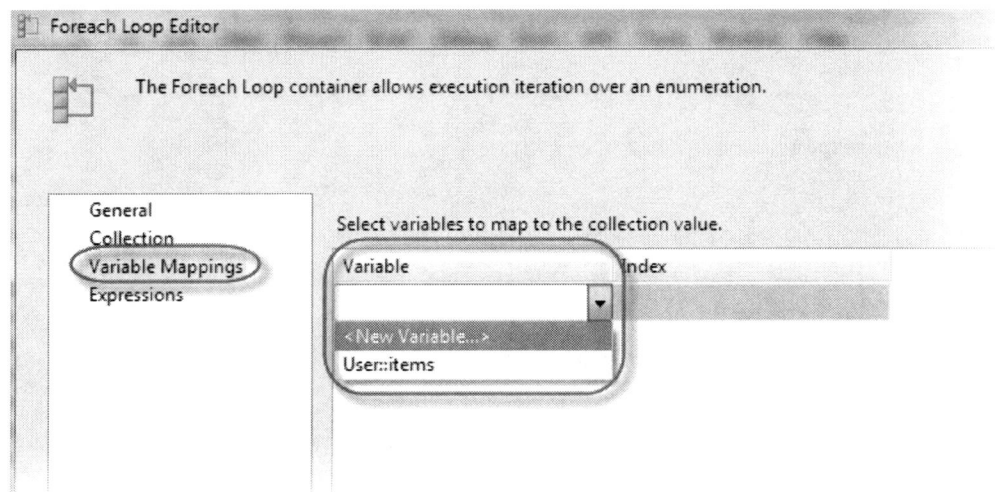

Figure 6-15: Configuring the **Variable Mappings** for the **Foreach Loop**.

From the **Variable** drop-down list, select **<New Variable>** to create a new variable and map it to the result set. This opens the **Add Variable** dialog box again; change the **Name** to `itemID`, the **Value type** to `Int32`, and the **Value** to 0 (Figure 6-16).

Chapter 6: FILESTREAM with SSIS and SSRS

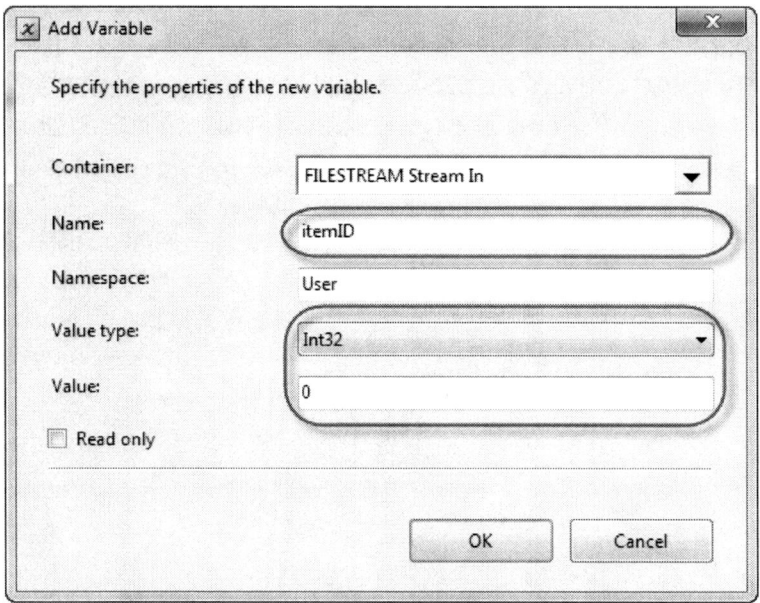

Figure 6-16: Adding the `itemID` variable to the **Foreach Loop**.

Click **OK** to save the changes. Make sure that the newly created variable is selected in the **Variable** column of the **Variable Mappings** page (Figure 6-17), and then click **OK** to save the configuration.

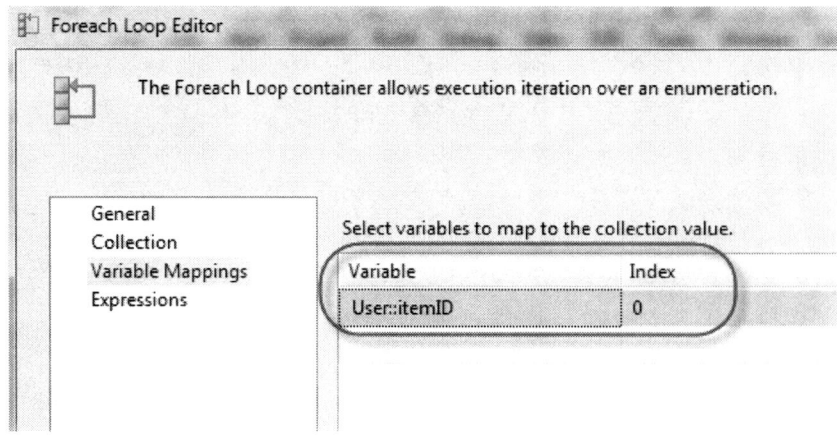

Figure 6-17: Mapping the new `itemID` variable.

Set the **Index** column to **0** to tell the **Foreach Loop** container to store the value from the first column of the result set in the `itemID` variable on each iteration. Click **OK** to save the configuration, and return to the Package Designer.

Adding a Script task to perform FILESTREAM operations

The next step is to add a **Script** task to the package, which we will use to write the .NET code to perform `FILESTREAM` operations using the `FILESTREAM` Managed API. You can find the **Script** task in the toolbox under **Control Flow Items**. Drag and drop it onto the Package Designer window, inside the **Foreach Loop Container** (Figure 6-18).

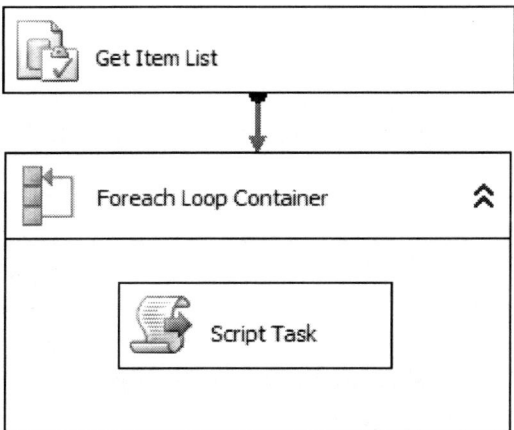

Figure 6-18: Adding the **Script Task** inside the **Foreach Loop Container**.

Next, we will write some .NET code to perform the `FILESTREAM` operations. Depending upon your preference, you can choose C# or VB, but note that this decision must be made before you make any changes to the script task; once the **Script** task has been modified, you cannot change the .NET language associated with it.

Chapter 6: FILESTREAM with SSIS and SSRS

Double-click on the **Script Task** to configure the properties of the script and start writing the FILESTREAM handling code (Figure 6-19).

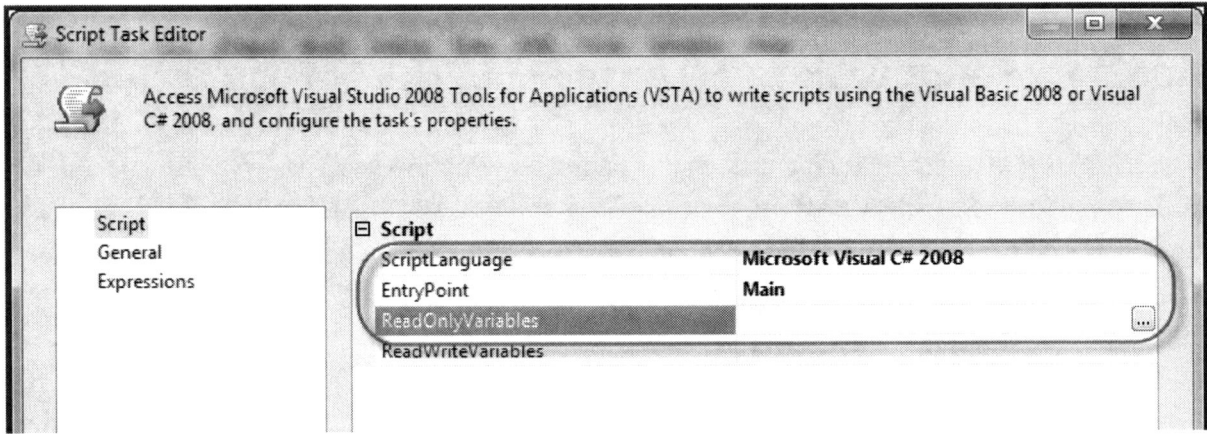

Figure 6-19: Configuring the **Script** task.

This property page allows you select the script language you wish to use. For the purpose of this example, let us go ahead with C#.

Once configured, the **Script** task will be executed at each iteration of the **Foreach Loop**. For each iteration, the **Foreach Loop** stores the value of the ItemID column in the itemID variable. We need to pass the itemID variable to the **Script** task so that we can write the code to process the item specified by the variable.

Click on the button to the right of **ReadOnlyVariables** to open the **Select Variables** dialog box. Then, locate the itemID variable and select it (Figure 6-20).

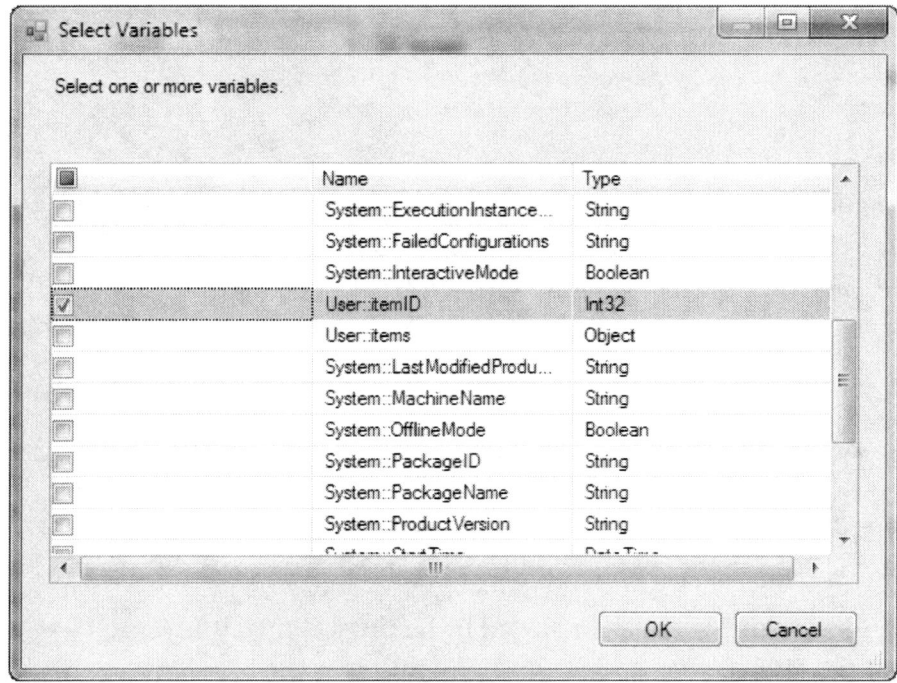

Figure 6-20: Selecting the `itemID` variable.

Click **OK** to save the changes. On the parent dialog box, click the **Edit Script** button. This will open the C# code editor in a new Visual Studio window.

Writing the FILESTREAM processing code

The next step is to write the code needed to perform the `FILESTREAM` operations. This is the most important part of this lab. We will modify the template code given by the Script task to suit our requirements.

To start with, we need to add a few additional namespace declarations to the existing namespace declarations, as shown in Listing 6-9.

Chapter 6: FILESTREAM with SSIS and SSRS

```
using System.Data.SqlClient;
using System.Data.SqlTypes;
using System.IO;
```

Listing 6-9: Additional namespace declarations.

Next, we need to create a connection to the target database. We already created a connection object earlier in this lab. Listing 6-10 demonstrates how to obtain a `SqlConnection` object from the Connection Manager we created using the Package Designer.

```
SqlConnection con;
con = Dts.Connections["NorthPole"].AcquireConnection(null) as SqlConnection;
```

Listing 6-10: Retrieving a `SqlConnection` object from the Connection Manager.

Add the above code (and all the sample codes provided in Listings 6-11 to 6-16) into the **void main()** method the Package Designer auto-generated, at the location where it says:

//TODO: Add your code here

Next, we need to determine the `ItemID` to be processed in the current iteration of the loop. We already created a package variable to which the `ItemID` will be assigned at each iteration of the loop. What we are doing here is assigning the value of the package variable `ItemID` to a local variable `ItemID` in the script for further use.

Listing 6-11 shows how to access the `ItemID` variable from the **Script** task.

```
Int32 ItemID = (int) Dts.Variables["User::itemID"].Value;
```

Listing 6-11: Reading the value of a package variable from the Script task.

Chapter 6: FILESTREAM with SSIS and SSRS

So far, we have obtained a Connection object pointing to the target database, and identified the ID of the item to be processed.

The approach presented in this lab does a round trip to the server at each iteration of the loop. This is to keep the duration of `FILESTREAM` transactions minimal. Remember that all access to the `FILESTREAM` data should be made within the scope of a transaction.

An alternative approach would be to start a transaction at the beginning of the process and fetch the `PathName()` of all the rows with a single database call. In this case, the additional round trips to the server can be avoided. However, this approach will keep a top level transaction open until the process completes, which could block the requests from other connections.

We now need a few local variables to store the `FILESTREAM` transaction context, the logical path name of the `FILESTREAM` data value, and the path to the disk file that we want to load into the `FILESTREAM` column, as shown in Listing 6-12.

```
byte[] FSContext = null;
string FSPathName = string.Empty;
string FileName = string.Empty;
```

Listing 6-12: Setting up the local variables.

Next, we'll start a database transaction and execute the stored procedure (Listing 6-13).

```
SqlCommand cmd = new SqlCommand();
cmd.Connection = con;
cmd.CommandText = "GetItemInfo";
cmd.CommandType = CommandType.StoredProcedure;
cmd.Parameters.AddWithValue("@ItemID", ItemID);
SqlTransaction transaction = con.BeginTransaction("ItemTran");
cmd.Transaction = transaction;
SqlDataReader reader = cmd.ExecuteReader();
```

Listing 6-13: Starting a database transaction and executing the stored procedure.

Chapter 6: FILESTREAM with SSIS and SSRS

The stored procedure will return the three critical pieces of information that we needed. The code in Listing 6-14 reads these values and assigns them to the local variables we created earlier.

```
reader.Read()
FSContext = (reader["FSContext"] as byte[]);
FSPathName = reader["FSPath"].ToString();
FileName = reader["ImageFileName"].ToString();
reader.Close();
```

Listing 6-14: Reading the values returned by the stored procedure.

Listing 6-15 opens the `FILESTREAM` data file for writing, and the image file for reading. It then reads from the disk file and writes into the `FILESTREAM` column.

```
// Open the FILESTREAM data file for writing
SqlFileStream fs = new SqlFileStream(FSPathName, FSContext,
                                    FileAccess.Write);

// Open the disk file for reading
FileStream localFile = new FileStream(FileName,
                                    FileMode.Open, FileAccess.Read);

// Start transfering data from disk file to FILESTREAM data file
BinaryWriter bw = new BinaryWriter(fs);
const int bufferSize = 4096;
byte[] buffer = new byte[bufferSize];
int bytes = localFile.Read(buffer, 0, bufferSize);
while (bytes > 0)
{
    bw.Write(buffer, 0, bytes);
    bw.Flush();
    bytes = localFile.Read(buffer, 0, bufferSize);
}
```

Listing 6-15: Reading from the disk file and writing to the `FILESTREAM` column.

It's now time to close the objects to release the resources and commit the transaction. Before we exit, we also set the **TaskResult** property of the `Dts` object to `Success`, to indicate that the process was successful (Listing 6-16).

```
// Close the files
bw.Close();
localFile.Close();
fs.Close();

// Commit the transaction
cmd.Transaction.Commit();
Dts.TaskResult = (int)ScriptResults.Success;
```

Listing 6-16: Closing the files and committing the transaction.

To keep the code listing simple, we have not included any error-handling code. It is recommended that you wrap your code within a `try-catch` block to handle any possible errors. The above snippet assumes that the code executes successfully and therefore commits the transaction and sets the task result to **Success**. Note that if an error occurs after the transaction is opened, you should explicitly roll back the transaction from your `catch/finally` block. You may also want to set the task status to **Failure** as demonstrated in Listing 6-17 to indicate that the script did not succeed.

```
cmd.Transaction.Rollback();
Dts.TaskResult = (int)ScriptResults.Failure;
```

Listing 6-17: Rolling back the transaction in the event of an error.

The complete listing of the C# source code is available in the download. The code listing for VB is also supplied; if you want to write your code using VB, remember you must change the **ScriptLanguage** in the property page of the Script task *before* the Script task is modified.

Congratulations! We have successfully completed the first SSIS lab. Execute the package and verify that it executes without error and the `FILESTREAM` columns are updated correctly.

The simplest way to verify that the image files are successfully loaded into the `FILESTREAM` column is to run the query in Listing 6-18 and look at the size of the BLOB value stored in each row.

```
SELECT
    ItemCode,
    ImageFileName,
    DATALENGTH(ItemImage) AS FileSize
FROM Items
/*
ItemCode  ImageFileName          FileSize
--------  ---------------------  --------
1001      C:\Images\IMG_5383.jpg 5303
3001      C:\Images\IMG_5384.jpg 5344
4005      C:\Images\IMG_5385.jpg 7489
6009      C:\Images\IMG_5386.jpg 6470
*/
```

Listing 6-18: Verifying that image files are successfully loaded into the `FILESTREAM` column.

You can match the `FileSize` value returned by the query with the size of the disk file to verify that the image files have been successfully loaded into the `FILESTREAM` column.

We will also cross-verify this in the next lab, where we will perform the reverse operation. We will export the BLOB values from the `FILESTREAM` column into a series of disk files.

Debugging the code

If you want to debug your code, you can set break points within the code and the execution will stop there. If your script task has a break point, it will show a red circle in the designer window as shown in Figure 6-21.

Chapter 6: FILESTREAM with SSIS and SSRS

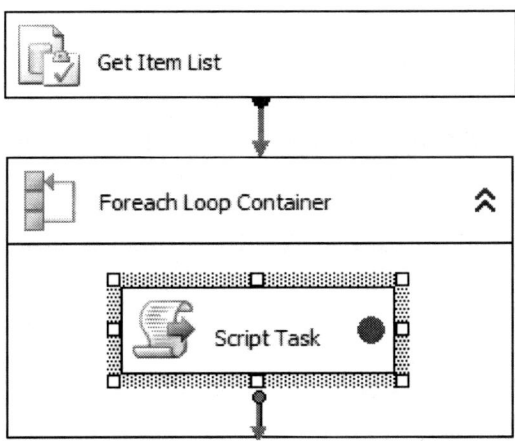

Figure 6-21: A break point in the Script Task.

If you are on a 64-bit computer, you may not be able to debug the package. From the Debugging tab in the properties of the project, you need to change the **Run64BitRuntime** property to **False** (Figure 6-22).

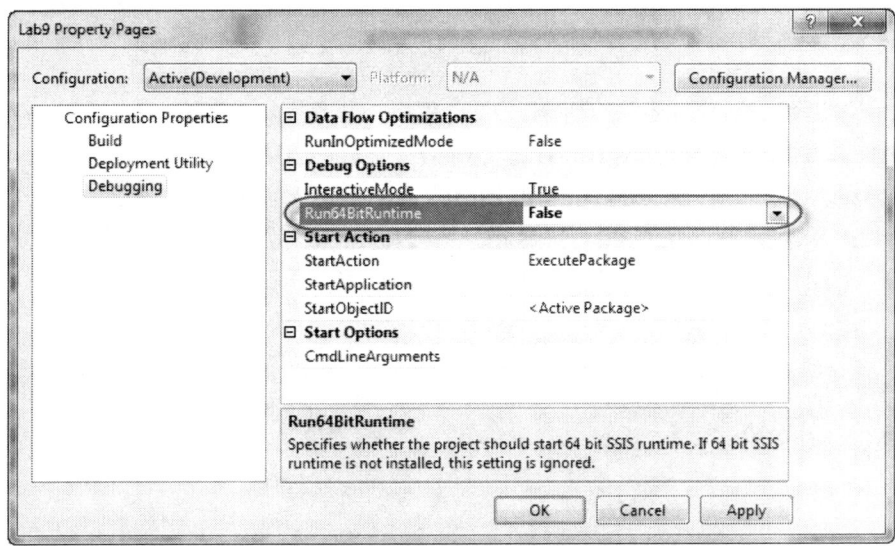

Figure 6-22: Changing the **Debug Options** in the project's properties.

Lab 11: Exporting BLOB Values from a FILESTREAM Column Using SSIS

In the previous lab, we saw how to load the content of disk files into the `FILESTREAM` column of a table using an SSIS package. In this lab, we will do the reverse of this; we will copy the BLOB values from the `FILESTREAM` column to disk files.

Creating the SSIS package

Most of the code for this lab is the same as for the previous lab, so an easy way to start this lab is to make a copy of the SSIS package we created in Lab 10, and modify it.

Make a copy of the **FILESTREAM Stream In.dtsx** package, and then rename it to **FILESTREAM Stream Out.dtsx**.

Setting the output folder

We'll assume that the content of the `FILESTREAM` column needs to be copied to a specific location on the local disk. We'll keep the name of the target location in a variable, instead of hard-coding it in our script. Select the **Variables** option from the **SSIS** menu to create a new variable. In the **Variables** dialog box, click the **New Variable** button to add a new variable to the list of existing variables (Figure 6-23).

Chapter 6: FILESTREAM with SSIS and SSRS

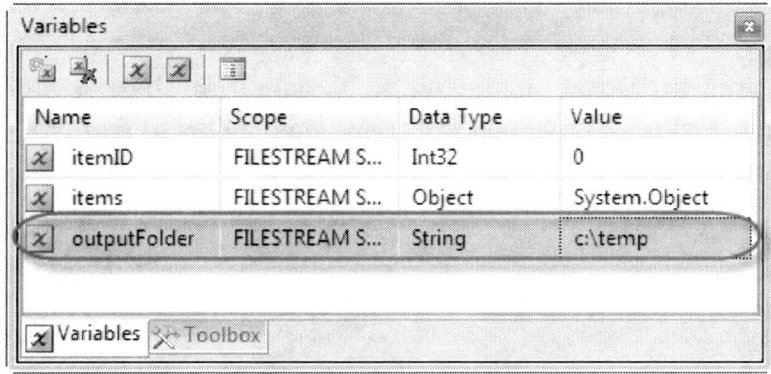

Figure 6-23: Creating a new variable.

When the variable has been added, edit the information as follows:

- **Name**: outputFolder
- **Scope**: FILESTREAM Stream Out
- **Data Type**: String
- **Value**: c:\temp

The Execute SQL task

The **Execute SQL** task does not need any changes. We will use the same stored procedure that we used in Lab 10, which returns a result set containing the ItemID of all the rows to be processed.

The Foreach Loop container

The **Foreach Loop** container does not need any changes either; it will iterate over each row returned by the **Execute SQL** task.

Chapter 6: FILESTREAM with SSIS and SSRS

The Script task

The Script task needs a lot of reworking. Instead of copying BLOB data from the disk file into the `FILESTREAM` column, the version that we need to create now will read from the `FILESTREAM` column and write into disk files.

The new variable that we just added needs to be passed into the script. In the **Script Task Editor**, for **ReadOnlyVariables**, select `outputFolder` (Figure 6-24).

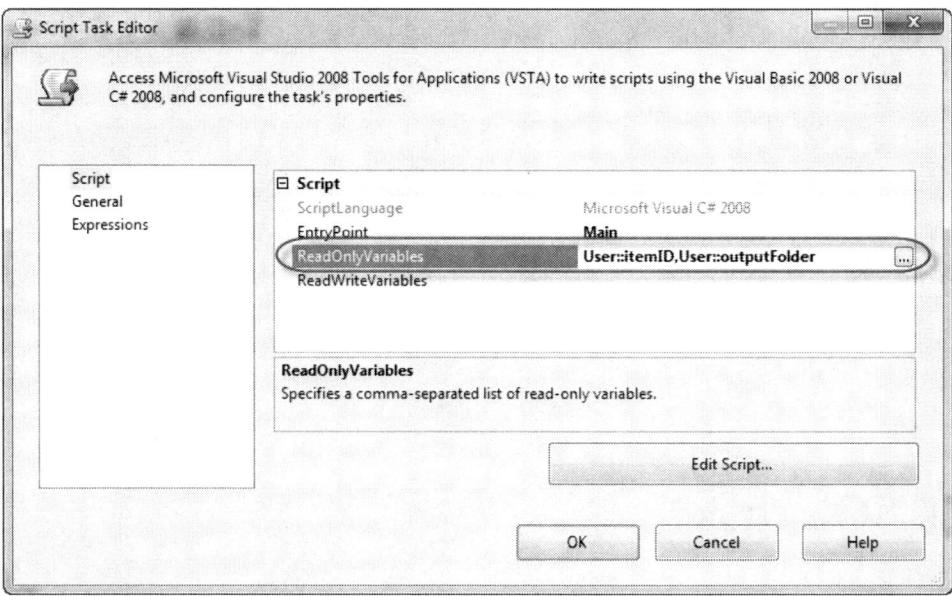

Figure 6-24: Adding a variable to the **Script** task.

The script also needs a number of changes. To start with, we have to retrieve the value of the package variable `outputFolder` and store it into a .NET string data type variable (Listing 6-19).

```
string OutputFolder = Dts.Variables["User::outputFolder"].Value.ToString();
```

Listing 6-19: Retrieving and storing the `outputFolder` variable.

In this lab, the `FILESTREAM` file must be opened for reading, and the disk file needs to be created and opened for writing.

The data stored in the table contains the full path and file name, for example: **c:\filestream\images\abc.jpeg**. We created a package variable earlier to store the location in which the image files need to be created, so we now need to build a new path based on the file path stored in the table and the target folder location stored in the package variable. Listing 6-20 shows how to do this.

```
// Open the FILESTREAM data file for reading
SqlFileStream fs = new SqlFileStream(FSPathName, FSContext,
                                    FileAccess.Read);

// Open the disk file for writing
string OnlyFilename = System.IO.Path.GetFileName(FileName);
FileStream localFile = new FileStream(OutputFolder + OnlyFilename,
                                      FileMode.Create, FileAccess.Write);

// Note that the BinaryWriter should be initialized with the
// localFile object
BinaryWriter bw = new BinaryWriter(localFile);
```

Listing 6-20: Building a path to the target location.

When you have completed the changes, execute the SSIS package and verify that the `FILESTREAM` data is correctly exported to the target location specified in the package.

The complete listings for the C# and VB source code to export BLOB values from a `FILESTREAM` column into disk files in the specified location are available in the download.

Lab 12: Displaying FILESTREAM Data in SSRS Reports

Images stored in the `FILESTREAM` column of a SQL Server database can be displayed using SSRS reports. You can display an image control to render the images on the report.

We have discussed, several times, that accessing `FILESTREAM` data through T-SQL is much less efficient than using the streaming APIs (Win32 or Managed APIs) provided by SQL Server. However, SSRS does not provide a way to access the `FILESTREAM` data using the streaming APIs. All access to the `FILESTREAM` data must go through T-SQL, and the `FILESTREAM` columns must be accessed as though they are `VARBINARY(MAX)` values. So, when creating a report that uses images stored in the `FILESTREAM` column of a SQL Server database, you do nothing that is `FILESTREAM`-specific.

In Labs 9 and 10, we looked at the example of a product catalog application used by North Pole Corporation and we saw how to import and export `FILESTREAM` data using SSIS. Now let's look at another requirement that is part of the product catalog application project: building the catalog.

In this lab, we'll create a SSRS report that will list the items in the catalog application database along with a thumbnail image of the items. The images are stored in the `FILESTREAM` column of the `Items` table. Note that this lab focuses only on the basic report design features required for completing the walk-through; detailed coverage of the SSRS features is beyond the scope of this book.

To complete this lab we will:

- create a new SSRS project
- create a data source to connect to the catalog application database
- create a dataset to retrieve product information
- design the report
- preview the report.

Chapter 6: FILESTREAM with SSIS and SSRS

In a typical report development environment you would go further, and deploy the report, but this and all the other steps in a typical report development cycle remain the same as for a non-`FILESTREAM` column, and therefore they are not discussed in detail in this lab.

Creating an SSRS report project

To create a new SSRS project, start Business Intelligence Development Studio and select **New Project** from the **File** menu (Figure 6-25).

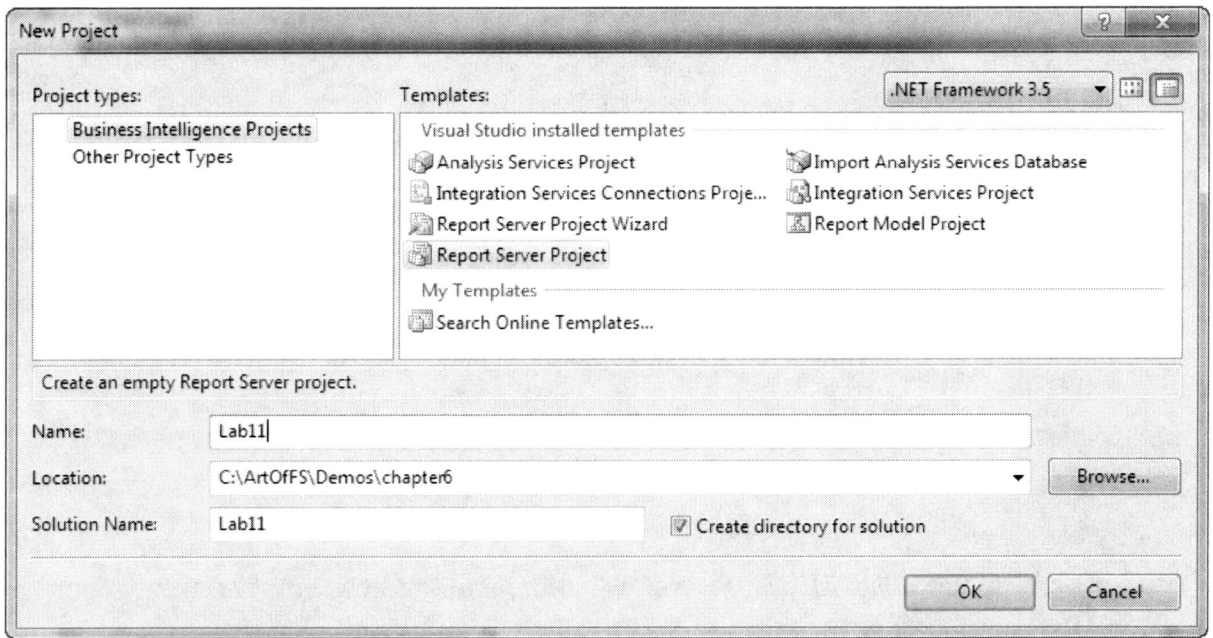

Figure 6-25: Creating a new SSRS project.

From the **Business Intelligence Projects**, select **Report Server Project**. Click **OK** to create an empty solution and project. Once the project has been created, the next step is to add a new report to the project. In the Solution Explorer, right-click on the **Reports** node and select **Add | New Item**. Then, from the **Report Project** templates, select **Report** (Figure 6-26).

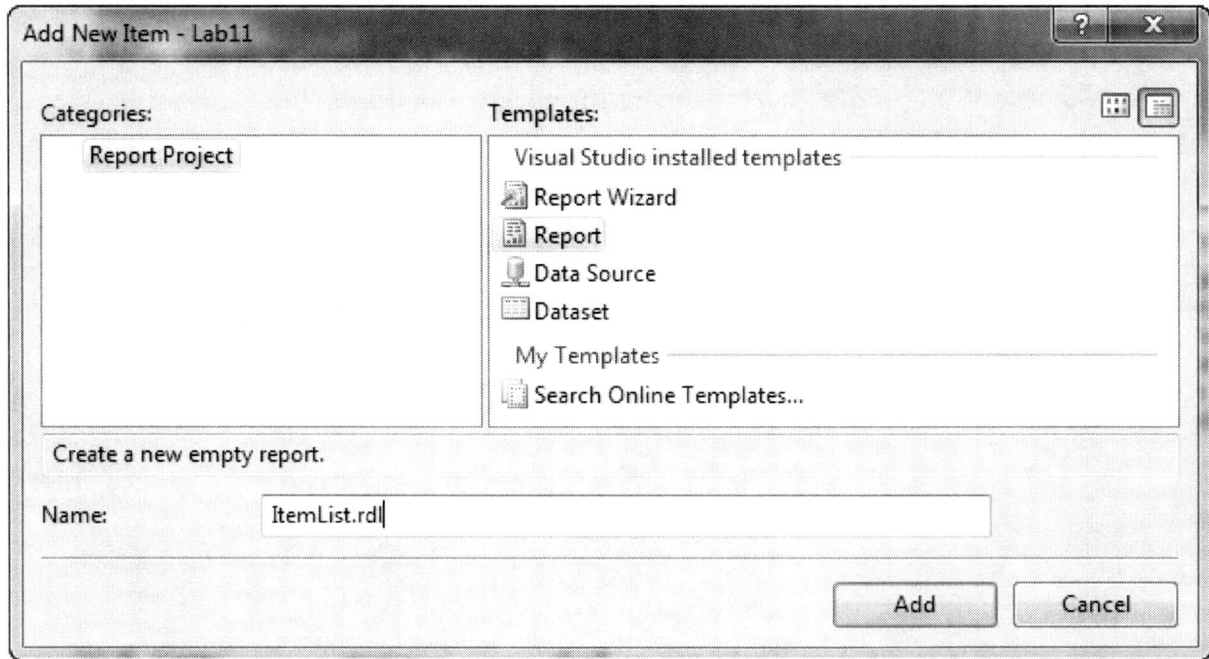

Figure 6-26: Creating a new report.

Name the report **ItemList.rdl**, and then click **Add** to add the new, empty report to our project. We are now ready to get started.

Creating a data source

The next step is to create a data source pointing to the database of the product catalog application. Note that, in most real world reporting service projects, you will create shared data sources and shared datasets so that the object definitions can be reused. However, for this example we will specify an embedded connection.

In the Report Data window, right-click the **Data Sources** node and select **Add Data Source**. When the **Data Source Properties** dialog box opens, either enter the connection string, or click **Edit** to build a connection string (Figure 6-27). Specify the SQL Server instance that hosts the product catalog database. When we created the data source for our SSIS lab, we were very careful to use Windows authentication in order to be able to access the data using the streaming APIs. Since SSRS does not support accessing the FILESTREAM data using Win32 or Managed APIs, we are free to choose between Windows authentication and SQL Server authentication.

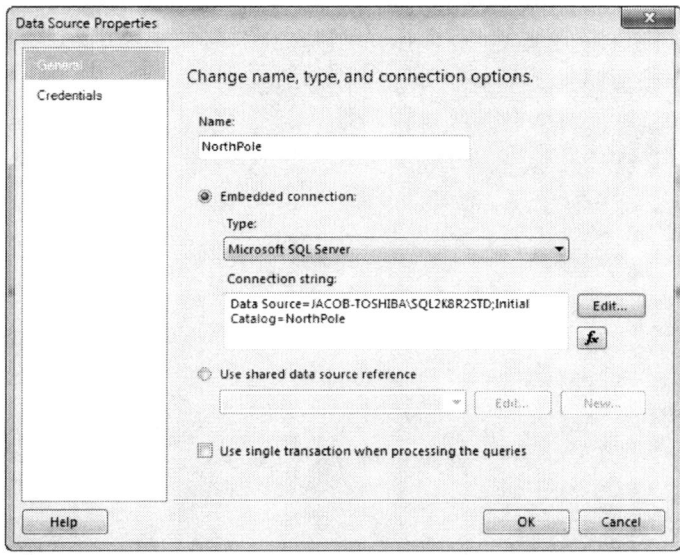

Figure 6-27: Creating the data source.

Click **OK** on the **Data Source Properties** dialog box to save the newly created data source and return to the Report Designer.

Creating a dataset

This is the first step in which we are going to do something that touches the FILESTREAM data: we'll create a dataset that fetches the product information and images from the Items table.

To begin, right-click on the **Datasets** node in the **Report Data** window and select **Add Dataset** in order to open the **Dataset Properties** dialog box (Figure 6-28). We'll configure the dataset as an embedded dataset – fill out the properties as follows:

- **Name**: ProductCatalog
- **Type**: Use a dataset embedded in my report
- **Data source**: NorthPole
- **Query type**: Text
- **Query**: SELECT ItemCode, ItemName, ItemImage FROM items

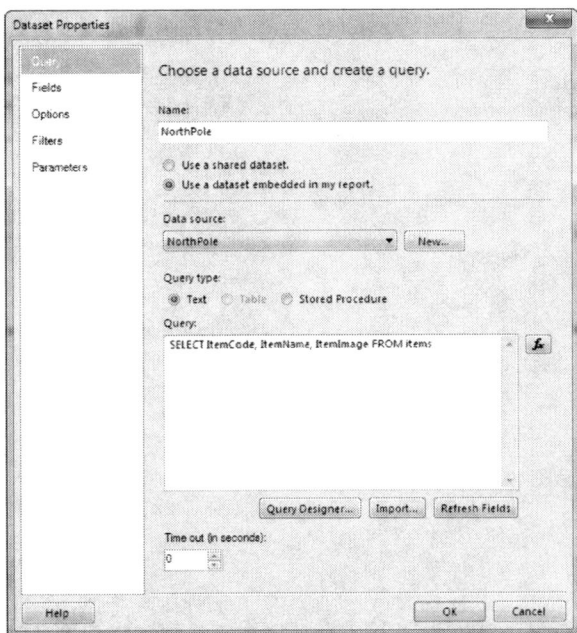

Figure 6-28: Adding a dataset to retrieve the product information.

Click **OK** to save the dataset properties and return to the Report Designer. In the **Report Data** explorer, you will see the new dataset along with the data columns (Figure 6-29).

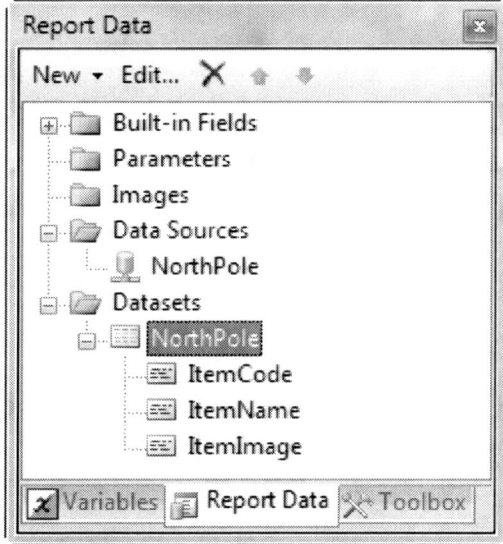

Figure 6-29: The **Report Data** explorer showing the new dataset.

We will use this dataset to build our product catalog.

Designing the report

The next step is to design the report. What we need is a tabular representation of the item information. One way to achieve this is by using a **Table** control. In the **Report Items** toolbox, locate the **Table** control and then drag and drop it into the Report Designer. This adds an empty table to the report.

Now we'll bind the columns to the columns returned by our dataset. Drag and drop the `itemcode` and `itemname` columns from the Report Data explorer into the first and second columns, respectively, of the table control (Figure 6-30).

Chapter 6: FILESTREAM with SSIS and SSRS

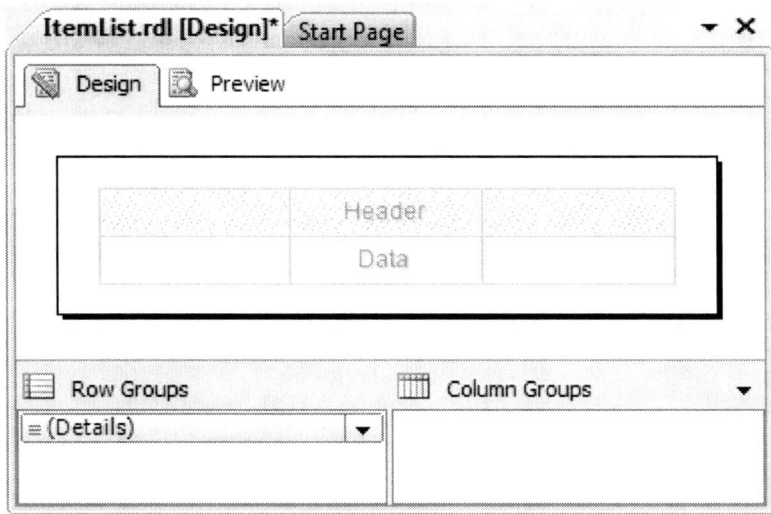

Figure 6-30: Binding the columns returned by the dataset to the Table control.

In the third column, we will display a thumbnail image of the product, so add an `Image` control to the third column: Locate the **Image** control in the toolbox, then drag and drop it into the third column of the **Table** control. When you drop an image control, it opens the **Image Properties** dialog box, shown in Figure 6-31 (if it does not open, right-click on the image control and select **Image Properties**), which needs to be configured as follows:

- **Name**: `ItemImage`
- **Select the image source**: `Database`
- **Use this field**: `ItemImage`
- **Use this MIME type**: select the type of image – in this example, we used `image/jpeg`.

Chapter 6: FILESTREAM with SSIS and SSRS

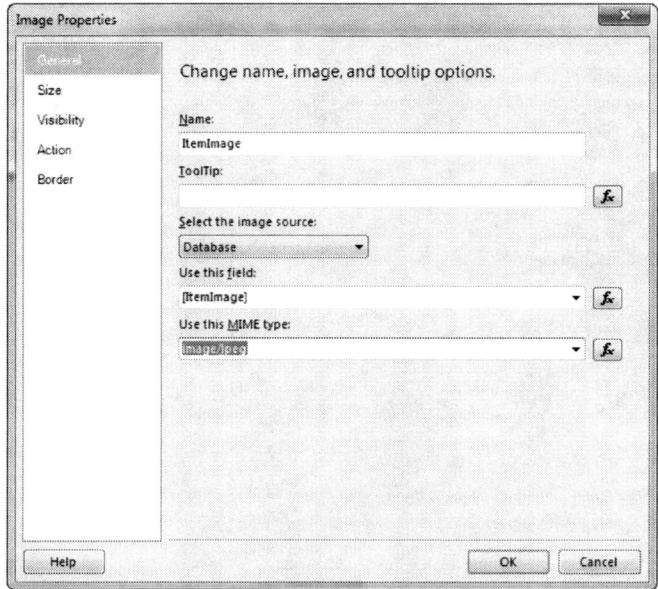

Figure 6-31: Setting the image properties.

With this, we have completed the report design. You can improve the appearance by modifying the display attributes such as font, size, border, background, color, and so on, as required.

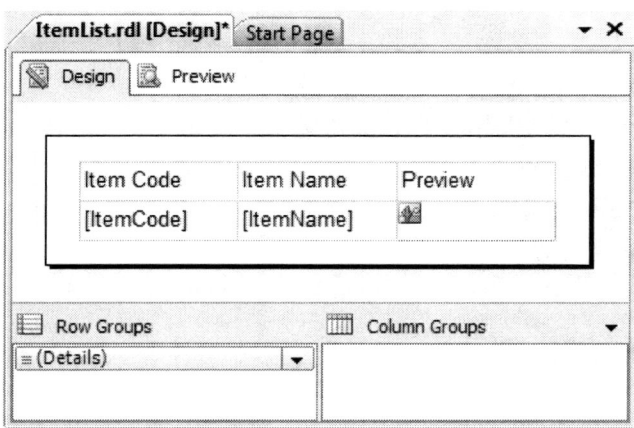

Figure 6-32: The completed report design.

Previewing the report

I'm sure you will agree that this is the easiest part of the process. If the report is designed correctly and the configuration is correct, it is just a matter of clicking the **Preview** tab (Figure 6-33).

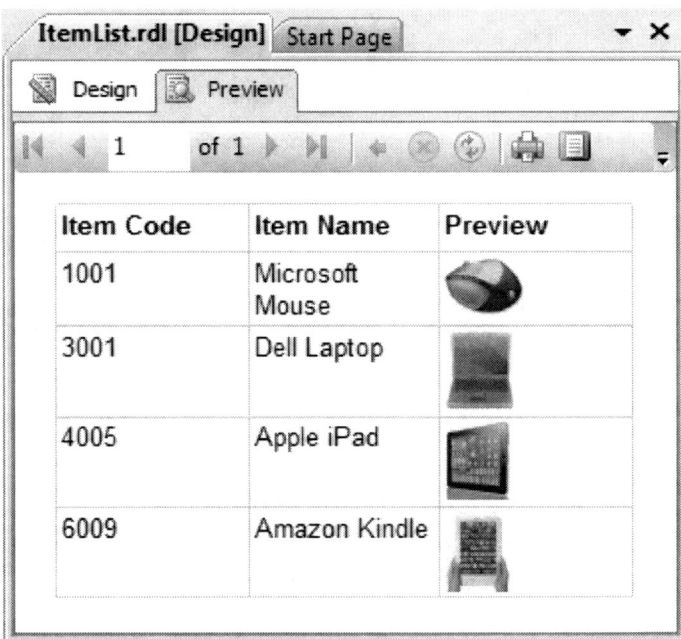

Figure 6-33:   Previewing the report.

The goal of this lab is to help you get started with building SSRS reports that use images stored in `FILESTREAM` columns. Remember that you are accessing the `FILESTREAM` data over T-SQL, and the performance benefits offered by I/O streaming are not available when using `FILESTREAM` data in SSRS reports.

Summary

The chapter presented three labs to help you to get started with creating SSRS and SSIS applications that deal with `FILESTREAM` data.

`FILESTREAM` columns can be accessed using the streaming APIs from SSIS using a **Script** task, which means that you can write .NET code that uses the Managed APIs to read and write `FILESTREAM` data. The first two labs demonstrated how to import and export `FILESTREAM` data using SSIS.

Though `FILESTREAM` columns can be accessed from SSRS, it does not provide a way to use the Win32 or Managed APIs; all access to the `FILESTREAM` data is done through T-SQL. An SSRS report must access the `FILESTREAM` columns as though they are `VARBINARY(MAX)` columns, as we saw in Lab 12.

Chapter 7: FILESTREAM Database Administration

The previous chapters have discussed development with the `FILESTREAM` feature in quite some detail. Here, we begin a sequence of four chapters dedicated to the administration and management of `FILESTREAM`-enabled databases. In this chapter, we'll examine some special considerations for `FILESTREAM`-enabled databases, and how the presence of `FILESTREAM` data might affect common database administrative tasks. Specifically, we will cover the points below.

- **Transaction isolation levels** – The behavior of `FILESTREAM`-enabled databases under each of the available levels, and where and how this differs from standard databases.

- **Moving `FILESTREAM`-enabled databases from one location to another** – The main difference is the need to move the `FILESTREAM` data container as well as data and log files.

- **`FILESTREAM` garbage files** – Possible issues associated with creation of an excessive number of `FILESTREAM` disk files, due to frequent modification of `FILESTREAM` data, and how SQL Server manages garbage collection of these files.

- **Common causes of a corrupt `FILESTREAM` database** – And how to use DBCC checks to examine and possibly repair damaged databases.

- **Coping with growth of `FILESTREAM` databases** – How to move `FILESTREAM` data partially or fully to new disk volumes, by rebuilding a clustered index in a new filegroup, and by partitioning `FILESTREAM` tables.

- **Migrating `FILESTREAM` data** – Moving large databases using scripting, or the Database Publishing Wizard, in cases where restoring a backup is not feasible.

FILESTREAM and Database Transaction Isolation Levels

With SQL Server 2008, it was not possible to enable the snapshot isolation level for databases that contained `FILESTREAM` data. Hence, it is only possible to operate such SQL 2008 `FILESTREAM` databases using one of the standard ANSI transaction isolation levels (`READ COMMITTED, READ UNCOMMITTED, REPEATABLE READ, SERIALIZABLE`). However, in SQL Server 2008 R2, and later, the snapshot isolation level has been extended to support `FILESTREAM` data.

If the row to be accessed is not locked by another process, `FILESTREAM` data can be accessed for reading or writing under all the transaction isolation levels.

If the row being accessed is locked (shared or exclusive mode) by another process, a write operation will fail under all the transaction isolation levels.

If the row being accessed is locked in Shared (S) mode by another process, `FILESTREAM` data can be accessed for reading under all the transaction isolation levels. However, if the row is locked in Exclusive (X) mode by another process, `FILESTREAM` data can be read only using the snapshot isolation level, and you will get the previous version of the `FILESTREAM` data value, if the other process has modified the `FILESTREAM` value.

READ COMMITTED, REPEATABLE READ and SERIALIZABLE isolation levels

The behavior of `FILESTREAM` data is the same for `READ COMMITTED`, `REPEATABLE READ` and `SERIALIZABLE`. If the row that contains the required `FILESTREAM` value is exclusively locked by another process, a call to `PathName()` to read this data, or write to it, will be blocked.

If the X lock is held for longer than the timeout duration, an error will be returned such as the following (when using ADO.NET):

```
Timeout expired. The timeout period elapsed prior to completion of the operation or the
server is not responding.
```

If the row is not locked at the time of retrieving the `PathName()` value and the `FILESTREAM` transaction context, but another process obtains an exclusive lock on the row right after that and before the Win32 API call is made, the attempt to open the `FILESTREAM` data file for read or write operation will fail with the following message:

```
The process cannot access the file specified because it has been opened in another
transaction.
```

If the row that contains the `FILESTREAM` value is locked in Shared (S) mode, a call to `PathName()` will succeed. In such a case, `FILESTREAM` data will be available for reading. However, if an attempt is made to write to the `FILESTREAM` data file, the operation will fail with the same message.

READ UNCOMMITTED isolation level

Under the `READ UNCOMMITTED` isolation level, a call to `PathName()` returns `NULL` if the row is exclusively locked by another process, and neither read nor write operations can be performed on the `FILESTREAM` cell using Win32/Managed APIs or TSQL.

If there is a shared lock on the row, `PathName()` returns the correct value, and you can access the `FILESTREAM` data for reading. If you attempt to open the `FILESTREAM` data file for writing, SQL Server will generate the same error as seen previously.

Snapshot isolation level

This new versioning-based isolation was introduced in SQL Server 2005 but has only been available since SQL Server 2008 R2 for `FILESTREAM` databases. When a database is operating in snapshot isolation, a client application can read `FILESTREAM` values stored on rows that are exclusively locked by another process, using T-SQL or the Win32 API; in other words, unlike with the standard transaction isolation levels, a call to `PathName()` is not blocked in this case. If the other transaction has modified the `FILESTREAM` value, the version of the `FILESTREAM` data file returned will be as it existed at the time the current transaction started.

Note that for databases containing only relational data, the snapshot isolation level introduces new possible new `SNAPSHOT` modes of operation:

- `SNAPSHOT` mode – queries return committed data as of the beginning of the transaction
- `READ_COMMITTED_SNAPSHOT` mode – queries return committed data as of the beginning of the current statement.

However, for `FILESTREAM`-enabled databases with `READ_COMMITTED_SNAPSHOT` mode enabled, data will be returned as it existed at the start of the transaction. In other words, there is effectively only one mode of snapshot isolation available for `FILESTREAM` databases.

Note that snapshot isolation level is disabled by default; the query in Listing 7-1 will confirm whether or not it is enabled on a named database.

```
SELECT
    snapshot_isolation_state_desc
FROM sys.databases
WHERE name = DB_NAME()
/*
snapshot_isolation_state_desc
------------------------------
OFF
*/
```

Listing 7-1: Determining whether snapshot isolation level is enabled.

If the snapshot isolation level is disabled (`OFF`), we can enable it by running the query in Listing 7-2. Note, again, that SQL Server 2008 does not allow you to enable snapshot isolation level on databases having `FILESTREAM` filegroups. This restriction has been removed in SQL Server 2008 R2.

```
ALTER DATABASE NorthPole
SET ALLOW_SNAPSHOT_ISOLATION ON
```

Listing 7-2: Enabling snapshot isolation level on a database.

Therefore, starting from SQL Server 2008 R2, we can use snapshot isolation to access a `FILESTREAM` data value for read operations even if the row being read is locked (shared or exclusive). However, write operations are not permitted on the rows that are already locked (shared or exclusive) by another session. If any attempt is made to do so, SQL Server will display the following error:

```
The process cannot access the file specified because it has been opened in another
transaction.
```

Summary of FILESTREAM behavior under transaction isolation levels

The following table summarizes the behavior of `FILESTREAM` operations under various transaction isolation levels, when the row being accessed is locked by another process.

Row is locked by another process	Isolation level	T-SQL		Win32	
		Read	Write	Read	Write
EXCLUSIVE	READ COMMITTED	No	No	No	No
EXCLUSIVE	READ UNCOMMITTED	Yes	No	No	No
EXCLUSIVE	REPEATABLE READ	No	No	No	No
EXCLUSIVE	SERIALIZABLE	No	No	No	No
EXCLUSIVE	SNAPSHOT(SQL Server 2008 R2 or later)	Yes	No	Yes	No
SHARED	READ COMMITTED	Yes	No	Yes	No
SHARED	READ UNCOMMITTED	Yes	No	Yes	No
SHARED	REPEATABLE READ	Yes	No	Yes	No
SHARED	SERIALIZABLE	Yes	No	Yes	No
SHARED	SNAPSHOT(SQL Server 2008 R2 or later)	Yes	No	Yes	No

Table 7-1: Summary of behavior of `FILESTREAM` operations with isolation levels.

Detaching and Attaching FILESTREAM Databases

It is common practice to detach and attach database files in order to move a database from one location to another. In a typical detach-attach process, you detach the database, move the MDF and LDF files to the new location, and then perform an attach operation. The only difference for a FILESTREAM-enabled database is that, along with your data (MDF) and log (LDF) files, you also need to move the FILESTREAM data container.

> **SSMS does not fully support attaching FILESTREAM-enabled databases**
>
> The **Attach Databases** dialog box does not allow you to specify the location of the FILESTREAM data file. As a result, you cannot attach a FILESTREAM-enabled database using SSMS if the path to the FILESTREAM container is different from the original location.

Let's see this in action. Listing 7-3 re-creates our, by now familiar, NorthPole database and loads an image into a FILESTREAM column. As usual, change the locations and paths as required.

```
USE master
GO

-- If the sample database exists, drop it and re-create it
IF DB_ID('NorthPole') IS NOT NULL
    DROP DATABASE NorthPole
GO

CREATE DATABASE NorthPole ON PRIMARY (
    NAME = NorthPole,
    FILENAME = 'C:\ArtOfFS\Demos\Chapter7\NorthPole.mdf'
), FILEGROUP NorthPole_fs CONTAINS FILESTREAM(
    NAME = NorthPole_fs,
    FILENAME = 'C:\ArtOfFS\Demos\Chapter7\NorthPole_fs') LOG ON (
    NAME = NorthPole_log,
    FILENAME = 'C:\ArtOfFS\Demos\Chapter7\NorthPole_log.ldf')
GO
```

```sql
-- Create a table with a FILESTREAM column
USE NorthPole
GO

CREATE TABLE [dbo].[Items]
    (
      [ItemID] UNIQUEIDENTIFIER ROWGUIDCOL
                                NOT NULL
                                UNIQUE ,
      [ItemNumber] VARCHAR(20) ,
      [ItemDescription] VARCHAR(50) ,
      [ItemImage] VARBINARY(MAX) FILESTREAM
                                NULL
    )
GO

-- INSERT a row with FILESTREAM data and insert the data to the table
INSERT  INTO Items
        ( ItemID ,
          ItemNumber ,
          ItemDescription ,
          ItemImage
        )
        SELECT  NEWID() ,
                'MS1001' ,
                'Microsoft Mouse' ,
                bulkcolumn
        FROM    OPENROWSET(BULK 'C:\ArtOfFS\Demos\Images\MicrosoftMouse.jpg',
                        SINGLE_BLOB) AS x
```

Listing 7-3: T-SQL script to create a sample database.

Let's assume that this database underpins a successful application and we need to move the data and log files to new, bigger hardware. To simulate this in our example, we'll move the primary data file and log file to `C:\temp\data`, and the `FILESTREAM` container to `C:\temp\FS`. First, however, we need to detach the database, as shown in Listing 7-4 (alternatively, you can right-click the database in SSMS Object Explorer and select **Tasks | Detach…**).

```
-- Detach the database
USE master
GO
EXEC sp_detach_db @dbname = 'NorthPole'
```

Listing 7-4: Detaching a `FILESTREAM`-enabled database.

Next, locate the primary data file, log file and `FILESTREAM` data container, and move them to their new locations. Now we're ready to reattach the database to our SQL Server instance. This could be the same instance, a different instance on the same computer, or a different instance on a different computer. Note, though, that if the database is being attached to a different SQL Server instance, we must ensure that `FILESTREAM` is enabled on the target server (see Appendix A) and that the target SQL Server instance should be running the same, or a later, version of SQL Server. You can detach a SQL Server 2008 and attach it to a SQL Server 2012 instance, but you cannot detach a SQL Server 2012 database and attach it to a SQL Server 2008/R2 instance.

Once these files have been moved to the new location, we are ready to attach the database as shown in Listing 7-5.

```
-- Attach the FILESTREAM database
CREATE DATABASE NorthPole ON
PRIMARY (
    NAME = NorthPole,
    FILENAME = 'C:\Temp\Data\NorthPole.mdf'),
FILEGROUP NorthPole_fs CONTAINS FILESTREAM(
    NAME = NorthPole_fs,
    FILENAME = 'C:\Temp\FS\NorthPole_fs')
LOG ON  (
    NAME = NorthPole_log,
    FILENAME = 'C:\Temp\Data\NorthPole_log.ldf')
FOR ATTACH
GO
```

Listing 7-5: Attaching a `FILESTREAM`-enabled database.

To verify success, connect to the `NorthPole` database and fire off a simple query to retrieve the data from the `items` table.

FILESTREAM and Garbage Files

SQL Server does not support in-place updates of the disk file storing the BLOB data for a `FILESTREAM` column. A disk file is created for every non-`NULL` `FILESTREAM` data value stored in every `FILESTREAM` column of every table in the database. When you update the BLOB value stored in a `FILESTREAM` cell, the associated disk file also needs to be updated. What SQL Server does internally is to create a new file with the modified value. The old version of the file will lie around in the folder until the file is no longer needed. Unwanted files are later deleted by an asynchronous garbage collection process that runs in the background. An old version of a `FILESTREAM` data file is available for garbage collection when a database `CHECKPOINT` occurs after the transaction log is truncated past the LSN (Log Sequence Number) which generated the new file.

For this reason, `FILESTREAM` storage is not ideal for cases where the BLOB data stored in the `FILESTREAM` column is frequently updated. Every time the `FILESTREAM` value is updated (from a non-`NULL` value to another non-`NULL` value) SQL Server will have to create a new file with the modified value. If the frequency of such update operations is high, you might experience severe performance problems. In such a case, storing the BLOB data in the file system and storing the path to the disk file in a table might be more efficient than using a `FILESTREAM` column.

Garbage files and recovery models

Under the `SIMPLE` recovery model, the `FILESTREAM` garbage collector is triggered when a database `CHECKPOINT` occurs. You can issue a `CHECKPOINT` to trigger the garbage collection thread to clean up the unwanted files in the `FILESTREAM` data container.

Under the `FULL` and `BULK_LOGGED` recovery models, you might notice that issuing a `CHECKPOINT` does not clean up the unwanted files in the `FILESTREAM` data container. A `CHECKPOINT` may still run the garbage collector, but it may not remove the file as you would normally expect. This is because the transaction log virtual log file (VLF) that contains the record is still active, and will remain so until the log is backed up. Every `FILESTREAM` operation is mapped to a transaction LSN in the transaction log. Under `FULL` and `BULK_LOGGED` recovery models, the garbage collector will remove a file only after the transaction log VLF that contains the LSN associated with the `FILESTREAM` operation is not part of the active log.

FILESTREAM garbage collection and tombstone tables

As we have seen, SQL Server does not support in-place updates of `FILESTREAM` data. If we modify a BLOB value stored in a `FILESTREAM` column, SQL Server will create a new disk file with the modified value. The old file will stay around for some time until it is "no longer needed" and the garbage collector steps in and deletes it.

It is interesting to note how SQL Server keeps track of the garbage files. If we modify a few `FILESTREAM` data values and look into the `FILESTREAM` data folder, we'll find many more files than the number of rows in the table. So the question is, "Which are garbage files and which are not?" SQL Server creates an internal table called the `FILESTREAM` **tombstone table** to hold the details of garbage files to be removed. The garbage collector queries this table to identify the garbage files and removes them when those files are no longer needed.

To see this in action, run the script in Listing 7-6 to create a sample database containing a table with two `FILESTREAM` columns.

```
USE master
GO

IF DB_ID('NorthPole') IS NOT NULL
    DROP DATABASE NorthPole
GO
```

Chapter 7: FILESTREAM Database Administration

```
CREATE DATABASE NorthPole ON PRIMARY (
    NAME = NorthPole,
    FILENAME = 'C:\ArtOfFS\Demos\Chapter7\NorthPole.mdf'
), FILEGROUP NorthPole_fs CONTAINS FILESTREAM(
    NAME = NorthPole_fs,
    FILENAME = 'C:\ArtOfFS\Demos\Chapter7\NorthPole_fs') LOG ON (
    NAME = NorthPole_log,
    FILENAME = 'C:\ArtOfFS\Demos\Chapter7\NorthPole_log.ldf')
GO

USE NorthPole
GO

CREATE TABLE [dbo].[Items]
    (
      [ItemID] UNIQUEIDENTIFIER ROWGUIDCOL
                                NOT NULL
                                UNIQUE ,
      [ItemNumber] VARCHAR(20) ,
      [ItemDescription] VARCHAR(50) ,
      [ItemImage1] VARBINARY(MAX) FILESTREAM
                                NULL ,
      [ItemImage2] VARBINARY(MAX) FILESTREAM
                                NULL
    )
```

Listing 7-6: Creating an example database with two FILESTREAM columns.

Now we'll insert a row into the FILESTREAM table (Listing 7-7).

```
INSERT  INTO Items
        ( ItemID ,
          ItemNumber ,
          ItemDescription ,
          ItemImage1 ,
          ItemImage2
        )
        SELECT  NEWID() ,
                'MS1001' ,
                'Microsoft Mouse' ,
                0x1 ,
                0x1
```

Listing 7-7: Inserting a row into the table.

Run the code in Listing 7-8 to update the FILESTREAM columns. The first column is updated to NULL and SQL Server discards the FILESTREAM data file associated with the field. The second column is updated with a new value, and SQL Server creates a new version of the file containing the new value, and discards the previous file.

```
UPDATE  Items
SET     ItemImage1 = NULL ,
        ItemImage2 = 0x2
```

Listing 7-8: Updating the columns to create garbage files.

After the UPDATE operation, you will see three files in the FILESTREAM data container. Out of the three, two are no longer needed. Those two files will be registered in the FILESTREAM tombstone table. We can try to read the names of those files from that table, but first we need to find out its name, as shown in Listing 7-9.

```
SELECT
    name
FROM sys.internal_tables
WHERE name LIKE 'FILESTREAM_tomb%'
/*
name
-------------------------------
FILESTREAM_tombstone_2073058421
*/
```

Listing 7-9: Retrieving the name of the FILESTREAM tombstone table.

However, the tombstone table cannot be accessed from the user mode queries. To read information from this table, we need to connect to the server using Dedicated Administrator Connection (DAC).

Chapter 7: FILESTREAM Database Administration

To make a DAC via SSMS:

- from the **File** menu, select **New, Database Engine Query**
- in the connection dialog box, enter `ADMIN:your-server-name`; for example, if your server name is Server1, enter `ADMIN:Server1` (Figure 9-1)
- enter the credentials
- write your queries in the new query window.

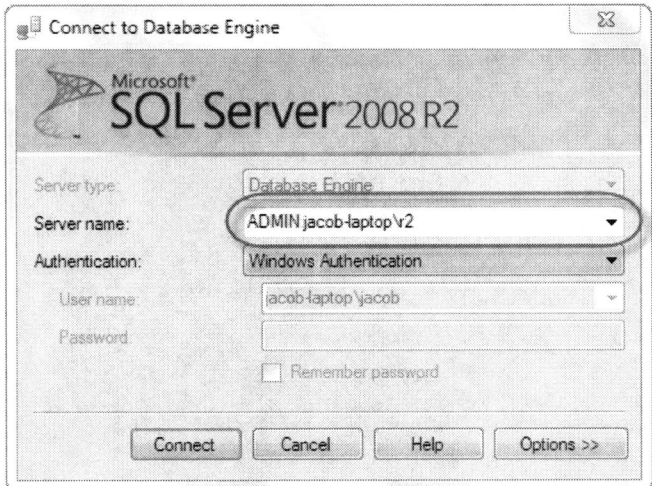

Figure 7-1: Making a DAC using SSMS.

Please note that DAC is for diagnostic/debugging purposes and should not be misused. Also note that only one DAC connection is possible at any given time, which means that the Object Explorer window cannot display the tree view of the database to which you are connected, and this is why you will get an error when trying to connect using DAC from the **New Query** button, or the **Connect to Database Engine** option of the Object Explorer.

Connect to your instance using DAC and run the query in Listing 7-10, which will retrieve the list of garbage files in the current database. If you have followed the example, the query will return details of two garbage files.

```sql
SELECT
    physical_name AS FILESTREAMFolder,
    rowset_guid AS TableFolder,
    column_guid AS ColumnFolder,
    FILESTREAM_value_name AS FILESTREAMFile
FROM sys.filestream_tombstone_2073058421 ft
INNER JOIN sys.database_files df
    ON df.file_id = ft.file_id

/*
FILESTREAMFolder         TableFolder     ColumnFolder    FILESTREAMFile
---------------------    ------------    ------------    --------------
C:\Demos\FS\NorthPoleFS  448BFCA8-6...   91DFDC80-E...   00000018-000...
C:\Demos\FS\NorthPoleFS  448BFCA8-6...   2A7202BA-4...   00000018-000...
*/
```

Listing 7-10:   Retrieving the list of garbage files.

FILESTREAM Data Corruption and DBCC Checks

One of the most undesirable situations for a database administrator is database corruption. In most cases, regular database checks and maintenance activities will help a database administrator to ensure that the databases are healthy and free from corruption.

A common cause of a corrupted `FILESTREAM` database is an "over-enthusiastic" administrative user who wants to play with the `FILESTREAM` data files directly. Remember that all access to the `FILESTREAM` data should be made through SQL Server. Direct access to the `FILESTREAM` data using the file system tools may corrupt your database.

Chapter 7: FILESTREAM Database Administration

The following sections examine a few common causes of a corrupt `FILESTREAM` database, and how to use `DBCC CHECKDB` or `DBCC CHECKTABLE` to check the consistency of your database along with the `FILESTREAM` data, and try to fix any corruption issues.

Corruption caused by missing FILESTREAM data files

The recommended way to delete a `FILESTREAM` data file is by setting the value of the column to `NULL` by performing a T-SQL `UPDATE` operation. If a user or software process directly deletes a file from the `FILESTREAM` data container, you will end up with a corrupted database. Let's replicate this scenario here (we're about to deliberately corrupt a database, so only do this on a test database on a test server).

Run the script in Listing 7-11 to create a new `FILESTREAM`-enabled database with a `FILESTREAM` column and two rows.

```
USE master
GO

IF DB_ID('NorthPole') IS NOT NULL
    DROP DATABASE NorthPole
GO

CREATE DATABASE NorthPole ON PRIMARY (
    NAME = NorthPole,
    FILENAME = 'C:\ArtOfFS\Demos\Chapter7\NorthPole.mdf'
), FILEGROUP NorthPole_fs CONTAINS FILESTREAM(
    NAME = NorthPole_fs,
    FILENAME = 'C:\ArtOfFS\Demos\Chapter7\NorthPole_fs') LOG ON (
    NAME = NorthPole_log,
    FILENAME = 'C:\ArtOfFS\Demos\Chapter7\NorthPole_log.ldf')
GO

USE NorthPole
GO
```

Chapter 7: FILESTREAM Database Administration

```sql
CREATE TABLE [dbo].[Items]
    (
        [ItemID] UNIQUEIDENTIFIER ROWGUIDCOL
                                    NOT NULL
                                    UNIQUE ,
        [ItemNumber] VARCHAR(20) ,
        [ItemDescription] VARCHAR(50) ,
        [ItemImage] VARBINARY(MAX) FILESTREAM
                                    NULL
    )
GO

INSERT INTO Items
        ( ItemID, ItemNumber, ItemDescription, ItemImage )
VALUES  ( NEWID(), 'MS1001', 'Microsoft Mouse', 0x1 ),
        ( NEWID(), 'MS1002', 'Microsoft Keyboard', 0x2 )
```

Listing 7-11: Creating a FILESTREAM database with a FILESTREAM column and two rows.

Navigate to the FILESTREAM data container using Windows Explorer and you will see the two FILESTREAM data files in the folder associated with the Items table. Go ahead and delete one of those files.

Let's fire off a few queries to confirm that the database has indeed been corrupted. Listing 7-12 reads data from the Items table.

```sql
SELECT
    itemNumber,
    ItemDescription
FROM Items
/*
itemnumber            ItemDescription
-------------------   -------------------
MS1001                Microsoft Mouse
MS1002                Microsoft Keyboard
*/
```

Listing 7-12: Reading relational data from the corrupted Items table.

287

Chapter 7: FILESTREAM Database Administration

That worked… but we did not touch the `FILESTREAM` data in the query. Listing 7-13, on the other hand, will try to read from the `FILESTREAM` columns.

```
SELECT
    itemnumber,
    itemImage
FROM Items
/*
itemnumber              ItemImage
--------------------    --------------------------------
Msg 233, Level 20, State 0, Line 0
A transport-level error has occurred when receiving
results from the server. (provider: Shared Memory
Provider, error: 0 - No process is on the other
end of the pipe.)
*/
```

Listing 7-13: Attempting to read `FILESTREAM` data from the corrupted `Items` table.

There is a fatal error with Level 20. In SQL Server 2008 and R2 the connection will be terminated when such an error occurs. However, in SQL Server 2012 this error does not terminate the connection.

Note that the error occurs only if you try to access a `FILESTREAM` value that is having a problem (in this case, missing from the `FILESTREAM` data container). Querying a valid `FILESTREAM` value will work correctly, as shown in Listing 7-14.

```
SELECT
    itemNumber,
    DATALENGTH(ItemImage)
FROM items
WHERE itemNumber = 'MS1002'
/*
item                    number
--------------------    --------------------
MS1002                  4
*/
```

Listing 7-14: Reading uncorrupted `FILESTREAM` data in a corrupted database.

Checking for database consistency

Consistency of the `FILESTREAM` data can be checked using `DBCC CHECKDB` for the entire database, or `DBCC CHECKTABLE` to validate a single table. In Listing 7-15, we run `DBCC CHECKTABLE` to scan the table that we just corrupted by deleting the `FILESTREAM` data file using Windows Explorer.

```
DBCC CHECKTABLE('Items')

/*
DBCC results for 'sys.FILESTREAM_tombstone_2073058421'.
There are 0 rows in 1 pages for object
"sys.FILESTREAM_tombstone_2073058421".
DBCC results for 'Items'.
Msg 7904, Level 16, State 2, Line 1
Table error: Cannot find the FILESTREAM file
"00000015-0000005e-0004" for column ID 4 (column directory
ID 4d8cb114-f573-490e-adfa-e4583889b836) in object ID 2105058535,
index ID 0, partition ID 72057594038779904, page ID (1:157),
slot ID 0.
There are 2 rows in 1 pages for object "Items".
CHECKTABLE found 0 allocation errors and 1 consistency errors
in table 'Items' (object ID 2105058535).
repair_allow_data_loss is the minimum repair level for the
errors found by DBCC CHECKTABLE (NorthPole.dbo.Items).
DBCC execution completed. If DBCC printed error messages, contact
your system administrator.
*/
```

Listing 7-15: Scanning the corrupted table.

As expected, the `DBCC CHECKTABLE` command scanned the entire table and detected that a `FILESTREAM` data file is missing from the `FILESTREAM` data container.

Fixing corrupted data

One of the key features offered by `FILESTREAM` is consistency between `FILESTREAM` data and relational data. We just deleted a `FILESTREAM` data file directly (outside SQL Server) and so lost the consistency of data. The only way to fix this is either by deleting the row that contains the `FILESTREAM` data file (recommended), or by adding the lost file back to the `FILESTREAM` data container.

If you do not want to lose the relational data, you could fix the corruption by copying back the correct file directly into the `FILESTREAM` data container. This requires that you have the ability to locate a backup copy somewhere, possibly by restoring from a backup. SQL Server allows you to query the relational data even though the `FILESTREAM` data is corrupted, which may help you to identify which data value is missing. Note that the file name of the new file must be the same; the file name and location can be identified from the DBCC error message.

If you cannot locate a copy of the missing or corrupt file, you can put a dummy file with the expected file name into the `FILESTREAM` data folder, and this will "fix" the corruption so that you do not have to delete the relational data (which may be hard to get back). For example, if your table stores the avatar of users and you lost the image of one record due to a mistake, you could put an anonymous image file into the `FILESTREAM` data folder.

To use a dummy file, locate an existing file or create a new file that is of the same type as the missing file. Copy the dummy file to the `FILESTREAM` data container and rename it to match the name of the missing file (as reported by `DBCC CHECKDB`). Having done so, rerun `DBCC CHECKDB` or `DBCC CHECKTABLE`, and you will see that the corruption is fixed.

If you can tolerate some degree of data loss, then the alternative solution is to delete the row from the table to make the data consistent; we can do this by running `DBCC CHECKDB` with `repair_allow_data_loss`, which is about as scary as it sounds; we're about to lose some data! In this case, it will delete the associated row(s) from the table and restore the consistency of the data.

Chapter 7: FILESTREAM Database Administration

To see this working, go back to the **FILESTREAM** data folder and delete the file we just created. Run **DBCC CHECKTABLE** again, and you will see that the error is reported again. Run the script in Listing 7-16 to fix the corruption by deleting the records that have corrupted **FILESTREAM** values. The first action the script performs is to take the database into single user mode. The database needs to be in single user mode to perform a repair operation.

```
ALTER DATABASE NorthPole SET SINGLE_USER
WITH ROLLBACK IMMEDIATE
GO

DBCC CHECKDB('NorthPole', repair_allow_data_loss)
/*
Msg 7904, Level 16, State 2, Line 2
Table error: Cannot find the FILESTREAM file "00000015-0000005e-0004"
for column ID 4 (column directory ID 4d8cb114-f573-490e-adfa-e4583889b836) in
object ID 2105058535, index ID 0, partition ID 72057594038779904, page ID (1:157),
slot ID 0.

The error has been repaired.
Msg 8945, Level 16, State 1, Line 2

Table error: Object ID 2105058535, index ID 2 will be rebuilt.
The error has been repaired.
*/
```

Listing 7-16: Fixing **FILESTREAM** corruption by deleting the affected rows.

If you run a query on the **Items** table, you will see that it now has only one row; the row from which the **FILESTREAM** data was missing has been deleted as part of the repair process. Again, keep in mind that this approach may or may not be acceptable, depending upon the nature of your application and sensitivity of the data.

Corruption caused by orphaned files

Creating or copying unwanted files in the `FILESTREAM` data container can also cause corruption in a database.

Let us see what happens when an unwanted file is present in the `FILESTREAM` data container. Go to the `FILESTREAM` data container and create a new file, or copy an existing file from another folder. For this demonstration, I copied the **MicrosoftMouse.jpg** into the `FILESTREAM` data container's folder structure. Then, run `DBCC CHECKDB` or `DBCC CHECKTABLE` and you should see an error message similar to the following:

```
Table error: The file "\12f4b92b-6c51-43a5-9a32-71d1b0de0646\MicrosoftMouse.jpg" in the
rowset directory ID 4443b7d5-904c-475d-bcc8-20bc0e09b887 is not a valid FILESTREAM file.
```

Note that SQL Server complains that there is a file present that is not a valid `FILESTREAM` file. One could probably argue that this is because the file is not correctly named. Files in the `FILESTREAM` data folder do not have extensions, and they are named following a certain pattern. Go back to your `FILESTREAM` folder and rename the file so that it follows the same naming pattern as the other files in the `FILESTREAM` folder, and then run `DBCC CHECKTABLE` again.

```
Table error:  The orphaned file "0000001b-0000015c-0005" was found in the FILESTREAM directory
ID 12f4b92b-6c51-43a5-9a32-71d1b0de0646 for object ID 21575115, index ID 0, partition ID
72057594039042048, column ID 4.
```

Note that the error is different now. This time, SQL Server detected that there is an orphan file in the `FILESTREAM` directory. Let's see if `DBCC CHECKDB` can fix this by deleting the orphaned file; rerun `DBCC CHECKDB` with `repair_allow_data_loss` (Listing 7-16).

```
Table error: The orphaned file "0000001b-0000015c-0005" was found in the FILESTREAM directory
ID 12f4b92b-6c51-43a5-9a32-71d1b0de0646 for object ID 21575115, index ID 0, partition ID
72057594039042048, column ID 4.
```

As you can see, SQL Server cannot fix an inconsistency error of this type. If it finds a foreign file in the `FILESTREAM` data container, it will return an error, but `DBCC CHECKTABLE` or `DBCC CHECKDB` will not remove the unwanted file. You must remove it yourself to fix the corruption.

> **Corruption can leak into your backup files**
>
> Note that, if you take a backup of the database, the backup will also include the orphaned file. If you subsequently restore the backup, the new database will be corrupted as well.

Before moving on, delete the orphaned file from the `FILESTREAM` data container, then run `DBCC CHECKDB` again, to make sure that the database is no longer in a corrupted state.

Corruption caused by deleting the garbage files manually

As discussed earlier in the *Garbage files and recovery models* section, there is sometimes a delay before garbage files are deleted. If you lose patience and delete garbage files yourself, you may create a problem for the garbage collector, as it will try to remove files that no longer exist.

If you have been following through with the example over the previous sections, the `Items` table in `NorthPole` database has only one record. Go to the `FILESTREAM` data container and note down the name of the file. Next, run the script in Listing 7-17 to update the `FILESTREAM` data value. The update operation will generate a new file with the modified value and the old file will become garbage.

```
UPDATE TOP (1) Items SET
    ItemImage  = CAST(REPLICATE('A', 2048) AS VARBINARY(MAX))
```

Listing 7-17: Updating a `FILESTREAM` data value to create a garbage file.

After the update, you will see that there are two files in the `FILESTREAM` data container. A new file has been generated with the modified value, and the previous file (whose name you noted) is now garbage.

My tests show that deleting this garbage file manually, without waiting for the garbage collector, does not corrupt the database in present versions of SQL Server. After deleting the garbage files, I ran `DBCC CHECKDB` and no error was reported. This was surprising to me, because the garbage files are tracked internally through the `FILESTREAM` tombstone table and I would expect SQL Server to report an error if one goes missing.

As has been stressed several times already, it is not a good idea to touch the `FILESTREAM` data container directly. All access to the `FILESTREAM` data should be done through SQL Server – either using T-SQL or through the Win32 API calls. Do not ever attempt to clean `FILESTREAM` garbage by yourself, unless there is an emergency where you are running out of storage space and you badly need some of those garbage files to be removed (and, of course, you fully understand the risks of touching `FILESTREAM` data directly).

Querying FILESTREAM Databases

SQL Server has a number of `FILESTREAM`-related system views that you can use to query additional information about the `FILESTREAM` storage and activities. They are listed in Chapter 9: *Investigating FILESTREAM Databases*, along with coverage of a few new system wait types to deal with the various `FILESTREAM`-related operations and some of the common `FILESTREAM` metadata queries that you might find very helpful while working with `FILESTREAM`-enabled databases.

FILESTREAM Data and Space Management

The `FILESTREAM` feature enables the storage of large BLOB values in the database, and one of the challenges that database administrators will face is space management. Moving a copy of the production database to a secondary location or to the development environment will be a real challenge in many cases, so it is very important to plan carefully when you decide to go with a `FILESTREAM` implementation.

> **`FILESTREAM` *database and backups***
>
> *As we will discuss in Chapter 8: Back Up and Restore for `FILESTREAM` Databases, the backup of a `FILESTREAM` database will also include the `FILESTREAM` data, so large backup sizes / long backup times are also a potential issue.*

If the expected workload and use cases are known in advance, it will be easier to decide the number of `FILESTREAM` filegroups needed, as well as to identify any data partitioning requirements for handling storage and retrieval. However, there may be many cases where this information is not known in advance or the actual workload and usage scenarios may overshoot all the estimations made at design time.

These scenarios may lead to the requirement to move `FILESTREAM` data partially or fully to new disk volumes with the minimum possible downtime. We'll examine a few options that will allow us to do this.

Changing the FILESTREAM filegroup location

In this example, let's imagine that our database started small, and we expected the `FILESTREAM` data to grow to 100 GB in three years. Therefore, we put the `FILESTREAM` data file on a 148 GB disk volume. After a year, it's clear that the data is growing faster than expected and we have already used over 120 GB on the disk volume and need to move the `FILESTREAM` data to a larger disk.

Run the T-SQL code provided in Listing 7-18 to rebuild our sample database.

```sql
USE master
GO

IF DB_ID('NorthPole') IS NOT NULL
    DROP DATABASE NorthPole
GO

CREATE DATABASE NorthPole ON
PRIMARY (
    NAME = NorthPole,
    FILENAME = 'C:\ArtOfFS\Demos\Chapter7\NorthPole.mdf'
), FILEGROUP NorthPole_fs CONTAINS FILESTREAM(
    NAME = NorthPole_fs,
    FILENAME = 'C:\ArtOfFS\Demos\Chapter7\NorthPole_fs')
LOG ON (
    NAME = NorthPole_log,
    FILENAME = 'C:\ArtOfFS\Demos\Chapter7\NorthPole_log.ldf')
GO
```

Listing 7-18: Creating the sample database.

This creates a `FILESTREAM` database with a single `FILESTREAM` filegroup and sets the `FILESTREAM` data container to `C:\ArtOfFS\Demos\Chapter7\NorthPole_fs`. The next step is to create a `FILESTREAM`-enabled table (Listing 7-19).

```
USE NorthPole
GO
CREATE TABLE [dbo].[Items](
    [ItemID] [int] IDENTITY(1,1) NOT NULL,
    [ItemGuid] [uniqueidentifier] ROWGUIDCOL  NOT NULL UNIQUE,
    [ItemNumber] [varchar](20) NULL,
    [ItemDescription] [varchar](50) NULL,
    [ItemImage] [varbinary](max) FILESTREAM  NULL,
    CONSTRAINT PKEY_Items PRIMARY KEY CLUSTERED
    ([ItemID] ASC)
)
```

Listing 7-19: Creating a FILESTREAM table.

This table is a bit different from the previous examples; this time, the Items table has an IDENTITY column called ItemID, which has a PRIMARY KEY defined on it. The next step is to insert a few rows into the table (Listing 7-20).

```
INSERT INTO Items(ItemGuid, ItemNumber, ItemDescription, ItemImage) VALUES
(NEWID(), 'ITM001', 'Item 1', 0x),
(NEWID(), 'ITM001', 'Item 1', 0x)
```

Listing 7-20: Populating the table with zero-length files.

In this simple example, there will only be two files in the FILESTREAM data container. However, imagine that the database has grown very large and the folder contains a large number of FILESTREAM data files, necessitating the move of the FILESTREAM filegroup to a new disk volume. For the purpose of keeping this example simple, let's assume that the new location is C:\ArtOfFS\Demos\Chapter7\NorthPole_fs2. Of course, in reality, the new location would be on a separate disk volume.

The approach we will take here is to add a new FILESTREAM filegroup at this new location, and rebuild the clustered index on the FILESTREAM table, which will move the FILESTREAM data to this new location. Listing 7-21 adds a new FILESTREAM filegroup into the NorthPole database.

Chapter 7: FILESTREAM Database Administration

```
ALTER DATABASE NorthPole
ADD FILEGROUP NorthPole_fs2
CONTAINS FILESTREAM
```

Listing 7-21: Adding a new `FILESTREAM` filegroup.

Next, associate the filegroup with the location to which we want to move the `FILESTREAM` data (Listing 7-22).

```
ALTER DATABASE NorthPole
ADD FILE
(
    NAME= NorthPole_fs2,
    FILENAME = 'C:\ArtOfFS\Demos\Chapter7\NorthPole_fs2'
)
TO FILEGROUP NorthPole_fs2
```

Listing 7-22: Adding a file to the newly created `FILESTREAM` filegroup.

The next step is to drop the clustered index (which is also the primary key of the table) using the script in Listing 7-23. If there is currently no clustered index on the table, then move on to the next step, which is creating a clustered index.

```
ALTER TABLE [dbo].[Items] DROP CONSTRAINT [PKEY_Items]
```

Listing 7-23: Dropping the clustered index on the `Items` table.

Now, in Listing 7-24, we can re-create the clustered index, specifying the location of the new `FILESTREAM` filegroup. SQL Server will move the `FILESTREAM` data to the new location while the clustered index is being built.

```
ALTER TABLE [dbo].[Items]
ADD CONSTRAINT [PKEY_Items]
PRIMARY KEY CLUSTERED ([ItemID] ASC)
FILESTREAM_ON [NorthPole_fs2]
```

Listing 7-24: Rebuilding the clustered index to move the `FILESTREAM` data.

Notice the usage of the `FILESTREAM_ON` clause in Listing 7-24. By specifying the `FILESTREAM_ON` clause, you instruct SQL Server to move the `FILESTREAM` data to the specified filegroup.

Note that this approach requires attention to an important detail. If, for some reason, the clustered index is rebuilt again, the `FILESTREAM_ON` clause must be used again, to avoid the `FILESTREAM` data container from moving back to the default filegroup.

An alternative to moving the data by using the `FILESTREAM_ON` clause to the `ALTER TABLE` command, when we add the new clustered index, is to first specify the new target `FILESTREAM` filegroup as the default filegroup for the database, and then simply add the clustered index, as shown in Listing 7-25.

```
ALTER DATABASE NorthPole MODIFY FILEGROUP NorthPole_fs2 DEFAULT
GO
ALTER TABLE [dbo].[Items]
ADD CONSTRAINT [PKEY_Items]
PRIMARY KEY CLUSTERED ([ItemID] ASC)
```

Listing 7-25: Setting the default `FILESTREAM` filegroup to move the data.

Whichever technique you use, once you have rebuilt the clustered index, look in the new `FILESTREAM` data location and you will see two `FILESTREAM` data files. Now look in the original `FILESTREAM` location and will see two files there, too. The reason for this is that the garbage collector has not yet run; the next time it does, those files will be deleted.

To verify that new `FILESTREAM` data is going to the new location, run the code in Listing 7-26, which adds two more rows to the `FILESTREAM` table.

```
INSERT INTO Items(itemguid, itemnumber, itemdescription, ItemImage) VALUES
(NEWID(), 'ITM001', 'Item 1', 0x),
(NEWID(), 'ITM001', 'Item 1', 0x)
```

Listing 7-26: Adding two more rows to the `FILESTREAM` table.

The new `FILESTREAM` data location contains two new files, which are not present in the original location. If you no longer need the original filegroup, you can remove it, by first removing the `FILESTREAM` data container and then the filegroup itself. Listing 7-27 shows how.

```
ALTER DATABASE NorthPole
REMOVE FILE NorthPole_fs ;

ALTER DATABASE NorthPole
REMOVE FILEGROUP NorthPole_fs ;
```

Listing 7-27: Removing the `FILESTREAM` data container and filegroup.

Note that the demonstrated behavior has an important consequence: because only one `FILESTREAM` filegroup can be marked as the default for the database, if you are intentionally spreading the `FILESTREAM` data over multiple filegroups (as discussed next), then creating or recreating a clustered index on a table with `FILESTREAM` data stored in a non-default filegroup will cause the data to be moved, which may be undesired.

Adding a new partition to share the FILESTREAM storage load

We can partition a `FILESTREAM` table so as to distribute the `FILESTREAM` storage to multiple disk volumes. By designing the table in this way, it is quite easy to add a new partition to a `FILESTREAM` table, in order to add more storage space, or balance the I/O load across multiple storage systems.

In this example, we'll create a partitioned `FILESTREAM` table and then add a new partition to move some of the `FILESTREAM` data to a new filegroup. First, run the script in Listing 7-28 to re-create the sample database.

```
USE master
GO

IF DB_ID('NorthPole') IS NOT NULL
    DROP DATABASE NorthPole
GO

CREATE DATABASE NorthPole ON
PRIMARY (
    NAME = NorthPole,
    FILENAME = 'C:\ArtOfFS\Demos\Chapter7\NorthPole.mdf'),
FILEGROUP NorthPole2(
    NAME = NorthPole2,
    FILENAME = 'C:\ArtOfFS\Demos\Chapter7\NorthPole2.ndf'),
FILEGROUP NorthPole_fs1 CONTAINS FILESTREAM DEFAULT(
    NAME = NorthPole_fs1,
    FILENAME = 'C:\ArtOfFS\Demos\Chapter7\NorthPole_fs1'),
FILEGROUP NorthPole_fs2 CONTAINS FILESTREAM(
    NAME = NorthPole_fs2,
    FILENAME = 'C:\ArtOfFS\Demos\Chapter7\NorthPole_fs2')
LOG ON (
    NAME = NorthPole_log,
    FILENAME = 'C:\ArtOfFS\Demos\Chapter7\NorthPole_log.ldf')
GO
```

Listing 7-28: Creating a FILESTREAM database with multiple FILESTREAM filegroups.

This database contains a primary filegroup (NorthPole) containing the primary data file, a filegroup called NorthPole2, containing a secondary data file, two FILESTREAM filegroups, NorthPole_fs1 and NorthPole_fs2, and the log file. Purely for convenience, all of these are stored on the same disk volume but, in a real-world scenario, you'd probably put all these files on different disk volumes.

Next, we're going to create two partitions to store the FILESTREAM data. Listing 7-29 shows the partition function and partition schemes to do this, assuming we're going to partition the table by the ID column. Take a look at the code and then we'll discuss how it works.

Chapter 7: FILESTREAM Database Administration

```
USE NorthPole
GO

CREATE PARTITION FUNCTION NPPartFN (INT) AS
RANGE RIGHT FOR VALUES (4)

CREATE PARTITION SCHEME NPPartDBSch AS
PARTITION NPPartFN TO([PRIMARY],[NorthPole2])
GO

CREATE PARTITION SCHEME NPPartFSSch AS
PARTITION NPPartFN TO(NorthPole_fs1, NorthPole_fs2)
GO
```

Listing 7-29: Creating a partition function and scheme.

First, this code creates a partition function, `NPPartFN`, which will split data across two filegroups; relational data will be split across the primary and secondary data files, and the `FILESTREAM` data will be divided across the two `FILESTREAM` filegroups.

We will associate this function with the `ItemID` column of the `Items` table, such that rows with `ItemID` less than 4 will go to the first filegroup (`PRIMARY` for relational data and `NorthPole_fs1` for `FILESTREAM` data), and those with 4 and above will go to the second filegroup (`NorthPole2` for relational data and `NorthPole_fs2` for `FILESTREAM` data). Of course, these numbers are very small and are used only for demonstration purposes. In the real world, you could use a larger value, or you might want to partition based on date, or some other value.

The second part of the code creates two partition schemes; one for the relational data and the other for the `FILESTREAM` data. Note that the partition switching of `FILESTREAM` data works only when the `RIGHT` operator is used in the partition function. It does not work with `LEFT`, which is a confirmed bug in the current versions of SQL Server.

The next step is to create the `Items` table, exploiting our new partition scheme, as shown in Listing 7-30.

```
USE NorthPole
GO
CREATE TABLE [dbo].[Items](
    [ItemID] [int] IDENTITY(1,1) NOT NULL,
    [ItemGuid] [uniqueidentifier] ROWGUIDCOL
        NOT NULL UNIQUE ON [PRIMARY],
    [ItemNumber] [varchar](20) NULL,
    [ItemDescription] [varchar](50) NULL,
    [ItemImage] [varbinary](max) FILESTREAM  NULL
) ON NPPartDBSch(ItemID)
FILESTREAM_ON NPPartFSSch
```

Listing 7-30: Creating the `Items` table on the partition scheme.

Listing 7-31 inserts six rows into the `Items` table. Based on our partition rules, the first three rows should go to the first filegroup and the rest should go to the second filegroup.

```
INSERT INTO Items(itemguid, itemnumber, itemdescription, ItemImage)
SELECT NEWID(), 'ITM001', 'Item 1', 0x1
UNION ALL
SELECT NEWID(), 'ITM002', 'Item 2', 0x2
UNION ALL
SELECT NEWID(), 'ITM003', 'Item 3', 0x3
UNION ALL
SELECT NEWID(), 'ITM004', 'Item 4', 0x4
UNION ALL
SELECT NEWID(), 'ITM005', 'Item 5', 0x5
UNION ALL
SELECT NEWID(), 'ITM006', 'Item 6', 0x6
```

Listing 7-31: Creating six new rows in the `Items` table.

Go to the `FILESTREAM` data container and verify that you see three files in the location associated with the first filegroup and another three files in the location associated with the second `FILESTREAM` filegroup.

Chapter 7: FILESTREAM Database Administration

Now, let's assume that this database has been running for years, and we are about to run out of space on the disk volume holding the filegroup `NorthPole_fs2`. To mimic this scenario, we'll simply add three more rows into the sample database so that the first filegroup still has three `FILESTREAM` data files and the second filegroup is "overloaded" with six `FILESTREAM` data files (Listing 7-32).

```sql
INSERT INTO Items(itemguid, itemnumber, itemdescription, ItemImage)
SELECT NEWID(), 'ITM007', 'Item 7', 0x7
UNION ALL
SELECT NEWID(), 'ITM008', 'Item 8', 0x8
UNION ALL
SELECT NEWID(), 'ITM009', 'Item 9', 0x9
```

Listing 7-32: Creating three more rows in the `Items` table.

What we want to do is create a new `FILESTREAM` filegroup (on a separate disk), then create a new partition scheme that makes sure all subsequent data will be stored in this new filegroup, and finally modify our partition function so that the three rows created in Listing 7-32 are moved to the new partition scheme.

The first step is to add the new filegroups. It's not technically required to add a new data filegroup for every new `FILESTREAM` filegroup. This practice is used here only to make the code examples clear to follow. Thus, we will create two new filegroups, one for the relational data and the other for the `FILESTREAM` data (Listing 7-33).

```sql
ALTER DATABASE NorthPole
ADD FILEGROUP NorthPole_fs3 CONTAINS FILESTREAM

ALTER database NorthPole
ADD FILE
(
    NAME = 'NorthPole_fs3',
    FILENAME = 'C:\ArtOfFS\Demos\Chapter7\NorthPole_fs3'
)
TO FILEGROUP NorthPole_fs3
```

```
ALTER DATABASE NorthPole
ADD FILEGROUP NorthPole3

ALTER database NorthPole
ADD FILE
(
    NAME = 'NorthPole3',
    FILENAME = 'C:\ArtOfFS\Demos\Chapter7\NorthPole3.mdf'
)
TO FILEGROUP NorthPole3
```

Listing 7-33: Adding two new filegroups to the sample database.

Now we'll add the newly created filegroups into the partition scheme and mark them as the NEXT filegroup to be used (Listing 7-34).

```
ALTER PARTITION SCHEME NPPartFSSch
NEXT USED NorthPole_fs3

ALTER PARTITION SCHEME NPPartDBSch
NEXT USED NorthPole3
```

Listing 7-34: Adding the new filegroups into the partition scheme.

We can now reconfigure the partition function to add another split at 7; this will move all the rows with ItemID 7 out of the NorthPole2 and NorthPole_fs2 filegroups and into the NorthPole3 and NorthPole_fs3 filegroups.

```
ALTER PARTITION FUNCTION NPPartFN()
SPLIT RANGE (7);
```

Listing 7-35: Modifying the partition function.

Take a look in the FILESTREAM data container. You will see that three FILESTREAM data files have been added to the new location. The FILESTREAM data container belonging to the second filegroup still contains six files, but three of them are garbage and will be removed when the garbage collector runs next time.

Throughout this example, we've partitioned the relational data according to the same scheme as the FILESTREAM data. However, it is also possible to partition only the FILESTREAM data, and leave all the relational data in a single database file. Listing 7-29 can be modified to use the PRIMARY filegroup twice in the NPPartDBSch partition scheme, as shown in Listing 7-36.

```
USE NorthPole
GO

CREATE PARTITION FUNCTION NPPartFN (INT) AS
RANGE RIGHT FOR VALUES (4)

CREATE PARTITION SCHEME NPPartDBSch AS
PARTITION NPPartFN TO([PRIMARY],[PRIMARY])
GO

CREATE PARTITION SCHEME NPPartFSSch AS
PARTITION NPPartFN TO(NorthPole_fs1, NorthPole_fs2)
GO
```

Listing 7-36: Creating a partition function and scheme to partition FILESTREAM data but not relational data.

Listings 7-33 and 7-34 can be modified similarly. In Listing 7-33, you would not create the filegroup NorthPole3 or the associated file. In Listing 7-34, you would not use the second ALTER PARTITION statement.

Migrating FILESTREAM Data

The recommended way to move or copy large databases from one location to another is to restore a full backup (see Chapter 8). However, in cases where restoring backups is not allowed, such as in a shared hosting location, or when only selected objects need to be restored, we can resort to scripting of the schema and data to transport SQL Server objects from one location to another. It is possible to script tables with `FILESTREAM` data but it is only recommended in cases where the database size is relatively small, and scripting data of `FILESTREAM`-enabled databases is recommended only if the BLOB values are small.

SSMS scripting

The scripting functionality offered by SSMS allows us to create `INSERT` scripts that can be executed on another location to re-create the `FILESTREAM` data. You can do this by setting the export option **Type of data to script** to *Schema and data* or *Data only*, as shown in Figure 7-2.

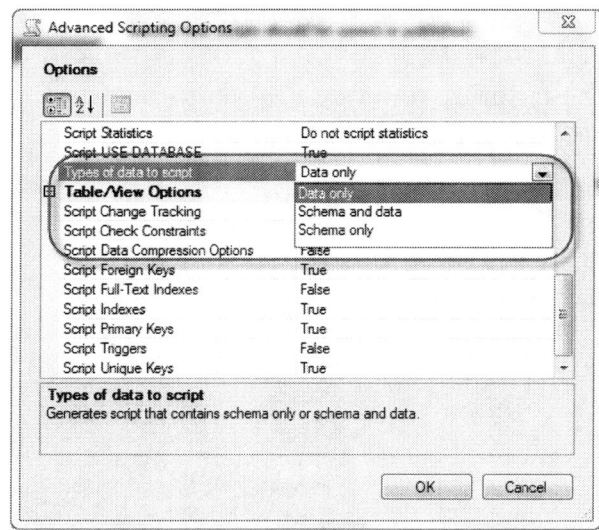

Figure 7-2: Selecting the types of data to script.

Chapter 7: FILESTREAM Database Administration

The scripting process does not require any `FILESTREAM`-specific changes; it is the same as the process for a non-`FILESTREAM` database. SSMS generates `INSERT` statements to populate the target database with the same values as the source table, including the `FILESTREAM` columns. `FILESTREAM` columns are exported as a hex string, as shown in Listing 7-37.

```
INSERT [dbo].[Items] (
    [ItemID],
    [ItemNumber],
    [ItemDescription],
      [ItemImage])
VALUES (
    N'f326ed65-5131-4ef7-891a-89fad516b856',
    N'MS1001', N'Microsoft Mouse',
    0xFFD8FFE000104A464946000101000001000010000FFDB004
    30009060708070609080708000A0A090B0D160F0D0C0C0D1B14
    151016201D2222201D1F1F2428342C242631271F1F2D3D2D3
    35373A3A3A232B3F443F384334393A37FFDB0043010A0A0A0
    ........................................
    37373737373737373737FFC00011080067007A030122000)
```

Listing 7-37: `INSERT` statement for a `FILESTREAM` column.

The Scripting Wizard allows us to generate scripts to be deployed on a different version of SQL Server. This is one of the areas where the scripting functionality adds value over regular backups, as we cannot, for example, restore a SQL Server 2008 R2 backup on SQL Server 2008.

We select the target database in the **Advanced Scripting Options** screen (Figure 7-3).

Chapter 7: FILESTREAM Database Administration

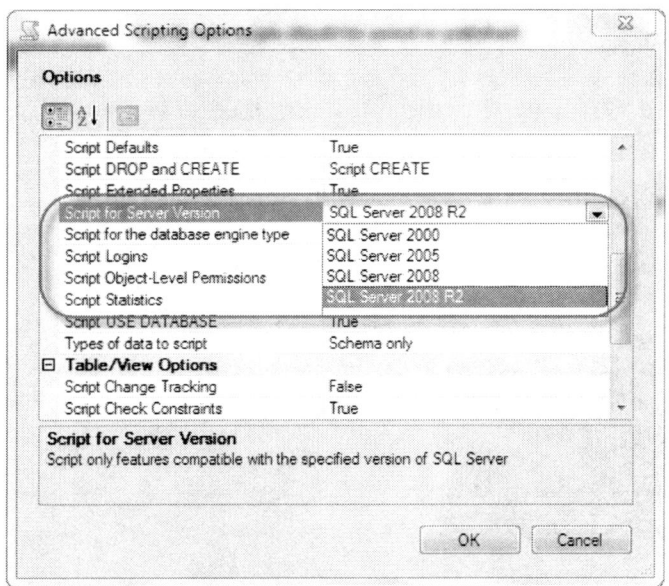

Figure 7-3: Selecting the target SQL Server version for scripting.

We can generate scripts of a SQL Server 2008 `FILESTREAM` database and deploy to a SQL Server 2005 instance. The `FILESTREAM` columns will be deployed as `VARBINARY(MAX)` columns on the target database. However, we cannot script a `FILESTREAM` column for deployment to SQL Server 2000.

It appears that SSMS cannot script `FILESTREAM` values larger than 2 GB. However, this is unlikely to be a problem because, in the real world, I would not expect anyone to attempt to generate scripts for BLOB values larger than about 100 MB.

The Database Publishing Wizard

Using the SQL Server Database Publishing Wizard, we can deploy database scripts and data to another local or remote server. The Database Publishing Wizard (versions 1.3 and 1.4) is integrated with Visual Studio, and allows us to publish directly from the Visual Studio IDE (Figure 7-4).

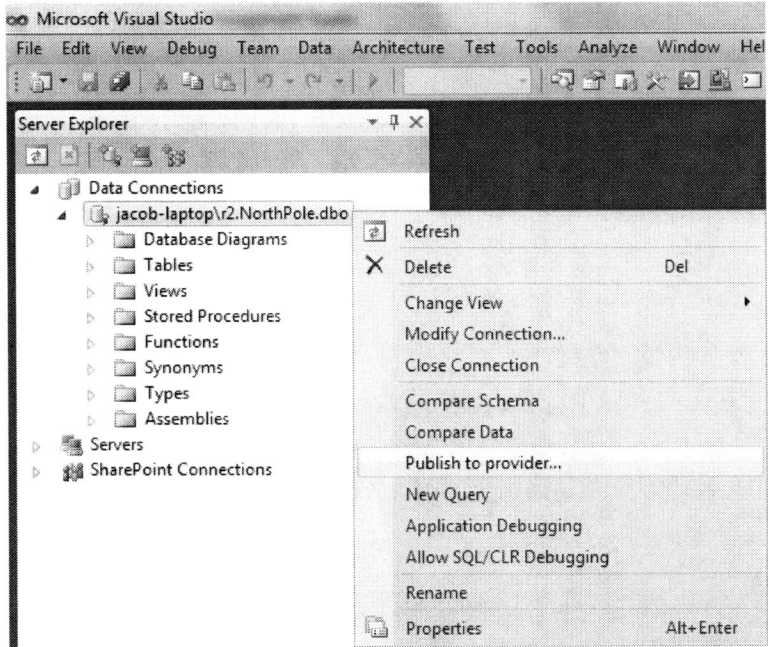

Figure 7.4: The Database Publishing Wizard.

The functionality offered by the Database Publishing Wizard is very much similar to the Database Scripting Wizard we examined earlier.

> **Database Publishing Wizard**
>
> *The current version of Database Publishing Wizard can be downloaded from:* HTTP://BRURL.COM/FS23.

The Database Publishing Wizard allows us to publish a SQL Server 2008 database to a SQL Server 2008 or 2005 database. When publishing from SQL Server 2008 to 2005, `FILESTREAM` columns will be created as `VARBINARY(MAX)` columns. We cannot publish a SQL Server 2008 database with `FILESTREAM` columns for deployment to a SQL Server 2000 instance.

Summary

This chapter walked through quite an array of database administration topics that are relevant to people managing `FILESTREAM` databases. Here's a brief summary of what we covered.

- How to detach and attach `FILESTREAM` databases and, in the process, move the `FILESTREAM` files to a new location.

- The behavior of `FILESTREAM` data under the transaction isolation levels.

- How the database recovery model of the database affects the way the garbage collector steps in and removes the garbage files. We also looked at the `FILESTREAM` tombstone table, which keeps track of the garbage files; the garbage collector uses this table to identify the files to be removed.

- Why it is not recommended that you touch the `FILESTREAM` data files on the NTFS folder directly, and why all access to the `FILESTREAM` data should be made through SQL Server only. Deleting files from the `FILESTREAM` data container or creating new files in the `FILESTREAM` data container can cause corruption in the database.

Chapter 7: FILESTREAM Database Administration

- How to detect corruption of `FILESTREAM` data using `DBCC CHECKDB` or `DBCC CHECKTABLE`, and how to fix corruption using the `repair_allow_data_loss` flag, although repairs involve deleting the relational data that was stored in the same row as the corrupted `FILESTREAM` data.

- Various methods for `FILESTREAM` database space management, including how to move `FILESTREAM` storage location of a table that is not partitioned, and how to add a new partition to a partitioned `FILESTREAM` table to distribute the `FILESTREAM` storage load.

- How to script `FILESTREAM` tables and data using the built-in SSMS Scripting Wizard as well as the Database Publishing Wizard.

Chapter 8: Backup and Restore for FILESTREAM Databases

One of the benefits of the `FILESTREAM` feature over the traditional methods of storing the BLOB data in the file system is that a `FILESTREAM` database backup contains both the relational data *and* the BLOB data stored in the `FILESTREAM` data container. This removes the administrative overhead of having to maintain separate backups of the disk files, which is necessary when using traditional BLOB storage methods. Likewise, when the full backup of a `FILESTREAM` database is restored to another location, the `FILESTREAM` data is also restored, and is available along with the relational data.

The backup process for a `FILESTREAM`-enabled database is the same as that for a non-`FILESTREAM` database; the `BACKUP` statement is the same, regardless of whether or not the database being processed has the `FILESTREAM` feature enabled. The restore operation, however, is a little different for a `FILESTREAM`-enabled database since we need to specify the path where the `FILESTREAM` filegroups should be restored.

In this chapter, we will examine the points below.

- How to perform full, differential, and log backups for `FILESTREAM` databases; this is no different than for any standard database.

- How to restore a `FILESTREAM` database from a full backup, and how to perform a point-in-time restore.

- File backups and piecemeal restores to bring a database back online with only the relational data.

- Data and backup compression for `FILESTREAM` databases.

- The issue of garbage files being included in `FILESTREAM` database backups.

Creating and Populating the Sample Database

As usual, our preparatory step for the examples is to re-create our `NorthPole` database, the `Items` table, with the `FILESTREAM` column, and populate it with some fresh data. We've performed this step many times now so, without further ado, the script is in Listing 8-1. The only additional point to note is that, immediately after creating the database, we `ALTER` it to stipulate use of the `FULL` recovery model because we wish to perform transaction log backups for this database. It is not possible to perform transaction log backups for a database operating in `SIMPLE` recovery model.

The script below starts with dropping the database if it already exists. In case you intend to repeatedly execute this script and subsequent exercises provided below, as part of your tests/experiment, you might want to consider dropping the database from SSMS. When you drop a database from SSMS, it will also remove the backup history from the `MSDB` database, resulting in a cleaner environment for the new database.

```
USE master
GO

-- If the database already exists, drop and re-create it
IF DB_ID('NorthPole') IS NOT NULL BEGIN
    DROP DATABASE NorthPole
END
GO

-- Create a FILESTREAM-enabled database
CREATE DATABASE NorthPole ON
PRIMARY (
    NAME = NorthPole,
    FILENAME = 'C:\ArtOfFS\Demos\Chapter8\NorthPole.mdf'
), FILEGROUP NorthPole_fs CONTAINS FILESTREAM(
    NAME = NorthPole_fs,
    FILENAME = 'C:\ArtOfFS\Demos\Chapter8\NorthPole_fs')
LOG ON (
    NAME = NorthPole_log,
    FILENAME = 'C:\ArtOfFS\Demos\Chapter8\NorthPole_log.ldf')
GO
```

```sql
-- Set the database recovery model to full
ALTER DATABASE NorthPole SET RECOVERY FULL
GO


-- Create a table with a FILESTREAM column
USE NorthPole
GO


-- Create the "Items" table
CREATE TABLE [dbo].[Items](
    [ItemID] UNIQUEIDENTIFIER ROWGUIDCOL NOT NULL UNIQUE,
    [ItemNumber] VARCHAR(20),
    [ItemDescription] VARCHAR(50),
    [ItemImage] VARBINARY(MAX) FILESTREAM NULL,
    [CreatedDate] DATETIME DEFAULT GETDATE()
)
GO


-- Insert the data into the table
INSERT INTO Items (ItemID, ItemNumber, ItemDescription, ItemImage)
SELECT
    NEWID(), 'MS1001', 'Microsoft Mouse',
    CAST(bulkcolumn AS VARBINARY(MAX))
FROM OPENROWSET(
    BULK 'C:\ArtOfFS\Demos\Images\MicrosoftMouse.jpg', SINGLE_BLOB
) AS x
```

Listing 8-1: T-SQL script to create the sample database for the examples in this chapter.

Backing up FILESTREAM Databases

In this section we'll consider the three most common types of database backup.

- **Full database backup** – Backs up all the data and objects in all the data files associated with a database.

- **Differential database backup** – Backs up any data and objects in all the data files for a given database that have changed since the last full backup.

- **Transaction log backup** – Copies into a backup file all the log records inserted into the transaction log file since the last transaction log backup.

No `FILESTREAM`-specific commands or keywords are required to create any of these backup types.

Full backups

A full database backup is the cornerstone of most SQL Server Backup and recovery schemes, and a full backup of a `FILESTREAM` database always includes the `FILESTREAM` data, as well as all the relational data.

Listing 8-2 takes a full backup of the `NorthPole` database and stores the backup file on the same drive as the database files. Of course, this is purely for convenience in this demo; in reality, you would always back up to a separate disk drive. Feel free to alter the path as required.

```
-- Take a full backup
USE master
GO
BACKUP DATABASE NorthPole
    TO DISK = 'C:\ArtOfFS\Demos\Chapter8\bak\NorthPole.bak'
GO
```

Listing 8-2:   T-SQL code to take a full backup of a `FILESTREAM`-enabled database.

Differential backups

A differential backup of a SQL Server database contains all changes since the previous full backup. Differential backups are especially useful when the database is large, and `FILESTREAM` databases are obviously expected to be large, since a full database backup process for such databases will be a time- and resource-consuming process. A typical backup scheme might consist of weekly full backups interspersed with nightly differential backups (plus transaction log backups, as required).

Again, the behavior of differential backups is the same with `FILESTREAM` as with non-`FILESTREAM` databases. Listing 8-3 inserts a new row into the `NorthPole` database and then captures a differential backup.

```
-- Insert another row into the table
USE NorthPole
GO
INSERT INTO Items (ItemID, ItemNumber, ItemDescription, ItemImage)
SELECT
    NEWID(), 'MS1002', 'Microsoft Mouse 2',
    CAST(bulkcolumn AS VARBINARY(MAX))
FROM OPENROWSET(
    BULK 'C:\ArtOfFS\Demos\Images\MicrosoftMouse.jpg', SINGLE_BLOB
) AS x

-- Take a differential backup
USE master
GO
BACKUP DATABASE NorthPole
    TO DISK = 'C:\ArtOfFS\Demos\Chapter8\bak\NorthPole_Diff.bak'
WITH DIFFERENTIAL
GO
```

Listing 8-3: Capturing a differential database backup.

Transaction log backups

A transaction log backup captures every record in the log that has been generated since the last log backup. We can combine these log backups with full (and any differential) backups to restore a database to any point in time before the last log backup was taken, assuming we have an unbroken chain of log files, taken after the relevant full backup.

Once again, no `FILESTREAM`-specific additional steps or commands are needed to take transaction log backups of `FILESTREAM` databases. Listing 8-3 inserts a third row into the `NorthPole` database, then captures a transaction log backup.

```
-- Insert another row into the table
USE NorthPole
GO
INSERT INTO Items (ItemID, ItemNumber, ItemDescription, ItemImage)
SELECT
    NEWID(), 'MS1003', 'Microsoft Mouse 3',
    CAST(bulkcolumn AS VARBINARY(MAX))
FROM OPENROWSET(
    BULK 'C:\ArtOfFS\Demos\Images\MicrosoftMouse.jpg', SINGLE_BLOB
) AS x

-- Take a log backup
USE master
GO

BACKUP LOG NorthPole
    TO DISK = 'C:\ArtOfFS\Demos\Chapter8\bak\NorthPole_Log.trn'
GO
```

Listing 8-4: Capturing a log backup.

Next, to set the scene for our various restore examples, we're going to add a fourth row to the table, note the current time (we'll need this later), and then simulate a disaster in the form of someone accidentally deleting the contents of the `Items` table. Finally, we take a second log backup.

```
-- Insert another row into the table
USE NorthPole
GO
INSERT INTO Items (ItemID, ItemNumber, ItemDescription, ItemImage)
SELECT
    NEWID(), 'MS1004', 'Microsoft Mouse 4',
    CAST(bulkcolumn AS VARBINARY(MAX))
```

```
FROM OPENROWSET(
    BULK 'C:\ArtOfFS\Demos\Images\MicrosoftMouse.jpg', SINGLE_BLOB
) AS x

SELECT GETDATE() AS Date
/*
Date
----------------------
2012-03-08 14:22:28.040
*/

-- Oops!No WHERE clause?!
BEGIN TRAN
DELETE FROM Items
COMMIT TRAN

-- Take a second log backup
USE master
GO

BACKUP LOG NorthPole
    TO DISK = 'C:\ArtOfFS\Demos\Chapter8\bak\NorthPole_Log2.trn'
GO
```

Listing 8-5: Fourth insert, accidental deletion from `Items` table, second log backup.

Restoring FILESTREAM Databases

Restoring a `FILESTREAM` database *may* require a little more attention than the backup process because, while restoring, we need to specify the location of the `FILESTREAM` filegroups in addition to the data and log files, if restoring to a new database. When performing an in-place restore, no additional parameters are required. In addition, `FILESTREAM` must be enabled on the SQL Server instance to which the database is being restored.

Restoring from a full backup

The simplest `RESTORE` operation involves just a single full backup file. This type of restore is relatively common when, for example, refreshing a development environment with the latest version of a production database.

Currently, following our "accidental" deletion, the `Items` table is empty. Listing 8-5 restores our full database backup over the top of the existing `NorthPole` database and recovers the database.

```
USE [master]
GO

RESTORE DATABASE NorthPole FROM
DISK = 'C:\ArtOfFS\Demos\Chapter8\bak\NorthPole.bak'
WITH REPLACE, RECOVERY
GO
```

Listing 8-6:   Restoring a full database backup over the existing database.

We have restored our `NorthPole` database, but so far only recovered one of the missing rows in our `Items` table. Fortunately, with the other backup files we've captured, we can repeat the restore operation and this time roll the database forward to recover the other three missing rows.

Point-in-time restore

Our current `NorthPole` database contains an `Items` table with just a single row of data, and our goal here is to restore the database to the point where it contained all four rows of data.

Our complete backup scheme for the `NorthPole` database consists of a full backup, a differential backup and two transaction log backups. With these backup files, we could perform another restore operation to completely restore the `NorthPole` database; in other words, we could restore each backup file in sequence, rolling the database forward to the state it existed in at the end of the second log backup, and then recover the database. In fact, in this very simple case, we can perform a complete restore simply using the full backup and the two transaction log backups; remember that a log backup captures all contents in the log file since the last **log backup** and so, in this case, the first transaction log backup will contain the log records for both the rows added after the full backup, and the second log backup will contain the details of the final insert. In a more realistic backup scheme, there would likely have been transaction log backups taken at regular intervals in the time between the full backup and the differential backup. In such a case, the differential backup would have allowed us to avoid having to restore those log backups, and our restore operation would instead have used just the full backup, the differential backup, and any subsequent log backups.

In any event, the problem we have here is that a complete restore would return the database to the state where the contents of the `Items` table were deleted since, when we restore the second log backup, it would roll forward, not only the fourth insert, but also the transaction that deleted the contents of `Items`. What we want to do instead, to get all the contents of our `Items` table back, is restore to a **specific point in time** within that second log backup; namely, the time that we recorded after the fourth insert, but before the accidental delete.

Fortunately, SQL Server supports point-in-time recovery of `FILESTREAM` databases; when you restore a `FILESTREAM`-enabled database from a certain point in time, the `FILESTREAM` data will be consistent with the relational data in the restored database.

Let's look at an example that performs a point-in-time restore of a `FILESTREAM` database. This time, instead of restoring over the top of the existing `NorthPole` database, we're going to restore to a new database, called `NothPole2`. At the end of this operation what we should have is a `NorthPole` database, with one row in the `Items` table, and a `NorthPole2` database with all four rows back in the `Items` table.

Chapter 8: Backup and Restore for FILESTREAM Databases

The first step is to restore the full backup to create the `NorthPole2` database, as shown in Listing 8-7. Notice the use of the `NORECOVERY` option; this instructs SQL Server to leave the database in a restoring state, ready to receive more backup files.

```
-- Restore the full backup
RESTORE DATABASE NorthPole2
    FROM DISK = 'C:\ArtOfFS\Demos\Chapter8\bak\NorthPole.bak'
    WITH NORECOVERY,
    MOVE 'NorthPole' TO 'C:\ArtOfFS\Demos\Chapter8\NorthPole2.mdf',
    MOVE 'NorthPole_log' TO 'C:\ArtOfFS\Demos\Chapter8\NorthPole2_log.ldf',
    MOVE 'NorthPole_fs' TO 'C:\ArtOfFS\Demos\Chapter8\NorthPole2_fs',
GO
```

Listing 8-7: Restoring a full backup.

The code uses the `MOVE` option three times, to specify the location of the data file, log file, and `FILESTREAM` data container, respectively. Note that the leaf-level folder (`NorthPole2_fs` in this example) should not exist already, but the containing folder (`C:\ArtOfFS\Demos\Chapter8`) must exist! SQL Server reserves the "exclusive" rights to create and configure `NorthPole2_fs` folder as part of the restore operation.

The next step is to completely restore the first transaction log backup, again leaving the `NorthPole2` database in a restoring state.

```
RESTORE LOG NorthPole2
FROM DISK = 'C:\ArtOfFS\Demos\Chapter8\bak\NorthPole_log.trn'
WITH NORECOVERY
```

Listing 8-8: Restoring the transaction log backup.

The final step is the interesting one; we apply the second log backup, but stop the restore at the point just before the data was accidentally deleted, and then recover the database. If you are following this example on your own system, insert the date and time from Listing 8-9.

```
RESTORE LOG NorthPole2
FROM DISK = 'C:\ArtOfFS\Demos\Chapter8\bak\NorthPole_log2.trn'
WITH RECOVERY,
-- Replace the date and time with the date and time you noted earlier
STOPAT = '2012-03-08 14:22:28.040'
```

Listing 8-9: Restoring the transaction log to a specified point in time.

Now, if we run a `SELECT` query on the `Items` table in the restored `NorthPole2` database, you will see that there are four rows. If you run the same query on the original `NorthPole` database, you will see that the table contains one row (or no rows if you didn't run Listing 8-6).

You can verify that the `FILESTREAM` data is restored correctly to the point prior to the "wrong operation," by doing one of the following:

- run a `SELECT` query on the `Items` table and look at the `ItemImage` column; you will see that the column contains BLOB values which reference the `FILESTREAM` data
- go to Windows Explorer and look at the `FILESTREAM` data container; you will notice that there are four files in the folder.

Point-in-time recovery for `FILESTREAM`-enabled databases gives database administrators one more reason for moving to `FILESTREAM` storage from the traditional storage methods.

File Backups and Piecemeal Restores

Generally speaking, the fact that a database backup includes the `FILESTREAM` data files is a bonus; it reduces the administrative overhead for DBAs, as they no longer need to worry about separately backing up disk files.

Chapter 8: Backup and Restore for FILESTREAM Databases

However, there may be times when a DBA does not want the `FILESTREAM` data to be part of the regular database backups. For example, you may want to grab a most recent copy of the production database and send it to the development/test team. A production database with `FILESTREAM` data could be quite large, and you might only need the relational data for your development or test environment.

It is possible to create a full file backup of a `FILESTREAM` database to exclude the `FILESTREAM` filegroups. This is helpful when you do not care about the `FILESTREAM` data and only want to deal with the relational data. When you restore such a backup using the Enterprise edition of SQL Server, you will be able to query all the relational data. However, any query that tries to access the `FILESTREAM` data will obviously fail.

Let's go ahead and run some scripts to see this in action. First, rerun the script in Listing 8-1 to re-create the sample database, and then run the script provided in Listing 8-10 to take a backup of the `PRIMARY` filegroup (excluding the `FILESTREAM` filegroup).

```
-- Take a backup
BACKUP DATABASE NorthPole
    FILEGROUP = 'PRIMARY'
    TO DISK = 'C:\ArtOfFS\Demos\Chapter8\bak\NorthPolePrimary.bak'
GO
```

Listing 8-10: Creating a file backup that excludes the `FILESTREAM` filegroup.

Now let's go ahead and create a new database from this partial backup.

```
-- Restore
RESTORE DATABASE NorthPolePartial
    FROM DISK = 'C:\ArtOfFS\Demos\Chapter8\bak\NorthPolePrimary.bak'
    WITH RECOVERY,
    PARTIAL,
    MOVE 'NorthPole' TO 'C:\ArtOfFS\Demos\Chapter8\NorthPolePartial.mdf',
    MOVE 'NorthPole_log' TO 'C:\ArtOfFS\Demos\Chapter8\NorthPolePartial_log.ldf',
GO
```

Listing 8-11: Restoring a partial backup that excludes `FILESTREAM` filegroups.

Chapter 8: Backup and Restore for FILESTREAM Databases

The script in Listing 8-11 restores the file backup that we created earlier. Note the usage of the **PARTIAL** option in the restore process. When the script has successfully executed, the new database will be online and you will be able to query all the data that is available in the primary filegroup.

Any filegroups that were not part of the restore will be piecemeal restored and, in the case below, the **FILESTREAM** filegroup will be marked as **RECOVERY_PENDING**, as shown from the query against the system catalog view **sys.database_files** in Listing 8-12.

```
USE NorthPolePartial
GO
SELECT
    type_desc,
    name,
    physical_name,
    state_desc
FROM sys.database_files

/*
type_desc    name           physical_name                              state_desc
----------   ------------   ----------------------------------------   ----------------
ROWS         NorthPoleDB    C:\ArtO..\NorthPolePartial.mdf             ONLINE
LOG          NorthPoleLOG   C:\..\NorthPolePartial_log.ldf             ONLINE
FILESTREAM   NorthPoleFS    C:\ArtOfFS\Dem...\NorthPole_fs             RECOVERY_PENDING
*/
```

Listing 8-12: Retrieving the list of filegroups associated with a database.

The **FILESTREAM** filegroup will become a "ghost" and, unless you have a file backup of the **FILESTREAM** filegroup and associated transaction logs, there is no way to get rid of it. The data stored in such ghost filegroups will not be available to the database.

In this example, all the data in the **Items** table except the **FILESTREAM** columns will be available for reading and writing. However, if we attempt to access the **FILESTREAM** data, SQL Server will generate an error. Therefore, the **SELECT *** on the **Items** table will fail because this operation attempts to read the **FILESTREAM** column along with all the other columns, as illustrated in Listing 8-13.

Chapter 8: Backup and Restore for FILESTREAM Databases

```
USE NorthPolePartial
GO

SELECT  *
FROM    Items
/*
Msg 670, Level 16, State 1, Line 2
Large object (LOB) data for table "dbo.Items" resides on an
offline filegroup ("NorthPoleFS") that cannot be accessed.
*/
```

Listing 8-13: A SELECT * query on a FILESTREAM table will fail if the FILESTREAM filegroup is not available.

If only the relational data is selected, the query will be successful. If a partial restore sequence excludes any FILESTREAM filegroup, point-in-time restore is not supported. For more information see *Piecemeal Restores (SQL Server)* at HTTP://BRURL.COM/FS24.

Data and Backup Compression for FILESTREAM Databases

One of the primary concerns with regard to having a database storing large amounts of BLOB data is the storage challenge, since FILESTREAM-enabled databases are expected to store huge amounts of data.

SQL Server 2008 introduced a data compression feature with compression of relational data at the page or row level. However, it does not compress the FILESTREAM data associated with the relational data.

It is possible to mark a FILESTREAM data container as "compressed" at the Windows level, which ultimately compresses the FILESTREAM data stored in the folder. However, this option is beneficial only if the data in the FILESTREAM data container is further compressible. If the data is already compressed (such as a zip file, jpeg, etc.) enabling compression at the NTFS level will incur unwanted CPU overhead. Though the early FILESTREAM documentation such as the FILESTREAM white paper at HTTP://BRURL.COM/FS7 does not explicitly discourage using NTFS compression on FILESTREAM data containers, this blog post from the Microsoft Customer Service and Support team counsels against it (HTTP://BRURL.COM/FS8).

However, it is possible to take a compressed backup of a FILESTREAM-enabled database. When taking a compressed backup, FILESTREAM data will also be compressed and you will notice a difference in the backup size, depending upon how compressible the FILESTREAM data is.

Beware of Garbage Files in FILESTREAM Backups

In my experience, it's possible that a full backup of a FILESTREAM-enabled database will also include the garbage files present in the FILESTREAM data container at the time of taking the backup. SQL Server does not filter out the garbage files when creating the backup file. Even if the transaction that generated the garbage file is committed, the garbage files will still be part of the backup until they are removed by the garbage collector thread.

The following example demonstrates this behavior. Begin by recreating our sample database using the script provided in Listing 8-1. Once the database is created, run the script in Listing 8-14, which updates the FILESTREAM value 100 times to generate 100 garbage files.

```
-- Update the data 100 times
DECLARE @i INT = 1
WHILE @i <= 100 BEGIN
    UPDATE Items SET ItemImage = 0x
    SET @i = @i + 1
END
```

Listing 8-14: Updating a non-NULL FILESTREAM value to generate new garbage files.

Chapter 8: Backup and Restore for FILESTREAM Databases

Each iteration of the loop updates the value stored in the `ItemImage` column of the `Items` table, and each `UPDATE` operation generates a new garbage file. After the execution completes, you can see the garbage files by looking into the `FILESTREAM` data container associated with the `ItemImage` column. You will see 101 files in the folder, of which 100 are garbage files.

We have seen how to locate the `FILESTREAM` data container associated with a database/table/column in the earlier chapters. If you still find it difficult, you can find a number of useful queries in Chapter 9: *Investigating FILESTREAM Databases*.

We now take a full backup of the `NorthPole` database by running the script shown in Listing 8-15. We are using the `WITH INIT` option to overwrite any previous backup sets in the backup file.

```
-- Take a backup
BACKUP DATABASE NorthPole
    TO DISK = 'C:\ArtOfFS\Demos\Chapter8\bak\NorthPole.bak'
    WITH INIT
GO
```

Listing 8-15: Generating a full backup file.

This full backup will include all the 100 garbage files we generated in the previous step. To verify this, we can restore the backup to create a new database, `NorthPole3`, and put the `FILESTREAM` data into `C:\ArtOfFS\Demos\Chapter8\NorthPole3_fs` (or any other folder that you prefer).

```
-- Restore
RESTORE DATABASE NorthPole3
    FROM DISK = 'C:\ArtOfFS\Demos\Chapter8\bak\NorthPole.bak'
    WITH RECOVERY,
    MOVE 'NorthPole' TO 'C:\ArtOfFS\Demos\Chapter8\NorthPole3.mdf',
    MOVE 'NorthPole_log' TO 'C:\ArtOfFS\Demos\Chapter8\NorthPole3_log.ldf',
    MOVE 'NorthPole_fs' TO 'C:\ArtOfFS\Demos\Chapter8\NorthPole3_fs',
    FILE=1
GO
```

Listing 8-16: Restoring a `FILESTREAM` database.

When the backup has been restored, go to the `FILESTREAM` data container and you will see 101 files instead of just the 1 that you would normally expect to see. It is quite surprising to see that all the garbage files came along with the backup, and they all got restored in the new location.

The garbage files unnecessarily increase the backup time and size, and increase the disk space requirements on the target location. My tests showed that a transaction log backup followed by a full backup on the target database clears the garbage files the next time the garbage collector runs.

Summary

We have seen that taking a backup of a `FILESTREAM` database is no different from backing up a non-`FILESTREAM` database. However, a restore operation may need a little bit more attention when restoring to a different database because you have to specify the location to which the `FILESTREAM` data is to be restored. In addition, you need to make sure that the `FILESTREAM` feature is enabled on the target database. SQL Server supports point-in-time recovery of `FILESTREAM`-enabled databases and this chapter presented an example to demonstrate this feature.

SQL Server allows the creation of full file backups of `FILESTREAM` databases that do not include the `FILESTREAM` filegroups. When such a backup is restored, all the relational data will be accessible. If you attempt to access the `FILESTREAM` data, SQL Server will generate an error.

The backup of a `FILESTREAM` database includes the garbage and orphaned files that are present in the `FILESTREAM` data container at the time of the backup. These files will be restored on the target location when the database is restored.

Chapter 9: Investigating FILESTREAM Databases

In the previous two chapters, we examined `FILESTREAM` database administration in some detail. To complete the discussion, we examine here our various options for investigating the `FILESTREAM` database and configuration metadata.

This chapter focuses on exposing a number of `FILESTREAM`-related system catalog views, along with a number of useful queries that help you to retrieve various valuable pieces of information about the `FILESTREAM` configuration. We also take a brief look at some of the in-depth information available from the `FILESTREAM`-related Dynamic Management Views (DMVs), and the available wait types that might help you troubleshoot various `FILESTREAM` performance issues.

Relevant System Catalog Views

SQL Server has a number of `FILESTREAM`-related system views that we can use to find information about `FILESTREAM` tables and columns.

We'll briefly review the system views that contain metadata relevant to `FILESTREAM` columns, and then take a look at some useful queries based on these views, which can give us such information as the location of the `FILESTREAM` data container, the names of all tables in a database that contain `FILESTREAM` columns, and so on.

sys.all_columns, sys.columns and sys.system_columns

The `sys.all_columns` view contains the columns belonging to all the user-defined objects and system objects in the current database.

The `sys.columns` view is essentially a subset of `sys.all_columns` and contains the columns belonging to all the table valued assembly functions, inline table valued functions, internal tables, system tables, table valued functions, user tables and views, again, in the current database.

Both views contain the `is_filestream` column, which returns 1 for `FILESTREAM` columns, and so can be used to determine all the `FILESTREAM` columns in the current database, as shown in Listing 9-1.

```
SELECT
    s.name AS SchemaName,
    t.name AS TableName,
    c.name AS ColumnName
FROM SYS.columns c
INNER JOIN sys.tables t ON t.object_id = c.object_id
INNER JOIN sys.schemas s ON s.schema_id = t.schema_id
WHERE is_filestream = 1
/*
SchemaName  TableName  ColumnName
----------  ---------  ----------
dbo         Items      ItemImage
*/
```

Listing 9-1: Retrieving all the `FILESTREAM` columns from the current database.

This `sys.sytem_columns` view contains a row for every column in all system objects and also has an `is_filestream` column which is expected to return 1 for all `FILESTREAM` columns. However, since none of the system tables in the SQL Server versions up to and including 2012 have `FILESTREAM` columns, this column will always contain 0. It is possible that a future version of SQL Server may have system tables with `FILESTREAM` columns.

sys.computed_columns

The system view `sys.computed_columns` contains a record for every computed column in the current database.

`sys.computed_columns` has a column `is_filestream`, which indicates whether the column has a `FILESTREAM` attribute or not. Although SQL Server (2008, 2008 R2, and 2012) allows the creation of computed columns based on `FILESTREAM` columns, it does not allow the creation of computed columns with the `FILESTREAM` attribute. Therefore, the `is_filestream` column on every row in `sys.computed_columns` will always be 0.

sys.identity_columns

This view contains a list of all the columns in the current database that are marked as `IDENTITY` columns. This view has a column `is_filestream`, which will be always 0 because an `IDENTITY` column cannot have the `FILESTREAM` attribute.

sys.dm_repl_traninfo

This system view returns information about each replicated transaction on a database that is configured for replication.

This view has a `FILESTREAM`-related column `fsinfo_address` which is a `VARBINARY(8)` value that stores the in-memory address of the cached `FILESTREAM` information structure.

sys.tables

The system catalog view `sys.tables` contains a row per user-defined table in the current database. The column `filestream_data_space_id` refers to the data space ID of a `FILESTREAM` filegroup or a partition scheme that consists of `FILESTREAM` filegroups.

sys.internal_tables

The system catalog view `sys.internal_tables` contains one row for every internal table in the current database. According to Books Online, internal tables are automatically generated by SQL Server to support specific features; they are generated when those features are enabled, and removed when the features are disabled. It looks like this is not true for the `FILESTREAM`-specific internal table, `FILESTREAM_TOMBSTONE`. It is also found in the `model` database and automatically added to every new database, whether or not the `FILESTREAM` feature is enabled.

This view has a number of columns that are relevant to the `FILESTREAM` feature.

- **internal_type** – A `TINYINT` column that specifies the type of the internal table being referenced by the current row. If the current database has a `FILESTREAM` tombstone table, it will show up in this view and the `internal_type` column will be set to 208. (For more information about the tombstone table, refer back to Chapter 7.)
- **internal_type_desc** – The text description of the `internal_type` column. For `FILESTREAM` tombstone tables, the value will be `FILESTREAM_TOMBSTONE`.
- **name** – The name of the table. `FILESTREAM` tombstone tables are named as `filestream_tombstone_nnnnn`, where nnnnn is a number that points to the `object_id` of the table.
- **filestream_data_space_id** – An integer value that is reserved for future use.

sys.partitions

This view contains a row for each partition of all the tables and indexes in the given database. One of the columns in this view is `filestream_filegroup_id`, which points to the filegroup ID in the `sys.filegroups` table.

sys.data_spaces

This view returns a row for every filegroup, partition schema, and `FILESTREAM` filegroup. The query in Listing 9-2 retrieves all the `FILESTREAM` filegroups in the current database.

```
SELECT
    *
FROM sys.data_spaces
WHERE type_desc = 'FILESTREAM_DATA_FILEGROUP'
/*
name          data_space_id type type_desc                 is_default
------------  ------------- ---- ------------------------- ----------
NorthPole_fs  2             FD   FILESTREAM_DATA_FILEGROUP 1
*/
```

Listing 9-2:   Retrieving all the `FILESTREAM` filegroups in the current database.

The following columns of this view are related to the `FILESTREAM` feature.

- **name** – The name of the filegroup, partition schema, or `FILESTREAM` filegroup.
- **data_space_id** – The unique data space ID.
- **type** – The type of data space. For `FILESTREAM` filegroups, this will be set to `FD`.
- **type_desc** – A description of the data space. For `FILESTREAM` filegroups, this will be `FILESTREAM_DATA_FILEGROUP`.
- **is_default** – If the filegroup is marked as the default filegroup, this will be set to 1.

sys.database_files

The `sys.database_files` view lists all files defined in the current database. There are three columns of particular interest when querying for `FILESTREAM`-related information. First, the `type` and `type_desc` columns indicate the type of file. A `type` of 2 or `type_desc` of `FILESTREAM` indicates a `FILESTREAM` data container (which, as we know, is actually a folder in the file system and not a file). The `physical_name` column contains the full path in the file system where the database file is located. In the case of a `FILESTREAM` data container, it is the root of the `FILESTREAM` data container.

Upon close investigation, one will also find that the `maxsize` and `growth` columns contain values of 0, which is never the case for data or log files.

sys.filegroups

This view inherits from `sys.data_spaces` and contains all the columns in the parent view and a few additional ones. The columns that are of interest for `FILESTREAM` are those that are inherited from `sys.data_spaces`, described above.

sys.system_internals_partition_columns

This system view contains a number of internal columns copied from the catalog of the relational engine. One of the columns relevant to this discussion is the `is_filestream` column that specifies whether the column being described has a `FILESTREAM` attribute. However, the information retrieved from this view is redundant and is available in other system views.

Books Online warns that this view is reserved for the internal system usage only and future compatibility is not guaranteed. This view is included for completeness only.

sys.system_internals_partitions

This is another internal view that contains some `FILESTREAM`-related information. Two columns that are relevant to the `FILESTREAM` feature are `filestream_filegroup_id` and `filestream_guid`. `filestream_filegroup_id` refers to the filegroup ID of the `FILESTREAM` filegroup.

Again, Books Online warns that this view is reserved for the internal system usage only and future compatibility is not guaranteed. Personally, however, I found this view very helpful and have used it a number of times to retrieve various pieces of information related to the location of the `FILESTREAM` folders (see, for example, Listings 9-10 and 9-11).

sys.filestream_tombstone_*

This is an internal table that the `FILESTREAM` feature uses to keep track of the garbage files. When a garbage file is generated, it is recorded in this table and the garbage collector reads information from the tombstone table and cleans the garbage based on it.

A detailed explanation of this table is provided in Chapter 7.

Useful FILESTREAM Metadata Queries

While working with `FILESTREAM`-enabled databases, you might very often come across cases where you need to query the `FILESTREAM` metadata to retrieve information. This section provides some `FILESTREAM` metadata queries, using many of the system catalog views discussed previously, which you might find very helpful.

SQL Server instance-level queries

Let's start with a few queries that are helpful for retrieving FILESTREAM-related information on the SQL Server instance level. These make extensive use of the system function, SERVERPROPERTY().

Is FILESTREAM enabled?

The system function SERVERPROPERTY() can be used to determine whether the FILESTREAM feature is enabled on the current SQL Server instance, as shown in Listing 9-3.

```
IF SERVERPROPERTY('FilestreamEffectiveLevel') > 0
    PRINT 'FILESTREAM is enabled'
ELSE
    PRINT 'FILESTREAM is disabled'
```

Listing 9-3:   Determining whether FILESTREAM is enabled.

Identify the FILESTREAM access level

The system function SERVERPROPERTY() can be used to determine the FILESTREAM access level in the current SQL Server instance, as shown in Listing 9-4.

```
SELECT
    SERVERPROPERTY('FilestreamConfiguredLevel')
        AS FilestreamConfiguredLevel,
    SERVERPROPERTY('FilestreamEffectiveLevel')
        AS FilestreamEffectiveLevel
```

Chapter 9: Investigating FILESTREAM Databases

```
/*
FilestreamConfiguredLevel     FilestreamEffectiveLevel
-------------------------     ------------------------
3                             3
*/
```

Listing 9-4: Identifying the `FILESTREAM` access level at the Windows level.

Both `FilestreamConfiguredLevel` and `FilestreamEffectiveLevel` return a numeric value that indicates the current configuration value, as follows:

- **0** – `FILESTREAM` is disabled
- **1** – `FILESTREAM` is enabled for T-SQL access
- **2** – `FILESTREAM` is enabled for T-SQL and Win32 streaming access (local only)
- **3** – `FILESTREAM` is enabled for T-SQL and Win32 streaming access (local and remote) (Undocumented).

The difference between `FilestreamConfiguredLevel` and `FilestreamEffectiveLevel` is found in how `FILESTREAM` requires configuration changes at the Windows level, through Configuration Manager, and at the SQL Server instance level through SSMS or the `sp_configure` stored procedure (see Appendix A for more details).

Note that at time of writing (March 2012) the description of these server properties given in Books Online was not accurate.

The `FilestreamConfiguredLevel` property returns the value as configured in Configuration Manager. `FilestreamEffectiveLevel` returns the actual ("effective") level of `FILESTREAM` access that is enabled. `FilestreamEffectiveLevel` can be less than or equal to `FilestreamConfiguredLevel`. If the configuration at the instance level is different from the configuration at the Windows level, the lower access level will prevail. Let's examine this in the matrix below.

Chapter 9: Investigating FILESTREAM Databases

Instance \ Windows	0	1	2 (local only)	3 (local and remote)
0: Disabled	0	0	0	0
1: T-SQL access only	0	1	1	1
2: T-SQL and streaming access	0	1	2	3

The matrix shows how the values configured at the instance level (rows) and those configured at the Windows level (columns) result in the `FilestreamEffectiveLevel`. You'll notice that the lower of the two always wins. For example, if the Windows configuration allows T-SQL and Win32 streaming access but the instance is configured for T-SQL access only, then the effective configuration is T-SQL access only. In plain terms, if the desired access level is remote streaming access, this will need to be configured as such, both at the Windows level and at the instance level.

The matrix also shows that it's not possible to control the difference between local and remote streaming access at the instance level. That difference can only be controlled at the Windows level. (Early CTP versions of SQL Server 2008 did have that ability, but for unknown reasons it was removed before the release.)

You can check the output of the following T-SQL statement to find the configured value at the SQL Server instance level (Listing 9-5).

```
EXEC sp_configure 'filestream_access_level'
/*
name                          minimum maximum config_value run_value
----------------------------- ------- ------- ------------ ---------
filestream access level       0       2       2            2
*/
```

Listing 9-5: Identifying the FILESTREAM access level at the instance level.

Chapter 9: Investigating FILESTREAM Databases

The column `config_value` contains the current configured value at the SQL Server instance level:

- **0** – FILESTREAM is disabled
- **1** – FILESTREAM is enabled for T-SQL access
- **2** – FILESTREAM is enabled for T-SQL and Win32 streaming access.

Unlike the `FilestreamEffectiveLevel` and `FilestreamConfiguredLevel` server properties, the possible values for `config_value` do not include '3'.

Identify the FILESTREAM share name

The `FILESTREAM` share name can be retrieved from the `SERVERPROPERTY()` system function using the `FilestreamShareName` parameter, as shown in Listing 9-6.

```
SELECT
    SERVERPROPERTY('FilestreamShareName')
    AS FilestreamShare
/*
FilestreamShare
---------------
MSSQLSERVER
*/
```

Listing 9-6: Retrieving the `FILESTREAM` share name.

Identify the FILESTREAM-enabled databases

To determine whether a database is `FILESTREAM`-enabled, we need to check whether the database has a `FILESTREAM` filegroup or not. This can be identified from the system view `sys.filegroups`. The T-SQL code in Listing 9-7 checks for a `FILESTREAM` filegroup in each database in the current SQL Server instance.

Chapter 9: Investigating FILESTREAM Databases

```
CREATE TABLE #db (dbname SYSNAME)
EXECUTE sp_MSforeachdb '
    INSERT INTO #db(dbname)
    SELECT ''?'' FROM [?].sys.filegroups
    WHERE type = ''FD'''

SELECT * FROM #db
DROP TABLE #db
```

Listing 9-7: Identifying all the FILESTREAM-enabled databases.

Database-level queries

These queries retrieve specific FILESTREAM-related information from the current database.

Identifying the FILESTREAM data container location

The path to the FILESTREAM data container(s) associated with the current database can be identified by looking at the physical_name column of the system view sys.database_files, as shown in Listing 9-8.

```
SELECT
    db_name() AS DatabaseName,
    physical_name AS FilestreamFolder
FROM sys.database_files
WHERE type_desc = 'FILESTREAM'
/*
DatabaseName    FilestreamFolder
------------    ------------------------------------
NorthPole       C:\ArtOfFS\Demos\Chapter9\NorthPole_fs
*/
```

Listing 9-8: Identifying the FILESTREAM data container of a database.

Identifying the tables with FILESTREAM columns

A `FILESTREAM` column can be identified by looking at the `is_filestream` column of the system view `sys.columns`, as shown in Listing 9-9.

```
SELECT DISTINCT
    OBJECT_NAME(OBJECT_ID) AS TableName
FROM sys.columns c
WHERE c.is_filestream = 1
/*
TableName
---------
Items
Items2
Items3
Items4
*/
```

Listing 9-9: Retrieving a list of all tables with `FILESTREAM` fields in a database.

Identifying the FILESTREAM folder names associated with each FILESTREAM table

SQL Server creates a root folder for every `FILESTREAM` table in the database. Since the folders are named using GUID values, it will often be very confusing when you have several `FILESTREAM` tables in the database. Listing 9-10 shows a query that can be used to determine the folder names associated with each `FILESTREAM` table.

```
SELECT
    t.name AS TableName,
    d.name AS FileGroup,
    p.filestream_guid AS FolderName
FROM sys.tables t
INNER JOIN sys.system_internals_partitions p
    ON p.object_id = t.object_id
```

Chapter 9: Investigating FILESTREAM Databases

```
INNER JOIN sys.data_spaces d
    ON d.data_space_id = t.filestream_data_space_id
WHERE p.filestream_filegroup_id > 0
/*
TableName  FileGroup       FolderName
---------  -------------   -----------------------------------
Items1     NorthPole_fs1   041C0478-8EB6-4C65-B0AD-12E29DF69D09
Items2     NorthPole_fs2   AEA2F2A4-4CA5-4790-AB16-1F78379D69C8
*/
```

Listing 9-10: Retrieving the FILESTREAM folders associated with each table in the current database.

Note that, without the WHERE clause, two rows are returned for each table with FILESTREAM columns. The second row contains NULL as the filestream_guid value. There are two rows in sys.system_internals_partitions for a single table with FILESTREAM columns. The difference seems to be in the filestream_filegroup_id field that is set to "0" for the row that has the NULL in the filestream_guid field.

If the FILESTREAM table is partitioned, SQL Server will create a root folder per partition in the table. If you have partitioned FILESTREAM tables, you might need a slightly modified version of the above query to determine the FILESTREAM folder names of each partition, as shown in Listing 9-11. It is interesting to note that SQL Server does not list the NULL row we saw earlier when the table is partitioned; therefore, this query does not have the same WHERE clause.

```
SELECT
    t.Name AS TableName,
    sip.partition_number AS PartitionNumber,
    sip.filestream_guid AS FilestreamFolder
FROM sys.system_internals_partitions sip
INNER JOIN sys.partitions p ON p.partition_id = sip.partition_id
    AND sip.filestream_guid IS NOT NULL
INNER JOIN sys.tables t
    ON t.object_id = p.object_id
```

```
/*
TableName  PartitionNumber   FilestreamFolder
---------  ---------------   ------------------------------------
Items      1                 8C2E5B76-40E9-4F14-81D1-809DD2AB377E
Items      2                 9410B335-DF04-48B1-BC14-6B7DE5022133
Items      3                 5C3C61C5-978B-4014-A8BA-B35FE79127DA
*/
```

Listing 9-11: Retrieving the FILESTREAM folders of each partition.

Identifying the FILESTREAM filegroup associated with each FILESTREAM table

Listing 9-12 retrieves all the FILESTREAM tables in the current database and shows the FILESTREAM filegroups associated with each table.

```
SELECT
    t.name AS TableName,
    f.name AS FilestreamFileGroup,
    fl.physical_name AS FilestreamFolder
FROM sys.tables t
INNER JOIN sys.filegroups f
    ON f.data_space_id = t.filestream_data_space_id
INNER JOIN sys.database_files fl
    ON fl.data_space_id = f.data_space_id
/*
TableName  FilestreamFileGroup  FilestreamFolder
---------  -------------------  ------------------------------------
Items2     NorthPole_fs         C:\ArtOfFS\Demos\Chapter9\NorthPole_fs
Items3     NorthPole_fs         C:\ArtOfFS\Demos\Chapter9\NorthPole_fs
Items4     NorthPole_fs         C:\ArtOfFS\Demos\Chapter9\NorthPole_fs
Items      NorthPole_fs         C:\ArtOfFS\Demos\Chapter9\NorthPole_fs
*/
```

Listing 9-12: Retrieving all the FILESTREAM tables and their FILESTREAM filegroups.

Chapter 9: Investigating FILESTREAM Databases

If the table is partitioned, you will need a different version of the above query to retrieve the same information. This is given in Listing 9-13.

```
SELECT
    t.name AS [Table],
    f.name AS FilestreamFG,
    f.physical_name AS FilestreamFolder
FROM sys.tables t
INNER JOIN sys.partitions p
    ON p.object_id = t.object_id
INNER JOIN sys.database_files f
    ON f.data_space_id = p.filestream_filegroup_id
    AND f.type_desc = 'FILESTREAM'

/*
Table  FilestreamFG   FilestreamFolder
-----  -------------  ------------------------------------
Items  NorthPole_fs1  C:\ArtOfFS\Demos\Chapter7\NorthPole_fs1
Items  NorthPole_fs2  C:\ArtOfFS\Demos\Chapter7\NorthPole_fs2
Items  NorthPole_fs3  C:\ArtOfFS\Demos\Chapter7\NorthPole_fs3
*/
```

Listing 9-13: Retrieving all the FILESTREAM tables and their FILESTREAM filegroups on the partitioned database (from Chapter 7).

Identifying the FILESTREAM folder name associated with each FILESTREAM column

If a table has more than one FILESTREAM column, it will often be very confusing to identify the folder associated with each column. Listing 9-14 retrieves a list of all FILESTREAM columns in a table, along with the FILESTREAM folder associated with the column.

Chapter 9: Investigating FILESTREAM Databases

```sql
DECLARE @objectID INT
SELECT @objectID = OBJECT_ID('Items4')

SELECT
    cp.name AS [ColumnName],
    p.partition_number AS [Partition],
    CAST(rs.colguid AS UNIQUEIDENTIFIER) AS [FolderName]
FROM sys.sysrscols rs
INNER JOIN sys.partitions p ON rs.rsid = p.partition_id
    AND rs.colguid IS NOT NULL
    AND p.object_id = @objectID
INNER JOIN sys.syscolpars cp ON cp.colid = rs.rscolid
    AND cp.id = @objectID

/*
ColumnName  Partition   FolderName
----------  ---------   ------------------------------------
ItemImage1  1           BE0F0AE1-03CB-45EA-93E6-AE9CE4C3C875
ItemImage2  1           5F14959C-36A7-4A6F-9BC7-567A9B8CB5DB
ItemImage3  1           A505E6F6-2B34-454B-BF60-A142294349E0
ItemImage4  1           BB9EE893-0CDB-4849-B0FB-4E0DBCF57864
ItemImage5  1           D14A7768-8FCC-4B32-B776-89C2CDD8BB1F
*/
```

Listing 9-14: Retrieving the FILESTREAM folders associated with each FILESTREAM column in a table.

This query tries to read from a few "internal" tables that are not accessible to regular user queries. If you copy and paste the above query into your query window and run it, you will receive the following error:

```
Msg 208, Level 16, State 1, Line 4
Invalid object name 'sys.sysrscols'.
```

This happens because the view **sys.sysrscols** is not accessible to user mode queries. To run queries that are not accessible to user mode queries, you need to make a DAC to the database. Connecting to SQL Server using a DAC was discussed in Chapter 7.

Identifying the FILESTREAM file name associated with each FILESTREAM value

SQL Server names `FILESTREAM` files based on the transaction LSN that created the file. SQL Server keeps track of this value internally and uses it to identify the correct file when a read/write request comes in.

Though it is possible to identify the disk file associated with each `FILESTREAM` value on your `FILESTREAM` column, it is a lengthy process. SQL Server MVP Paul Randal has written a detailed blog post which explains how to do this. I would recommend you take a look at it (HTTP://BRURL.COM/FS9).

FILESTREAM-related DMVs

SQL Server has a number of `FILESTREAM`-related DMV views that we can use to find very detailed information regarding `FILESTREAM` storage and activity against `FILESTREAM` databases.

sys.dm_filestream_file_io_handles

This DMV returns all the open `FILESTREAM` handles which any client application has opened using the Win32 API function `OpenSqlFilestream` or the `SqlFilestream` managed class. It has a number of columns providing detailed information about the open I/O handles. You can find a complete reference of all the columns in MSDN at HTTP://BRURL.COM/FSIO. The columns below may be particularly helpful.

- **filestream_transaction_id** – Shows the ID of the transaction associated with the given handle. This is the value returned by the GET_FILESTREAM_TRANS-ACTION_CONTEXT() T-SQL function. This field can be joined with the **sys.dm_FILESTREAM_file_io_requests** view to retrieve additional information.

- **access_type**
    - **R**: file opened for read operation
    - **W**: file opened for write operation
    - **RW**: file opened for read and write operation.

- **logical_path** – Shows the logical path name of the file that is associated with the **FILESTREAM** handle. This is the same value that is returned by the PathName() method.

- **physical_path** – shows the actual NTFS path name of the file being accessed. It is enabled by tracing Flag 5556.

- **creation_client_process_id** – This shows the ID of the Windows process which is responsible for the **FILESTREAM** transaction. That can help narrow down which application is misbehaving, and so on.

sys.dm_filestream_file_io_requests

This DMV displays a list of the **FILESTREAM** I/O requests being processed at the given moment. This view can be joined with **sys.dm_filestream_file_io_handles** on the filestream_transaction_id column to retrieve additional information about the **FILESTREAM** operations going on.

You may want to query this DMV to retrieve extended information about the **FILESTREAM** processing going on your server. You can find more information in Books Online at HTTP://BRURL.COM/FSII.

sys.dm_tran_active_transactions

This DMV returns the active transactions in all the databases in the given SQL Server instance. If one or more `FILESTREAM` transactions are in progress, the `filestream_transaction_id` of this will be non-`NULL`.

This view can be joined with `sys.dm_filestream_file_io_handles` on `filestream_transaction_id` to retrieve additional information.

The T-SQL code in Listing 9-15 shows how to retrieve all the active `FILESTREAM` transactions in the current instance.

```sql
SELECT  *
FROM    sys.dm_tran_active_transactions
WHERE   filestream_transaction_id IS NOT NULL
```

Listing 9-15:   Retrieving all the active `FILESTREAM` transactions in the current instance.

FILESTREAM and Wait Types

The `FILESTREAM` feature introduced a few new system **wait types** to deal with the various `FILESTREAM`-related operations, available through the `sys.dm_os_wait_stats` DMV.

FS_FC_RWLOCK

This wait type is generated by the `FILESTREAM` garbage collector. It occurs when garbage collection is disabled prior to a backup or restore operation, or when a garbage collection cycle is being executed.

FS_GARBAGE_COLLECTOR_SHUTDOWN

This wait type occurs during the cleanup process of a garbage collection cycle. It indicates that the garbage collector is waiting for the cleanup tasks to be completed.

FS_HEADER_RWLOCK

This wait type indicates that the process is waiting to obtain access to the FILESTREAM header file for read or write operation. The FILESTREAM header is a disk file located in the FILESTREAM data container and is named filestream.hdr. This file contains important metadata information that SQL Server uses to manage the FILESTREAM data associated with a given database. Unlike FILESTREAM data files, SQL Server keeps an exclusive lock on the filestream.hdr file.

FS_LOGTRUNC_RWLOCK

This wait type indicates that the process is trying to access FILESTREAM log truncation, either to perform a log truncate operation, or to disable log truncation prior to a backup or restore operation.

FSA_FORCE_OWN_XACT

This wait type occurs when a FILESTREAM file I/O operation needs to bind to the associated transaction, but the transaction is currently owned by another session.

FSAGENT

`FSAgent` is part of the `FILESTREAM` subsystem which sits between the storage engine and the `FILESTREAM` data. `FSAgent` manages the handling of `FILESTREAM` data files in a transparent manner so that the rest of the storage engine feels that they are real `VARBINARY(MAX)` values. This wait type occurs when a `FILESTREAM` file I/O operation is waiting for `FSAgent` to perform an I/O operation. In the RTM version of SQL Server 2008, this wait type showed up in Activity Monitor, which may make performance troubleshooting more difficult. This issue is documented in Microsoft KB article 958942 (HTTP://BRURL.COM/FSI2) and fixed in Cumulative Update 2 for SQL Server 2008.

FSTR_CONFIG_MUTEX

This wait type occurs when there is a wait for another `FILESTREAM` feature reconfiguration to be completed.

FSTR_CONFIG_RWLOCK

This wait type occurs when there is a wait to serialize access to the `FILESTREAM` configuration parameters.

Summary

SQL Server exposes a number of system catalog views, as well as DMVs, which provide a good deal of insight into the internal metadata of `FILESTREAM` storage and configuration. We have examined those views that are particularly helpful in investigating `FILESTREAM`-enabled databases.

Chapter 10: Integrating FILESTREAM with other SQL Server Features

As we have seen in the previous chapters, the `FILESTREAM` feature is implemented as an additional attribute added to a `VARBINARY(MAX)` column. This model keeps `FILESTREAM` features and the complexities associated with managing BLOB data completely transparent to the T-SQL programming interface; T-SQL code can access `FILESTREAM` data just as if it were a regular `VARBINARY(MAX)` column. Mostly, this means that existing SQL Server features that work with `VARBINARY(MAX)` columns work with `FILESTREAM` columns without requiring modification.

In this chapter, we will look at how well the `FILESTREAM` feature aligns with the SQL Server features below.

- Replication
- Log shipping
- Full-text indexing
- Database snapshots
- Change Data Capture (CDC)
- Data compression
- Transparent data encryption
- Database mirroring
- High Availability Disaster Recovery – Always On (HADRON).

FILESTREAM and Replication

Replication technologies provide a means to copy data from a primary database (publisher) to one or more secondary databases (subscribers). Even though replication wasn't designed for all the functions DBAs use it for today, it is nevertheless widely used as a solution for reporting, load balancing, synchronization, high availability, disaster recovery, and so on. SQL Server supports replicating **FILESTREAM** data but, of course, **FILESTREAM** data is stored outside the database (in the file system) and is often used to store very large data files, so it is interesting to examine *how* replication of **FILESTREAM**-enabled databases works.

Replicating FILESTREAM columns

When replicating SQL Server 2008 **FILESTREAM**-enabled databases, **FILESTREAM** columns can be replicated either with or without the **FILESTREAM** attribute.

If you replicate **FILESTREAM** columns with the **FILESTREAM** attribute, **FILESTREAM** data values on the publisher column will go to a **FILESTREAM** column on the subscriber. When you replicate a **FILESTREAM** database to a SQL Server 2008 or later instance, in most cases you would want to replicate the **FILESTREAM** attribute along with the **FILESTREAM** columns.

If you replicate **FILESTREAM** columns without the **FILESTREAM** attribute, **FILESTREAM** data values on the publisher will be replicated as **VARBINARY(MAX)** columns on the subscriber. In this way, it's possible to replicate a table with **FILESTREAM** columns to a SQL Server 2005 subscriber, which doesn't support **FILESTREAM**. However, it is not possible to replicate **FILESTREAM** columns to SQL Server 2000 subscribers. Table 10-1 summarizes the **FILESTREAM** replication support with previous versions of SQL Server.

Chapter 10: Integrating FILESTREAM with other SQL Server Features

Publication	SQL Server 2008 and later	SQL Server 2005	SQL Server 2000 or earlier
Replicate as FILESTREAM	Supported	Not supported	Not supported
Replicate as VARBINARY(MAX)	Supported	Supported	Not supported

Table 10-1: FILESTREAM replication support for SQL Server versions.

Note that it is not possible to create a single publication that replicates FILESTREAM columns with the FILESTREAM attribute to SQL Server 2008 subscribers and without the FILESTREAM attribute to SQL Server 2005 subscribers.

Size limits when replicating* FILESTREAM *columns as* VARBINARY(MAX) *columns

When replicating FILESTREAM *values as* VARBINARY(MAX) *columns to SQL Server 2008, and later, subscribers, the maximum data size supported is 2 GB. However, replicating large data values from SQL Server 2008 publishers to SQL Server 2005 subscribers is limited to a maximum of 256 MB of data. Replication will fail if the data value is larger.*

By default, FILESTREAM columns are configured to replicate as VARBINARY(MAX) values. You can change this setting from the property page of the publication using SSMS. To do this, open the publication properties dialog box by right-clicking on the publication and selecting **Properties**. Then, on the **Articles** tab, right-click on the desired table article and select the **Set Properties** menu item. Change the property value **Convert filestream to MAX data types** to **False** (Figure 10-1).

Chapter 10: Integrating FILESTREAM with other SQL Server Features

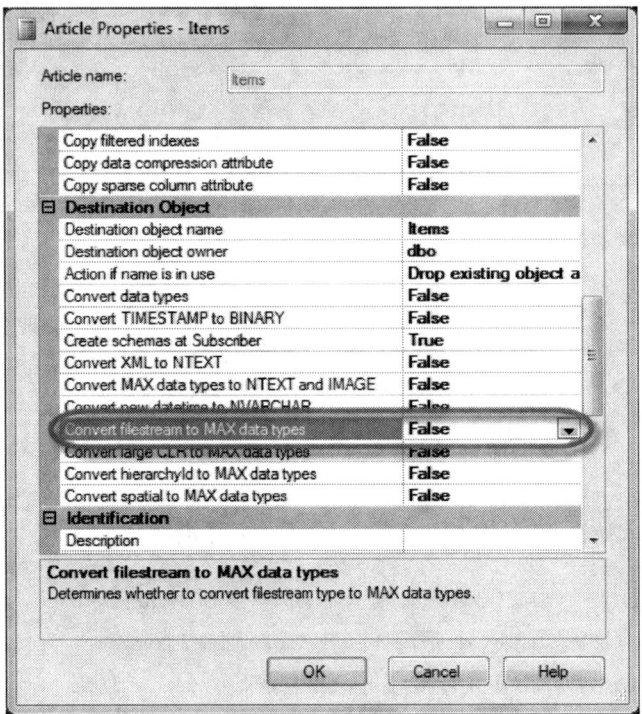

Figure 10-1: Choosing to replicate FILESTREAM columns with the FILESTREAM attribute.

Click **OK** on the **Article Properties** dialog box and then again on the **Publication Property** dialog box to save the changes. You must then reinitialize the subscriptions for the changes to take effect.

You can also use T-SQL to specify that you want to replicate FILESTREAM columns with the FILESTREAM attribute; details are provided later in the section, *Managing the FILESTREAM replication flag using T-SQL*.

Maximum replication data size

While configuring replication for FILESTREAM columns to VARBINARY(MAX) columns, one of the most important configuration parameters that needs attention is the *maximum replication data size* setting. This is a SQL Server instance-level configuration which, by default, is set to 64 KB.

Therefore, under the default maximum replication data size, and default FILESTREAM to VARBINARY(MAX) conversion settings, transactional or merge replication of a FILESTREAM () column, or any other large-value type, will fail if we attempt to store values larger than 64 KB. And not only the replication, but also the INSERT or UPDATE operation will fail; SQL Server will abort the INSERT or UPDATE operation and generate the following error:

```
Length of LOB data (nnnn) to be replicated exceeds configured maximum 65536.
The statement has been terminated.
```

As we have seen several times in the previous chapters, FILESTREAM columns are ideal only if the values you expect to store in the FILESTREAM column are 1 MB or larger. This obviously means that when you set up transactional replication, you should either replicate to FILESTREAM, or change the maximum replication data size configuration setting so that values larger than 64 KB can be stored and replicated.

To change the maximum replication size configuration setting, right-click on the SQL Server instance in SSMS Object Explorer and click **Properties**, navigate to the **Advanced** tab and edit the setting, as shown in Figure 10-2.

Once the maximum replication data size setting has been increased, you will be able to replicate FILESTREAM data values to VARBINARY(MAX) that are less than, or equal to, the size specified.

Chapter 10: Integrating FILESTREAM with other SQL Server Features

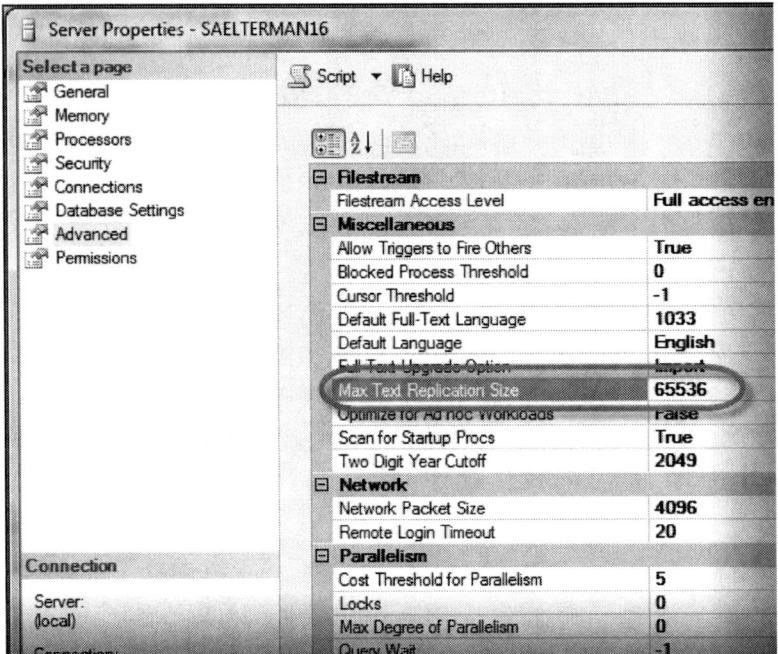

Figure 10-2: Using SSMS to change the maximum data replication size.

To change the maximum replication data size using T-SQL, you configure the `max text repl size` setting using the system stored procedure, `sp_configure`. You can specify any value within the range of 0 to 2147483647 bytes, or simply specify 1 to instruct SQL Server to impose a restriction depending on the maximum storage capacity of the associated data type as shown in Listing 10-1. As noted earlier, this raises the size limit to 2 GB when replicating to SQL Server 2008, and later, instances, but the limit remains only 256 MB when replicating to SQL Server 2005 instances.

```
sp_configure 'show advanced options', 1;
GO
RECONFIGURE;
GO
sp_configure 'max text repl size', -1;
GO
RECONFIGURE;
GO
```

Listing 10-1: Using T-SQL to change the maximum replication data size.

FILESTREAM replication and the UNIQUEIDENTIFIER column

In Chapter 2, we discussed the fact that `FILESTREAM` columns can be added to a table only if it has a `UNIQUEIDENTIFIER` column that is marked as a `ROWGUIDCOL` with a `UNIQUE` constraint. When replicating `FILESTREAM` columns with the `FILESTREAM` attribute, we must ensure that the `UNIQUEIDENTIFIER` column is also selected for replication and that the `UNIQUE` constraint replicated along with the `UNIQUEIDENTIFIER` column.

If we remove the `UNIQUEIDENTIFIER` column from the publication, or decide not to replicate the `UNIQUE` constraint, the `FILESTREAM` attribute will not be replicated to the subscriber; it will be replicated as a `VARBINARY(MAX)` column, even if we set the **Convert FILESTREAM to MAX data types** to `FALSE`.

When a replication requirement exists, it is especially important to consider how to generate the values for the `UNIQUEIDENTIFIER` column of `FILESTREAM` tables. A new GUID value can be generated using either `NEWID()` or `NEWSEQUENTIALID()`. Using `NEWSEQUENTIALID()` is recommended over `NEWID()` because it provides better replication performance and less fragmentation of the data. It should be noted that using `NEWSEQUENTIALID()` is only supported in a `DEFAULT` constraint and this may not be appropriate for a particular scenario.

Chapter 10: Integrating FILESTREAM with other SQL Server Features

When creating a merge or transactional publication with updatable subscriptions, SQL Server will automatically add a `UNIQUEIDENTIFIER` column, with a `ROWGUIDCOL` attribute if the table does not already have one. On `FILESTREAM` tables, SQL Server will use the existing GUID column.

When adding a `FILESTREAM` column to a table that is already published for merge or transactional replication with updatable subscriptions, we don't need to add a new `UINQUEIDENTIFIER` column because the replication process will already have done so when the table was published for two-way replication. However, we must ensure that the `UINQUEIDENTIFIER` column has a `UNIQUE` constraint; if the column does not have a `UNIQUE` constraint, you need to add one before creating the `FILESTREAM` column on the table.

By default, merge replication and transactional replication are configured to replicate schema changes to the subscriber. If this setting is changed, the `UNIQUE` constraint will not be replicated to the subscribers and an error will be raised when the `FILESTREAM` column is replicated.

The current schema replication settings can be reviewed in the **Subscription Options** page of the **Publication Properties** dialog box: right-click on the publication and select **Properties**, and then select the **Subscription Options** tab. The **Schema Replication** section is at the bottom of the property table (Figure 10-3).

Chapter 10: Integrating FILESTREAM with other SQL Server Features

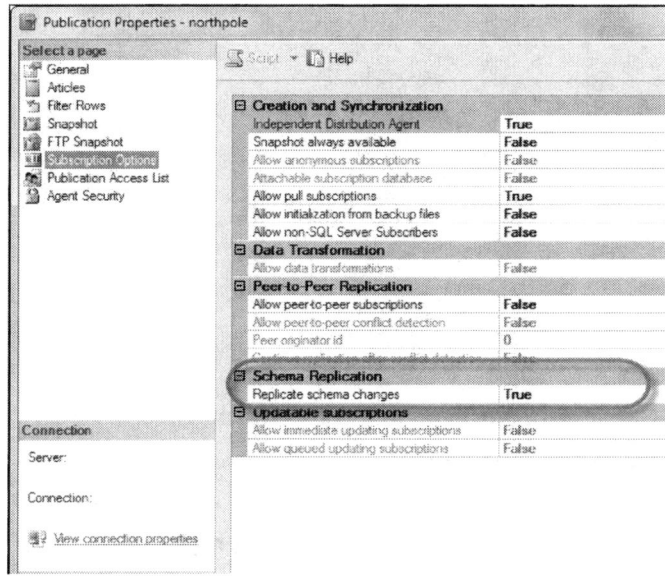

Figure 10-3: Setting the **Schema Replication** option.

We can also set this option by running the following replication stored procedures:

- for merge replication – `sp_helpmergepublication`
- for transactional replication with or without updatable subscriptions – `sp_helppublication`.

One of the columns returned by these stored procedures is `replicate_ddl`. If the publication is configured to replicate schema changes, the value in this column will be 1; otherwise, it will be 0.

We can use the replication stored procedures to change the `replicate_ddl` setting:

- for merge replication – `sp_changemergepublication`
- for transactional replication with or without updatable subscriptions – `sp_changepublication`.

Chapter 10: Integrating FILESTREAM with other SQL Server Features

Listing 10-2 shows how to set this option to `true` using T-SQL for a merge publication.

```
EXEC sp_changemergepublication
  @publication = 'northpole',
  @property = N'replicate_ddl',
  @value = 1,
  @force_invalidate_snapshot = 0,
  @force_reinit_subscription = 0;
```

Listing 10-2: T-SQL script to update the `replicate_ddl` option of a publication.

MSDN documentation says that, if a `UNIQUE` constraint has been added manually and you wish to remove replication, the `UNIQUE` constraint should be removed first. If the `UNIQUE` constraint is not removed before attempting to drop the publication, the drop operation will fail. I could not replicate this behavior during my testing, but keep this in mind while replicating `FILESTREAM` columns.

Managing the FILESTREAM replication flag using T-SQL

In the previous section we learned that a `FILESTREAM` column can be replicated with or without the `FILESTREAM` attribute. Then we saw how to change the configuration to replicate the `FILESTREAM` attribute or disable the replication of the `FILESTREAM` attribute using the SSMS dialog boxes. Here, we examine how the `FILESTREAM` replication flag can be managed using T-SQL; in other words, how to enable and disable the replication of the `FILESTREAM` attribute using the replication system stored procedures.

The configuration settings of any article that is part of a publication can be changed using the stored procedures:

- for merge replication – `sp_changemergearticle`
- for transactional replication with or without updatable subscriptions – `sp_changearticle`.

Both of these stored procedures accept the `schema_option` parameter; this parameter is a bitmap value, where every bit (or "flag") in this parameter represents the status of a specific configuration setting, one of which determines whether or not SQL Server will replicate the `FILESTREAM` attribute. The value returned for this parameter is the bitwise OR product of one or more of the values of these bits.

To replicate a `FILESTREAM` column along with the `FILESTREAM` attribute, the bit represented by 0x100000000 should be set; to disable replication of the `FILESTREAM` attribute, this bit should be cleared, being careful not to set or clear any bits other than the intended one.

The recommended way to change the `FILESTREAM` replication flag is as follows:

- read the existing value of the `schema_option` configuration setting
- set or clear the `FILESTREAM` replication flag (0x100000000)
- write the modified configuration value back to the publication.

Read the current configuration setting

The first step is to read the current value of the `schema_option` configuration setting, using either the `sp_helpmergearticle` system stored procedure for merge replication or `sp_helparticle` for transactional replication, as shown in Listing 10-3.

```
-- Look for the previous settings. Run sp_helparticle and
-- look for the "schema_option" column.
exec sp_helparticle 'northpole', 'items'
```

Listing 10-3: Querying the current settings of an article in a transactional publication.

Read the value of the `schema_option` column from the output of this statement. This can be automated by storing the output of the stored procedure in a temp table and reading from that temp table. The default value of the `schema_option` is 0x000000000803509F.

Setting the FILESTREAM replication flag

Having retrieved the current configuration value of the `schema_option` setting, we can go ahead and set the FILESTREAM replication flag. First, we can determine the current status of the FILESTREAM flag by performing a bitwise AND operation on the current `schema_option` configuration value returned by Listing 10-3, as shown in Listing 10-4.

```
DECLARE @val BIGINT
-- Assume that the current value is 0x000000010803509F
SELECT @val = 0x000000010803509F

-- Check whether FILESTREAM replication flag is enabled
IF @val & 0x100000000 <> 0
    PRINT 'FILESTREAM option is ON'
ELSE
    PRINT 'FILESTREAM option is OFF'
```

Listing 10-4: Checking whether the FILESTREAM replication flag is currently enabled.

Having determined the current status of the FILESTREAM flag, you can set or clear the flag as required. As previously mentioned, the FILESTREAM replication setting is turned on by setting the appropriate bit in the `schema_option` bitmap value. A specific bit on a byte (or byte stream) can be turned on by performing a bitwise OR operation. However, a bitwise operation cannot be performed on a VARBINARY value, so we have to start with a

Chapter 10: Integrating FILESTREAM with other SQL Server Features

BIGINT value, perform the required bitwise operation and then convert the new value to a VARBINARY so that a string representation of the hex value can be created from that, as shown in Listing 10-5.

```
DECLARE
    @options VARBINARY(8),
    @prev BIGINT

-- Set the flag to replicate FILESTREAM flag using a bitwise OR
-- We'll assume that the previous value is 0x000000000803509F
SELECT @prev = 0x000000000803509F

SELECT @prev = @prev | 0x100000000
SELECT @options = CAST(@prev AS VARBINARY(8))
SELECT @options
-- Original Value: 0x000000000803509F
-- New Value    : 0x000000010803509F
-- Note the flag :  ---------^--------
```

Listing 10-5: Turning the FILESTREAM replication flag on by performing a bitwise OR operation.

To turn off the FILESTREAM replication flag, we need to run the reverse operation and to clear a specific bit in the configuration value using a bitwise NOT operation. Listing 10-6 shows how to do this.

```
DECLARE
    @options VARBINARY(8),
    @prev BIGINT

-- Clear the FILESTREAM repl flag using a bitwise NOT operation
-- We'll assume that the previous value is 0x000000010803509F
SELECT @prev = 0x000000010803509F

SELECT @prev = @prev ^ 0x100000000
SELECT @options = CAST(@prev AS VARBINARY(8))
SELECT @options
-- Original Value: 0x000000010803509F
-- New Value    : 0x000000000803509F
-- Note the flag :  ---------^--------
```

Listing 10-6: Turning the FILESTREAM replication flag off by performing a bitwise NOT operation.

Writing back the modified configuration value

The final step is to write the modified configuration value back to the publication, using either the `sp_changemergearticle` stored procedure for merge replication or `sp_changearticle` for transactional replication. This is a little more complicated than you might think, since the `schema_option` parameter is an **NVARCHAR** parameter, which expects a hex representation of the configuration value.

Creating the string representation of a hex value is a little tricky, too. One method is to use the XML data type methods; Listing 10-7 shows how to use the `xs:hexBinary()` function to build a string representation of a hex value.

```
DECLARE @optInt BIGINT

-- Assume that the original value is 0x000000000803509F
SELECT @optInt = 0x000000000803509F

-- Turn ON the FILESTREAM replication flag
SELECT @optInt = @optInt | 0x100000000

-- Build a VARBINARY(8) value from the INT value
DECLARE @optHex VARBINARY(8)
SELECT @optHex = CAST(@optInt AS VARBINARY(8))

-- Covert the VARBINARY value to a hex string
DECLARE @optNv NVARCHAR(30)
SELECT @optNv = master.dbo.fn_varbintohexstr(@OptHex)
SELECT @optNv
--returns '0x000000010803509F'
```

Listing 10-7: Building a string representation of a hex value.

Having built an **NVARCHAR** value from the modified `schema_option` configuration value, we can go ahead and execute the replication stored procedures to write the value back to the publication, as shown in Listing 10-8.

```
exec sp_changearticle
    @publication = N'northpole',
    @article = N'Items',
    @property = N'schema_option',
    @value = @optNv,
    @force_invalidate_snapshot = 1,
    @force_reinit_subscription = 1
```

Listing 10-8: Writing back the modified `schema_option` value into the publication.

Impact of FILESTREAM replication configuration changes

Changing the FILESTREAM replication flag requires regenerating a new replication snapshot and reinitializing all the subscribers. Turning the FILESTREAM replication flag off is relatively harmless, but turning it on needs some careful thought.

When you turn the FILESTREAM replication flag on:

- any SQL Server 2005 subscribers to the publication will break; a publication cannot be replicated to SQL Server 2005 subscribers if the FILESTREAM replication flag is turned on
- any SQL Server 2008 subscribers will break if the subscription database is not FILESTREAM enabled and does not have a default FILESTREAM filegroup.

Replication log reader and the FILESTREAM garbage collector

As discussed in Chapter 7, SQL Server does not allow in-place updates of FILESTREAM values. If you attempt to modify a FILESTREAM value either using T-SQL or using the streaming APIs, SQL Server creates a completely new copy of the FILESTREAM data file with the modified value. The old file stays around in the `FILESTREAM` data container until the garbage collector steps in and deletes it.

Every `FILESTREAM` operation is linked to an LSN in the database transaction log. The garbage collector will remove a file marked for garbage collection only when the transaction log is truncated past the LSN that created the `FILESTREAM` garbage file.

When a `FILESTREAM` database is published, the transaction log cannot be truncated until the replication log reader agent reads the information from the transaction log. This can delay the `FILESTREAM` garbage collection, because the garbage collector cannot delete the files until the transaction log is truncated.

It is therefore possible that you will notice `FILESTREAM` garbage files lying around for a longer period if the `FILESTREAM` columns are replicated and the replication log reader agent does not run frequently.

FILESTREAM and synchronization methods

It is important to note that, if a publication includes tables having `FILESTREAM` columns, the *snapshot* synchronization methods offered by SQL Server Enterprise Edition cannot be used.

SQL Server Enterprise Edition provides two efficient synchronization methods for building the replication snapshot, namely *database snapshot* and *database snapshot character*, which generates the snapshot based on a database snapshot, resulting in no locks being applied on the tables when the replication snapshot is being created. Database snapshots cannot include `FILESTREAM` filegroups (explained later in this chapter) and therefore, if the publication includes `FILESTREAM` columns, snapshot synchronization methods are not supported.

Replicating databases with multiple FILESTREAM filegroups

Most real-world `FILESTREAM` databases will have more than one `FILESTREAM` filegroup, and it is important to understand how replication works with multiple `FILESTREAM` filegroups.

By default, when you replicate a `FILESTREAM` database, all `FILESTREAM` data will go to the default `FILESTREAM` filegroup. However, we can configure the publication to replicate `FILESTREAM` data to its own filegroup in the subscriber by setting another flag in the `schema_option` configuration value.

In the previous section, we saw how to set or clear flags in the `schema_option` configuration value. In a similar way, we can modify an article to replicate `FILESTREAM` data to the same filegroups in the subscriber by turning on the bit represented by `0x800000000`.

Note that the replication process does not create `FILESTREAM` filegroups on the subscriber database. If you use this option, you must create the required `FILESTREAM` filegroups on the target database before applying the initial snapshot.

The option to set the `FILESTREAM` filegroup is available only through T-SQL. The SSMS property page does not have this option.

FILESTREAM and the different replication types

Here, we examine briefly the behavior of `FILESTREAM` columns specific to each replication type.

Transactional replication

`FILESTREAM` works beautifully with transactional replication (with or without updatable subscriptions). For either type of transactional replication, setting up publishers and subscribers for `FILESTREAM` columns is not much different from what we would usually do for any other column.

One difference is the option that allows us to decide whether `FILESTREAM` columns should be replicated with the `FILESTREAM` attribute, which we have already discussed. Another is the option that determines whether the `FILESTREAM` columns should go to the default `FILESTREAM` filegroup or to filegroups with the same name in the subscriber. In the **Article Properties** dialog box (shown in Figure 10-1), the **Copy filegroup associations** property determines whether replicated data is stored in the default filegroups at the subscriber or in the filegroups with matching names from the publisher. The default value is **False**, meaning that the replicated data will be stored in the subscribers' default filegroups.

Merge replication

Merge replication allows two-way synchronization of data between the publisher and subscribers. The `FILESTREAM`-related configuration changes that you might need to do when setting up a merge replication are pretty much the same as what you do for a transactional replication.

Chapter 10: Integrating FILESTREAM with other SQL Server Features

Aside from the additional options relating to FILESTREAM columns noted in the previous section, one specific difference when using merge replication is that if you have SQL Server 2005 (or earlier) subscribers, the option to replicate FILESTREAM as VARBINARY(MAX) is not available in the SSMS wizard page (Figure 10-4) or the article properties page.

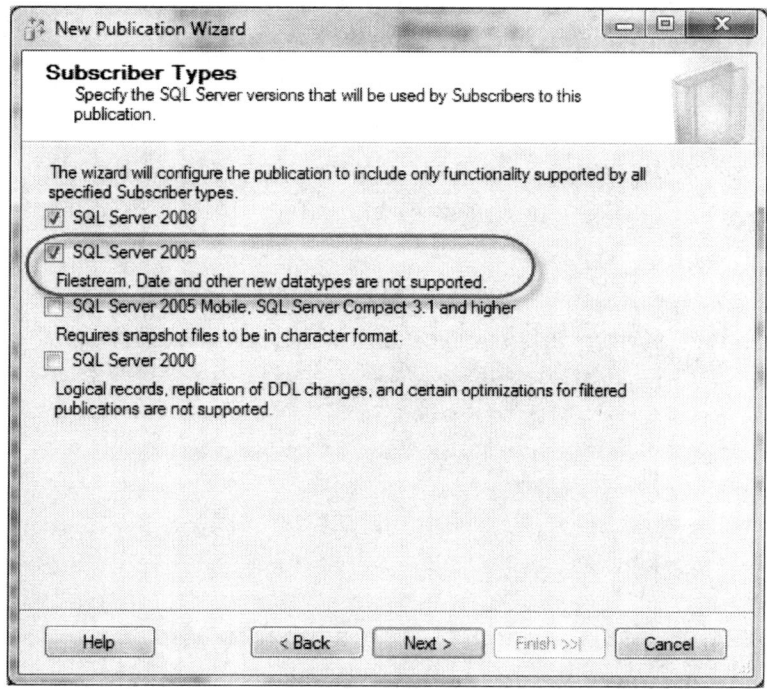

Figure 10-4: Replicate FILESTREAM is not supported for merge replication.

If you select **SQL Server 2005**, you can still replicate FILESTREAM columns; the publication will be configured to replicate FILESTREAM columns as VARBINARY(MAX) columns and the SSMS property page will not allow you to change it. If you select **SQL Server 2000** and include FILESTREAM columns, the publication wizard will fail because a FILESTREAM column cannot be replicated to a SQL Server 2000 database.

Merge replication includes memory optimization, which is controlled by the `stream_blob_columns` parameter of the `sp_addmergearticle` and `sp_changemergearticle` stored procedures. Turning this option on while replicating large BLOB values significantly improves replication performance. It is therefore recommended to have this option turned on when you are replicating `FILESTREAM` columns. It is especially important when the `FILESTREAM` column is added to a table that is already published, because it can happen that this setting was not turned on when the table was originally published. In such a case, you need to turn this flag on explicitly.

The current status of this setting can be determined by running the replication stored procedure `sp_helpmergearticle` and looking at the `stream_blob_columns` column in the output.

When using merge replication with web synchronization over HTTPS protocol, the maximum size of data values is limited to 50 MB. A runtime error will be raised if the data size is larger than 50 MB.

Snapshot replication

Creating snapshot replication for `FILESTREAM` columns is very similar to what we have seen with transactional replication. One immediate difference that you might notice is that the `max text repl size` option is ignored by snapshot replication. This configuration option is explained earlier in this chapter.

FILESTREAM and Log Shipping

Log shipping is a popular way of ensuring high availability of databases by sending transaction logs to one or more secondary SQL Server servers at specified intervals. SQL Server allows log shipping of `FILESTREAM`-enabled databases.

To configure log shipping of `FILESTREAM`-enabled databases, the secondary servers must be running on SQL Server 2008 and have `FILESTREAM` enabled. Beyond this, one point you might need to pay attention to is the connectivity between the primary and secondary servers. Transaction logs shipped using log shipping will include `FILESTREAM` data as well, which will make the shipped logs very big if your database deals with a lot of `FILESTREAM` operations involving large BLOB values. It is also important to understand that, when a `FILESTREAM` value is updated, SQL Server creates a new file with the modified value. This new copy of the file will be included in the transaction log backup which has an impact on the overall size of the transaction log backups.

FILESTREAM and Full-Text Indexing

Full-text indexing works with `FILESTREAM` columns in just the same way as with `VARBINARY(MAX)` columns, with the only difference being that the 2 GB limit is not applicable when indexing `FILESTREAM` columns.

Just like `VARBINARY(MAX)` columns that do not have the `FILESTREAM` attribute, full-text indexing requires a column that stores the extension of the documents stored in the `FILESTREAM` column. SQL Server looks at this column to determine the document type, loads the appropriate IFilter, and indexes it.

> **More about full-text indexing**
>
> *A detailed explanation of full-text indexing is beyond the scope of this book. For more information, I would suggest you take a look at Books Online at:* HTTP://BRURL.COM/FSI3.

For a quick look at how SQL Server indexes `FILESTREAM` columns using full-text indexing, let's create a table with a few `FILESTREAM` data values, as shown in Listing 10-9.

Chapter 10: Integrating FILESTREAM with other SQL Server Features

```
USE master
GO

IF DB_ID('NorthPoleFT') IS NOT NULL
    DROP DATABASE NorthPoleFT
GO

CREATE DATABASE NorthPoleFT ON PRIMARY (
    NAME = NorthPoleFT,
    FILENAME = 'C:\ArtOfFS\Demos\Chapter10\NorthPoleFT.mdf'
), FILEGROUP NorthPoleFT_fs CONTAINS FILESTREAM(
    NAME = NorthPoleFT_fs,
    FILENAME = 'C:\ArtOfFS\Demos\Chapter10\NorthPoleFT_fs') LOG ON (
    NAME = NorthPoleFT_log,
    FILENAME = 'C:\ArtOfFS\Demos\Chapter10\NorthPoleFT_log.ldf')
GO
```

Listing 10-9: Creating a sample database for full-text indexing.

We'll now create a table to store some office documents, which we'll use for testing the full-text indexing (Listing 10-10).

```
USE NorthPoleFT
GO

CREATE TABLE [dbo].[Documents]
    (
      [DocID] [uniqueidentifier] ROWGUIDCOL
                                 NOT NULL ,
      [DocName] [varchar](128) NULL ,
      [DocType] [varchar](10) NULL ,
      [DocBody] [varbinary](MAX) FILESTREAM
                                 NULL ,
      CONSTRAINT [PK_Documents] PRIMARY KEY CLUSTERED ( [DocID] ASC )
    )
ON  [PRIMARY] FILESTREAM_ON [NorthPoleFT_fs]
```

Listing 10-10: Creating a table with FILESTREAM columns.

Chapter 10: Integrating FILESTREAM with other SQL Server Features

And finally, let's insert two rows into this table: a Word document and an Excel file (Listing 10-11). If you are following the example, ensure you create these files, or change the paths to point to files that exist on your computer.

```sql
SELECT  NEWID() ,
        'FILESTREAM Book - List of Chapters' ,
        '.xls' ,
        bulkcolumn
FROM    OPENROWSET(BULK 'c:\temp\FILESTREAM Book - List of Chapters.xls',
                SINGLE_BLOB) AS x

-- Insert the data to the table
INSERT  INTO Documents
        ( [DocID] ,
          [DocName] ,
          [DocType] ,
          [DocBody]
        )
        SELECT  NEWID() ,
                'Chapter 10 - Integrating FILESTREAM' ,
                '.doc' ,
                bulkcolumn
        FROM    OPENROWSET(BULK 'c:\temp\Chapter 10 - Integrating FILESTREAM.doc',
                        SINGLE_BLOB) AS x
```

Listing 10-11: Loading documents into the `FILESTREAM` column of a table.

It is now time to create a full-text index catalog. This can be done either using the SSMS wizard or using T-SQL (Listing 10-12).

```sql
CREATE FULLTEXT CATALOG
DocumentCatalog
AS DEFAULT ;
```

Listing 10-12: Creating a full-text catalog.

We can now create a full-text index on the `DocBody` column, in which we have stored the content of the Office documents (Listing 10-13).

```
CREATE FULLTEXT INDEX ON
    dbo.Documents(
        DocName,
        DocBody TYPE COLUMN DocType
    )
KEY INDEX PK_Documents
ON DocumentCatalog
WITH CHANGE_TRACKING AUTO;
```

Listing 10-13: Creating a full-text index.

Note that we have specified the column that stores the document extension using the `TYPE COLUMN` clause. This allows SQL Server to understand the document type and use the appropriate IFilter to index it.

That is all we need to do, so Listing 10-14 shows how to search for the keyword `Replication` within the indexed documents.

```
USE NorthPoleFT
GO
SELECT  *
FROM    documents
WHERE   CONTAINS ( DocBody, 'Replication' )
```

Listing 10-14: Searching a full-text index.

When creating a full-text index (using either T-SQL or the SSMS wizard), we can specify the filegroup on which the index should be created. We cannot select a `FILESTREAM` filegroup as the target filegroup for the full-text index. If a filegroup is not specified, the default data filegroup of the database is used.

When using the SSMS wizard, *don't* select the `FILESTREAM` filegroup, otherwise the full-text index creation will fail.

FILESTREAM and Database Snapshots

Database snapshot is a very interesting feature, introduced in SQL Server 2005, providing a read-only static view of a database that exists in the same SQL Server instance. A database can have multiple snapshots pointing to it, but all should reside on the same SQL Server instance. Each database snapshot is transactionally consistent with the source database as of the time at which the snapshot is created.

SQL Server allows the creation of a database snapshot of a FILESTREAM-enabled database. However, the snapshot should not include the FILESTREAM filegroups. If we attempt to include a FILESTREAM filegroup in the database snapshot, the operation will fail with an error, as shown in Listing 10-15.

```
CREATE DATABASE NorthPoleSnapshot ON PRIMARY (
    NAME = NorthPole,
    FILENAME = 'C:\ArtOfFS\Demos\Chapter10\NorthPoleSnapshot.mdf'
), FILEGROUP NorthPoleSnapshot_fs CONTAINS FILESTREAM(
    NAME = NorthPoleSnapshot_fs,
    FILENAME = 'C:\ArtOfFS\Demos\Chapter10\NorthPoleSnapshot_fs') AS SNAPSHOT
    OF NorthPole

/*
Msg 1815, Level 16, State 5, Line 1
The FILESTREAM property cannot be used with database snapshot files.
*/
```

Listing 10-15: Snapshot of a FILESTREAM-enabled database cannot include FILESTREAM filegroups.

The T-SQL code in Listing 10-16 creates a snapshot of a FILESTREAM database without the FILESTREAM filegroups.

```
CREATE DATABASE NorthPoleSnapshot ON PRIMARY (
    NAME = NorthPole,
    FILENAME = 'C:\ArtOfFS\Demos\Chapter10\NorthPoleSnapshot.mdf'
) AS SNAPSHOT OF NorthPole
```

```
/*
Command(s) completed successfully.
*/
```

Listing 10-16: Creating a database snapshot from a `FILESTREAM`-enabled database.

Be careful when querying the database snapshot of a `FILESTREAM` database. If a query tries to read from the `FILESTREAM` columns, it will fail, because the `FILESTREAM` filegroup is not available with the database snapshot, as shown in Listing 10-17.

```
USE NorthPole20100817
GO

SELECT * FROM Items
/*
Msg 601, Level 12, State 3, Line 1
Could not continue scan with NOLOCK due to data movement.
*/
```

Listing 10-17: Reading from `FILESTREAM` columns is not allowed when using a database snapshot.

With the limitation that the `FILESTREAM` columns are not available, `FILESTREAM` database snapshots behave like the snapshots of regular databases. Listing 10-18 reads values from non-`FILESTREAM` columns in the database snapshot.

```
USE NorthPole20100817
GO

SELECT ItemNumber, ItemDescription
FROM Items
/*
ItemNumber              ItemDescription
--------------------    -----------------------
MS1002                  Microsoft Keyboard
*/
```

Listing 10-18: Reading non-`FILESTREAM` columns from a database snapshot.

In most cases, it will be tedious to selectively exclude the `FILESTREAM` columns while querying a database snapshot. It would have been much easier if SQL Server simply returned `NULL` for the `FILESTREAM` columns instead of raising an error, but it is possible that this was not done because one of the main features of the `FILESTREAM` storage is the transactional consistency between the relational data and `FILESTREAM` data.

FILESTREAM and Change Data Capture

Change Data Capture (CDC) was introduced with SQL Server 2008. When this feature is enabled, SQL Server keeps track of the modifications (inserts, updates, and deletions) on the tables being tracked. The data capture takes place asynchronously (by reading the transaction log), which eliminates the additional overhead you may have with a trigger-based custom data capture framework. CDC can be configured to capture data modifications at the table level as well as at the column level.

> **More on CDC**
>
> *For a more detailed discussion of CDC, see the Microsoft article, Tuning the Performance of Change Data Capture in SQL Server 2008 at:* HTTP://BRURL.COM/FS25.

Books Online states that CDC does not support any of the new data types introduced in SQL Server 2008. If you decide to enable CDC on your `FILESTREAM`-enabled tables, you must exclude the `FILESTREAM` columns from the capture list.

So what happens if you enable CDC on a table that contains `FILESTREAM` columns? CDC will capture those columns as `VARBINARY(MAX)` columns.

Chapter 10: Integrating FILESTREAM with other SQL Server Features

> **A warning on enabling CDC on FILESTREAM columns!**
>
> *It may affect the performance of the system. In addition, it is an unsupported operation and you might end up with a number of problems, for example, large-value type columns may generate a huge volume of change data if those columns are frequently inserted/updated/deleted.*

However, it will be interesting to see what happens when CDC is enabled on a **FILESTREAM** column. To start with, let us create a **FILESTREAM**-enabled database (Listing 10-19).

```sql
USE master
GO

IF DB_ID('NorthPole') IS NOT NULL
    DROP DATABASE NorthPole
GO

CREATE DATABASE NorthPole ON PRIMARY (
    NAME = NorthPole,
    FILENAME = 'C:\ArtOfFS\Demos\Chapter10\NorthPole.mdf'
), FILEGROUP NorthPole_fs CONTAINS FILESTREAM(
    NAME = NorthPole_fs,
    FILENAME = 'C:\ArtOfFS\Demos\Chapter10\NorthPole_fs') LOG ON (
    NAME = NorthPole_log,
    FILENAME = 'C:\ArtOfFS\Demos\Chapter10\NorthPole_log.ldf')
GO

USE NorthPole
GO

CREATE TABLE [dbo].[Items]
    (
        [ItemID] UNIQUEIDENTIFIER ROWGUIDCOL
                                NOT NULL
                                UNIQUE ,
        [ItemNumber] VARCHAR(20) ,
        [ItemDescription] VARCHAR(50) ,
        [ItemImage] VARBINARY(MAX) FILESTREAM
                                NULL
    )
```

Chapter 10: Integrating FILESTREAM with other SQL Server Features

```
GO

INSERT   INTO Items
         ( ItemID ,
           ItemNumber ,
           ItemDescription ,
           ItemImage
         )
         SELECT   NEWID() ,
                  'MS1001' ,
                  'Microsoft Mouse' ,
                  bulkcolumn
         FROM     OPENROWSET(BULK 'C:\temp\MicrosoftMouse.jpg',
                             SINGLE_BLOB) AS x
```

Listing 10-19: Creating a FILESTREAM-enabled database to test CDC.

The next step is to enable CDC by running the CDC system stored procedures (Listing 10-20).

```
USE NorthPole
GO

-- Enable CDC on the NorthPole database
EXEC sys.sp_cdc_enable_db

-- Enable CDC on the Items table
EXEC sys.sp_cdc_enable_table @source_schema = 'dbo',
                             @source_name = 'items',
                             @role_name = 'cdc_items',
                             @supports_net_changes = 0
```

Listing 10-20: Enabling CDC on a table.

Note that you need to have the SQL Server Agent service running to have the CDC data captured. If SQL Agent is not running, you will not see the data until you run SQL Agent and the capture jobs populate CDC tables with the data. To verify if the SQL Server Agent service is running, open **Control Panel | Administrative Tools | Services**. Scroll down the list of services until you see the SQL Server Agent service for your instance (the instance name is between parentheses). Check the value in the **Status** column. If it is blank, then the service is stopped. Right-click the service name and select **Start**. If you want the service to start automatically when Windows starts, modify the **Properties** of the service and change the **Startup type** to **Automatic**.

Once CDC is enabled, we can make some data modifications and see the results in the captured tables (Listing 10-21).

```
-- Update the content of the ItemImage column
UPDATE  Items
SET     ItemImage = CAST(1 AS VARBINARY(MAX))

-- Delete the record
DELETE  FROM Items
```

Listing 10-21: Updating the `FILESTREAM` value to generate some CDC log entries.

Now, let's go to the CDC tables and see whether the data has been captured (Listing 10-22).

```
DECLARE
    @LSNFrom BINARY(10) = sys.fn_cdc_map_time_to_lsn(
                               'smallest greater than or equal',
                               GETDATE() - 1) ,
    @LSNTo BINARY(10) = sys.fn_cdc_map_time_to_lsn(
                               'largest less than or equal',
                               GETDATE())

SELECT  CASE [__$operation]
            WHEN 1 THEN 'Delete'
            WHEN 2 THEN 'Insert'
            WHEN 3 THEN 'Update (Old Values)'
            WHEN 4 THEN 'Update (New Values)'
        END AS Operation ,
        ItemNumber ,
        ItemDescription ,
        DATALENGTH(ItemImage) AS ImageSize
FROM    cdc.fn_cdc_get_all_changes_dbo_Items(@LSNFrom, @LSNTo,
                               'all update old') ;
```

```
/*
Operation                 ItemNumber  ItemDescription  ImageSize
------------------------  ----------  ---------------  ---------
Update (Old Values)       MS1001      Microsoft Mouse  499988
Update (New Values)       MS1001      Microsoft Mouse  4
Delete                    MS1001      Microsoft Mouse  4
*/
```

Listing 10-22: Querying the CDC logs for data modification history.

Note that the maximum replication text size configuration setting also affects CDC. We examined this setting in detail when we discussed replication, earlier in this chapter. When CDC is enabled on a table, if you try to insert or update a data value larger than the size specified, the INSERT or UPDATE operation will fail.

To summarize, it is possible to enable CDC on FILESTREAM columns, but CDC will capture the column as VARBINARY(MAX), not as FILESTREAM. Enabling CDC on FILESTREAM columns is not recommended or supported. Before moving on, let's disable CDC on the NorthPole database. Listing 10-23 shows how. It's not necessary to disable CDC on individual tables first.

```
USE NorthPole
GO

-- Disable CDC on the NorthPole database
EXEC sys.sp_cdc_disable_db
```

Listing 10-23: Disabling CDC on a database.

FILESTREAM and Data Compression

SQL Server 2008 introduced page-level and row-level compression of relational data, but it does not compress FILESTREAM data stored in the FILESTREAM filegroup(s) of the database. On the other hand, SQL Server will allow you to store the FILESTREAM data container on a compressed disk volume. However, as discussed in the *Data and Backup Compression for FILESTREAM Databases* section in Chapter 8, documentation from the Microsoft support engineers indicates that this is not a recommended configuration.

Another compression feature introduced in SQL Server 2008 is backup compression. This feature allows you to take a compressed backup by issuing the WITH COMPRESSION command in your backup script. Fortunately, SQL Server does compress the FILESTREAM data when you take a compressed backup of the database, which can possibly save a significant amount of backup storage space and shorten the backup time.

FILESTREAM and Transparent Data Encryption

One of the very interesting data security features added in SQL Server 2008 is Transparent Data Encryption (TDE), enabling encryption of an entire database. The encryption is transparent to application code; SQL Server takes care of encryption and decryption at the storage level and you do not need to do anything other than enabling this feature on the database.

However, note that TDE does not encrypt the FILESTREAM data stored in a FILESTREAM database.

FILESTREAM and Database Mirroring

SQL Server does not allow mirroring of a `FILESTREAM`-enabled database. We cannot add a `FILESTREAM` filegroup to a SQL Server database that is already mirrored. If a database already has a `FILESTREAM` filegroup, SQL Server will not allow it to be mirrored.

What is very interesting is that the **Mirroring** option is still available in the property page of a `FILESTREAM`-enabled database. The **Mirroring** page will guide us step by step through configuring the principal, mirror, and witness servers, and we might even get a message saying that mirroring has been successfully configured. However, when we actually start mirroring, an error is raised, as shown in Figure 10-5.

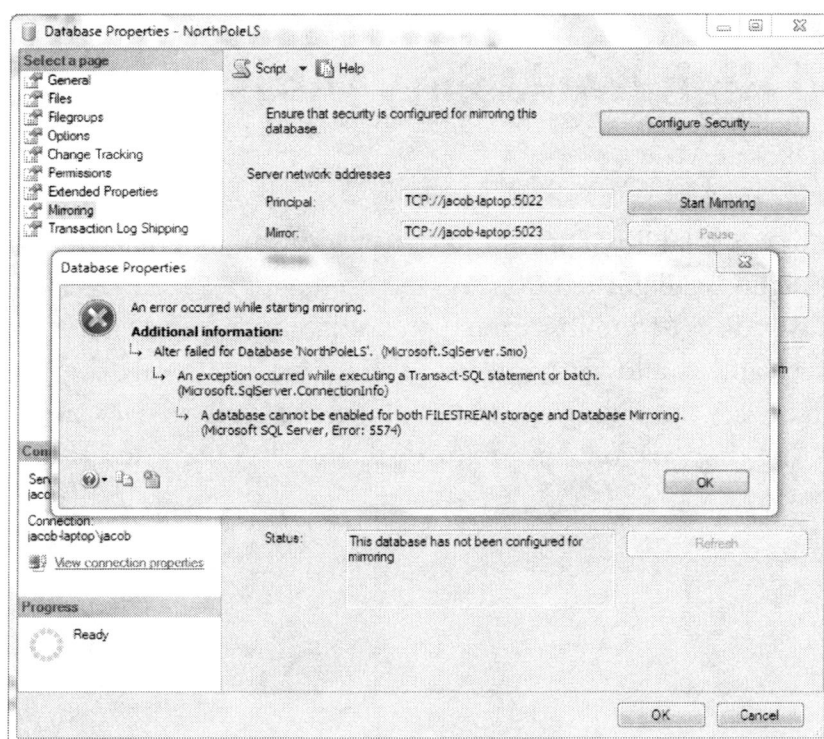

Figure 10-5: Error when attempting to mirror a `FILESTREAM`-enabled database.

Chapter 10: Integrating FILESTREAM with other SQL Server Features

If we attempt the same using T-SQL, SQL Server will generate the following error when the `SET PARTNER` command is issued:

```
A database cannot be enabled for both FILESTREAM storage and Database Mirroring.
```

One of the reasons for not allowing mirroring of a `FILESTREAM`-enabled database could be the excessive amount of `FILESTREAM` log data that might need to be ransferred to the mirror server if a lot of `FILESTREAM` activity takes place on the database. Since SQL Server does not allow in-place update of `FILESTREAM` data values, every modification generates a new file, which has to be transferred to the mirror server.

FILESTREAM and High Availability Disaster Recovery

In SQL Server 2012, the new High Availability Disaster Recovery – Always On (HADRON) feature does support creating highly available database nodes, even with `FILESTREAM`-enabled databases. HADRON was designed to meet the high availability needs of a wide variety of SQL Server users, and so allow other features that were being used for high availability and disaster recovery (including replication, log shipping, and database mirroring discussed earlier in this chapter) to focus on the problems they were designed to solve.

Summary

This chapter focused on examining how `FILESTREAM` works with other popular SQL Server features. Some of these features work well with `FILESTREAM`.

- `FILESTREAM` works very well with replication; `FILESTREAM` columns can be replicated with or without the `FILESTREAM` attribute, and they can be replicated as `VARBINARY(MAX)` columns to SQL Server 2005 subscribers.
- SQL Server supports log shipping of `FILESTREAM`-enabled databases. There is no change in the configuration process except that you need to make sure that the target SQL Server instances have `FILESTREAM` enabled.
- Full-text indexing works with `FILESTREAM` columns in a similar way to that of `VARBINARY(MAX)` columns, but with the 2 GB limitation of data size removed.

However, some of them are only partially supported and a few of the very interesting features introduced in SQL Server 2005 and SQL Server 2008 do not support `FILESTREAM` at all.

- Database snapshots of `FILESTREAM` databases can be created. However, you cannot include `FILESTREAM` filegroups in the database snapshot. When querying the database snapshot, if you attempt to read from the `FILESTREAM` columns, SQL Server will generate an error.
- Change Data Capture does not "officially" support `FILESTREAM` columns. If you configure CDC on a `FILESTREAM` column, the data will be captured as `VARBINARY(MAX)` columns. Enabling CDC on `FILESTREAM` columns is not recommended.

Chapter 10: Integrating FILESTREAM with other SQL Server Features

- SQL Server does not allow mirroring `FILESTREAM` databases.

- Compressing data using row-level or page-level compression does not compress `FILESTREAM` data.

- TDE does not encrypt `FILESTREAM` data.

However, Microsoft's commitment to providing first-class support for `FILESTREAM` does show in the new SQL Server 2012 High Availability Disaster Recovery – Always On feature. It can make `FILESTREAM` data highly available by copying it to secondary servers.

Chapter 11: FileTable

The addition of the FileTable feature in SQL Server 2012 heralded the first significant change to `FILESTREAM` since its introduction in SQL Server 2008. A FileTable is basically just a "normal" SQL Server table for storing `FILESTREAM` data, via a `VARBINARY(MAX)` column called `file_stream`, but which also stores metadata regarding the underlying files and directories. This allows Windows applications to access `FILESTREAM` data exactly as if it were stored directly on the file system, and addresses the need to access the `FILESTREAM` data outside of the context of a SQL Server transaction. It also supports features such as full-text and semantic search on `FILESTREAM` data.

In this chapter, we'll investigate how a FileTable is different from tables with `FILESTREAM` columns and how to create and access FileTables. We'll also look behind the covers of FileTable to understand better how the `FILESTREAM` feature is used to implement FileTables.

Introduction to FileTable

FileTable is solidly based on many concepts found in the `FILESTREAM` feature. Just like normal `FILESTREAM` tables, FileTables are meant to store BLOB data on an NTFS volume, while keeping that data integrated with the relational data found in the SQL Server database. FileTable also retains full compatibility with existing SQL Server tools, services, and query options. However, unlike data stored in a traditional `FILESTREAM` column, client applications do not require modifications in order to access data stored in a FileTable. Contrast this to the requirement of using the Win32 or .NET streaming APIs in client applications that use normal `FILESTREAM` tables, and you'll agree that FileTables have an advantage.

Chapter 11: FileTable

FileTables can be accessed from any Windows application, including Windows Explorer. This means that users can navigate to a file share that exists on the network and use that file share like they would a traditional file share hosted on a file server. Recall that the file share created for `FILESTREAM` purposes is visible when browsing to the SQL Server host on the network, but it's not accessible.

Another significant difference between `FILESTREAM` and FileTable is that FileTables support storing data in a hierarchical fashion using a folder structure. Data in a `FILESTREAM`-enabled table is flat unless you include some form of hierarchy in the table's design.

Beyond these differences, `FILESTREAM` data stored in FileTables has the same benefits and restrictions as any other `FILESTREAM` data, including integrated backup and recovery.

FileTable Concepts

Before we create a FileTable, let's review some of the concepts underlying the FileTable feature, in order to achieve a good understanding of the FileTable architecture, including its limitations.

Fixed schema

FileTables use a predefined and fixed schema, which defines, not only the characteristics of the file data itself, but also metadata describing the underlying file or folder. Table 11-1 lists every field in the FileTable schema with a brief explanation of each one. For selected columns, sample values are also provided.

Column Name	Column Description	Sample Value(s)
`stream_id`	This is the `rowguidcol` that is required of all tables with `FILESTREAM` columns.	
`file_stream`	The `FILESTREAM` data column that stores the actual file contents.	`0x` (empty file) `NULL` (folder)
`Name`	The file or folder name.	
`path_locator` (PK)	The hierarchy identifier of the file or folder. See below for more information about the hierarchy structure. This is the primary key of the table.	
`parent_path_locator`	This is a persisted computed column that contains the `path_locator` of the parent folder. The computation uses the `GetAncestor()` function on the `path_locator` field. This must be a valid `path_locator` value and this requirement is enforced using a foreign key constraint.	
File and Folder Metadata Columns		
`file_type`	This is a computed column that represents the type of file based on the file extension. The computation uses the undocumented `GETFILEEXTENSION()` T-SQL function to determine the extension of the file. This column is useful when configuring fulltext indexes, as discussed later in this chapter.	

Column Name	Column Description	Sample Value(s)
cached_file_size	The size of the file in bytes. This is a computed column. It uses the DATALENGTH() T-SQL function to calculate the file size. The Books Online documentation notes that, in unusual circumstances, the value of this column can get out of sync. The T-SQL DATALENGTH() function will always return the correct file size in bytes.	NULL for folders ≥ 0 for files
creation_time	The date and time the file was created, which can be set by Windows APIs. Like the next two "_time" fields below, it is stored as a datetime2(4) value, which means the time zone offset is included in the value.	
last_write_time	The date and time the file contents were last updated. Like creation_time and last_access_time, this value can also be set by Windows APIs and thus may not reflect the actual time.	
last_access_time	The date and time the file contents were last accessed. Just like this metadata attribute on the NTFS file system, it is important to note that it would be accessing an application that is responsible for updating this value. Many applications do not change this value when opening a file.	
is_directory	Indicates if the row refers to a folder instead of a file.	0 for files 1 for folders

Column Name	Column Description	Sample Value(s)
is_offline	Reflects the NTFS extended file attribute "offline." When this attribute is set, it means that the file is only available when working online. This attribute is best left unmodified.	
is_hidden	Reflects the hidden attribute of the file system.	
is_readonly	Reflects the read-only attribute of the file system.	
is_archive	Reflects the archive attribute of the file system. Usually, the archive bit is reset by full and incremental backup operations and set by the Windows APIs when the file contents are changed. It's important to note that when modifying the file_stream value using T-SQL, the archive bit is not set automatically by SQL Server.	
is_system	Reflects the system file attribute of the file system.	
is_temporary	Reflects the NTFS extended file attribute "temporary."	

Table 11-1: Overview of the FileTable schema.

You'll notice that the majority of the columns in the schema are metadata columns. In a traditional file system, this metadata would be stored in the file system's metadata area (like the MFT for NTFS). This metadata is used by the SQL Server component that exposes the FileTable's contents as a file share to set the file and folder attributes. They do not influence how the files can be used. For example, if the is_readonly bit is set to 1, it does not mean that SQL Server will enforce that the file contents cannot be changed. These metadata attributes are only present to provide compatibility with the NTFS file system.

In addition to the predefined, fixed schema of FileTables, several additional database objects are created when creating FileTables. These objects include `DEFAULT` constraints to set appropriate values for many of the metadata columns in the FileTable, `CHECK` constraints to ensure that no invalid column values can be added (such as a non-`NULL` `file_stream` column if the row refers to a folder and not a file) and `UNIQUE` constraints to ensure that each full path is unique. There is even a foreign key for the `parent_path_locator` column to ensure that it refers to a valid folder.

Creating folder structures using the HIERARCHYID data type

FileTable supports folder structures with a maximum depth of 15 subfolders. Even though a maximum of 15 subfolders is supported, you will probably create a maximum of 14 subfolders, because it's not possible to create a file in the 15th-level subfolder (as it would create a 16th-level item).

The folder structure is implemented using the `HIERARCHYID` feature introduced with SQL Server 2008. While a complete discussion of the `HIERARCHYID` data type is beyond the scope of this book, it is valuable to review some of the concepts and basic queries that can be performed using `HIERARCHYID` fields.

In a FileTable, the primary key is a field of type `HIERARCHYID` and even though it's easy to query the parent of a given `HIERARCHYID` value, the parent in the hierarchy is stored in the `parent_path_locator` field. To keep this discussion focused on the basics of `HIERARCHYID`, and since we have yet to discuss how to create FileTables, we'll use a sample table that does not actually contain any `FILESTREAM` data, but just the hierarchy structure and a name field, as shown in Listing 11-1.

```
USE NorthPole
GO

CREATE TABLE Hierarchy
    (
        path_locator HIERARCHYID NOT NULL
                                 PRIMARY KEY CLUSTERED ,
        parent_path_locator AS ( CASE WHEN path_locator.GetLevel() = 1
                                      THEN NULL
                                      ELSE path_locator.GetAncestor(1)
                                 END )
            PERSISTED
            FOREIGN KEY REFERENCES Hierarchy ( path_locator ) ,
        name NVARCHAR(255) NOT NULL
    )
```

Listing 11-1: Create a sample hierarchy in SQL Server.

The script creates a new table containing three fields with names also found in FileTables. The `path_locator` is the primary key, and the `parent_path_locator` is a computed column. In addition, the `parent_path_locator` is also a foreign key which references the primary key of the same table. This is to ensure we cannot add a child for a non-existing parent. The `name` is the would-be name of the file or folder stored in the FileTable.

Listing 11-2 demonstrates how a new row can be added to the `Hierarchy` table. It is up to the application to create the `HIERARCHYID` values. A `HIERARCHYID` can be written as a string representation, whereby each level in the hierarchy is separated using `'/'`. A `HIERARCHYID` value always starts and ends with a forward slash.

```
INSERT INTO Hierarchy
       ( path_locator, name )
VALUES ( '/1/', '1.txt' )
```

Listing 11-2: Adding a row to the hierarchy.

When querying the table contents (Listing 11-3), you find that a `HIERARCHYID` is a binary type. Using a simple `CAST`, we can get back the string representation of the `HIERARCHYID`.

```
SELECT   path_locator ,
         CAST(path_locator AS NVARCHAR) 'path' ,
         parent_path_locator ,
         name
FROM     Hierarchy
/*
path_locator    path    parent_path_locator    name
------------    ----    -------------------    -----
0x58            /1/     NULL                   1.txt
*/
```

Listing 11-3: Querying a `HIERARCHYID`.

The value of `parent_path_locator` is `NULL` because this row was added at the first level. Listing 11-4 shows how to add a row at the second level. The updated output of the `SELECT` statement from Listing 11-3 is also shown.

```
INSERT   INTO Hierarchy
         ( path_locator, name )
VALUES   ( '/1/1/', '1.1.txt' )
/*
path_locator    path     parent_path_locator    name
------------    -----    -------------------    -------
0x58            /1/      NULL                   1.txt
0x5AC0          /1/1/    0x58                   1.1.txt
*/
```

Listing 11-4: Adding a row to a second level.

Assuming the name `1.txt` refers to a file, the preceding code would be nonsensical in a FileTable scenario, because file system files cannot have children. Also, in FileTables, you would not determine the `path_locator` yourself; rather, it is the result of the position of the file or folder in the file system's structure.

> **More on using hierarchies**
>
> Books Online has a tutorial available at HTTP://BRURL.COM/FSI4.

Root folder

A single SQL Server instance can host multiple FileTables, across multiple databases, so each database must be assigned a root folder. This root folder becomes a child folder of the `FILESTREAM` share on the SQL Server host. By default, the name of the file share is **MSSQLSERVER** (or the SQL Server instance name, if you use named instances).

The root folder must be unique across all databases in the same instance, and can be configured from SSMS or using T-SQL. Using SSMS, simply right-click on the database's node in Object Explorer and click **Properties** and then, in the **Database Properties** dialog box, go to the **Options** page, locate the **FILESTREAM Directory Name** option and type in the folder name.

Listing 11-5 shows how to set the root folder using a T-SQL script. Note that the folder name can be different from the database name, but it must be a valid Windows folder name.

```
-- Configure the root folder
ALTER DATABASE NorthPole SET FILESTREAM (DIRECTORY_NAME = 'NorthPole')
```

Listing 11-5: Set the FileTable root folder name using T-SQL.

This method can also be used to change the name of the root folder, if previously set. This change takes effect immediately, although it requires that all active connections to the database are closed. You cannot reset the `FILESTREAM` directory name to `NULL` as long as there are FileTables in the database.

Non-transactional access

Transactional access to the BLOB data stored in a FileTable is supported like it is with any `FILESTREAM` column. The ability to access the files and folders in the FileTable using traditional Windows API-based applications requires that access is also allowed outside the bounds of a SQL Server transaction. Access to traditional `FILESTREAM` columns still requires a transaction context for reading and writing, even in SQL Server 2012, and this is regardless of any database-level configuration for non-transactional access.

This non-transactional access is configured at the database level, meaning that we can have multiple databases on the same SQL Server instance with different configurations for non-transactional access of FileTables. The options for non-transacted access are:

- **Off** – Non-transactional access to FileTables is not allowed; any access to the `FILESTREAM` data stored in all FileTables in the database follows the same rules as regular `FILESTREAM`.

- **ReadOnly** – Non-transactional access to FileTable data is only possible for reading; client applications cannot create or modify files and folders unless they use traditional `FILESTREAM` techniques.

- **Full** – Non-transactional access to FileTables is allowed for both reading and writing; client applications can open and save files and create folders using the standard Windows or .NET file I/O APIs.

Internally, SQL Server will use the Read Committed transaction isolation level to enforce locking or concurrency semantics.

To configure non-transactional access using SSMS, open the **Database Properties** window for the database in question, and in the **Options** page locate the **FILESTREAM Non-Transacted Access** option and select the appropriate value as shown in Figure 11-1.

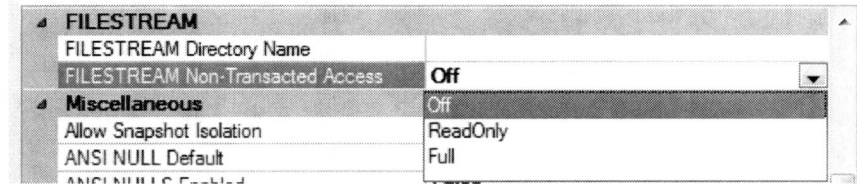

Figure 11-1: Setting non-transactional access level using SSMS.

After selecting the appropriate option, close the **Database Properties** dialog. SSMS will warn you that, in order to change database properties, all connections to that database must be closed. You must click **Yes** in order to save your changes. If you click **No**, the **Database Properties** dialog is not closed, and you can cancel the changes instead.

To configure non-transactional access using a T-SQL script, refer to Listing 11-6.

```
-- Configure non-transactional access to FileTables in the current DB
ALTER DATABASE NorthPole SET FILESTREAM (NON_TRANSACTED_ACCESS = FULL)
```

Listing 11-6: Configuring non-transactional access using T-SQL.

The valid values for the NON_TRANSACTED_ACCESS are OFF, READ_ONLY and FULL, as described previously.

While non-transactional access to FileTable data is a requirement for interoperability with client applications that only use Windows file I/O APIs, there is also a risk of consistency problems. For example, it is possible for a client application to "see" a file and read the file attributes (but not read the file contents) while a transaction that is creating the file is still in progress. Should the transaction roll back and the file be removed, the application might be acting on incorrect information. I have not found a way to avoid this possibility, although I did have to work hard to make it happen.

A noteworthy difference between non-transactional access and transactional access is related to garbage files. Garbage files are not created when updating files using non-transactional access. Rather, the original FILESTREAM data file is written to directly.

Chapter 11: FileTable

This allows for in-place (or partial) updates to the files, potentially resulting in significant performance enhancements over other `FILESTREAM` scenarios. This enhancement comes at the cost of transactional integrity. When a file is deleted using non-transactional access, the `FILESTREAM` file will remain and follow the same rules for garbage collection as other garbage files.

FileTable namespace

The namespace of a FileTable refers to its file and folder structure. In order to navigate to a FileTable's root folder, you need to know the machine name, the instance-level `FILESTREAM` share name, the database-level folder name and the FileTable-level folder name. The root path can then be constructed like this:

`\\servername\instance-share\database-directory\FileTable-directory`

SQL Server 2012 provides several functions to obtain the correct names of the share and folders. Assuming a default SQL Server instance with default `FILESTREAM` share name, a database called `NorthPole` with default `FILESTREAM` directory name, and a FileTable called `Documents` with a default FileTable directory name, the UNC path would be:

`\\servername\MSSQLSERVER\NorthPole\Documents`

In order to implement an NTFS-compatible structure in SQL Server tables (referred to as "FileTable semantics" in Books Online), FileTable uses many constraints, computed columns and defaults.

Constraints and computed columns can cause a lot of overhead if many operations are performed on a FileTable in short order. You might be performing more operations than usual if the namespace of the FileTable is being reorganized, such as when you are moving files from one folder to another. Another example might be a bulk load operation. On those occasions, you may consider disabling the constraints to achieve better performance while these tasks are being completed. Disabling the constraints is accomplished by disabling the FileTable's namespace. You will need to re-enable the namespace before the FileTable contents will be available again.

Before the FileTable's namespace will be re-enabled (and the contents be available using Windows APIs), SQL Server will perform a consistency check on the FileTable. If the consistency check fails, then the namespace will not be re-enabled and the inconsistency must be fixed.

To disable a FileTable's namespace in SSMS, right-click on the FileTable, open the **Table Properties** dialog box, and go to the **FileTable** page. Change the value of the **FileTable namespace enabled** option to **False**.

The code in Listing 11-7 disables and then re-enables the FileTable namespace for the `Documents` table. Barring a rogue DML operation that takes place between the disable and enable operations, this simple action will not result in inconsistencies.

```
-- Disable the Documents FileTable namespace
ALTER TABLE Documents DISABLE FILETABLE_NAMESPACE
GO

-- Enable the Documents FileTable namespace
ALTER TABLE Documents ENABLE FILETABLE_NAMESPACE
```

Listing 11-7:   Disabling and enabling a FileTable's namespace using T-SQL.

Since disabling the FileTable namespace disables constraints, this should not be done without thoroughly considering the potential implications of data consistency problems.

FileTable security

`FILESTREAM` data can only be accessed in the context of SQL Server, so SQL Server exercises control over who can access the data. For `FILESTREAM` columns, the same permissions can be set as for other columns, thereby allowing or denying access to roles or users.

SQL Server also maintains control over the `FILESTREAM` data that is stored in FileTables. As such, an important restriction on the use of FileTables must be noted: SQL Server security can work at the table and column level, but not at the row level. In FileTables, each row is a file or folder and, as such, these cannot be secured individually (unlike with NTFS permissions). It is not possible to create an access control list on a file or folder stored in a FileTable, and Windows Explorer will not show the **Security** tab in the file or folder properties dialog.

In order for a user to have access to FileTable data using Windows APIs, the user's Windows logon account will have to be granted permissions on all columns in the FileTable (or the user account will need to be a member of a role that has such permissions).

It is possible to prevent users from performing certain tasks in a FileTable by modifying the permissions on the FileTable. This is best accomplished by creating database roles, such as `FileTable_nodelete` and `FileTable_noinsert`, to which you can then add logins or other roles. If you have multiple FileTables, you may consider creating a role for each set of FileTables with specific access restrictions.

Prevent creating and deleting files or folders

To prevent users from deleting files and folders, you can explicitly deny the `Delete` permission on the FileTable(s). The affected logins will be able to access and modify the files and folders in the FileTable as well as create new ones, but will not be able to delete any files or folders, even those they created themselves. If a user attempts to delete a file or folder, it will appear to succeed, but a simple refresh of the folder shows that the item is still there. No error message is shown to the user. This, again, is a departure from the way NTFS permissions are normally set up: the `CREATOR OWNER` of an object usually has full control over that object, including delete permission.

Denying the `Delete` permission to users is effective only to prevent accidental deletion. As we'll discover below, it's not possible to make files read-only on a user-by-user basis. That means that a user with malicious intent can still destroy the contents of the file, even if the file itself cannot be deleted.

It is also possible to prevent users from creating new files and folders in a FileTable by denying the `Insert` permission in a similar fashion as for the `Delete` permission. When a user attempts to create a new file or folder in the FileTable, they will receive an error message that looks like the one below (Figure 11-2). This error message is unfortunately not very polished.

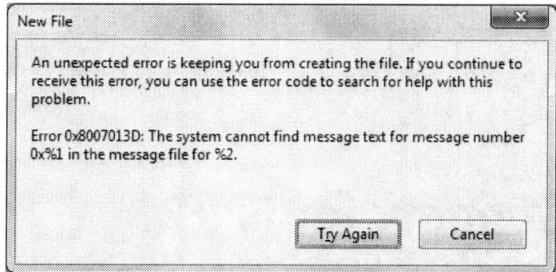

Figure 11-2: Error message when attempting to create a new file or folder.

No read-only access

Unfortunately, it is not possible to provide read-only access to certain users or roles while providing read and write access to others. When explicitly denying the `Update` permission on the FileTable to a role or user, users are still able to open files and folders, make changes and save those changes using Windows file I/O APIs. However, because the

Update permission is denied, the metadata fields in the FileTable do not get updated. So, the `last_write_time` and `cached_file_size` values of that row in the FileTable will not reflect accurate values. At the time of going to press, Microsoft confirmed that this is a bug and that they intend to issue an update to address it.

It is possible that these shortcomings in the security features of FileTable will be a deal breaker for some environments, and you will have to review these and discuss the potential implications with the stakeholders.

Setting Up the Server for FileTable

FileTable is based on `FILESTREAM`, so the SQL Server machine and instance need to be configured to support `FILESTREAM`. Specifically, the use of FileTables requires the `FILESTREAM` access level to be set to allow remote streaming access. Complete details of how to set up and verify `FILESTREAM` configuration are found in Appendix A.

It is also important to note that, just like `FILESTREAM`, to access FileTable data using the Windows API, Windows authentication must be enabled for the SQL Server instance.

Creating a Database with Support for FileTable

In order to create a FileTable, the hosting database must be configured to support `FILESTREAM` and FileTable. A complete discussion about creating databases with `FILESTREAM` support is provided in Chapter 2.

In addition to support for `FILESTREAM`, the database must also have the **FILESTREAM Directory Name** option set to a valid folder name. It is also most likely that you will enable non-transactional access to the FileTables in your database. The T-SQL script in Listing 11-8 creates a database that has support for FileTable enabled. Review the section on *FileTable Concepts*, above, to learn how to configure the FileTable settings using SSMS.

Chapter 11: FileTable

```sql
-- If the 'NorthPole' exists, drop it
IF DB_ID('NorthPole') IS NOT NULL BEGIN
    DROP DATABASE NorthPole;
END

-- Create NorthPole database
CREATE DATABASE NorthPole ON
PRIMARY (
    NAME = NorthPole,
    FILENAME = 'C:\ArtOfFS\Demos\Chapter11\NorthPole.mdf'
), FILEGROUP NorthPole_fs CONTAINS FILESTREAM(
    NAME = NorthPole_fs,
    FILENAME = 'C:\ArtOfFS\Demos\Chapter11\NorthPole_fs' )
LOG ON (
    NAME = NorthPole_log,
    FILENAME = 'C:\ArtOfFS\Demos\Chapter11\NorthPole_log.ldf')

-- Configure non-transactional access
ALTER DATABASE NorthPole SET FILESTREAM (NON_TRANSACTED_ACCESS = FULL)

-- Configure the root folder
ALTER DATABASE NorthPole SET FILESTREAM (DIRECTORY_NAME = 'NorthPole')
```

Listing 11-8: T-SQL script to create a database with FileTable enabled and configured.

If you have an existing database, you can verify its readiness to support FileTable by querying the `sys.database_filestream_options` catalog view as shown in Listing 11-9.

```sql
SELECT non_transacted_access, non_transacted_access_desc,
    directory_name
FROM sys.database_filestream_options
WHERE database_id = DB_ID('NorthPole')
/*
non_transacted_access  non_transacted_access_desc  directory_name
---------------------  --------------------------  --------------
2                      FULL                        NorthPole
*/
```

Listing 11-9: Querying a catalog view to verify FileTable support.

If the `directory_name` column is `NULL`, then you will need to change that option, using either SSMS or T-SQL. Both methods are discussed in the earlier *FileTable Concepts* section.

Creating a FileTable

When we have a database that meets the prerequisites, we can create our first FileTable.

Create a FileTable using T-SQL

A FileTable has a fixed schema, so the T-SQL statement to create one is as simple as shown in Listing 11-10.

```
USE NorthPole
GO

CREATE TABLE Documents AS FILETABLE
```

Listing 11-10: T-SQL statement to create a FileTable.

You'll notice there is no need to specify field names, but we specify a new clause: `AS FILETABLE`. This clause indicates to SQL Server that the standard schema is to be used.

With the FileTable created, use Windows Explorer to navigate to the FileTable's folder, using the path below. This path assumes that you have a default instance of SQL Server, you did not change the `FILESTREAM` share name and you configured the `FILESTREAM` directory name to be the same as the database name (`NorthPole`):

\\localhost\MSSQLSERVER\NorthPole\Documents

By default, the folder name of the FileTable is the table name. You can change the name of the directory (which is a subfolder of the database's root folder discussed above) by adding the `FILETABLE_DIRECTORY` option in the `CREATE TABLE` statement (Listing 11-11).

```
CREATE TABLE Documents AS FILETABLE
    WITH (FILETABLE_DIRECTORY = 'NorthPole Documents')
```

Listing 11-11: Creating a FileTable with a specific directory name.

If you need to change the directory name, you can use the `ALTER TABLE` statement in Listing 11-12.

```
ALTER TABLE Documents SET (FILETABLE_DIRECTORY = 'Documents')
```

Listing 11-12: Change the directory name of a FileTable.

The directory name of a FileTable must be a valid Windows directory name, which means that certain characters are not allowed. For example, a directory name cannot contain the pipeline character (|). While it's probably not common, it is possible in SQL Server to create a table with a pipeline character in the name. If you try to create a FileTable with the name **Documents|Confidential**, you will receive an error message like the one below.

```
Msg 33402, Level 16, State 1, Line 1
An invalid directory name 'Documents|Confidential' was specified. Use a valid Windows
directory name.
```

At that point, you will need to decide if you want to change the table name to match the requirements of Windows naming conventions or if you want to override the default folder name using the `FILETABLE_DIRECTORY` option.

The FileTable data in a new FileTable will be stored on the default `FILESTREAM` filegroup defined in your database. You may have a need to place the FileTable data on a specific filegroup that is not the default filegroup in the database. Listing 11-13 shows how this can be done.

```sql
-- Create a new FILESTREAM filegroup
ALTER DATABASE NorthPole
    ADD FILEGROUP NorthPole_fs2 CONTAINS FILESTREAM

-- Create a new FILESTREAM data container
ALTER DATABASE NorthPole
    ADD FILE (NAME = 'NorthPole_fs2',
        FILENAME = 'C:\ArtOfFS\Demos\ChapterX\NorthPole_fs2')
    TO FILEGROUP NorthPole_fs2

USE NorthPole
GO

-- Place the FileTable data on a specific FILESTREAM filegroup
CREATE TABLE Documents AS FILETABLE
    FILESTREAM_ON NorthPole_fs2
```

Listing 11-13: Creating a FileTable that uses a specific FILESTREAM filegroup.

You will notice the FILESTREAM_ON clause is the same clause you would use when changing the FILESTREAM filegroup on a regular table.

Create a FileTable using SSMS

In other chapters, we have highlighted that it's not possible to create FILESTREAM columns using SSMS. However, SSMS does offer some support for creating FileTables by providing a shortcut menu entry and **Create FileTable** template code.

To create a FileTable using SSMS, right-click on the **Tables** node and select the **New FileTable** item. If you already have a FileTable defined in the database, you can also right-click on the **FileTables** node. SSMS will create a new query window and include a **Create FileTable** template. Unfortunately, the default template requires a lot of work to customize, including selecting the correct database to create the FileTable in as well as replacing placeholder values in more than 20 locations.

It is possible to customize the template and reduce the number of placeholders that need to be replaced. On a 64-bit system, the file containing the template can be found at:

```
C:\Program Files (x86)\Microsoft SQL Server\110\Tools\Binn\
ManagementStudio\SqlWorkbenchProjectItems\Sql\Table\
Create FileTable.sql
```

After creating a precautionary backup, you can edit this file to your liking. For example, you can remove the USE statement, change occurrences of the schema_name placeholder to dbo and comment out the parts that set the optional values for FILETABLE_DIRECTORY and FILETABLE_COLLATE_NAME.

Listing 11-14 shows a suggested Create FileTable template after the edits described above are made.

```
-- ==========================================
-- Create FileTable template
-- (customized 2012-01-06, Art of FILESTREAM)
-- ==========================================

IF OBJECT_ID('dbo.<table_name>', 'U') IS NOT NULL
  DROP TABLE dbo.<table_name>
GO

CREATE TABLE dbo.<table_name> AS FILETABLE
-- WITH
-- (
--    FILETABLE_DIRECTORY = '<file_table_directory_name>',
--    FILETABLE_COLLATE_FILENAME = <file_table_filename_collation, sysname, database_default>
-- )
GO
```

Listing 11-14: Create FileTable template with fewer placeholders.

Chapter 11: FileTable

Work with a FileTable using SSMS

While SSMS has only limited support for creating FileTables, there are some commands and elements that have been added to the GUI that can come in handy while working with FileTables.

SSMS lists FileTables in their own node in the Object Explorer tree. It lists all the FileTables in the database and provides a context menu that contains the **New FileTable** entry. When drilling down into the FileTables node, it acts just like the Tables node (Figure 11-3).

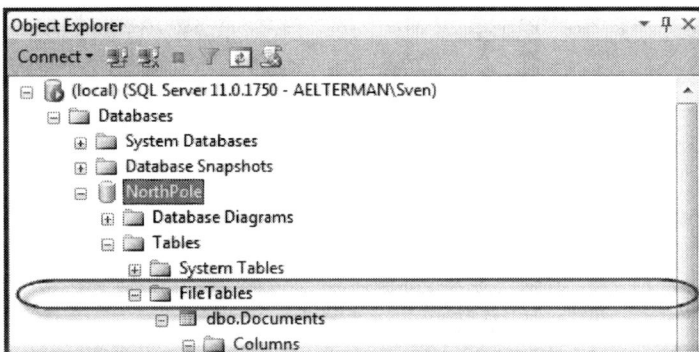

Figure 11-3:   FileTables node in SSMS (trimmed full column list for brevity).

Using SSMS, it is possible to change the FileTable's directory name. This change takes effect immediately, but can only be made if no files are open in that FileTable. To change the directory name, right-click on the FileTable and select **Properties**, then in the **Table Properties** dialog, go to the **FileTable** page and change the value of the **FileTable directory name** property to a valid Windows directory name (Figure 11-4).

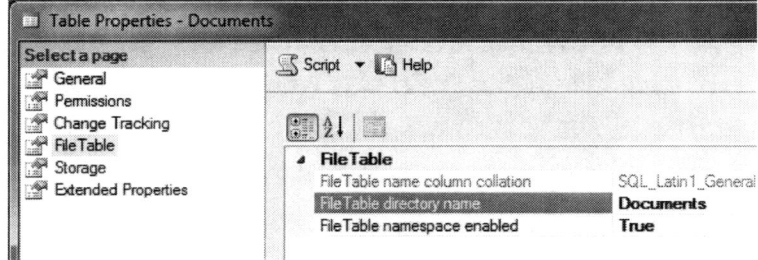

Figure 11-4: Changing the FileTable directory name using SSMS.

To help you quickly open a Windows Explorer window showing the contents of the FileTable, right-click on the FileTable name and select **Explore FileTable Directory**. This menu option will be grayed out if the database is not set up for non-transactional access or if the FileTable's namespace is disabled.

Adding constraints to the FileTable

It's not possible to create constraints on the FileTable at creation time, but you can add constraints later, using an `ALTER TABLE` statement. Note that you cannot remove the constraints that are created by default.

By way of example, let's add a constraint to the FileTable that would prevent files from being created at the FileTable root folder. A constraint like this might be useful if you have defined folders in the FileTable and you do not want users to create files unless they're in one of those subfolders. Listing 11-15 shows how to define such a constraint on a FileTable.

```
ALTER TABLE Documents
    ADD CONSTRAINT CK__Documents__NoFilesInRoot
    CHECK
        (is_directory = 1 OR path_locator.GetLevel() > 1)
```

Listing 11-15: Creating a constraint on a FileTable.

In Listing 11-15, the constraint checks that either the value of the `is_directory` column is 1 (we'll allow creating folders at any level) or that the level in the hierarchy is greater than 1. This will prevent users from creating files at the FileTable's root, but not at any other level. When attempting to create a new file at the root, the error message shown in Figure 11-5 will appear.

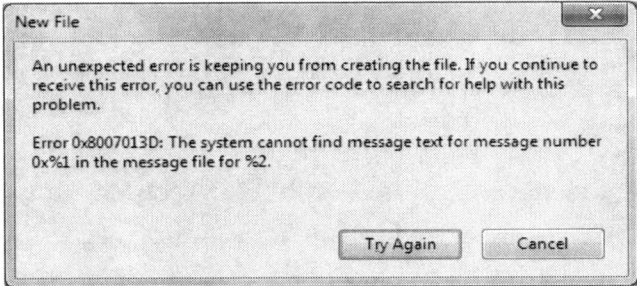

Figure 11-5: Error message when attempting to create a file at Level 1 after applying a constraint.

If you have plans to apply the same constraint to multiple FileTables in the database, it would be a good idea to extract the logical expression into a user-defined function. For now, however, let's remove this constraint from the table (Listing 11-16).

```
ALTER TABLE Documents
    DROP CONSTRAINT CK_Documents_NoFilesInRoot
```

Listing 11-16: Drop a user-defined constraint from a FileTable.

Restrictions on creating FileTables

While most operations that can be performed on regular tables can be performed on FileTables, there are a few restrictions. Foremost, of course, is the notion that the schema is predefined and fixed. You cannot add or remove columns from a FileTable. Usually, it's possible to work around that limitation by defining another table and creating a one-to-one relationship between the FileTable and the table containing the additional data.

Furthermore, it's also not possible to create a FileTable in the `tempdb` database or create a FileTable as a temporary table (which is expected, based on the first restriction, as temporary tables are created in `tempdb`). That restriction also applies to `FILESTREAM` in general, as it's not possible to modify `tempdb` to add a `FILESTREAM` filegroup.

Accessing a FileTable with Windows Explorer and Other Client Applications

Once you have created a FileTable, it is ready for use. If you intend to use your FileTable to store data used by an application that is not `FILESTREAM`-aware (i.e. the application will not be modified to support transactional access to the files), you do not need to take any further action.

By way of example, let's create a new file and folder and examine the effect in SQL Server. Using Windows Explorer, navigate to the file share where your FileTable is located. If you followed the example from Listings 11-8 and 11-10, this will be your path name:

`\\localhost\MSSQLSERVER\NorthPole\Documents`

Alternatively, you can also right-click on the FileTable in SSMS and choose the **Explore FileTable Directory** from the shortcut menu.

Creating files

At this time, the folder should be empty. Right-click the right pane and select **New | Text Document**. Provide a filename for the new file, such as `Letter.txt` and confirm.

Now open (or return to) SSMS and select all rows from the **Documents FileTable**. You will find that one row is returned. You can verify the value of the name column to make sure the correct file is returned. Also note the value of the cached_file_size column, which should read 0 (as the file is empty). A full discussion of the FileTable schema is included above.

It is possible that you set a value for the **FILESTREAM Non-Transacted Access** to **ReadOnly**. In that case, you will not be able to create new files. Windows Explorer will show an error message like the one in Figure 11-6.

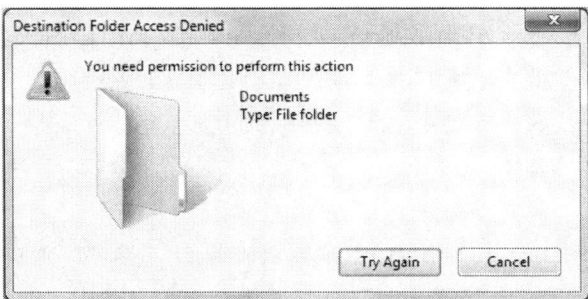

Figure 11-6: Windows Explorer error message if **FILESTREAM Non-Transacted Access** is set to **ReadOnly**.

The error message states that destination folder access is denied, but there really isn't a permission issue. It may be more constructive to think about it as a configuration issue.

If you successfully created the new text file, open it in your favorite text editor (which is likely not FILESTREAM-aware!) and add some text to the file. Use the **Save** command in your text editor to save your changes. Rerun the SELECT query in SSMS and review the results. You will find that the cached_file_size column has been updated to reflect the new file size. Close the text editor.

Creating folders

One of the major benefits of FileTable is the ability to store the data hierarchically, meaning in folders. Let's create a new child folder and examine the effect in the FileTable. In Windows Explorer, right-click in the right pane, select **New | Folder**, provide a name for the new folder and confirm. Rerun the `SELECT` statement to retrieve all rows from the FileTable, and note that you now have two results. The second row is your folder. The best way to distinguish between a folder and a file row in a FileTable is using the `is_directory` field. The value is 0 for a file and 1 for a folder. You can also check for a `NULL` in the `file_stream` column.

Memory-mapped files

One major caveat of FileTable is that memory-mapped files are not supported. A discussion of memory-mapped files is beyond the scope of this text, but suffice it to say that some popular Windows utilities (including Notepad and Paint) use it when opening files on the local system, even if the path is a UNC path (like `\\systemname\MSSQLSERVER\NorthPole`). While those utilities likely do not make or break a FileTable adoption, let's look at a workaround.

If you created a new, zero-length text file, you will be able to successfully open the file with Notepad, make changes to it, and save it. However, once you close the file and then try to reopen it, you will receive this error message from Notepad:

```
The request is not supported.
```

Notepad will no longer be able to open the file. This is because Notepad uses memory-mapped files. You can work around this issue by mapping a drive letter to the `FILESTREAM` share. Also, when accessing the files from another host than the SQL Server machine, memory-mapped files are not used.

Empty database folder

If a user account has only been granted **select**, **insert**, **update** and/or **delete** permission on the FileTables in a database, the shared folder for that database will appear empty when browsing to it. When typing in the name of the folder associated with a FileTable, you can navigate further.

As an example, consider John, who has been given **select** permission only on the FileTable in the database `NorthPole` on the server SQL01. (Assume the `FILESTREAM` directory name and the FileTable directory name are the same as the database and table names).

When John uses Windows Explorer to navigate to the database's folder at `\\SQL01\MSSQLSERVER\NorthPole`, the folder will appear empty. By appending the folder name to the path `\\SQL01\MSSQLSERVER\NorthPole\DocumentStore`, John will have access to the FileTable.

This symptom is caused by the fact that the user was not granted the **View definition** permission on the FileTable. The commonly used built-in database roles `db_datareader` and `db_datawriter` are also not granted those permissions.

So, in order for your users to have a fluent experience while accessing FileTable shares, they should be given the **View definition** permission.

Programming FileTable

In this section, we'll cover how to read and update FileTable data using application code. We'll use both T-SQL and the .NET file I/O APIs to read, create, modify, and delete files and folders in a FileTable.

Adding rows using T-SQL

Although it will probably be uncommon to add rows to a FileTable using T-SQL, it is possible to do so. Applicable scenarios may include hydrating default rows to a new database instance or, perhaps, the creation of new folders using your application's custom GUI.

In the next few examples, we will prepare our Documents FileTable for use by an order entry application. We will create some files and folders in the table by using the T-SQL INSERT statement and specifying values for the required fields that don't have default values. The file we will create in the root of the FileTable is a README file, which one might use to inform end-users about the proper use of the file share.

Listing 11-17 shows the minimum required T-SQL code to create a new file in our Documents FileTable. Successfully executing this statement requires that you dropped the user-defined constraint using the code in Listing 11-16.

```
INSERT INTO Documents ([name], file_stream)
VALUES ('ReadMe.txt', 0x)
```

Listing 11-17: Creating an empty file in the root folder using T-SQL.

There is no default value defined for the `file_stream` column, and a NULL is not allowed unless the row refers to a folder, so we specify 0x to create a zero-length file. Listing 11-18 shows how to create a new folder using T-SQL. The folder will be used to store documents about each order that is placed. In a real-world scenario, this might include an image of the shipping label. In our scenario, we will use only dummy file contents.

```
INSERT INTO Documents ([name], is_directory)
VALUES ('Order Files', 1)
```

Listing 11-18: Creating a new folder in the FileTable root folder using T-SQL.

Chapter 11: FileTable

We may also need to create a new file in a subfolder. We must ensure that we create this new file in a valid hierarchy, which means that we must include the folder's `path_locator` in the `path_locator` of this new record. As an example, Listing 11-19 shows a simplified view of the structure we just created using Listing 11-17 and Listing 11-18.

```
SELECT CAST(path_locator AS VARCHAR(4000)), name,
    path_locator.GetLevel() AS 'level', is_directory
FROM Documents

/*
path_locator   name          level  is_directory
------------   -----------   -----  ------------
/1.1.1/        ReadMe.txt    1      0
/2.2.2/        Order Files   1      1
*/
```

Listing 11-19: Querying the contents of the `Documents` table.

While the `path_locator` values you will find are more complex, the point is to illustrate that the file and the folder have a different `hierarchyid` (`path_locator`) value, but that the level in the hierarchy is both 1. The new file we want to add should have a `path_locator` and `level` value like the ones shown in Table 11-2.

path_locator	name	level
/2.2.2/3.3.3/	NewFile.txt	2

Table 11-2: `path_locator` value for the new file.

We must create the new file record as a child of the **Order Files** folder, so we cannot use the `DEFAULT` constraint on the `path_locator` column to let SQL Server create a `path_locator` value located in the FileTable root. Instead, we must first find the parent folder's `path_locator` value and construct a new `path_locator` value that is a child value of the parent folder's `path_locator`. Listing 11-20 shows how this can be done.

```
-- Find the path_locator value for the parent directory
DECLARE @parent_path_locator HIERARCHYID

SELECT @parent_path_locator = path_locator
FROM Documents
WHERE name = 'Order Files'
    AND path_locator.GetLevel() = 1
    AND is_directory = 1

-- Create a new path_locator value that places the new file
-- as a child of the parent directory
DECLARE @path_locator VARCHAR(675)
SET @path_locator = @parent_path_locator.ToString() +
    CONVERT(VARCHAR(20), CONVERT(BIGINT, SUBSTRING(
        CONVERT(BINARY(16), NEWID()), 1, 6))) + '.' +
    CONVERT(VARCHAR(20), CONVERT(BIGINT, SUBSTRING(
        CONVERT(BINARY(16), NEWID()), 7, 6))) + '.' +
    CONVERT(VARCHAR(20), CONVERT(BIGINT, SUBSTRING(
        CONVERT(BINARY(16), NEWID()), 13, 4))) + '/'

-- Insert a new record, specifying the new path_locator
INSERT INTO Documents (name, file_stream, path_locator)
VALUES ('OrderFile.txt', 0x, @path_locator)
```

Listing 11-20: Create a zero-length file in a subfolder using T-SQL.

We are creating the HIERARCHYID value by calling the NEWID() function three times.

- Firstly, extracting a specific number of bytes from it (6 the first time, 6 the second time and 4 the third time).

- Secondly, converting the binary value to a 64-bit integer.

- Thirdly, converting the integer to a variable-length string of maximum 20 characters (though the true maximum length is 15 characters the first two times and 8 characters the third time).

Each of these values is then concatenated and separated with a period. At the end, a forward slash is added. This is the same way in which the SQL Server default constraint creates the path_locator value. Unfortunately, the NEWID() function cannot be used in a user-defined function. Otherwise, the smart developer would undoubtedly create a reusable function to create a `path_locator` value for a new child given the parent's `path_locator`.

Also, Microsoft uses the `NEWID()` function three times in the constraint, because it's not possible to declare a variable there to hold the value of a single call. If you plan to create a stored procedure, you might just make one call to `NEWID()` and store the value in a temporary variable. Listing 11-21 shows what such a stored procedure could look like.

```
CREATE PROCEDURE dbo.CreateFileTableFile
  @name NVARCHAR(255),
  @parent_name NVARCHAR(255),
  @parent_level tinyint
AS
BEGIN
  SET NOCOUNT ON;

  DECLARE @parent_path_locator HIERARCHYID;
  DECLARE @temp_id BINARY(16);

  -- Find the path_locator of the parent of the new file
  SELECT @parent_path_locator = path_locator
  FROM Documents
  WHERE name = @parent_name
    AND path_locator.GetLevel() = @parent_level
    AND is_directory = 1;

  -- If the parent's path_locator was found
  IF (@parent_path_locator IS NOT NULL)
  BEGIN
    SET @temp_id = CONVERT(BINARY(16), NEWID());

    -- Create a new path_locator value that places the new file
    -- as a child of the parent directory
    DECLARE @path_locator VARCHAR(675)
    SET @path_locator = @parent_path_locator.ToString() +
      CONVERT(VARCHAR(20), CONVERT(BIGINT, SUBSTRING(
        @temp_id, 1, 6))) + '.' +
      CONVERT(VARCHAR(20), CONVERT(BIGINT, SUBSTRING(
        @temp_id, 7, 6))) + '.' +
      CONVERT(VARCHAR(20), CONVERT(BIGINT, SUBSTRING(
        @temp_id, 13, 4))) + '/';
```

```
    -- Insert a new record, specifying the new path_locator
    INSERT INTO Documents (name, file_stream, path_locator)
    VALUES (@name, 0x, @path_locator);
  END
  ELSE
  BEGIN
    -- Raise error because the specified parent folder does not exist
    RAISERROR ('The parent name does not exist in the FileTable at the specified
level.', 16, 1);
  END
END
```

Listing 11-21: A stored procedure to insert a new row in a FileTable.

It is possible to create simpler values for the `path_locator` field, such as just appending `1/` to the `parent_path_locator` value, but then your values are deviating from the default structure. Also, you have to provide some mechanism to ensure uniqueness of the `path_locator`, which will likely involve a call to `NEWID()` anyway.

In the same fashion, we can now create a second-level subfolder using Listing 11-22. The only difference from Listing 11-21 is found in the `INSERT` statement, where the `file_stream` column has been replaced by the `is_directory` column.

```
-- Find the path_locator value for the parent directory
DECLARE @parent_path_locator HIERARCHYID

SELECT @parent_path_locator = path_locator
FROM Documents
WHERE name = 'Order Files'
    AND path_locator.GetLevel() = 1
    AND is_directory = 1

-- Create a new path_locator value that places the new file
-- as a child of the parent directory
DECLARE @path_locator VARCHAR(675)
SET @path_locator = @parent_path_locator.ToString() +
    CONVERT(VARCHAR(20), CONVERT(BIGINT, SUBSTRING(
        CONVERT(BINARY(16), NEWID()), 1, 6))) + '.' +
    CONVERT(VARCHAR(20), CONVERT(BIGINT, SUBSTRING(
        CONVERT(BINARY(16), NEWID()), 7, 6))) + '.' +
```

```
        CONVERT(VARCHAR(20), CONVERT(BIGINT, SUBSTRING(
            CONVERT(BINARY(16), NEWID()), 13, 4))) + '/'

-- Insert a new record, specifying the new path_locator
INSERT INTO Documents (name, is_directory, path_locator)
VALUES ('2013 Order Files', 1, @path_locator)
```

Listing 11-22: Create a new subfolder using T-SQL.

Some of the complexities in adding files and folders using T-SQL, specifically children of other folders, may lead many developers to choose to use the Windows APIs instead. The next section discusses using the standard .NET `System.File.IO` namespace classes to achieve the same results.

Using .NET file I/O APIs

In this section, we will use the traditional .NET file I/O APIs to access FileTable data. First, we will need to determine the path to the files and folders that are stored in the FileTable. There is a new T-SQL function that allows us to get the UNC path of a FileTable's `file_stream` column: `GetFileNamespacePath()`. This function takes two optional arguments; the first determines if a full path (which includes server name, share name and FileTable directory name) is returned or if a relative path is returned. The second argument determines the format in which the server name is returned, and is similar to the `PathName()` function found on a regular `FILESTREAM` column. (The `PathName()` function works on the `file_stream` column, but returns the path you would use to create a `SqlFileStream` instance in the context of a transaction.)

Listing 11-23 shows an ADO.NET code snippet to retrieve the full path of a file whose name and location in the hierarchy is known. There are other ways to initially find the `path_locator` of a file or folder, which can then be used to retrieve the UNC path.

```
string SqlText = @"SELECT file_stream.GetFileNamespacePath(1)
                   FROM Documents
                   WHERE name = 'MyFile.txt'
                   AND path_locator.GetLevel() = 1";
string FilePath = null;

using (SqlConnection conn = new SqlConnection(
       "server=.;database=NorthPole;integrated security=sspi;"))
using (SqlCommand cmd = new SqlCommand(SqlText, conn))
{
  conn.Open();
  FilePath = (string)cmd.ExecuteScalar();
}
```

Listing 11-23: ADO.NET code snippet to retrieve full path.

You'll note that this code does not use any of the `FILESTREAM`-related queries we've seen in previous chapters. This is a plain T-SQL query, with the only new addition the use of the `GetFileNamespacePath()` function. This function is discussed in more detail later in the chapter. We can use this file path to open the file for reading and output its contents to the console (Listing 11-22).

```
if (FilePath != null)
{
  using (System.IO.StreamReader sr = System.IO.File.OpenText(FilePath))
  {
    Console.WriteLine(sr.ReadToEnd());
  }
}
```

Listing 11-24: Open a file in a FileTable for read access using .NET file I/O APIs.

Listing 11-24 is not designed to demonstrate best practices in the use of the .NET file I/O APIs. Specifically, in this example, we are reading an entire file as a string without considering the file size. In a real-world scenario, we might be doing this to a multi-gigabyte file and causing significant performance issues. Using file streams would be a better practice.

Chapter 11: FileTable

You may also want to use the file I/O APIs to create new files and folders. First, you'll need to obtain the UNC path of a valid folder in the FileTable namespace. Listing 11-25 shows how to obtain the UNC path of the FileTable root folder. It uses the T-SQL `FileTableRootPath()` function to retrieve the UNC path. The argument to the function is the name of the FileTable. If this argument is not specified, the database's root directory is returned. This function is discussed in more detail in the section below on *Managing FileTables*.

```csharp
string SqlText = "SELECT FileTableRootPath('Documents')";
string RootPath = null;

using (SqlConnection conn = new SqlConnection(
        "server=.;database=NorthPole;integrated security=sspi;"))
using (SqlCommand cmd = new SqlCommand(SqlText, conn))
{
  conn.Open();
  RootPath = (string)cmd.ExecuteScalar();
}
```

Listing 11-25: Obtaining the root folder of a FileTable in .NET.

Listing 11-26 then uses this root folder value to create a folder and a file inside the new folder. In this code snippet, the `System.IO` namespace is not explicitly specified for the class names, so make sure you have a `using` statement (or `Imports` in Visual Basic) at the top of your code file before running this code.

```csharp
if (RootPath != null)
{
  DirectoryInfo di = Directory.CreateDirectory(RootPath +
    "\\Order Files");
  using (StreamWriter sw = File.CreateText(di.FullName +
    "\\ReadMe.txt"))
  {
    sw.WriteLine("Hello, World!");
  }
}
```

Listing 11-26: Creating a folder and file in a FileTable using .NET file I/O APIs.

As a best practice, consider writing code that is independent from the SQL Server configuration by using relative paths. If you are storing path values anywhere, store the value relative to the database-level directory. That way, a change to the configuration of SQL Server will not break the application.

You may be storing path values as part of an application's configuration data, which might allow the application to retrieve the folder where all order files are located. To avoid storing the full path: `\\servername\MSSQLSERVER\NorthPole\Documents\Order Files` store instead: `\Order Files`. Then, when the full path is needed, call the `FileTableRootPath()` function and concatenate your stored value to the return value of the function.

A more comprehensive discussion of the use of .NET file I/O APIs is beyond the scope of this book. However, below are some limitations that exist in the use of the APIs.

- It's not possible to rename the database or FileTable root directories using the I/O APIs.
- It's not possible to obtain an exclusive handle on the database or FileTable root directories.

Managing FileTables

In addition to the functions and views that apply to all `FILESTREAM`-enabled databases and tables, there are specific functions and views added to SQL Server 2012 to support the FileTable feature.

T-SQL functions

In addition to the `PathName()` function, which has existed since SQL Server 2008, three new documented T-SQL functions have been added to SQL Server 2012: `FileTableRootPath()`, `GetFileNamespacePath()` and `GetPathLocator()`.

FileTableRootPath

`FileTableRootPath()` returns the UNC path of the root directory of the current database and, with the use of the optional argument, appends the root directory of the specified FileTable. On a default server instance and assuming all default share and directory names, a call to `FileTableRootPath()` in the `NorthPole` database will yield this result:

```
\\SERVERNAME\MSSQLSERVER\NorthPole
```

A call to `FileTableRootPath('Documents')` will yield this result:

```
\\SERVERNAME\MSSQLSERVER\NorthPole\Documents
```

GetFileNamespacePath

This intrinsic function returns the UNC path of the file or folder referenced by the `file_stream` column. This function has two optional arguments.

The first argument determines if the computer name and share name are also included. If the argument is 0 (default), only the relative path starting with the database-level directory is returned. If the argument is 1, the full UNC path is returned.

The second argument determines if the computer name is converted. The default value of 0 converts the computer name to NetBIOS format, a value of 1 does not convert the computer name, and a value of 2 returns the fully qualified domain name of the server. (This argument and its values are identical to that found in the `PathName()` intrinsic function.)

Listing 11-27 shows the use of the `GetFileNamespacePath()` function with the default argument values and with non-default argument values.

```
SELECT file_stream.GetFileNamespacePath() 'Default',
    file_stream.GetFileNamespacePath(1, 2) 'Non-default'
FROM Documents
WHERE name = 'File.txt'
/*
Default               Non-default
------------------    --------------------------------------------
\Documents\File.txt   \\SQL.domain.us\MS...ER\NorthPole\Documents\File.txt
*/
```

Listing 11-27: Using the `GetFileNamespacePath()` function.

GetPathLocator

This function returns the `HIERARCHYID` associated with the specified, existing full path. You would use this function if you have a known FileTable path and need to locate the SQL Server data row associated with it. Books Online provides a migration scenario from a file server to FileTable as an example at HTTP://BRURL.COM/FSI5.

In addition, several undocumented T-SQL functions have been added. These functions are used in the constraints related to FileTables, but it appears they cannot be called from regular T-SQL code.

PathName

The `PathName()` function has been around since the introduction of `FILESTREAM` in SQL Server 2008. The function works on the `file_stream` column of a FileTable and you would use its value if you use transactional access to the FileTable and you want to use the `FILESTREAM` Win32 API calls. You cannot use the return value of the `PathName()` function to open a FileTable file for non-transactional access.

Chapter 11: FileTable

There has been a change to the `PathName()` function in SQL Server 2012 to support Availability Groups, a new feature in the latest release. Any discussion of Availability Groups is beyond the scope of this book, but `PathName()` now has a second optional argument that determines whether the returned name should be the virtual network name (VNN) (default) or the computer name.

Catalog and Dynamic Management Views

Three new catalog management views and one new DMV have been added to SQL Server 2012. One catalog view has been updated to support FileTable.

sys.tables

The `sys.tables` catalog view has been updated to include the `is_FileTable` column. A value of 1 in the `is_FileTable` column indicates that the table is a FileTable.

sys.database_filestream_options

We have already used this catalog view in Listing 11-9 to check the readiness of a database for FileTable creation. The view includes four columns.

- **database_id** – The ID of the database within the SQL Server instance. This is useful for filtering by a particular database. You can retrieve the ID of a database using the `DB_ID()` function.
- **directory_name** – The database-level directory name for all FileTables within the database. If this value is NULL, a database-level directory has not been set and the database cannot contain FileTables.

- **non_transacted_access** – A TINYINT representing the level of non-transactional access for the database. The values can be:
  - 0: Non-transactional access is disabled
  - 1: Non-transactional access is only enabled for read-only access
  - 2: Non-transactional access if fully enabled
  - 5: Non-transactional access is in transition to read-only access
  - 6: Non-transactional access is in transition to disabled.
- **non_transacted_access_desc** – The description of the value in the non_transacted_access column. The possible values and their numeric equivalents are:
  - NONE (0)
  - READ_ONLY (1)
  - FULL (2)
  - IN_TRANSITION_TO_READ_ONLY (5)
  - IN_TRANSITION_TO_OFF (6).

sys.filetable_system_defined_objects

This catalog view returns a list of all the system-defined objects that have been created when the FileTables in the current database were created. This includes the FileTable's primary key, foreign key, unique and check constraints, and defaults. A FileTable has 20 such system-defined objects.

The view contains two columns: object_id and parent_object_id. The object_id column contains the object ID of the system-defined object, and the parent_object_id column contains the object ID of the FileTable. Listing 11-28 shows how the object name of each object can be retrieved using the `OBJECT_NAME()` function. On your system, you should recognize the names of the objects, although the IDs and numeric values at the end of the names will be different.

```
select [object_id],
   OBJECT_NAME([object_id]) 'name',
   parent_object_id,
   OBJECT_NAME(parent_object_id) 'parent name'
from sys.filetable_system_defined_objects
/*
object_id  name                              parent_object_id  parent_name
---------  --------------------------------  ----------------  -----------
277576027  PK__Document__5A5B77D57DF9CB0A    261575970         Documents
...
581577110  DF__Documents__is_te__22AA2996    261575970         Documents
*/
```

Listing 11-28: Retrieving the names of the FileTable system-defined objects.

Note that the objects included in this catalog view cannot be deleted. They are an integral part of the FileTable and will be deleted by SQL Server only if the FileTable itself is deleted. The constraints can be disabled by disabling the FileTable namespace (see FileTable namespace, above).

sys.filetables

This view lists information about the FileTables in the current database. The columns in the `sys.FileTables` view are:

- **object_id** – The object ID of the FileTable.
- **is_enabled** – Returns 0 if the FileTable's namespace is not enabled and 1 if the namespace is enabled.
- **directory_name** – The name of the FileTable root directory.

- **filename_collation_id** – The ID of the SQL Server collation used to store the file or folder name.
- **filename_collation_name** – This column contains the name of the SQL Server collation used to store the file or folder name.

sys.dm_filestream_non_transacted_handles

This DMV returns a list of all the non-transactional file and folder handles that are currently open. On an active server, the results of querying this view will change constantly.

There are 32 columns in this view, and their description can be found in Books Online at HTTP://BRURL.COM/FS16. Here, we only discuss those that are most useful in resolving issues.

- **database_id** – The ID of the database where the item with the open handle is located.
- **object_id** – The ID of the FileTable where the item with the open handle is located.
- **handle_id** – A unique number that can be used with the sp_kill_filestream_non_transacted_handles stored procedure to kill the handle.
- **opened_file_name** – The relative path that was originally requested to be opened.
- **open_time** – The UTC time the handle was opened.
- **login_name** – The user name of the user who opened the handle.

Stored procedures

One new stored procedure which has also been added is sp_kill_filestream_non_transacted_handles. This stored procedure can be used to kill handles to files that have been opened using non-transactional access. The stored procedure takes two optional arguments, `table_name` and `handle_id`. If these arguments are not provided, or `NULL` is passed, all non-transactional file handles are closed. If `table_name` only is provided, all non-transactional file handles for that table are closed. If `table_name` is provided, then a `handle_id` can also be specified to close a specific file. The handle IDs of open files can be obtained from the dynamic management view `sys.dm_filestream_non_transacted_handles`, discussed previously.

Advanced FileTable Uses

In this section, we will demonstrate the use of FileTable with two other SQL Server features that are particularly well suited to be used in conjunction with it: full-text search and semantic search. Full-text search indexes the contents of columns of supported types (including `VARBINARY(MAX)` and `FILESTREAM`) and allows for fast searching of those contents. It is somewhat like the Windows Search feature. Semantic search is new in SQL Server 2012 and builds upon the full-text indexing feature.

Full-text search

FileTable is ideally suited as a document storage repository, so adding a full-text index to the table may help users locate documents. The schema of FileTables meets the requirements for full-text indexing.

- The file contents are in a `VARBINARY(MAX) FILESTREAM` column.
- The file extension is stored in a computed column, `file_type`. This column is used to map to the correct IFilter.
- There is a unique index on the FileTable that meets the requirements for full-text indexing: the primary key of the FileTable.

Chapter 11: FileTable

Listing 11-29 shows how to create a full-text catalog in the database and a full-text index on the `name` and `file_stream` columns of the `Documents` FileTable.

```sql
-- Create a full-text catalog
CREATE FULLTEXT CATALOG NorthPole_Catalog AS DEFAULT

-- Create a full-text index on the FileTable
CREATE FULLTEXT INDEX ON Documents
    (name LANGUAGE 1033,
    file_stream TYPE COLUMN file_type LANGUAGE 1033)
    KEY INDEX PK__Document__5A5B77D57DF9CB0A
    ON NorthPole_Catalog
```

Listing 11-29: Create a full-text catalog and full-text index.

Now we can query the full-text catalog for a list of files that contain the text **test** in the `file_stream` field (Listing 11-30). The `FREETEXT()` function is used to specify which column we are querying and the value we are looking for.

```sql
SELECT file_stream.GetFileNamespacePath(1)
FROM dbo.Documents
WHERE FREETEXT(file_stream, 'test')
```

Listing 11-30: Query a full-text catalog.

Just like with any full-text index, each indexed column has a specific language code associated with it (the `sys.fulltext_languages` catalog view returns a list of supported languages and their code). If your system has documents stored in different languages and you want those to be indexed correctly, you will need to create a separate FileTable for each language.

A more detailed discussion of full-text search, including the predicates that can be used and tips on maintaining the index and configuring IFilters for different file types is beyond the scope of this book.

Semantic search

Semantic search is a new feature in SQL Server 2012 and allows for writing more advanced queries that can include the relationship between words in the FileTable contents. Scenarios that are enabled by this feature include the automatic extraction of key words in a document (to populate a tag cloud, for example) or the creation of a document similarity index to compare documents with each other.

An exhaustive discussion of the semantic search feature and its linguistic underpinnings is not appropriate for this book. However, we will examine how to:

- enable semantic search on a FileTable which already has full-text indexing enabled
- write a basic query which identifies keywords in a specified document.

Prepare the server for semantic search

Books Online has a complete discussion of the prerequisites for semantic search (HTTP://BRURL.COM/FSI7). During installation, the **Full-Text and Semantic Extractions for Search** instance feature must be selected.

After installation, a semantic language statistics database must be installed to the system and attached to the SQL Server instance. This database is not installed with SQL Server 2012. Instead, you must execute a separate Windows Installer package to install the database. Afterwards, you must attach the database to your SQL Server instance.

Finally, the semantic language statistics database must be registered by calling the `sp_fulltext_semantic_register_language_statistics_db` stored procedure, specifying the semantic language statistics database.

Language support

Language support for semantic search is more limited than for full-text indexing. By querying the `sys.fulltext_semantic_languages` catalog view, a list of supported languages can be obtained.

Add a semantic search index

To add semantic search to the full-text index created in Listing 11-29, refer to the code in Listing 11-31.

```
ALTER FULLTEXT INDEX ON Documents
    ALTER COLUMN file_stream
        ADD Statistical_Semantics
```

Listing 11-31:   Create a semantic search index on an existing full-text index.

Execute a semantic query

By way of example, we will execute a semantic query on the **Documents** FileTable to identify keywords in a file called **Resume.docx** in the root folder of the FileTable (Listing 11-32).

```
-- Find the key value of the document to use
DECLARE @path_locator HIERARCHYID

SELECT @path_locator = path_locator
FROM Documents
WHERE name = 'Resume.docx'
    AND path_locator.GetLevel() = 1
```

Chapter 11: FileTable

```
-- If the document exists
IF (@path_locator IS NOT NULL)
    -- Select the top 10 keywords from the document
    SELECT TOP(10) KeyPhraseTable.keyphrase
    FROM SEMANTICKEYPHRASETABLE
        (
        Documents,      -- the table name containing the document
        file_stream,    -- the column name of the document
        @path_locator   -- the ID associated with the document
        ) AS KeyPhraseTable
    ORDER BY KeyPhraseTable.score DESC
```

Listing 11-32: Writing a semantic query to determine keywords in a document.

You will note that this code was written in multiple statements. This was done primarily for clarity, although the IF clause can be used to output a message in case the document does not exist in the FileTable. Without the IF clause, the semantic search statement would not return any results and would not provide a warning that the `path_locator` value was not found.

Practical semantic analysis

You may want to run your own résumé through this type of semantic analysis and see which keywords are identified. You may be surprised to learn that what your résumé is seen as focusing on is something entirely different from what you intended. You can safely assume that employers and employment agencies employ similar linguistic analysis to rank your résumé against others, or to compare your résumé to job descriptions.

Investigating FileTable

While end-users will view the files in the FileTables like they would view any file share, as a developer or database administrator it is still important to understand that the file contents are actually stored in the `FILESTREAM` data container associated with the `file_stream` column of the FileTable.

The same techniques used in Chapter 9 to investigate the location of the physical files on the SQL Server host can be used to locate the FileTable data. Note that the folder hierarchy in a FileTable is purely logical: the `FILESTREAM` data container is a flat structure that contains all file data, regardless of the folder they are located in according to the hierarchy structure of the FileTable.

The file names found in the `FILESTREAM` data container are LSNs, and not the file names found in the name column of the FileTable. Again, this is consistent with how `FILESTREAM` is implemented and this has not changed in SQL Server 2012.

The rules for updates to `FILESTREAM` data also apply. Most importantly, any modification to a FileTable file results in the creation of a new file in the `FILESTREAM` data container and the old file being marked as garbage by adding it to the `FILESTREAM` tombstone table.

Summary

In this chapter, we examined the newly introduced FileTable feature. Available in SQL Server 2012, FileTable expands the `FILESTREAM` concept, primarily by allowing non-transactional access to the stored BLOBs and by providing a hierarchical storage model, similar to folders on an NTFS volume.

To adequately understand FileTable, we first introduced several new concepts, including the fixed schema, non-transactional access, FileTable namespace and FileTable security. Next, we configured the server for FileTable and created a database with FileTable support.

We created a FileTable using T-SQL and examined the support for FileTables in SSMS. We used Windows Explorer to access the FileTable contents and create new files and folders. In the *Programming FileTable* section, we learned how to add data to a FileTable using T-SQL and the .NET file I/O APIs. We concluded that using the .NET file I/O APIs is preferable.

Then we looked at new SQL Server objects to support FileTable, including new functions, views and stored procedures. These objects help us to manage the FileTables in our environment by providing insight into the structure and contents of the FileTable data.

Finally, we examined two advanced features that are supported for FileTable data: full-text search and semantic search. The schema of FileTables lends itself well to being used with both full-text and semantic search.

Chapter 12: Planning, Configuration and Best Practices

Correct planning and configuration are vital ingredients in any successful technology implementation, and the `FILESTREAM` feature is no exception to this rule. To make sure the `FILESTREAM` feature is tuned for optimum performance and manageability, there are a number of factors to consider. The most important practices are included in this chapter. Readers may also wish to further refer to the seminal white paper by Paul Randal, *FILESTREAM Storage in SQL Server 2008* (HTTP://BRURL.COM/FS7). Even though the paper was written to target SQL Server 2008 and written around the original release, the information it presents is still valid and highly useful.

Planning

`FILESTREAM` is a great feature if implemented where it is really needed, but it should not be an automatic choice for every BLOB storage requirement. It is very important to understand this at the planning stage of your project. Keep in mind that there are cases where storing BLOB values in a `VARBINARY(MAX)` column will perform better than storing them in a `FILESTREAM` column, so we need to understand where `FILESTREAM` is ideal and where it is not.

As with many technology questions, the answer is "it depends." A Microsoft Research study (conducted before the introduction of the `FILESTREAM` feature) investigated the impact of storing BLOB values in the database versus the file system, and found the following:

- BLOB values over 1 MB in size provide best performance when stored in the file system (i.e. would benefit from storage in a `FILESTREAM` column).

- BLOB values smaller than 256 KB in size provide best performance when stored within the database (i.e. would benefit from storage in a `VARBINARY(MAX)` column).
- Performance stats of BLOB values between 256 KB and 1 MB largely depend upon the way the data is used.

Microsoft research

You can download the research paper, To BLOB or Not To BLOB: Large Object Storage in a Database or a Filesystem: HTTP://BRURL.COM/FS2.

This suggests that `FILESTREAM` is ideal only if the average size of BLOB values is over 1 MB. If the data is smaller, storing it in a `VARBINARY(MAX)` column will be more efficient.

The usage pattern and business requirements also play a crucial role in deciding whether to choose `FILESTREAM` storage. For example, if the BLOB data is modified frequently (partial updates) a `VARBINARY(MAX)` column might give better performance than a `FILESTREAM` column.

If the answer to the question whether or not to go with `FILESTREAM` is "Yes," then you need to work on the configuration to ensure that the storage environment is optimized for the best `FILESTREAM` performance.

Optimizing your Storage Configuration for FILESTREAM

Earlier chapters showed how to easily configure a SQL Server instance for experimenting with `FILESTREAM` storage. When it comes to setting up a production server for `FILESTREAM` storage, a number of additional configuration steps are recommended to make sure that the server is tuned for optimum `FILESTREAM` performance.

Keep FILESTREAM data containers on a separate disk volume

`FILESTREAM` operations can be very I/O intensive, so it is advisable to keep the `FILESTREAM` data container isolated from the data and log files of your database. If you have several `FILESTREAM`-enabled databases on the server, it is advisable to put each `FILESTREAM` container on a separate disk volume.

If you expect to store a huge number of data files in your `FILESTREAM` data container, you can partition the `FILESTREAM` table and split the `FILESTREAM` data across multiple disk volumes. We saw how to partition a `FILESTREAM` table in Chapter 2.

Disabling short file names

As we discovered in Chapter 2, for every `FILESTREAM` cell that is not `NULL`, SQL Server creates a disk file in the columns folder of the data container. If the table is large, it is quite possible that the folders associated with the `FILESTREAM` columns will contain a large number of disk files.

Chapter 12: Planning, Configuration and Best Practices

By default, NTFS creates a secondary file name for every file that you create in the NTFS volume. These secondary file names are called *short file names*, and they follow the legacy 8.3 naming convention. Creation of short file names on folders that have a large number of files is very resource intensive, because the system needs to ensure uniqueness. It does this by matching the newly created name with the short file name of all the other files present in the folder.

Short file name generation is turned on by default. However, short file names are needed only if you expect 16-bit applications to read your files, which is highly unlikely on today's production servers. In addition, the data you store in the `FILESTREAM` data container should not be directly accessed by any application other than SQL Server. This means that you can safely turn off short file name creation on disk volumes where you store the `FILESTREAM` data.

You can use the command line tool `fsutil.exe` to disable short file names on your system. To first check whether it is already disabled, you can query the current setting by running the query shown in Listing 12-1 in the command window.

```
fsutil.exe behavior query disable8dot3
```

Listing 12-1:   Querying the short file name setting.

This will return the current value configured for this setting, as shown in Figure 12-1.

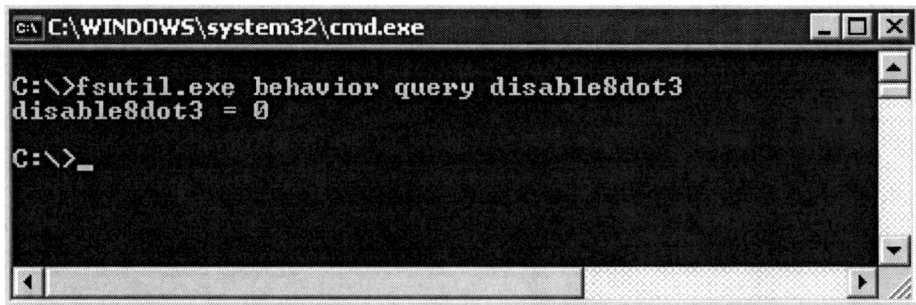

Figure 12-1:   The current setting for short file names.

If short file names are not disabled, you can disable them by running `fsutil.exe` with the `set` parameter (Listing 12-2).

```
fsutil.exe behavior set disable8dot3 1
```

Listing 12-2:   Changing the short file names setting.

You must reboot your computer for the changes to take effect.

While doing the research for this chapter, I came across a number of articles which mentioned that disabling short file names does not really provide any performance benefits. To verify this, I ran some tests which created a large number of files on a folder, and compared the performance differences.

The test script created 100,000 files in 20 laps, each lap creating 5,000 text files in a folder. At first, the test script was executed with short file names enabled. The script was run three times, and the average time it took to complete each lap was recorded. Then the test was run another three times with short file name generation disabled. (A server reboot was required for the change to take effect). My testing, summarized in Table 12-1, showed a considerable performance improvement after disabling 8.3 file names on the system.

Lap	Duration (in seconds) with short file names:		File names
	Enabled	Disabled	
1	4	1	File_1_1.txt to File_1_5000.txt
2	10	3	File_2_1.txt to File_2_5000.txt
3	9	4	File_3_1.txt to File_3_5000.txt
4	10	2	File_4_1.txt to File_4_5000.txt

Chapter 12: Planning, Configuration and Best Practices

Lap	Duration (in seconds) with short file names:		File names
	Enabled	Disabled	
5	11	4	File_5_1.txt to File_5_5000.txt
6	15	3	File_6_1.txt to File_6_5000.txt
7	21	4	File_7_1.txt to File_7_5000.txt
8	51	1	File_8_1.txt to File_8_5000.txt
9	106	3	File_9_1.txt to File_9_5000.txt
10	3	4	File_10_1.txt to File_10_5000.txt
11	4	2	File_11_1.txt to File_11_5000.txt
12	4	2	File_12_1.txt to File_12_5000.txt
13	5	1	File_13_1.txt to File_13_5000.txt
14	7	2	File_14_1.txt to File_14_5000.txt
15	7	2	File_15_1.txt to File_15_5000.txt
16	10	2	File_16_1.txt to File_16_5000.txt
17	10	1	File_17_1.txt to File_17_5000.txt
18	13	2	File_18_1.txt to File_18_5000.txt
19	14	2	File_19_1.txt to File_19_5000.txt
20	3	1	File_20_1.txt to File_20_5000.txt

Table 12-1:   Performance test results for short file names.

Initially, I was surprised that, when the test was run with short file names enabled, the duration went up with each lap (up to Lap 9) and then fell down to 3 seconds from 106. The same happened at Lap 19 too. Then I realized that the delay has to do with the amount of data NTFS has to look at before creating a new file. After Lap 9, the file name pattern changed and the same happened after Lap 19. It indicates that not only the number of files in the folder, but also the way files are named, affects the performance when short file names are enabled.

SQL Server names `FILESTREAM` data files based on the LSN that created the `FILESTREAM` data file. Based on the workload and usage pattern on your server, the file names on disk may or may not follow a specific pattern. The system overhead to create short file names depends on the number of files with similar names in the same folder.

If the file names created are similar, you might notice a performance difference after disabling short file names. It is important to note that the impact of short file names comes into the picture only when new files are created. If your application does not create new files, the impact of the change may often not be noticeable.

Compressing FILESTREAM data

When data is compressed, the I/O pressure on the system is reduced because less data is read from, and written to, the disk. On the other hand, CPU usage increases because the storage engine has to compress the data before writing to the disk, and decompress it on reading. Depending upon your workload, CPU, and I/O subsystem capabilities, compression may or may not help. In most cases, I have seen that compression helps if the data is compressible.

The SQL Server row- and page-level compression feature does not compress `FILESTREAM` data files. However, SQL Server allows `FILESTREAM` data files to be stored on compressed disk volumes. This will reduce the storage space needed for the data. The decision to go with compressed `FILESTREAM` storage should be taken only after clearly

Chapter 12: Planning, Configuration and Best Practices

analyzing the workload, system configuration, the type of BLOB values to be processed, and so on. Some file types use a compressed format, so trying to compress them again will add overhead without benefits.

Configuring NTFS cluster size

It is recommended that you format your NTFS volume with a larger-than-default cluster size (allocation unit). The default cluster size in Windows 2000, Windows Server 2003, and Windows Server 2008 is 4 KB. The recommended cluster size for optimum `FILESTREAM` performance is 64 KB, which is the maximum cluster size. If you intend to use NTFS file compression, you must keep the cluster size to 4 KB; NTFS file compression is not possible on volumes formatted with a cluster size greater than 4 KB. You can check the current cluster size of your disk by running `chkdsk.exe` without any parameters at the command prompt (Figure 12-2).

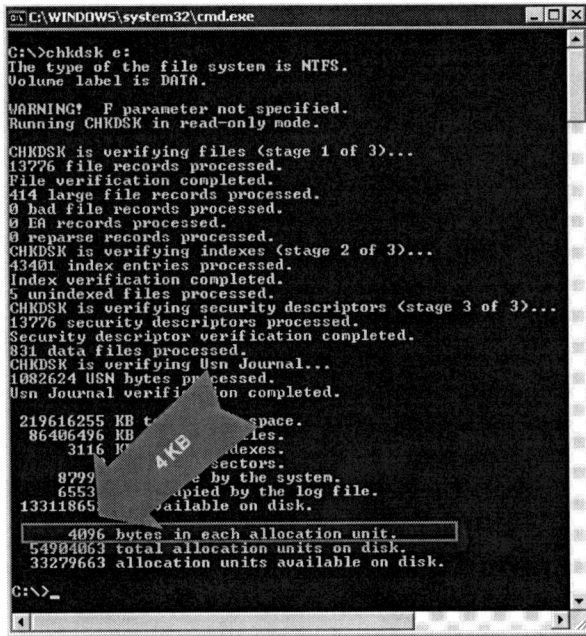

Figure 12-2: Running `chkdsk` to see the current cluster size.

Chapter 12: Planning, Configuration and Best Practices

It is important to consider the cluster size of your volume during the planning phase of the `FILESTREAM` implementation because, unless trusted third-party tools are used, it is not possible to change the cluster size without formatting the volume (and thus erasing all data).

Disabling the indexing service

Indexing usually slows down common file operations such as opening and closing. Because `FILESTREAM` data files should be accessed only through SQL Server, it is recommended that you disable indexing on the NTFS volumes where `FILESTREAM` data is stored.

Disabling indexing on an NTFS volume is quite easy. You can do this by right-clicking on the NTFS volume and selecting **Properties**. In the **General** tab, you can see an option to enable or disable the indexing service on the selected disk volume (Figure 12-4).

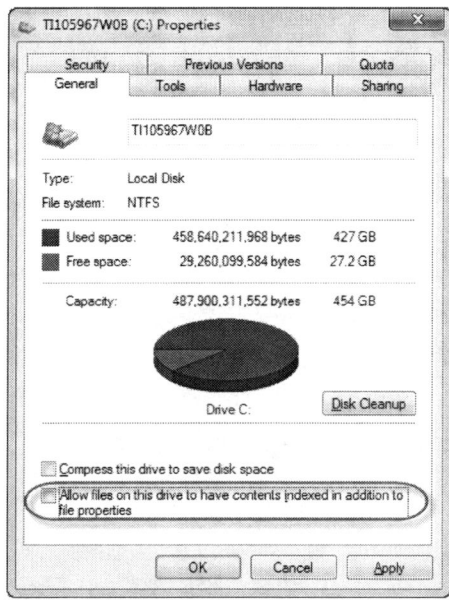

Figure 12-3: Disabling indexing on an NTFS volume.

Chapter 12: Planning, Configuration and Best Practices

Configuring antivirus

"Should I configure my antivirus software to scan the FILESTREAM data?" is a very interesting question. The answer depends upon various factors specific to the environment, such as the source of data, or the way `FILESTREAM` files are processed. If you are storing data that originated from untrusted sources (for example, end-user file uploads, perhaps even by users outside your own organization), you may want to enable virus scans. However, it is important to recognize that virus scanning software may not be 100% effective because it will not be able to determine the file type of the stored data if the scanner uses the file extension for that purpose.

If you decide to configure your antivirus software to scan the `FILESTREAM` data container, make sure you do not configure it to delete the infected files. If the antivirus software deletes an infected file from the `FILESTREAM` data container, you will end up with a corrupted database and it will be hard for you to figure out what went wrong and subsequently recover the database.

It is therefore recommended that you configure your antivirus software to quarantine the infected files rather than deleting them. If a `FILESTREAM` data file is infected and the antivirus software moves it to a quarantine folder, you can run `DBCC CHECKDB` to identify the missing files in the `FILESTREAM` data container and match it with the files in the quarantine folder. Chapter 7 included the options for recovering from missing `FILESTREAM` data files.

You may also consider an alternative approach, in which the virus scanning is done at the time of saving the `FILESTREAM` data. Many antivirus software vendors provide SDKs, which expose API functions that you can use to scan a memory stream. Such an API function can be called from your .NET or Win32 code just before writing the `FILESTREAM` data. This approach is most effective if your application writes data exclusively using the streaming I/O APIs and not using T-SQL statements.

Disabling the Last Access Time attribute

Each file in an NTFS volume has an attribute named `Last Access Time`. By default, NTFS tries to keep this attribute accurate by updating it every time the file is accessed. It means that even a read operation will result in a disk write operation (to update the `Last Access Time` attribute). Disabling this attribute on the `FILESTREAM` volume will give you considerable performance benefits if you deal with a large number of files that are frequently read. When the `Last Access Time` update is disabled, this attribute will show the same value as the `File Creation Time`.

You can disable `Last Access Time` by running `fsutil.exe` on computers running on Windows Server 2003 and later. You might want to first check the current setting of this configuration value. You can do it by running `fsutil.exe` in `query` mode (Listing 12-3).

```
fsutil.exe behavior query disablelastaccess
```

Listing 12-3:   Querying the `Last Access Time` setting.

If `Last Access Time` is not disabled, you will see a message that reads `disablelastaccess is not currently set`.

If the system is configured to disable the update of `Last Access Time`, your query will return `disablelastaccess = 1`.

If you see that your server is currently configured to update `Last Access Time`, you can disable it by running `fsutil.exe` with the `set` parameter (Listing 12-4).

```
fsutil.exe behavior set disablelastaccess 1
```

Listing 12-4:   Disabling `Last Access Time` update.

Chapter 12: Planning, Configuration and Best Practices

Configuring the disks with the correct RAID level

Configuring the correct RAID level is a complex subject, and a detailed discussion is beyond the scope of this chapter. Depending upon the environment, type of applications, and policies, the DBA team and storage administrators need to work together to identify the correct RAID level for the given environment and the performance objectives.

A detailed discussion of the RAID configuration is beyond the remit of this book. Below, however, are some general guidelines.

1. RAID 5 + striping (also referred to as RAID 50) is one of the best options, and gives very good read and write performance as well as good fault tolerance. However, this is one of the most expensive options because it requires the most disks to implement.

2. RAID 0 gives very good read and write performance, is cheaper than RAID 5 + striping, but provides no fault tolerance.

3. RAID 5 gives very good fault tolerance, but read and write operations are not as fast as with the other options.

Just like the other configuration parameters, correct planning before implementing `FILESTREAM` is crucial for ensuring optimum performance.

> **More on RAID configurations**
>
> *For a more detailed discussion of the different RAID configurations, see the Wikipedia articles on RAID at* HTTP://BRURL.COM/FS19, *and* HTTP://BRURL.COM/FS20.

Regular disk defragmentation

One of the regular database maintenance activities that you need to plan for FILESTREAM databases is defragmentation of the FILESTREAM disk volumes. If the FILESTREAM data files are large or frequently modified, the chances of fragmentation are higher, and regular defragmentation of the disk will improve performance.

Setting up FILESTREAM for Remote Access

Remote access to FILESTREAM data is one of the most misunderstood terms associated with FILESTREAM storage. Remote access to FILESTREAM data means "accessing FILESTREAM data from a client application that resides on a different computer from where the SQL Server instance is installed."

When you enable FILESTREAM for I/O streaming access in the FILESTREAM configuration, FILESTREAM data is accessible from client applications running on the same computer; an application running on the same computer as a SQL Server 2008 instance can access the FILESTREAM data either using the Win32 API or the Managed API exposed by SQL Server.

There is a further option, to allow remote clients to have streaming access to FILESTREAM data on the FILESTREAM configuration page of the SQL Server installer. You might have also noticed it in the FILESTREAM tab or the property sheet of the SQL Server instance opened from SQL Server Configuration Manager. In most real-world scenarios, the database and application will reside on different computers, therefore you should enable this option. Appendix A discusses fully the configuration of remote access.

Depending upon the security configuration of your network, you may or may not require additional changes to access FILESTREAM data remotely.

Access to `FILESTREAM` data from a remote computer uses the Server Message Block (SMB) protocol. SMB is a protocol used for sharing files and other resources such as printers between computers. The default port number used by SMB is 445. You need to make sure that the firewall is configured to allow access to these ports.

Configuring the client computer for remote access

Note that streaming access to the `FILESTREAM` data is available only when the client is authenticated using Windows authentication. So, when accessing `FILESTREAM` data remotely, it is very important to ensure that the Windows user account your application uses on the other computer has adequate permissions to log in to the SQL Server instance and access the `FILESTREAM` table using Windows authentication (Integrated Security).

As on the server side, to use `FILESTREAM` in a firewall-protected environment, the client must be able to resolve DNS names to the server that contains the `FILESTREAM` files.

Configuring the client application for remote access

On the application side, accessing `FILESTREAM` data remotely is no different from accessing it from the same computer. In Chapter 3, we saw several examples that demonstrated how to access the `FILESTREAM` data using the streaming APIs. You should be able to run those examples successfully against a remote SQL Server instance if `FILESTREAM` has been correctly configured for remote access.

MSDN documentation recommends doing fewer updates with bigger data chunks when accessing `FILESTREAM` data remotely. The recommended buffer size is 60 KB for the optimum performance.

Best Practices for FILESTREAM Development

In this section, we have included all best practices for developers working with `FILESTREAM`. Some of these practices are found in other chapters of the text as well, but this section may provide value for quickly evaluating an application's design or for use during a code review.

Use FILESTREAM streaming APIs to read and write FILESTREAM data

As we have seen, reading and writing `FILESTREAM` data using T-SQL is not efficient in most cases because, when `FILESTREAM` data is accessed using T-SQL, streaming capability is not available. In addition, T-SQL access uses SQL Server's memory for buffering the `FILESTREAM` data, which can significantly add to the memory pressure on the server.

For best performance, always use the Win32 or Managed API for reading and writing `FILESTREAM` data.

Avoid small partial updates

`FILESTREAM` does not support in-place update of the BLOB data. When you modify a `FILESTREAM` value, SQL Server will create a new copy of the entire file with the modified content and discard the old file. A new copy of the file needs to be created even for a small change in the `FILESTREAM` data file.

If your application requires modification of data, you might want to review the expected volume of changes when you are deciding whether `FILESTREAM` storage is ideal. If frequent modifications are required, you might benefit more from keeping the data in a

`VARBINARY(MAX)` column. To help you make this decision, do some performance tests to compare `FILESTREAM` and `VARBINARY(MAX)` storage options based on your specific workload and usage pattern.

Keep an additional column to store the type of file or extension

In many cases, a `FILESTREAM` column is expected to store more than one type of file. For example, a product catalog application might store multiple types of files (`.jpg`, `.png`, etc.) in the image column, and a document management application might store multiple types of documents (such as Word or Excel), and so on.

An additional column that specifies the file type can be beneficial. For example, in Chapter 10 we saw that full-text indexing expects an additional column in the table that stores the file extension. Based on the file type, the index component identifies the IFilter for the file and indexes the content. Even if you do not use full-text indexing, it may be helpful to keep a file type column, for example to identify the content type to the client application.

Identifying the type of file from a file header

Most file types have a header section that stores various pieces of information about the content of the file. For example, most image file types keep a file header that specifies the type of file, dimension of the image, and so on.

While it is recommended that you keep an additional column that specifies the file type, in the real world you may end up in a situation where there is no such column. For example, assume that the application stores different types of images in the `FILESTREAM` column of a product catalog table. In the absence of an extra column which stores

Chapter 12: Planning, Configuration and Best Practices

the file type or extension, you might need to read the file header (first few bytes of the `FILESTREAM` data) to determine the type of file.

When only a small piece of data is to be read from the beginning of the file, T-SQL access is found, in most cases, to be more appropriate and efficient than Win32 or Managed API access.

The code snippet in Listing 12-5 reads the header information from the image files stored in a `FILESTREAM` column and identifies the file types.

```sql
SELECT
    ItemNumber,
    ItemDescription,
    CASE
        WHEN SUBSTRING(itemimage, 1, 2) = 0XFFD8 THEN 'JPEG'
        WHEN SUBSTRING(itemimage, 1, 2) = 0X424D THEN 'BMP'
        WHEN SUBSTRING(itemImage, 1, 8) = 0x89504E470D0A1A0A THEN 'PNG'
        ELSE 'Other'
    END AS FileType
FROM Items

/*
ItemNumber   ItemDescription    FileType
----------   ----------------   --------
MM2001       Dell Laptop        JPEG
MS1002       Microsoft Mouse    PNG
MS1005       TVS Key Board      PNG
MS1007       XBOX 360           BMP
*/
```

Listing 12-5: Identifying file types from the file headers

In the above example, the column `FileType` shows the type of images stored in the `FILESTREAM` column by reading the header information stored in the first few bytes of the BLOB value.

Add a content-type column on FILESTREAM tables

If you intend to serve the `FILESTREAM` data from a web application, it may be beneficial to store the appropriate MIME type on each row. When the web application serves the `FILESTREAM` data to the client, it can set the appropriate content type in the HTTP Response header. Based on the content type, the client browser/application can open the file using the appropriate application.

In most cases, if you have a column that stores the file extension or file type, you can build the content type (such as "**application/msword**" for Word documents, "**image/jpeg**" for jpeg images, and so on). But if you deal with a large number of different file types, it may be a good idea to store the MIME type of the BLOB value stored in each row.

Add a timestamp or date column to track last modified date for cache control

If you are serving `FILESTREAM` data from web applications, caching is an important factor to consider. When a client browser and web server communicate over HTTP protocol, they exchange some caching information. The client tells the server about the copy of the file locally available (local cache) and the server instructs the client to use the local copy or to download a new copy of the file.

If the web server tells the client that the file on the server is the same as the copy that the client has in the local cache, the file is not downloaded again. Instead, the client browser serves it from the local cache. This significantly enhances the performance of web applications.

Caching information is exchanged between the client browser/application and web server using the HTTP cache headers. The client browser sends the `time stamp` or `etag` of the file it has in the local cache. After examining the cache header information of the incoming request, the web server tells the client whether the server has a newer version of the file or not. The file needs to be downloaded only if the server has a newer version or if the cache is expired.

In the case of a `FILESTREAM` application, the data is stored and managed within the database. The web server does not know about the modified status of the file. As a result, in most cases, the file is downloaded every time a request comes in. This adds considerable overhead to the application, the database, and the web server.

Having a time stamp or date column on the table that keeps track of modifications done on the `FILESTREAM` value will help you to implement cache control in your `FILESTREAM` web handler. When a request comes in from a client, you can examine the cache control headers to see whether the file on the server is newer than the file on the client. If the file has not been modified since the client downloaded it, your handler can send back an HTTP 304 response which tells the client to use its local copy of the file.

Use a computed column to retrieve the file size

While working with `FILESTREAM` databases, you might need to know the size of the BLOB value stored in the `FILESTREAM` column. To avoid calculating the length of each BLOB value every time you need to query, you might decide to create a column and update it at the time of writing the `FILESTREAM` value.

An easier option is to create a `PERSISTED` computed column that stores the length of the file. Listing 12-6 shows how to add a computed column that stores the size of the BLOB value stored in a `FILESTREAM` column.

```
ALTER TABLE Items
ADD FileSize AS DATALENGTH(ItemImage) PERSISTED;
```

Listing 12-6: Adding a computed column to store the size of the BLOB value in a `FILESTREAM` column.

Chapter 12: Planning, Configuration and Best Practices

As soon as the computed column is added, the sizes of the existing `FILESTREAM` values are automatically calculated and stored in the column. Whenever new `FILESTREAM` values are inserted or existing values are updated, the size is automatically recalculated and the computed column is updated. Listing 12-7 shows an efficient way to retrieve the file size from the computed column.

```
SELECT
    ItemNumber,
    ItemDescription,
    END AS FileType,
    FileSize
FROM Items

/*
ItemNumber  ItemDescription  FileSize
----------  ---------------  --------
MM2001      Dell Laptop         2290
MS1002      Microsoft Mouse     1753
MS1005      TVS Key Board       1930
MS1007      XBOX 360           28286
*/
```

Listing 12-7: Retrieving the file size from the computed column.

Keep a default constraint on FILESTREAM columns

We have already learnt, in Chapter 2, that a `FILESTREAM` table is populated using a two-step process. First, the relational data is inserted using a T-SQL query or stored procedure, then the `FILESTREAM` column is updated using Win32 or the Managed API.

To be able to write the `FILESTREAM` data using Win32 or the Managed API, the `FILESTREAM` cell must not be `NULL`. So the T-SQL query that inserts the relational data must insert a dummy value into the `FILESTREAM` column before the column can be updated using the `FILESTREAM` API. If you forget to insert this dummy value into the `FILESTREAM` column and try to update it using the streaming APIs, the operation will fail.

Chapter 12: Planning, Configuration and Best Practices

It is recommended in most cases that you add a `default` constraint to your `FILESTREAM` columns so that, when a new row is inserted, the `FILESTREAM` column will be populated with a non-`NULL` value. Listing 12-8 demonstrates how to add a `default` constraint to a `FILESTREAM` column.

```
ALTER TABLE Items
ADD CONSTRAINT ItemImage_Default DEFAULT 0x
FOR ItemImage
```

Listing 12-8: Adding a default constraint to a `FILESTREAM` column.

The default value for the `ItemImage` column is 0x, which indicates a zero-length binary value. This will effectively create a zero-length (empty) file in the `FILESTREAM` data container.

Summary

Correct planning and configuration are necessary to get the best performance from your `FILESTREAM`-enabled database. We examined a number of configuration settings that will significantly boost `FILESTREAM` performance.

In addition to configuring the disks with the correct RAID level, disabling short file names can help to improve performance considerably. It is recommended that you configure NTFS cluster size from 4 KB (default) to 64 KB if you do not intend to use NTFS file compression, and disable indexing and the `last access` attribute on the NTFS volume where you plan to store the `FILESTREAM` data.

If you would like to configure your antivirus software to scan the `FILESTREAM` data files, make sure that you configure it to only quarantine the infected files (not to delete them). If the antivirus software deletes `FILESTREAM` data files, the resulting database corruption may be harder to resolve.

Chapter 12: Planning, Configuration and Best Practices

Remote access to the **FILESTREAM** data uses SMB protocol and therefore the SMB ports (445 and 139) must be enabled on the firewall.

In most cases, it will be helpful to keep some additional columns, such as the file extension, MIME content type, and file size on the **FILESTREAM** tables, depending upon the type and usage pattern of your application.

Appendix A: Configuring FILESTREAM on a SQL Server Instance

In this appendix, we provide detailed instructions for how to enable the `FILESTREAM` feature, and how to disable it if necessary.

You can enable `FILESTREAM` while you are installing a SQL Server 2008 instance, either using the installation wizard, or unattended. Alternatively, you can change the configuration settings on an existing SQL Server instance to enable the feature.

As described in Chapter 1, the process requires both Windows Administrator-level actions (to enable the feature) and SQL Server Administrator-level actions (to set up the `FILESTREAM` access level). If you enable `FILESTREAM` as part of the installation, the access level is automatically set up based on the settings you select during installation. However, if you enable `FILESTREAM` post-installation, you will have to configure it in two places: in the SQL Server Configuration Manager to enable the feature, and in the SQL Server instance properties to set the access level.

In most cases, you might decide to enable `FILESTREAM` as part of the installation process if you know for sure that the feature is needed. If you do not know at the time of installation whether a particular feature is needed or not, then it is a better choice to install and configure just those features that are needed, and enable other features only when required.

It is important to note that a service restart is not needed to enable the `FILESTREAM` feature. So there is no harm in skipping the `FILESTREAM` configuration step during installation and enabling it only when needed. However, fully disabling `FILESTREAM` will require a service restart to take effect. Therefore, it's better not to enable it during installation if you do not really need it.

Appendix A: Configuring FILESTREAM on a SQL Server Instance

In this appendix, we will examine the actions below.

1. Understanding FILESTREAM configuration and access levels.
2. Enabling and configuring FILESTREAM during installation.
3. Enabling and configuring FILESTREAM after installation.
    a. Configuring FILESTREAM at the Windows level.
    b. Configuring FILESTREAM at the SQL Server instance level:
        i. using SSMS
        ii. using T-SQL.
4. Verifying FILESTREAM configuration.
    a. Verifying Windows-level FILESTREAM configuration.
    b. Verifying SQL Server instance-level FILESTREAM configuration.
    c. Using SSMS to check that FILESTREAM is enabled.
    d. Using T-SQL to check that FILESTREAM is enabled.
5. Disabling the FILESTREAM feature.
6. Advanced installation and configuration options.
    a. Unattended SQL Server installation and FILESTREAM configuration.
    b. Enabling and configuring FILESTREAM from the command line.
    c. Configuring FILESTREAM access level from the command line.
    d. Setting up FILESTREAM on a failover cluster.

Understanding FILESTREAM Configuration and Access Levels

As `FILESTREAM` is a hybrid feature which deals with relational data that resides in database files, and BLOB data that resides in the file system folders, it has to be configured at the SQL Server instance level as well as the Windows operating system level. The first step is to configure it at the Windows level, which requires Windows Administrator privileges. The second is to configure it at the SQL Server instance level, which requires SQL Server `sysadmin` privileges.

This configuration process has been designed as a two-step process, maybe because of the way roles and permissions are distributed among people who manage computers, networks, and SQL Server instances in the "real world." In most environments, Windows/Network administrators manage and administer the operating system and file system-level configurations, and database administrators manage SQL Server instance-level configurations.

If `FILESTREAM` is configured during the SQL Server installation, both parts of the process will be carried out during the installation process. If `FILESTREAM` is being configured on an existing instance, it becomes a two-step process, first enabling the feature, using the SQL Server Configuration Manager, and then setting the access level, using SSMS or T-SQL.

FILESTREAM access levels

The `FILESTREAM` feature can be configured to allow three different access levels:

- T-SQL access
- streaming access (local)
- streaming access (remote).

T-SQL access

This is the lowest FILESTREAM access level. When FILESTREAM is enabled at this level, you can create FILESTREAM-enabled databases and read/write FILESTREAM data only using T-SQL.

When FILESTREAM data is enabled for T-SQL access, a local or remote application that has a valid SQL Server connection open can access the FILESTREAM data just like any other relational data in the database.

Streaming access (local)

When the FILESTREAM feature is enabled for I/O streaming access, FILESTREAM data can be accessed using the Win32 APIs as well as .NET managed classes.

Note that at this level streaming access is enabled only to applications running on the same computer as the SQL Server instance. It is also important to understand that FILESTREAM streaming access is allowed only when using Windows authentication to connect to the database instance.

Streaming access (remote)

When the FILESTREAM feature is enabled for remote streaming access, FILESTREAM data can be accessed from client applications running on a different computer through the streaming APIs.

FILESTREAM access level configuration

As mentioned earlier, the FILESTREAM feature has to be enabled at the operating system level as well as SQL Server instance level. FILESTREAM configuration at the Windows level is done using SQL Server Configuration Manager. FILESTREAM configuration at the SQL Server instance level can be administered either through the SSMS GUI dialog or through T-SQL. The desired FILESTREAM access level needs to be configured at both places.

T-SQL access is the lowest FILESTREAM access level, followed by local streaming. Remote streaming is the highest FILESTREAM access level. If the Windows Administrator enables only T-SQL access and the SQL Server administrator enables full access, only T-SQL access will be permitted. Similarly, if the Windows Administrator enables remote streaming access and the SQL Server Administrator enables T-SQL access, then only T-SQL access will be allowed.

Local versus remote access

Local streaming access and remote streaming access has been a topic of great confusion to many people. Questions such as "Can a user accessing my website read FILESTREAM data when remote streaming access is enabled?" have appeared several times on forums. So let us try to understand them clearly.

Let us look at an example of a network/application configuration, and see how different FILESTREAM access levels affect different use cases.

Appendix A: Configuring FILESTREAM on a SQL Server Instance

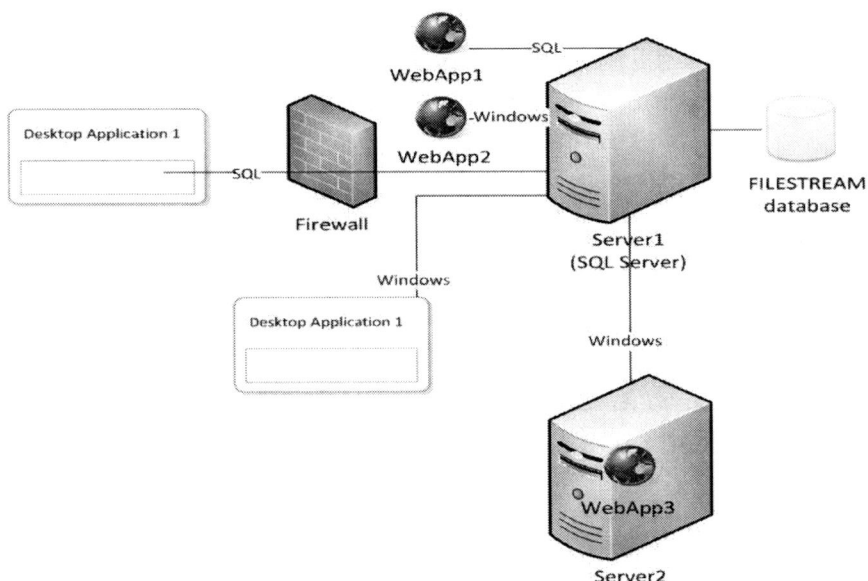

Figure A-1: Diagram demonstrating FILESTREAM local/remote configuration.

- SQL Server is installed on Server 1 and hosts a **FILESTREAM**-enabled database.

- Web Application 1 is installed on Server 1. The web application connects to SQL Server using SQL Server authentication.

- Web Application 2 is installed on Server 1. The web application connects to SQL Server using Windows authentication.

- Web Application 3 is configured on Server 2. The web application connects to SQL Server using Windows authentication.

- Desktop Application 1 is running on a computer at a remote location. The desktop application connects to the **FILESTREAM**-enabled SQL Server instance on Server 1 over the Internet using SQL Server authentication.

- Desktop Application 2 is running on a computer on the same network as the server. The desktop application connects to the **FILESTREAM**-enabled SQL Server instance on Server 1 over the LAN using Windows authentication.

Appendix A: Configuring FILESTREAM on a SQL Server Instance

Let's now see how each of the above applications behave under different `FILESTREAM` access levels.

1. **T-SQL Access is enabled**
   Because **only** T-SQL access is enabled:
   a. Web Applications 1, 2, and 3 can access `FILESTREAM` data through T-SQL.
   b. Desktop Applications 1 and 2 can access `FILESTREAM` data through T-SQL.
   c. None of the applications can access the `FILESTREAM` data through streaming APIs.

2. **Streaming Local Access is enabled**
   a. Web Application 1 can access `FILESTREAM` data only through T-SQL, because streaming access is only possible when using Windows authentication.
   b. Web Application 2 can access `FILESTREAM` data through T-SQL and streaming APIs.
   c. Web Application 3 can access `FILESTREAM` data through T-SQL only, because it is not running on the same server as the SQL Server instance hosting the database.
   d. Desktop Applications 1 and 2 can access `FILESTREAM` data through T-SQL only.
      i. Desktop Application 1 cannot use streaming access because it uses SQL Server authentication, and because the necessary ports are blocked on the firewall.
      ii. Desktop Application 2 cannot use streaming access because it runs on a computer other than the SQL Server.

3. **Streaming Remote Access is enabled**
   a. Web Application 1 can access `FILESTREAM` data only through T-SQL, because streaming access is only possible when using Windows authentication.
   b. Web Application 2 can access `FILESTREAM` data through T-SQL and streaming APIs.
   c. Web Application 3 can access `FILESTREAM` data through T-SQL and streaming APIs.

Appendix A: Configuring FILESTREAM on a SQL Server Instance

   d. Desktop Application 1 can access FILESTREAM data through T-SQL only, because it uses SQL Server authentication and because the necessary ports are blocked on the firewall.

   e. Desktop Application 2 can access FILESTREAM data through T-SQL and streaming APIs.

Enabling and Configuring FILESTREAM During Installation

Installing and configuring FILESTREAM during SQL Server installation is the easiest installation option because the entire configuration can be completed in a single step. All the desired options can be selected during the **Database Engine Configuration** step during installation.

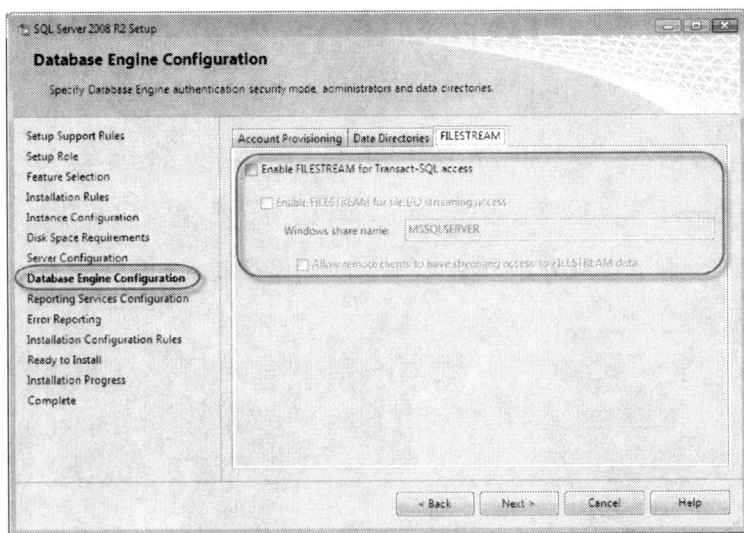

Figure A-2: Enabling FILESTREAM in the Database Engine Configuration installation step.

We'll briefly examine the different configuration options available on this page.

Enable FILESTREAM for Transact-SQL access

This is the primary level `FILESTREAM` configuration setting and it must be selected in order to enable the SQL Server instance to use the `FILESTREAM` capabilities. When this box is checked, the `FILESTREAM` feature will be enabled at the Windows and SQL Server instance levels. We can create, restore or attach `FILESTREAM`-enabled databases when the installation finishes, but we can only use T-SQL to read and write `FILESTREAM` data.

If the configuration is enabled, the installation process will automatically set `FILESTREAM` access level on the SQL Server instance to **Transact-SQL Access Enabled**.

Enable FILESTREAM for file I/O streaming access

When this configuration option is enabled, our SQL Server instance will allow I/O streaming access to the `FILESTREAM` data originating from the machine where the instance is installed. When I/O streaming is enabled, `FILESTREAM` data can be accessed using the Win32 API or .NET managed classes. Accessing the `FILESTREAM` data through the `FILESTREAM` API is much more efficient than T-SQL access and is always the recommended method.

When enabling `FILESTREAM` for I/O streaming access, we must specify a **Windows share name.** This Windows file share is not mapped to a directory on the system; it is simply a unique identifier that SQL Server uses to enable streaming access to the `FILESTREAM` data. This is internally (logically) linked to the actual file location. When we enable Win32 access to the `FILESTREAM` data, SQL Server installs and enables a Windows file system filter driver component. This component is responsible for doing the appropriate translation from the logical path to the file path as configured through `FILESTREAM` filegroup location.

If the configuration is enabled, the installation process will automatically set `FILESTREAM` access level on the SQL Server instance to **Full access enabled**.

Appendix A: Configuring FILESTREAM on a SQL Server Instance

Allow remote clients to have streaming access to FILESTREAM data

This option provides I/O streaming access to the `FILESTREAM` data from applications running on a different computer. Without this option, I/O streaming access to the `FILESTREAM` data will only be possible from an application that runs on the same computer as the SQL Server instance.

If the configuration is enabled, the installation process will automatically set `FILESTREAM` access level on the SQL Server instance to **Full access enabled**. Note that this is the same `FILESTREAM` access level we saw in the previous section when remote streaming access was not enabled. The fact is that there is no way to differentiate between the two settings at the instance level. We can verify these values by running the following T-SQL code after the SQL Server instance is installed.

```sql
SELECT
    SERVERPROPERTY('FilestreamEffectiveLevel') AS EffectiveValue,
    SERVERPROPERTY('FilestreamConfiguredLevel') AS WindowsConfiguredValue
```

Listing A-1: Checking FILESTREAM access level.

If remote I/O streaming is enabled, the server property value will be 3. If I/O streaming is enabled without remote access, it will be 2. These configuration settings are explained in detail later in this chapter.

Enabling and Configuring FILESTREAM After Installation

If `FILESTREAM` is not enabled during the SQL Server installation process, it is quite possible to perform the configuration post-installation. The most common reasons for not enabling `FILESTREAM` during installation are:

- the feature is not (currently) required in the environment
- the DBA or server administrator does not know whether `FILESTREAM` is needed or not, so it is better to keep it disabled and enable only when needed.

As discussed earlier, enabling and configuring `FILESTREAM` after installation requires two separate configuration actions, and we'll examine each in detail.

Configuring FILESTREAM at the Windows level

Windows level `FILESTREAM` feature configuration is administered from the SQL Server Configuration Manager. Follow the steps below to open the `FILESTREAM` configuration dialog.

1. Select **SQL Server Configuration Manager** from the **Configuration Tools** submenu.

Figure A-3: Starting SQL Server Configuration Manager.

Appendix A: Configuring FILESTREAM on a SQL Server Instance

2. From **SQL Server Configuration Manager**, right-click on the **SQL Server Service** and select **Properties** from the context menu.

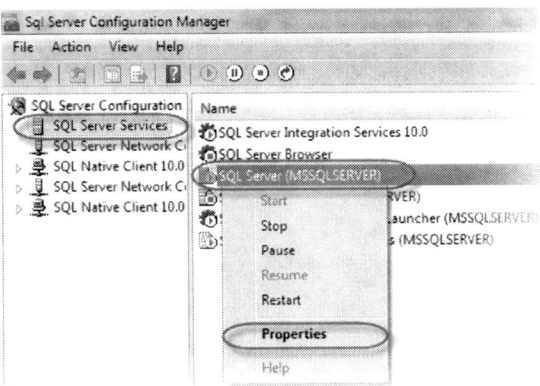

Figure A-4: Opening SQL Server Service Properties.

3. This will open the FILESTREAM configuration page which allows you to enable the FILESTREAM feature and select the desired access level.

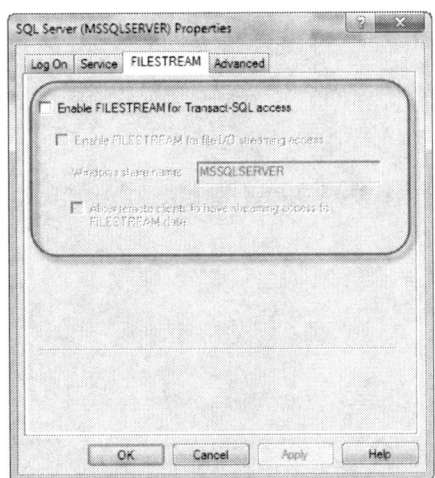

Figure A-5: Enabling the FILESTREAM feature.

4. The options available on this page are the same as what is available in the installation dialog. See the section above, where we discussed these options in detail.

Configuring FILESTREAM at the SQL Server instance level

`FILESTREAM` can be configured at the SQL Server instance level, either using the SSMS GUI dialog or through T-SQL.

Using SSMS to set FILESTREAM access level

SQL Server instance-level `FILESTREAM` configuration settings can be managed from the property page of the SQL Server instance.

1. In the **Object Explorer** window, right-click on the SQL Server instance and select **Properties** from the context menu.

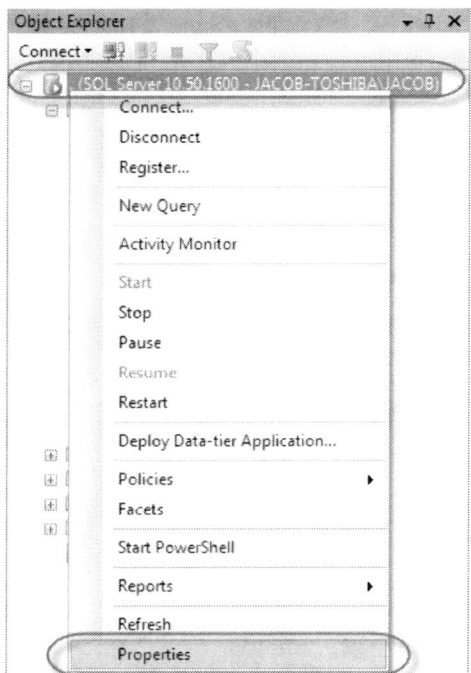

Figure A-6: Opening the SQL Server Instance Property Page.

Appendix A: Configuring FILESTREAM on a SQL Server Instance

2. Click on the **Advanced** tab on the left-hand-side control panel.

3. Look for the **Filestream** section on the top right-hand side of the property page.

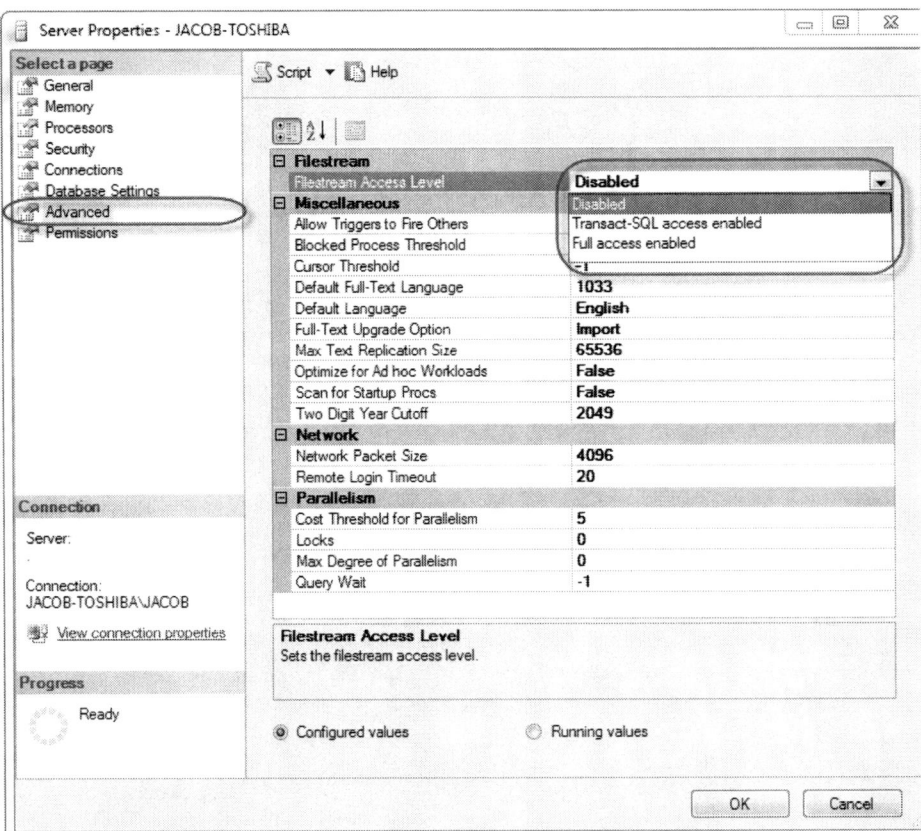

Figure A-7: Configuring the Filestream Access Level.

The **Filestream Access Level** option within the configuration dialog allows you to select one of the following options:

- **Disabled** – disables FILESTREAM access for the SQL Server instance
- **Transact-SQL access enabled** – enables FILESTREAM for T-SQL access
- **Full access enabled** – enables FILESTREAM for T-SQL and file I/O streaming access.

Appendix A: Configuring FILESTREAM on a SQL Server Instance

Making changes to the SQL Server `FILESTREAM` access level will require a service restart in some cases. Whenever you make changes to the `FILESTREAM` access level, SSMS will show a warning message indicating that the changes will not take effect until SQL Server is restarted (Figure A-8).

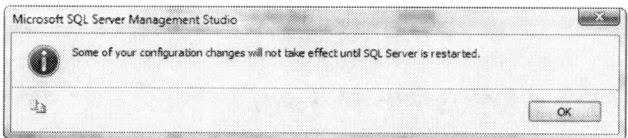

Figure A-8: Restart SQL Server message.

However, we can safely ignore this message when we select an "enable" access option; a service restart is not required when enabling `FILESTREAM` access on a SQL Server instance. If we completely disable access by selecting **Disabled**, a restart *is* required before the change will be effective.

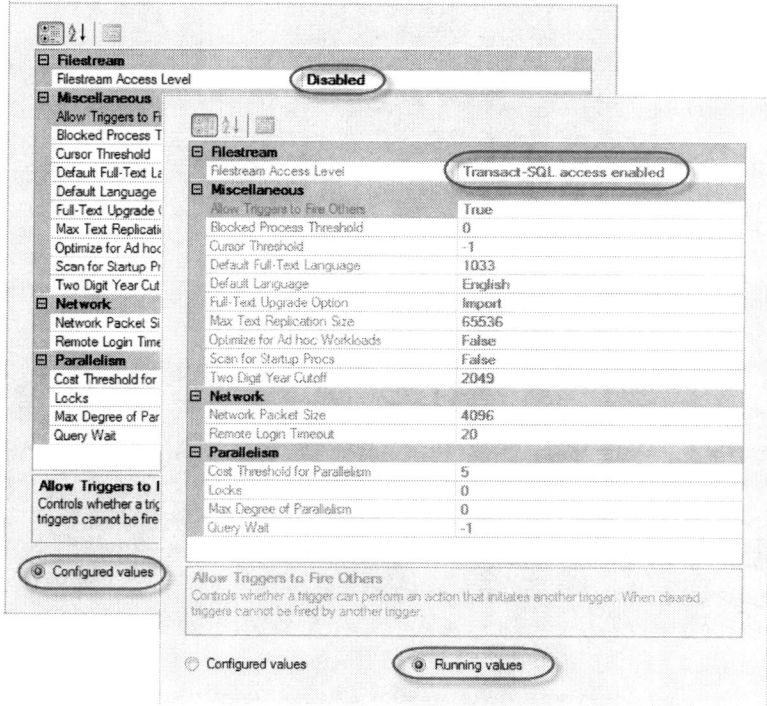

Figure A-9: Configured values and Running values.

475

Appendix A: Configuring FILESTREAM on a SQL Server Instance

Notice that the property page has two views: **Configured values** and **Running values**, as shown in Figure A-9. The **Running values** view shows the values currently being used by SQL Server. If an access level change requires a SQL Server restart, as in the case of **Disabled**, you will see the new value in **Configured values** and the old value in **Running values** until the instance is restarted.

Using T-SQL to set the FILESTREAM access level

We can use T-SQL to set the FILESTREAM access level. For example, run the T-SQL code in Listing A-2 to change the access level to **Full Access Enabled**.

```
EXEC sp_configure filestream_access_level, 2
GO
RECONFIGURE
GO
```

Listing A-2: Using T-SQL to change the FILESTREAM access level.

The second argument passed to sp_configure specifies the FILESTREAM access level.

- **0** – Disables FILESTREAM access.
- **1** – Enables FILESTREAM for T-SQL access.
- **2** – Enables FILESTREAM for full access (T-SQL and local I/O streaming). This option is not valid on clustered installations.

When you change the FILESTREAM access level using T-SQL, a message to restart SQL Server service is displayed only if you choose the "disable" FILESTREAM access level (parameter value 0).

Appendix A: Configuring FILESTREAM on a SQL Server Instance

Verifying FILESTREAM Configuration

We have seen various FILESTREAM configuration options and learned how to enable and configure FILESTREAM to the required access level. Let's verify that all the FILESTREAM settings are correctly configured before we start using them.

Verifying Windows-level FILESTREAM configuration settings

We know that the Windows-level FILESTREAM configuration is done from SQL Server Configuration Manager. So the first step is to check the **FILESTREAM** tab of the property page of the SQL Server service within the Configuration Manager.

Make sure that the FILESTREAM access is enabled to the desired level on the configuration page. If I/O streaming access to the FILESTREAM data is required, make sure that the FILESTREAM share name is configured in the configuration dialog.

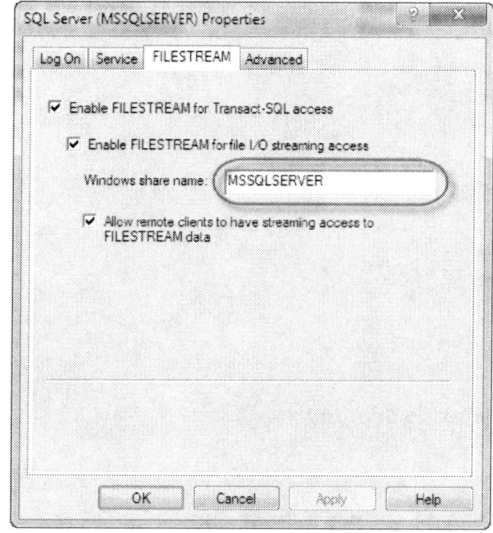

Figure A-10: Verifying FILESTREAM configuration.

Appendix A: Configuring FILESTREAM on a SQL Server Instance

It is also important to verify that a Windows share with the same name exists to ensure that the windows share is correctly configured.

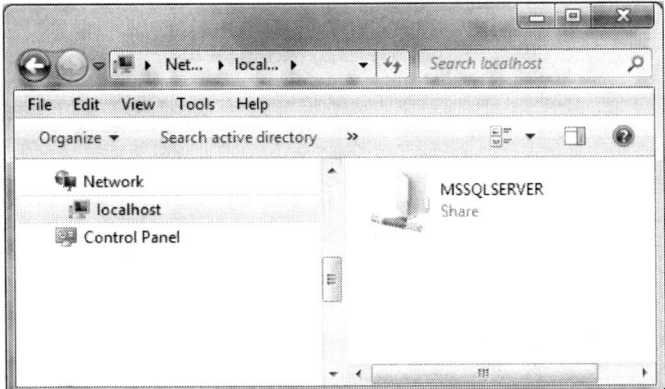

Figure A-11: Verifying FILESTREAM Windows share.

Please note that the Windows share does not point to a physical disk location; it points to a virtual identifier which allows SQL Server to map a SQL Server instance with its associated FILESTREAM data container. Attempting to open the Windows share will result in an error.

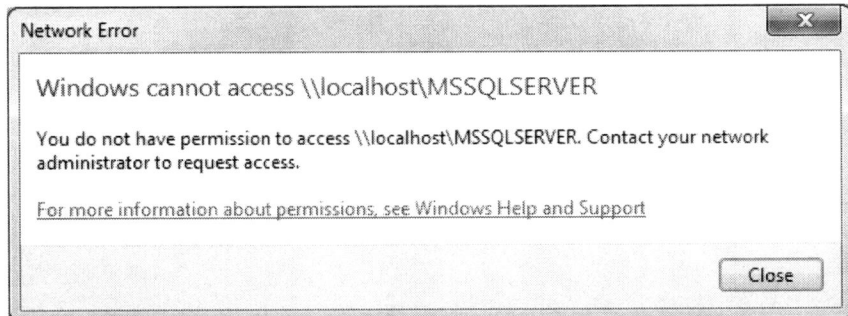

Figure A-12: The FILESTREAM Windows share is not accessible using Windows Explorer.

Verifying the Windows-level configuration can also be done using T-SQL, as discussed next.

Appendix A: Configuring FILESTREAM on a SQL Server Instance

Verifying SQL Server Instance-level FILESTREAM configuration settings

To ensure that the SQL Server instance is enabled and correctly set up for `FILESTREAM` storage, we can use SSMS or T-SQL.

Using SSMS to check that FILESTREAM is enabled

You can verify that `FILESTREAM` is correctly configured by looking at the SQL Server instance properties in SSMS. Select the **Advanced** page, then select the **Running values** view (Figure A-12).

Figure A-13: The **Running values** view shows the active configuration settings.

Then look at the **Filestream Access Level** as shown in Figure A-14.

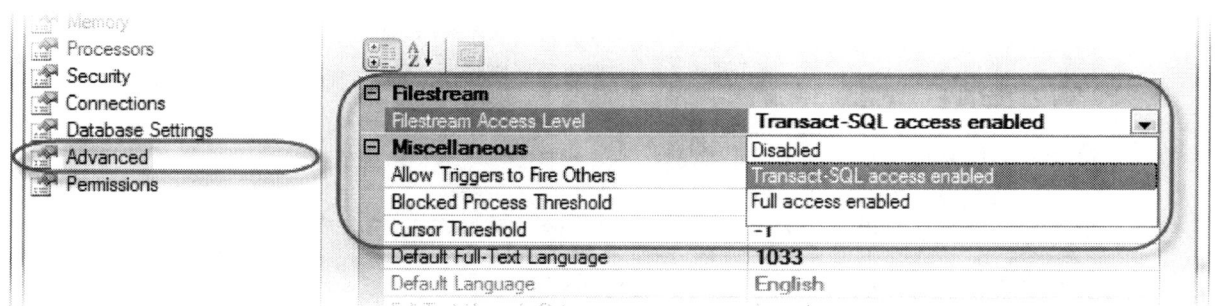

Figure A-14: Checking the **Filestream Access Level**.

Appendix A: Configuring FILESTREAM on a SQL Server Instance

The access level should show either **Transact-SQL access enabled** or **Full access enabled**. Note that, in the **Running values** view, there is no actual drop-down list.

The **Configured values** view will show the **Filestream Access Level** as configured at the SQL Server instance level. It is possible for the configured value to show **Full access enabled**, while the FILESTREAM feature can actually be disabled at the Windows level.

Using T-SQL to check that FILESTREAM is enabled

The T-SQL code in Listing A-3 retrieves the FILESTREAM configuration of the current SQL Server instance.

```
SELECT   SERVERPROPERTY('FilestreamEffectiveLevel') AS FilestreamEffectiveLevel
/*
FilestreamEffectiveLevel
---------------------------
1
*/
```

Listing A-3:   Query to retrieve the FILESTREAM configuration level of a SQL Server instance.

The possible return values of the above query are:

- **0** – FILESTREAM is disabled
- **1** – FILESTREAM is enabled for T-SQL access
- **2** – FILESTREAM is enabled for T-SQL and local streaming access only
- **3** – FILESTREAM is enabled for T-SQL and local and remote streaming access.

At the time of writing, neither the MSDN documentation nor Books Online mention configuration value 3. Configuration values 2 and 3 are used to differentiate between local and remote streaming access.

Appendix A: Configuring FILESTREAM on a SQL Server Instance

Disabling the FILESTREAM Feature

To disable the FILESTREAM feature at the Windows level, clear the **Enable FILESTREAM for Transact-SQL access** option in the **Properties** page of the SQL Server instance in **SQL Server Configuration Manager**.

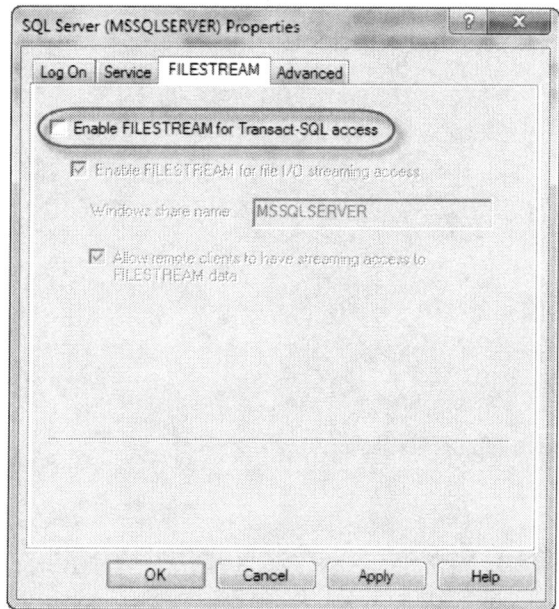

Figure A-15: Disabling the FILESTREAM feature.

A message will be displayed to inform you that a service restart is required before the changes can take effect, as shown in Figure A-16.

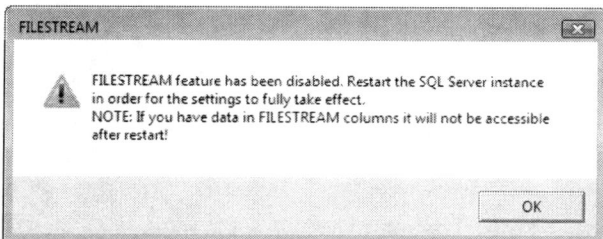

Figure A-16: Restart SQL Server instance message following disable.

Appendix A: Configuring FILESTREAM on a SQL Server Instance

Until the instance is restarted, the FILESTREAM-enabled databases can be queried using T-SQL (both relational and FILESTREAM data), but no longer using the streaming APIs. Access using the streaming APIs is disabled immediately because the file share is removed.

The restart is required because SQL Server has to take offline any FILESTREAM-enabled databases on the instance. Following the service restart, any FILESTREAM-enabled databases will not be accessible. You will be able to see the databases in the SSMS Object Explorer (Figure A-16), but you will not be able to establish a connection to them.

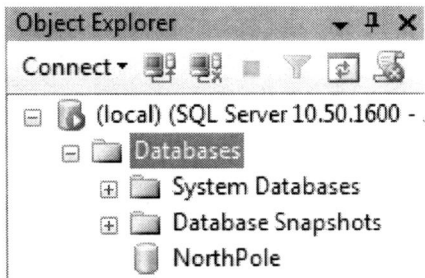

Figure A-17: Inaccessible FILESTREAM-enabled database in Object Explorer.

If we now try to run a query on a FILESTREAM-enabled database, we will get an error similar to the one shown in Listing A-4.

```
SELECT  *
FROM    NorthPole.dbo.items
/*
Msg 945, Level 14, State 2, Line 1
Database 'NorthPole' cannot be opened due to inaccessible
files or insufficient memory or disk space.
See the SQL Server errorlog for details.
*/
```

Listing A-4: Error message showing FILESTREAM-enabled database is inaccessible.

Advanced Installation and Configuration Options

We have examined the basic and the most commonly used `FILESTREAM` installation and configuration processes, and it is time for us to see some of the advanced configuration options.

Unattended SQL Server installation and FILESTREAM configuration

When installing SQL Server 2008 or later in unattended mode, we can use the `/FILESTREAMLEVEL` and `/FILESTREAMSHARENAME` configuration options to enable the `FILESTREAM` feature.

- **`/FILESTREAMLEVEL`** – This setting is optional. It specifies the required access level for the `FILESTREAM` feature. The following values are supported:
    - **0** – Disable `FILESTREAM` for the current instance. This is the default value.
    - **1** – Enable `FILESTREAM` for T-SQL access.
    - **2** – Enable `FILESTREAM` for T-SQL and I/O streaming access. This option is not valid for clusters.
    - **3** – Allow remote clients streaming access to `FILESTREAM` data.
- **`/FILESTREAMSHARENAME`** – This setting is required if `/FILESTREAMLEVEL` is 2 or 3. It specifies the Windows file share name to be used for storing the `FILESTREAM` data.

The example in Listing A-5 installs a new instance of SQL Server named `KATMAIUA` with `FILESTREAM` enabled, and sets the `FILESTREAM` share name to `KATMAIUA`.

Appendix A: Configuring FILESTREAM on a SQL Server Instance

```
Setup.exe
    /q
    /ACTION=Install
    /FEATURES=SQL
    /INSTANCENAME=KATMAIUA
    /SQLSVCACCOUNT="DOMAIN\User"
    /SQLSVCPASSWORD="mypwd"
    /SQLSYSADMINACCOUNTS="DOMAIN\User"
    /AGTSVCACCOUNT="DOMAIN\User"
    /AGTSVCPASSWORD="mypwd"
    /IAcceptSQLServerLicenseTerms
    /FILESTREAMLEVEL="3"
    /FILESTREAMSHARENAME="KATMAIUA"
```

Listing A-5: Example setup options for enabling FILESTREAM in unattended mode.

/IAcceptSQLServerLicenseTerms is a new parameter introduced in SQL Server 2008 R2. It is a mandatory parameter for unattended installations and the setup will fail if this value is not supplied.

Figure A-18 shows an example of the command line to enable FILESTREAM in unattended mode.

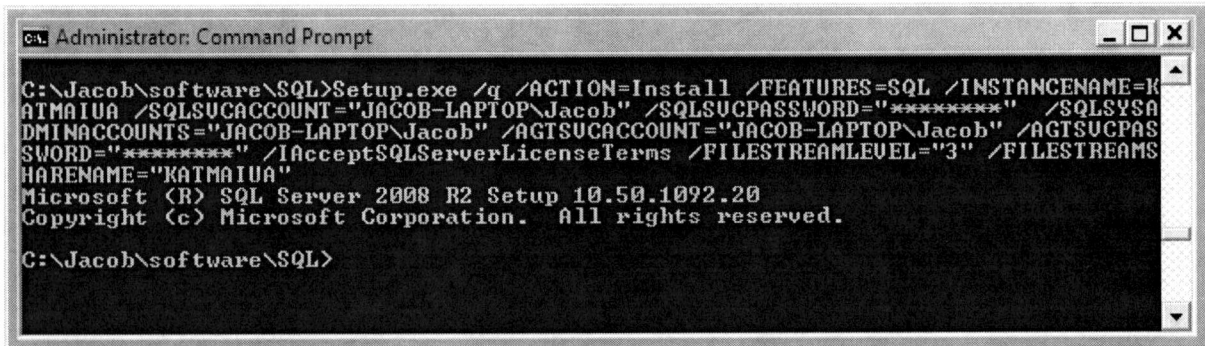

Figure A-18: Example of enabling FILESTREAM in unattended mode.

Once the installation script completes, we can verify the configuration settings of the newly installed SQL Server instance using the methods explained earlier in this chapter.

Enabling and configuring FILESTREAM from the command line

Sometimes, we need to enable and configure `FILESTREAM` using the command line, for example as part of the installation or upgrade of an application that intends to use the `FILESTREAM` features. It is quite easy to set the `FILESTREAM` access level by using SQL Server command line tools like **sqlcmd.exe**.

However, programmatically enabling the `FILESTREAM` feature is more complicated using a scripting language like VBScript. Luckily, a short VBScript is available for download at codeplex.com: HTTP://BRURL.COM/FS26.

Listing A-6 shows the syntax for running that script.

```
cscript filestream_enable.vbs
    [/Machine:MachineName]
    [/Instance:InstanceName]
    [/Level:level]
    [/Share:ShareName]
```

Listing A-6:   Syntax for running VBScript program to enable `FILESTREAM`.

Some debug messages are displayed; we can safely ignore these. Figure A-19 shows an example command line for enabling `FILESTREAM` programmatically.

```
filestream_enable.vbs /Machine:localhost /Instance:MSSQLSERVER /Level:3 /
Share:MSSQLSERVER
```

Once the script execution has completed, `FILESTREAM` is enabled at the Windows level, and we can then configure the access level on the SQL Server instance.

As of this writing, the CodePlex script mentioned does not work with SQL Server 2012. If you would like to run this script on SQL Server 2012, you need to edit the script and change `ComputerManagement10:FilestreamSettings` to `ComputerManagement11:FilestreamSettings` on lines number 37 and 110.

Configuring FILESTREAM access level from the command line

We can also configure the `FILESTREAM` access level from the command line using **sqlcmd.exe**. It allows us to run a T-SQL script on the specified SQL Server instance. As a first step, create a T-SQL script file containing the following code.

```
EXEC sp_configure filestream_access_level, 2
GO
RECONFIGURE
GO
```

Listing A-7: Creating a script file to configure `FILESTREAM` access level from the command line.

In this example, we are trying to set the `FILESTREAM` access level to **Full access**. See the reference earlier in this chapter for a detailed explanation of the values that can be passed as the second parameter into the system stored procedure `sp_configure`.

Save the script file as **c:\temp\set_filestream_access_level.sql**. This file can be passed as the query input to sqlcmd.exe. The following example demonstrates it.

```
sqlcmd -S . -E -I "c:\temp\set_filestream_access_level.sql"
```

Appendix A: Configuring FILESTREAM on a SQL Server Instance

When running this command, the T-SQL code we wrote within the script file will be executed against the specified SQL Server instance (in our case it is the default SQL Server instance on the local computer) and the output will be displayed in the command window.

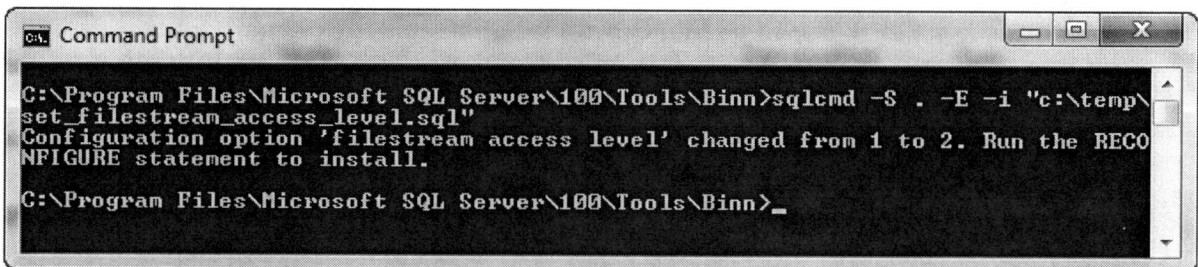

Figure A-19: Configuring FILESTREAM access level from command line.

We can use the various methods discussed earlier to verify that the configuration changes took place correctly on the specified SQL Server instance.

Setting up FILESTREAM on a failover cluster

When setting up the FILESTREAM feature on a failover cluster, we need to make sure that all the nodes are set up with the same configuration. The following steps are recommended for enabling and configuring FILESTREAM feature on a failover cluster.

1. Enable the FILESTREAM feature on the primary node using SQL Server Configuration Manager.

2. If I/O streaming access to the FILESTREAM data is required, enable it and specify the desired Windows share name or leave the default.

Appendix A: Configuring FILESTREAM on a SQL Server Instance

3. If remote access to the `FILESTREAM` data is required, enable the option. This action will also create a cluster file share resource.

4. Enable the `FILESTREAM` feature on each passive node using SQL Server Configuration Manager. The I/O streaming option on each of the passive nodes should be configured in the same way as on the primary node. All the passive nodes must use the same Windows share name as the primary node.

5. After `FILESTREAM` is enabled and configured using SQL Server Configuration Manager, configure the desired `FILESTREAM` access level on the primary node and all the passive nodes. It is important to make sure that you set the same `FILESTREAM` access level on all the nodes.

It is also important to configure the `FILESTREAM` data container(s) on a shared disk. The `FILESTREAM` data container must be accessible from all nodes in the cluster, hence the requirement to place it on a shared disk.

Summary

`FILESTREAM` can be enabled during installing of the SQL Server instance by selecting the appropriate options in the wizard. However, there may be times when you need to enable it on an existing SQL Server instance.

Enabling `FILESTREAM` post-installation is a two-step process. `FILESTREAM` must be enabled at the Windows Administrator level using SQL Server Configuration Manager, and it must be enabled at the SQL Server Administrator level either using SSMS or the **`sp_configure`** system stored procedure.

`FILESTREAM` can also be enabled as part of an unattended SQL Server installation by using the `/FILESTREAMLEVEL` and `/FILESTREAMSHARENAME` setup parameters. Additionally, a VBScript program, available at codeplex.com, can be used to programmatically enable the `FILESTREAM` feature at the Windows Administrator level.

Appendix A: Configuring FILESTREAM on a SQL Server Instance

If we disable `FILESTREAM` on a SQL Server instance that has one or more `FILESTREAM`-enabled databases, those databases will not be accessible after restarting the SQL Server service. The data on the database is unaffected, and will be available as normal if `FILESTREAM` is re-enabled and the SQL Server service is restarted. The message that SQL Server Configuration Manager provides is quite misleading. It says that, after disabling `FILESTREAM`, data in the `FILESTREAM` columns will not be available. However, the entire database will be inaccessible instead of just the `FILESTREAM` columns.

Index

Symbols

$FSLOG 48

A

Access FILESTREAM data 75
    configuring FILESTREAM access level from the command line 486-487
    FILESTREAM access level configuration 465
    from client applications 89-130
    from SQL Server Business Intelligence (BI) projects 227-269
    local versus remote access 465-468
    streaming access (local) 464
    streaming access (remote) 464
    T-SQL access 464

Access level, identification 338

ADO.NET connection, creating 237

ADO.NET Entity Framework (EF) 131, 132-157
    using T-SQL access 134-143

Advanced FILESTREAM DDL 79-85

Antivirus
    configuring 448

APIs
    data manipulation using the streaming APIs 102-105
    .NET file I/O APIs
        access FileTable data 422-425
    OpenSqlFilestream API reference 126-129
    SQL Server Win32 API functions 90, 129
    streaming 90

ASP.NET 165
    deploying and configuring a FILESTREAM web application on IIS 176-188
    displaying images stored in a FILESTREAM column 194-203
    uploading files from an ASP.NET web page 167-176

B

Backup
    and garbage files 327-329
    data and backup compression 326-327
    differential backup 316-317
    file backups 323-326
    full backup 316
    transaction log backup 317-319

Backup and restore 313-329. *See also* **Restore**

Binary Large Object (BLOB) 26
    BLOB data 27

C

Catalog views. *See* **System catalog views**

Change Data Capture (CDC) 379-383

Character Large Object (CLOB) 26
    CLOB data 26-27

Columns. *See* **Tables: creating with FILESTREAM columns**
    add FILESTREAM columns to existing table 62-65
    converting between FILESTREAM and VARBINARY(MAX) 65-67
    identifying tables with FILESTREAM columns 343

Index

Command line
    configuring FILESTREAM access level from 486-487
    enabling and configuring FILESTREAM from 485-486

Compressing FILESTREAM data 445-446

Compression. *See* **Backup: data and backup compression**

Configure FILESTREAM 461-489
    advanced options 483-488
    after SQL Server installation 471-476
    at SQL Server instance level 473-476
    at Windows level 471-472
    configuration and access levels 463-468
    during SQL Server installation 468-470
    from the command line 485-486
    verification 477-480
        of SQL Server instance-level configuration 479
        of Windows-level configuration 477-478

Consistency of FILESTREAM data 289

Creating FILESTREAM-enabled databases 52-59

D

Data and space management 295-306

Database
    enable FILESTREAM storage on an existing database 58-59
    FILESTREAM database administration 271-312
    FILESTREAM-enabled databases
        creating using SSMS 53-56
        creating using T-SQL 56-57
    investigating 331-352. *See also* Investigating FILESTREAM databases

Database-level FILESTREAM metadata queries 342-348

Database mirroring and FILESTREAM 385-386

Database Publishing Wizard and FILESTREAM 310-311

Database snapshots and FILESTREAM 377-379

Data compression and FILESTREAM 384

Data container (FILESTREAM) 47
    identifying location of 342

Data corruption and DBCC checks 285-294
    caused by manually deleting garbage files 293-294
    caused by missing FILESTREAM data files 286-291
    caused by orphaned files 292-293
    fixing corrupted data 290-291

Data manipulation using the streaming APIs 102-105
    deleting a row 105
    deleting the BLOB data 105
    insert a new record 102-103
    partial updates to FILESTREAM data 104
    reading information from the FILESTREAM store 105
    replace the FILESTREAM data completely 103-104

Data manipulation using T-SQL 69-79

Data migration 307-311

Data storage & management 21-45
    structured data 22-25
    unstructured data 25-27

Index

Dedicated Administrator Connection (DAC) 283–285
Default constraint for FILESTREAM columns 459
Defragmentation
    to improve performance 451
Deleting a row from a FILESTREAM-enabled table 105
Deleting BLOB data stored in FILESTREAM columns 77, 105
Disabling FILESTREAM storage 85–87
DML triggers and FILESTREAM 78
DMVs 348–350
    sys.dm_filestream_file_io_handles 348
    sys.dm_filestream_file_io_requests 349
    sys.dm_filestream_non_transacted_handles 431
    sys.dm_tran_active_transactions 350

E

Enable FILESTREAM for file I/O streaming access 469
Enable FILESTREAM for T-SQL access 469
Entity Data Model Wizard 137, 147
Entity Framework (EF). *See* ADO.NET Entity Framework (EF)

F

Failover cluster
    setting up FILESTREAM on 487–488
File backups 323–326
Filegroups 49. *See also* FILESTREAM: filegroups
    changing location of 296–300
    FILESTREAM filegroup queries 68–69
    identifying those associated with a table 345
    multiple 82–85
File names
    disabling short file names 441–445
    file header 454
    file name associated with each FILESTREAM value, identifying 348
FILESTREAM
    accessing data from client applications 89–130
    adding a FILESTREAM column 40
    adding FILESTREAM storage 39
    and garbage files 280–285. *See also* Garbage files
    and SSIS. *See* SQL Server Integration Services (SSIS)
    and synchronization methods 368
    and triggers 78–79
    best practices for development 453–459
    configuring on a SQL Server instance 461–489. *See also* Configure FILESTREAM
    converting columns to VARBINARY(MAX) 65–67
    data
        data and space management 295–306
        migrating 307–311
        updating and deleting 77
    databases
        administration 271–312
        attaching & detaching 277–279
        creating 52–59
    data container 47–49, 313
        and partitioned tables 79–82
        disabling 481–482

493

Index

enabling 38, 338
    identifying FILESTREAM enabled databases 341
filegroups 49-52
    and queries 68-69
    and tables 67-69
    multiple 82-85
getting started with 47-87
inserting BLOB data 41
integration with other SQL Server features 353-388
introducing 35-44
remote access. *See* Remote access
saving FILESTREAM data 173
serve images from a FILESTREAM database 189-193
setting the access level 39
share name, retrieving 341
storage
    configuration for 441-451
    disabling 85-87
when to use 42-44

FILESTREAM APIs 89

filestream.hdr 48, 51

FILESTREAM or VARBINARY(MAX)? 439-440

FILESTREAM replication flag 364-365

FileTable 389-438
    accessing with Windows Explorer and other client applications 413-416
        creating files 413-414
        creating folders 415
        empty database folder 416
        memory-mapped files 415
    adding constraints to 411-412
    advanced uses 432-436
        full-text search 432-433
        semantic search 434-436. *See also* Semantic search
    catalog and dynamic management views 428-431
    creating 406-413
        using SSMS 408-409
        using T-SQL 406-408
    creating a database with support for 404-406
    investigating 437
    managing FileTables 425-432
        T-SQL functions 425-428
    programming FileTable 416-425
        using .NET file I/O APIs 422-425
        using T-SQL 417-422
    restrictions on creating 412-413
    setting up the server for 404
    stored procedures 431-432
        sp_kill_filestream_non_transacted_handles 431-432
    underlying concepts 390-404
        creating folder structures 394-397
        FileTable namespace 400-401
        FileTable security 402-404
        fixed schema 390-394
        non-transactional access 398-400
        root folder 397
    work with a FileTable using SSMS 410-411

Folder names associated with FILESTREAM column, identifying 346

Index

Folder names associated with FILESTREAM table, identifying 343
Full-text indexing and FILESTREAM 373-376

G

Garbage files 280-285
    and recovery models 280-281
    collection and tombstone tables 281-286
    FILESTREAM garbage collector and the replication log reader 367-368
    in FILESTREAM backups 327-329

H

HIERARCHYID data type 394
High Availability Disaster Recovery - Always On (HADRON) 386

I

Images
    displaying thumbnail images of Items from a FILESTREAM Database on an ASP.NET web page 194-203
    serving from a FILESTREAM database 189-193
Index service
    disabling to improve performance 447
Insert a new record into a FILESTREAM-enabled table 102, 106-109
Insert a new record into a FileTable 417-422
Inserting a row with FILESTREAM data 71-76
Installation
    Advanced installation and configuration options 483-488
    enabling and configuring FILESTREAM 468-470
Integrated Security. *See* **SQL Server Integrated Security**
Internet Information Services (IIS)
    deploy & configure a FILESTREAM web application 176-188
Investigating FILESTREAM databases 331-352
Isolation levels
    FILESTREAM & database transaction levels 272-276
    snapshot isolation level 274-275

L

Labs
    1: Reads, writes and partial updates 106-115
    2: FILESTREAM and EF 132-157
    3: FILESTREAM and LINQ to SQL 158-163
    4: Upload files to a FILESTREAM Database from an ASP.NET web page 167-176
    5: Deploy and configure a FILESTREAM web application on IIS 176-188
    6: Create a web handler to serve images from a FILESTREAM database 189-193
    7: Display thumbnail images of items from a FILESTREAM database on an ASP.NET web page 194-203
    8: Use SqlFileStream in an N-Tier scenario 204-216
    9: Play video stored in a FILESTREAM database on a Silverlight application 216-225
    10: Load BLOB values into a FILESTREAM column using SSIS 228-255

Index

11: Export BLOB values from FILESTREAM column using SSIS 256-259
12: Display FILESTREAM data in SSRS reports 260-268

Large Object (LOB) 26
    manageability and recoverability 32
    performance 33
    security 33
    store in database or file system? 30-34
    storing in SQL Server 28-29
    storing in the file system 30

Last Access Time
    disabling 449

LINQ to SQL 131, 158-163
    querying FILESTREAM data 162-163

Local versus remote streaming access 465-468

Logical identifiers
    understanding the logical path to a FILESTREAM data file 115-122

Log shipping and FILESTREAM 372-373

M

Metadata queries 337-348
    database-level queries 342-348
    SQL Server instance-level queries 338-342

Microsoft IIS. *See* **Internet Information Services (IIS)**

Migrating FILESTREAM data 307-311

N

NTFS cluster size
    configuring 446-447

NVARCHAR(MAX) 28

O

Object relational mapping (ORM) 132
    configuring 139-141, 149-154, 159-161

OPENROWSET() 72

P

Partial updates to FILESTREAM data 104, 111-114
PARTITION 81
Partition a FILESTREAM table 300-306
PathName() 119, 120
PERSISTED computed column 457
Piecemeal restores 323-326
Planning, configuration and best practices 439-460
Publish Web dialog box 177

R

RAID level
    configuring 450

READ COMMITTED 272

Read information from the FILESTREAM store 105, 109-111

READ UNCOMMITTED 273

Relational model 21
    save relational data 172

Remote access
    configuring client application 452
    configuring client computer 452
    set up FILESTREAM for 451-452

Remote calling 211-215
REPEATABLE READ 272
Replacing FILESTREAM data 103

Index

Replication 354-372
    and the UNIQUEIDENTIFIER column 359-362
    different types 370-372
        merge replication 370
        snapshot replication 372
        transactional 370
    impact of FILESTREAM replication configuration changes 367
    log reader and the FILESTREAM garbage collector 367-368
    managing replication flag using T-SQL 362-367
    maximum replication data size 357-359
    replicating FILESTREAM columns 354-356
        size limits, VARBINARY(MAX) 355

Restore 319-323
    from full backup 320
    piecemeal restores 323-326
    point-in-time restore 320-323

Retrieving data using EF 143, 154-158

ROWGUIDCOL 61, 120

Rows
    inserting, with FILESTREAM data 71-76

S

Scripting. *See* SQL Server Management Studio (SSMS): scripting functionality

Script task 227, 247, 258

Semantic search 434-436
    add an index 435
    execute a semantic query 435-436
    language support 435
    prepare the server for 434

Semi-structured data 25

SERIALIZABLE 272

Set-based operations 114

Silverlight 165
    create an application 218-219

Snapshot isolation level. *See* Isolation levels

SqlFileStream
    class reference 123-126
    in an N-tier scenario 204-216
    instantiating a SqlFileStream object 123-126
    using with EF 144-157

SQL Server Database Publishing Wizard 310-311

SQL Server FILESTREAM configuration 461-489. *See also* Configure FILESTREAM

SQL Server instance-level queries 338-342

SQL Server Integrated Security
    and IIS 181-187

SQL Server Integration Services (SSIS) 227
    create the SSIS package 235-256
    export BLOB values 256-259
    load BLOB values 228-255

SQL Server Management Studio (SSMS)
    and FileTable 408, 410
    scripting functionality 307-309
    Using SSMS to check that FILESTREAM is enabled 479-480
    using SSMS to set FILESTREAM access level 473-476

SQL Server Reporting Services (SSRS) 227
    displaying FILESTREAM data in SSRS reports 260-268

Storage configuration for FILESTREAM 441-451

Storing unstructured data 28-34

Index

Streaming
    access to FILESTREAM data 90–101
        closing the FILESTREAM data file 101
        closing the transaction 101
        opening the FILESTREAM data file 95–97
        reading and writing FILESTREAM data 98–100
        retrieving logical path name and transaction context 92–95
        starting a transaction 91–92
    allow remote clients to have streaming access to FILESTREAM data 470
    definition 89
    enable FILESTREAM for file I/O streaming access 469
    streaming APIs 453

Streaming LOB data 34

Structured data 22–25

Synchronization methods
    and FILESTREAM 368

System catalog views 331–337. *See also* **Investigating FILESTREAM databases**
    sys.all_columns 332
    sys.columns 332
    sys.computed_columns 333
    sys.database_files 336
    sys.database_filestream_options 405, 428–429
    sys.data_spaces 335
    sys.dm_repl_traninfo 333
    sys.filegroups 336
    sys.filestream_tombstone_* 337
    sys.filetables 430–431
    sys.filetable_system_defined_objects 429–430
    sys.identity_columns 333
    sys.internal_tables 334
    sys.partitions 335
    sys.system_columns 332
    sys.system_internals_partition_columns 336
    sys.system_internals_partitions 337
    sys.tables 334, 428

T

Tables
    adding a new partition 300–306
    and FILESTREAM filegroups 67–69
    creating with FILESTREAM columns 59–69
        using SSMS table designer 59–60
        using T-SQL 60–62
    partitioned 79–82
    tombstone tables. *See* Garbage files

Tiers. *See* **SqlFileStream: in an N-tier scenario**

To BLOB or not to BLOB? 34, 42

Transactional consistency 31

Transaction isolation levels. *See also* **Isolation levels**
    summary of FILESTREAM behavior 276

Transparent Data Encryption (TDE) 384

Triggers
    and FILESTREAM columns 78

T-SQL
    add FILESTREAM column to existing table 62–65
    and FILESTREAM data manipulation 69–79
    and FileTable 406–408, 417–422, 425–428
        FileTableRootPath 426
        GetFileNamespacePath 426–427

GetPathLocator 427
PathName 427-428
creating FILESTREAM-enabled database with 60-87
creating tables with FILESTREAM columns 60-62
enabling FILESTREAM for T-SQL access 469
handling multiple FILESTREAM columns and rows 114-115
using T-SQL to check that FILESTREAM is enabled 480
using T-SQL to set FILESTREAM access level 476

U

Unattended SQL Server installation and FILESTREAM configuration 483-484
UNIQUEIDENTIFIER 61
Unstructured data 25-27
Updating FILESTREAM data 77

V

VARBINARY(MAX) 28, 60, 135
converting columns to FILESTREAM 65-67
VARCHAR(MAX) 28
Verifying FILESTREAM configuration 477-480
Video
handler, creating 219-222
play on a Silverlight application 216-225
Visual Studio 136, 146, 158, 176, 193, 205, 215
configuring the built-in web server port 223
running under administrator account 177

W

Wait types 350-352
FSA_FORCE_OWN_XACT 351
FSAGENT 352
FS_FC_RWLOCK 350
FS_GARBAGE_COLLECTOR_SHUTDOWN 351
FS_HEADER_RWLOCK 351
FS_LOGTRUNC_RWLOCK 351
FSTR_CONFIG_MUTEX 352
FSTR_CONFIG_RWLOCK 352
Web Handler 189
Win32 API functions 129
Windows Communication Foundation (WCF) 211-215
Windows level FILESTREAM feature configuration 471-472

SQL Server and .NET Tools
from Red Gate Software

Pricing and information about Red Gate tools are correct at the time of going to print. For the latest information and pricing on all Red Gate's tools, visit www.red-gate.com

redgate®
ingeniously simple tools

SQL Compare® Pro $595
Compare and synchronize SQL Server database schemas

- ↗ Eliminate mistakes migrating database changes from dev, to test, to production
- ↗ Speed up the deployment of new databse schema updates
- ↗ Find and fix errors caused by differences between databases
- ↗ Compare and synchronize within SSMS

> "Just purchased SQL Compare. With the productivity I'll get out of this tool, it's like buying time."
> **Robert Sondles** Blueberry Island Media Ltd

SQL Data Compare Pro $595
Compares and synchronizes SQL Server database contents

- ↗ Save time by automatically comparing and synchronizing your data
- ↗ Copy lookup data from development databases to staging or production
- ↗ Quickly fix problems by restoring damaged or missing data to a single row
- ↗ Compare and synchronize data within SSMS

> "We use SQL Data Compare daily and it has become an indispensable part of delivering our service to our customers. It has also streamlined our daily update process and cut back literally a good solid hour per day."
> **George Pantela** GPAnalysis.com

Visit **www.red-gate.com** for a 14-day, free trial

SQL Prompt Pro $295
Write, edit, and explore SQL effortlessly

- Write SQL smoothly, with code-completion and SQL snippets
- Reformat SQL to a preferred style
- Keep databases tidy by finding invalid objects automatically
- Save time and effort with script summaries, smart object renaming and more

> "SQL Prompt is hands-down one of the coolest applications I've used. Makes querying/developing so much easier and faster."
> **Jorge Segarra** University Community Hospital

SQL Source Control $395
Connect your existing source control system to SQL Server

- Bring all the benefits of source control to your database
- Source control schemas and data within SSMS, not with offline scripts
- Connect your databases to TFS, SVN, SourceGear Vault, Vault Pro, Mercurial, Perforce, Git, Bazaar, and any source control system with a capable command line
- Work with shared development databases, or individual copies
- Track changes to follow who changed what, when, and why
- Keep teams in sync with easy access to the latest database version
- View database development history for easy retrieval of specific versions

> "After using SQL Source Control for several months, I wondered how I got by before. Highly recommended, it has paid for itself several times over."
> **Ben Ashley** Fast Floor

Visit **www.red-gate.com** for a 28-day, free trial

SQL Backup Pro $795

Compress, encrypt, and strengthen SQL Server backups

- ↗ Compress SQL Server database backups by up to 95% for faster, smaller backups

- ↗ Protect your data with up to 256-bit AES encryption

- ↗ Strengthen your backups with network resilience to enable a fault-tolerant transfer of backups across flaky networks

- ↗ Control your backup activities through an intuitive interface, with powerful job management and an interactive timeline

> "SQL Backup is an amazing tool that lets us manage and monitor our backups in real time. Red Gate's SQL tools have saved us so much time and work that I am afraid my director will decide that we don't need a DBA anymore!"
>
> **Mike Poole** Database Administrator, Human Kinetics

Visit **www.red-gate.com** for a 14-day, free trial

SQL Monitor

from **$795**

SQL Server performance monitoring and alerting

- ↗ Intuitive overviews at global, cluster, machine, SQL Server, and database levels for up-to-the-minute performance data

- ↗ Use SQL Monitor's web UI to keep an eye on server performance in real time on desktop machines and mobile devices

- ↗ Intelligent SQL Server alerts via email and an alert inbox in the UI, so you know about problems first

- ↗ Comprehensive historical data, so you can go back in time to identify the source of a problem

- ↗ Generate reports via the UI or with Red Gate's free SSRS Reporting Pack

- ↗ View the top 10 expensive queries for an instance or database based on CPU usage, duration, and reads and writes

- ↗ PagerDuty integration for phone and SMS alerting

- ↗ Fast, simple installation and administration

> "Being web based, SQL Monitor is readily available to you, wherever you may be on your network. You can check on your servers from almost any location, via most mobile devices that support a web browser."
>
> **Jonathan Allen** Senior DBA, Careers South West Ltd

Visit **www.red-gate.com** for a 14-day, free trial

SQL Virtual Restore $495
Rapidly mount live, fully functional databases direct from backups

- ↗ Virtually restoring a backup requires significantly less time and space than a regular physical restore
- ↗ Databases mounted with SQL Virtual Restore are fully functional and support both read/write operations
- ↗ SQL Virtual Restore is ACID compliant and gives you access to full, transactionally consistent data, with all objects visible and available
- ↗ Use SQL Virtual Restore to recover objects, verify your backups with DBCC CHECKDB, create a storage-efficient copy of your production database, and more.

> "We find occasions where someone has deleted data accidentally or dropped an index, etc., and with SQL Virtual Restore we can mount last night's backup quickly and easily to get access to the data or the original schema. It even works with all our backups being encrypted. This takes any extra load off our production server. SQL Virtual Restore is a great product."
>
> **Brent McCraken** Senior Database Administrator/Architect, Kiwibank Limited

SQL Storage Compress $995
Silent data compression to optimize SQL Server storage

- ↗ Reduce the storage footprint of live SQL Server databases by up to 90% to save on space and hardware costs
- ↗ Databases compressed with SQL Storage Compress are fully functional
- ↗ Prevent unauthorized access to your live databases with 256-bit AES encryption
- ↗ Integrates seamlessly with SQL Server and does not require any configuration changes

Visit **www.red-gate.com** for a 14-day, free trial

SQL Toolbelt $1,995

The essential SQL Server tools for database professionals

You can buy our acclaimed SQL Server tools individually or bundled. Our most popular deal is the SQL Toolbelt: fourteen of our SQL Server tools in a single installer, with **a combined value of $5,930 but an actual price of $1,995**, a saving of 66%.

Fully compatible with SQL Server 2000, 2005, and 2008.

SQL Toolbelt contains:

- SQL Compare Pro
- SQL Data Compare Pro
- SQL Source Control
- SQL Backup Pro
- SQL Monitor
- SQL Prompt Pro
- SQL Data Generator

- SQL Doc
- SQL Dependency Tracker
- SQL Packager
- SQL Multi Script Unlimited
- SQL Search
- SQL Comparison SDK
- SQL Object Level Recovery Native

"The SQL Toolbelt provides tools that database developers, as well as DBAs, should not live without."
William Van Orden Senior Database Developer, Lockheed Martin

Visit **www.red-gate.com** for a 14-day, free trial

ANTS Memory Profiler $495
Find memory leaks and optimize memory usage

- ↗ Find memory leaks within minutes
- ↗ Jump straight to the heart of the problem with intelligent summary information, filtering options and visualizations
- ↗ Optimize the memory usage of your C# and VB.NET code

> "Freaking sweet! We have a known memory leak that took me about four hours to find using our current tool, so I fired up ANTS Memory Profiler and went at it like I didn't know the leak existed. Not only did I come to the conclusion much faster, but I found another one!"
> **Aaron Smith** IT Manager, R.C. Systems Inc.

ANTS Performance Profiler from $395
Profile your .NET code and boost the performance of your application

- ↗ Identify performance bottlenecks within minutes
- ↗ Drill down to slow lines of code thanks to line-level code timings
- ↗ Boost the performance of your .NET code
- ↗ Get the most complete picture of your application's performance with integrated SQL and File I/O profiling

> "ANTS Performance Profiler took us straight to the specific areas of our code which were the cause of our performance issues."
> **Terry Phillips** Sr Developer, Harley-Davidson Dealer Systems

> "Thanks to ANTS Performance Profiler, we were able to discover a performance hit in our serialization of XML that was fixed for a 10x performance increase."
> **Garret Spargo** Product Manager, AFHCAN

Visit **www.red-gate.com** for a 14-day, free trial

.NET Reflector ®   from **$35**

Decompile, browse, analyse and debug .NET code

- ↗ View, navigate and search through the class hierarchies of any .NET assembly, even if you don't have access to the source code.
- ↗ Decompile and analyse any .NET assembly in C#, Visual Basic and IL
- ↗ Step straight into decompiled assemblies whilst debugging in Visual Studio, with the same debugging techniques you would use on your own code

> "One of the most useful, practical debugging tools that I have ever worked with in .NET! It provides complete browsing and debugging features for .NET assemblies, and has clean integration with Visual Studio."
> **Tom Baker** Consultant Software Engineer, EMC Corporation

> "EVERY DEVELOPER NEEDS THIS TOOL!"
> **Daniel Larson** Software Architect, NewsGator Technologies

SmartAssembly ®   from **$795**

.NET obfuscation, automated error reporting and feature usage reporting

- ↗ **Obfuscation:** Obfuscate your .NET code and protect your IP
- ↗ **Automated Error Reporting:** Get quick and automatic reports on exceptions your end-users encounter, and identify unforeseen bugs within hours or days of shipping. Receive detailed reports containing a stack trace and values of the local variables, making debugging easier
- ↗ **Feature Usage Reporting:** Get insight into how your customers are using your application, rely on hard data to plan future development, and enhance your users' experience with your software

> "Knowing the frequency of problems (especially immediately after a release) is extremely helpful in prioritizing & triaging bugs that are reported internally. Additionally, by having the context of where those errors occurred, including debugging information, really gives you that leap forward to start troubleshooting and diagnosing the issue."
> **Ed Blankenship** Technical Lead and MVP

Visit **www.red-gate.com** for a 14-day, free trial

Performance Tuning with SQL Server Dynamic Management Views
Louis Davidson and Tim Ford

This is the book that will de-mystify the process of using Dynamic Management Views to collect the information you need to troubleshoot SQL Server problems. It will highlight the core techniques and "patterns" that you need to master, and will provide a core set of scripts that you can use and adapt for your own requirements.

ISBN: 978-1-906434-47-2
Published: October 2010

Defensive Database Programming
Alex Kuznetsov

Inside this book, you will find dozens of practical, defensive programming techniques that will improve the quality of your T-SQL code and increase its resilience and robustness.

ISBN: 978-1-906434-49-6
Published: June 2010

Brad's Sure Guide to SQL Server Maintenance Plans
Brad McGehee

Brad's Sure Guide to SQL Server Maintenance Plans shows you how to use the Maintenance Plan Wizard and Designer to configure and schedule eleven core database maintenance tasks, ranging from integrity checks, to database backups, to index reorganizations and rebuilds.

ISBN: 978-1-906434-34-2
Published: December 2009

The Red Gate Guide to SQL Server Team-based Development
Phil Factor, Grant Fritchey, Alex Kuznetsov, and Mladen Prajdić

This book shows how to use a mixture of home-grown scripts, native SQL Server tools, and tools from the Red Gate SQL Toolbelt, to successfully develop database applications in a team environment, and make database development as similar as possible to "normal" development.

ISBN: 978-1-906434-59-5
Published: November 2010

CPSIA information can be obtained at www.ICGtesting.com
Printed in the USA
BVOW06s0241190713

326193BV00006B/368/P